ETHICS
ORIGIN *AND* DEVELOPMENT

ETHICS

ORIGIN *AND* DEVELOPMENT

BY PRINCE KROPOTKIN

AUTHORIZED TRANSLATION FROM THE RUSSIAN BY LOUIS S. FRIEDLAND AND JOSEPH R. PIROSHNIKOFF

BENJAMIN BLOM New York/London 1968

First Published 1924
Reissued 1968
by Benjamin Blom, Inc. Bronx, New York 10452
and 56 Doughty Street London, W.C. 1

Library of Congress Catalog Card Number 68-56518

Printed in the United States of America

TRANSLATORS' PREFACE

Kropotkin's "Ethics: Origin and Development," is, in a sense, a continuation of his well-known work, "Mutual Aid as a Factor of Evolution." The basic ideas of the two books are closely connected, almost inseparable, in fact:—the origin and progress of human relations in society. Only, in the "Ethics" Kropotkin approaches his theme through a study of the ideology of these relations.

The Russian writer removes ethics from the sphere of the speculative and metaphysical, and brings human conduct and ethical teaching back to its natural environment: the ethical practices of men in their everyday concerns—from the time of primitive societies to our modern highly organized States. Thus conceived, ethics becomes a subject of universal interest; under the kindly eyes and able pen of the great Russian scholar, a subject of special and academic study becomes closely linked to whatever is significant in the life and thought of all men.

The circumstances leading to the conception and writing of this book are discussed by the Russian editor, N. Lebedev, whose Introduction is included in this volume. The present translators have availed themselves of Kropotkin's two articles on Ethics contributed to the *Nineteenth Century*, 1905–06. They found, however, that the author had made very many changes in the first three chapters of his book—in substance, a reproduction of the magazine articles—and they thought it best to make the necessary alterations and additions called for by the Russian text. These three chapters preserve the English and the turns of phrase of the magazine articles.

In preparing this edition the translators consulted all of the books mentioned by Kropotkin; they verified all his citations, and corrected a number of errors that crept into the Russian original owing to

iii

the absence of the author's supervising care. As is generally known, the book appeared after Kropotkin's death. The translators have added such additional footnotes as they thought would prove of value and interest to the English reader. They have made every attempt to discover and cite the best, most readily available English versions of the books referred to by the author. These added notes and comments are enclosed in brackets, and are usually marked,—*Trans. Note.* In addition, the Index has been carefully revised and augmented.

A multitude of books had to be consulted in the faithful discharge of the translators' duties. And for these, many librarians— those most obliging and patient of mortals—were pestered. The translators wish to record their thanks to Mr. Howson, Mr. Frederic W. Erb, Miss Erb, and Mr. Charles F. Claar—all of Columbia University Library, and to Mr. Abraham Mill of the Slavonic division of the New York Public Library. They and their assistants have been very helpful and kind. In the preparation of the manuscript the translators were fortunate to have the competent assistance of Miss Ann Bogel and Miss Evelyn Friedland—always vigilant in the discovery and eradication of errors.

Madam Sophie G. Kropotkin and Madam Sasha Kropotkin— wife and daughter of Peter Kropotkin—followed the progress of this edition; they have been ever gracious and helpful. It is their hope that, at some time in the near future, Kropotkin's last essays on Ethics will be issued in English translation. And indeed, our literature and thought will be richer for the possession of all of Kropotkin's writings. His work—fine and thorough and scholarly as it is—is only less inspiring than the ennobling memory of his life and character.

Louis S. Friedland

Joseph R. Piroshnikoff

New York
May 1924

TABLE OF CONTENTS

The progress of science and philosophy in the last hundred years. Modern technical progress. The possibility of developing an Ethics based on the natural sciences. The modern ethical theories. The fundamental defect of the modern ethical systems. The theory of struggle for existence: its mistaken interpretation. Mutual aid in Nature. Nature is not a-moral. Man receives his first lessons in morality from Nature.

What interferes with the progress of morality. The development of the social instinct. The inspiring force of the evolutionary ethics. Ideas and moral conceptions. The sense of duty. Two types of moral acts. The part played by individual initiative. The personal creative urge. Mutual Aid, Justice, Morality as the bases of the "naturalistic" ethics.

Darwin's theory of the origin of moral sentiment in man. Rudiments of moral sentiment in animals. Origin of the sense of duty in man. Mutual aid as the first source of ethical sentiments in man. Sociality in the animal kingdom. Intercommunication of the savages with animals. The origin of the conception of justice among primitive peoples.

Development of the social instinct among savages. Dual nature of moral requirements among the savage tribes: the fulfillment of some requirements is *obligatory*, while the fulfillment of others is merely *desirable*. Means of social compulsion of the individual among savages, in cases of non-fulfillment of the obligatory rules. Establishment of customs and of mode of life (*mœurs*) useful to society. Tribal manners and tribal justice. Division of society into classes and estates, and striving of separate groups for power and for domination over others. Evolution of the primitive moral conceptions. The necessity of studying this evolution and the determination of the fundamental principles of Ethics.

TABLE OF CONTENTS

TABLE OF CONTENTS

vii

INTRODUCTION BY THE RUSSIAN EDITOR

"ETHICS" is the swan song of the great humanitarian scientist and revolutionist-anarchist, and constitutes, as it were, the crowning work and the résumé of all the scientific, philosophical, and sociological views of Peter Alekseyevich Kropotkin, at which he arrived in the course of his long and unusually rich life. Unfortunately, death came before he could complete his work, and, according to the will and desire of Peter Alekseyevich, the responsible task of preparing "Ethics" for the press fell upon me.

In issuing the first volume of "Ethics", I feel the necessity of saying a few words to acquaint the reader with the history of this work.

In his "Ethics" Kropotkin wished to give answers to the two fundamental problems of morality: *whence originate man's moral conceptions?* and, *what is the goal of the moral prescriptions and standards?* It is for this reason that he subdivided his work into two parts: the first was to consider the question of the *origin and the historical development of morality,* and the second part Kropotkin planned to devote to the exposition of the *bases of realistic ethics, and its aims.*

Kropotkin had time to write only the first volume of "Ethics," and even that not in finished form. Some chapters of the first volume were written by him in rough draft only, and the last chapter, in which the ethical teachings of Stirner, Nietzsche, Tolstoi, Multatuli, and of other prominent contemporary moralists were to be discussed, remained unwritten.

For the second volume of "Ethics" Kropotkin had time to write only a few essays, which he planned to publish at first in the form of magazine articles,—and a series of rough drafts and notes. They are the essays: "Primitive Ethics," "Justice, Morality, and

Religion," "Ethics and Mutual Aid," "Origin of Moral Motives and of the Sense of Duty," and others.

Kropotkin began to occupy himself with moral problems as early as in the 'eighties, but he devoted particularly close attention to the questions of morality during the last decade of the nineteenth century, when voices began to be heard in literature proclaiming that morality is not needed and when the a-moralist doctrine of Nietzsche was gaining attention. At the same time, many representatives of science and of philosophic thought, under the influence of Darwin's teaching,—interpreted literally,—began to assert that there reigns in the world but one general law,—the "law of struggle for existence," and by this very assumption they seemed to lend support to philosophical a-moralism.

Kropotkin, feeling all the falseness of such conclusions, decided to prove from the scientific point of view that nature is not a-moral and does not teach man a lesson of evil, but that morality constitutes the natural product of the evolution of social life not only of man, but of almost all living creatures, among the majority of which we find the rudiments of moral relations.

In 1890 Kropotkin delivered, before the "Ancoats Brotherhood" of Manchester, a lecture on the subject "Justice and Morality," and somewhat later he repeated this lecture in amplified form before the London Ethical Society.

During the period 1891–1894 he printed in the magazine, *Nineteenth Century*, a series of articles on the subject of mutual aid among the animals, savages, and civilized peoples. These essays, which later formed the contents of the book "Mutual Aid, a factor of evolution," constitute, as it were, an introduction to Kropotkin's moral teaching.

In 1904–1905 Kropotkin printed in the magazine *Nineteenth Century* two articles directly devoted to moral problems: "The Ethical Need of the Present Day," and "The Morality of Nature." These essays, in somewhat modified form, constitute the first three chapters of the present volume. About the same time Kropotkin wrote in French a small pamphlet, "La Morale Anarchiste." In this pamphlet

INTRODUCTION BY THE RUSSIAN EDITOR

Kropotkin exhorts man to active participation in life, and calls upon man to remember that his power is not in isolation but in alliance with his fellow men, with the people, with the toiling masses. In opposition to anarchistic individualism he attempts to create *social morality*, the ethics of sociality and solidarity.

The progress of mankind, says Kropotkin, is indissolubly bound up with social living. Life in societies inevitably engenders in men and in animals the instincts of sociality, mutual aid,—which in their further development in men become transformed into the feeling of benevolence, sympathy, and love.

It is these feelings and instincts that give origin to human morality, i. e., to the sum total of moral feelings, perceptions, and concepts, which finally mould themselves into the fundamental rule of all moral teachings: "do not unto others that which you would not have others do unto you."

But not to do unto others that which you would not have others do unto you, is not a complete expression of morality, says Kropotkin. This rule is merely the expression of *justice*, equity. The highest moral consciousness cannot be satisfied with this, and Kropotkin maintains that together with the *feeling* of mutual aid and the *concept* of justice there is another fundamental element of morality, something that men call *magnanimity, self-abnegation* or *self-sacrifice*.

Mutual Aid, Justice, Self-sacrifice—these are the three elements of morality, according to Kropotkin's theory. While not possessing the character of generality and necessity inherent in logical laws, these elements, according to Kropotkin, lie, nevertheless, at the basis of human ethics, which may be regarded as the "physics of human conduct." The problem of the moral philosopher is to investigate the origin and the development of these elements of morality, and to prove that they are just as truly innate in human nature as are all other instincts and feelings.

Arriving in Russia after forty years of exile, Kropotkin settled at first in Petrograd, but soon his physicians advised him to change

xi

his residence to Moscow. Kropotkin did not succeed, however, in settling permanently in Moscow. The hard conditions of life in Moscow at the time compelled him, in the summer of 1918, to go to the tiny, secluded village of Dmitrov (60 *versts* from Moscow), where Kropotkin, almost in the literal sense of the word isolated from the civilized world, was compelled to live for three years, to the very day of his death.

Needless to say, the writing of such a work as "Ethics" and its exposition of the history and development of moral teachings, while the author was living in so isolated a place as Dmitrov, proved an extremely difficult task. Kropotkin had very few books at hand (all his library remained in England), and the verification of references consumed much time and not infrequently held up the work for long periods.

Owing to lack of means Kropotkin could not purchase the books he needed, and it was only through the kindness of his friends and acquaintances that he succeeded at times in obtaining with great difficulty this or that necessary book. Because of the same lack of means Kropotkin could not afford the services of a secretary or a typist, so that he was obliged to do all the mechanical part of the work himself, at times copying portions of his manuscript again and again. Of course, all this had its unfavourable influences on the work. To this must be added the circumstance that after coming to Dmitrov, Kropotkin, perhaps owing to inadequate nourishment, began often to feel physical indisposition. Thus, in his letter to me dated January 21, 1919, he writes: "I am diligently working on 'Ethics,' but I have little strength, and I am compelled at times to interrupt my work." To this a series of other untoward circumstances was added. For instance, Kropotkin was compelled for a long time to work evenings by a very poor light, etc.

Kropotkin considered his work on ethics a necessary and a revolutionary task. In one of his last letters (May 2, 1920) he says: "I have resumed my work on moral questions, because I consider that this work is absolutely necessary. I know that intellectual movements are not created by books, and that just the reverse is true. But I also know that for clarifying an idea the help of a book is needed, a book that expresses the bases of thought in their complete form. And in order to lay the bases of morality, liberated from religion, and standing higher than the religious morality . . . it is necessary to have the help of clarifying books." —"The need of such clarification is felt with particular insistence now, when human thought is struggling between Nietzsche and Kant. . . ."

In his conversations with me he often said, "Of course, if I were not so old I would not potter over a book on ethics during the Revolution, but I would, you may be sure, actively participate in the building of the new life."

A realist and a revolutionist, Kropotkin regarded Ethics not as an abstract science of human conduct, but he saw in it first of all a concrete scientific discipline, whose object is to inspire men in their practical activities. Kropotkin saw that even those who call themselves revolutionists and communists are morally unstable, that the majority of them lack a guiding moral principle, a lofty moral ideal. He said repeatedly that it was perhaps due to this lack of a lofty moral ideal that the Russian Revolution proved impotent to create a new social system based on the principles of justice and freedom, and to fire other nations with a revolutionary flame, as happened at the time of the Great French Revolution and of the Revolution of 1848.

And so he, an old revolutionist-rebel, whose thoughts were always bent on the happiness of mankind, thought with his book on Ethics to inspire the young generation to struggle, to implant in them faith in the justice of the social revolution, and to light in their hearts the fire of self-sacrifice, by convincing men that "happiness is not in personal pleasure, not in egotistic, even in higher joys, but in struggle for truth and justice among the people and together with the people."

Denying the connection of morality with religion and metaphysics, Kropotkin sought to establish ethics on purely naturalistic bases,

xiii

and endeavoured to show that only by remaining in the world of reality may one find strength for a truly moral life. In his "Ethics," Kropotkin, like the poet, gives to mankind his last message:

> "Dear friend, do not with weary soul aspire
> Away from the gray earth—your sad abode;
> No! Throb with th' earth, let earth your body tire,—
> So help your brothers bear the common load."

Many expect that Kropotkin's "Ethics" will be some sort of specifically "revolutionary" or "anarchist" ethics, etc. Whenever this subject was broached to Kropotkin himself, he invariably answered that his intention was to write a purely *human* ethics (sometimes he used the expression "realistic").

He did not recognize any *separate* ethics; he held that ethics should be one and the same for all men. When it was pointed out to him that there can be no single ethics in modern society, which is subdivided into mutually antagonistic classes and castes, he would say that any "bourgeois" or "proletarian" ethics rests, after all, on the common basis, on the common ethnological foundation, which at times exerts a very strong influence on the principles of the class or group morality. He pointed out that no matter to what class or party we may belong, we are, first of all, *human beings,* and constitute a part of the general animal species, *Man.* The genus "Homo Sapiens," from a most cultured European to a Bushman, and from the most refined "bourgeois" to the last "proletarian," in spite of all distinctions, constitutes a logical whole. And in his plans for the future structure of society Kropotkin always thought simply in terms of human beings—without that sediment of the social "table of ranks," which has thickly settled upon us in the course of the long historical life of mankind.

Kropotkin's ethical teaching may be characterized as the teaching of *Brotherhood,* although the word "brotherhood" is scarcely ever met with in his book. He did not like to use the word *brotherhood,* and preferred the term *solidarity.* Solidarity, in his opinion, is something more "real" than brotherhood. As a proof of his thought he pointed out that brothers frequently quarrel among themselves, hate one another, and even go as far as murder. In fact, according to the Biblical legend, the history of the human race begins with fratricide. But the conception of solidarity expresses the physical and the organic relation among the elements in every human being, and in the world of moral relations solidarity is expressed in sympathy, in mutual aid, and in *co*-miseration. Solidarity harmonizes with freedom and equity, and solidarity and equity constitute the necessary conditions of *social justice*. Hence Kropotkin's ethical formula: *"Without equity there is no justice, and without justice there is no morality."*

Of course, Kropotkin's ethics does not solve all the moral problems that agitate modern humanity (and it is not within expectation to think that they will ever be completely solved, for with every new generation the moral problem, while remaining unchanged in its essence, assumes different aspects, and engenders new questions). In his "Ethics" Kropotkin merely indicates the path and offers his solution of the ethical problem. His work is an attempt by a revolutionist-anarchist and a learned naturalist to answer the burning question: *why must I live a moral life?* It is extremely unfortunate that death prevented Kropotkin from writing in final, finished form the second part of his work, in which he planned to expound the bases of the naturalistic and realistic ethics, and to state his ethical credo.

Kropotkin, in his search for the realistic bases of ethics, seems to us an inspired reconnoiterer in the complicated world of moral relations. To all those who strive to reach the promised land of freedom and justice, but who are still subjected to the bitter pains of fruitless wanderings in the world of oppression and enmity, to all those Kropotkin stands out as a steadfast way-mark. He points the path to the new ethics, to the morality of the future which will not tolerate an immoral subdivision of human beings into "masters" and "slaves," into "rulers" and "subjects," but will be the expression of the free, collective co-operation of all for the common good, of that co-operation which alone will permit the establishment on earth of a real, and not an ephemeral, kingdom of brotherly labour and freedom.

A few last words. In editing, I endeavoured to be guided by the remarks that Peter Alekseyevich himself made in the course of our conversations and discussions, and also by the directions which he left among his documents, *"Instructions as to the disposition of my papers,"* and in a brief sketch, *"À un continuateur."* In the latter paper, Kropotkin writes, among other things: "si je ne réussi pas a terminer mon Éthique,—je prie ceux qui tâcheront peut-être de la terminer, *d'utiliser mes notes."*

For the purpose of the present edition these notes have remained unutilized, in the first place because the relatives and friends of the late Peter Alekseyevich decided that it is much more important and more interesting to publish "Ethics" in the form in which it was left by the author, and secondly, because the sorting and arranging of these notes will require much time and labour, and would have considerably retarded the appearance of "Ethics" in print.

In subsequent editions all the material left by Kropotkin pertaining to Ethics, will, of course, be utilized in one form or another.

N. LEBEDEV.

Moscow
May 1, 1922

xvi

ETHICS: ORIGIN AND DEVELOPMENT

CHAPTER I

THE PRESENT NEED OF DETERMINING THE BASES OF MORALITY

WHEN we cast a glance upon the immense progress realized by the natural sciences in the course of the nineteenth century, and when we perceive the promises they contain for the future, we cannot but feel deeply impressed by the idea that mankind is entering upon a new era of progress. It has, at any rate, before it all the elements for preparing such a new era. In the course of the last one hundred years, new branches of knowledge, opening entirely new vistas upon the laws of the development of human society, have grown up under the names of anthropology, prehistoric ethnology (science of the primitive social institutions), the history of religions, and so on. New conceptions about the whole life of the universe were developed by pursuing such lines of research as molecular physics, the chemical structure of matter, and the chemical composition of distant worlds. And the traditional views about the position of man in the universe, the origin of life, and the nature of reason were entirely upset by the rapid development of biology, the appearance of the theory of evolution, and the progress made in the study of human and animal psychology.

Merely to say that the progress of science in each of its branches, excepting perhaps astronomy, has been greater during the last century than during any three or four centuries of the ages preceding,

1

would not be enough. We must turn back 2000 years, to the glorious times of the philosophical revival in Ancient Greece, in order to find another such period of the awakening of the human intellect. And yet, even this comparison would not be correct, because at that early period of human history, man did not enter into possession of all those wonders of industrial technique which have been lately arrayed in our service. The development of this technique at last gives man the opportunity to free himself from slavish toil.

At the same time modern humanity developed a youthful, daring spirit of invention, stimulated by the recent discoveries of science; and the inventions that followed in rapid succession have to such an extent increased the productive capacity of human labour as to make at last possible for modern civilized peoples such a general well-being as could not be dreamt of in antiquity, or in the Middle Ages, or even in the earlier portion of the nineteenth century. For the first time in the history of civilization, mankind has reached a point where the means of satisfying its needs are in excess of the needs themselves. To impose, therefore, as has hitherto been done, the curse of misery and degradation upon vast divisions of mankind, in order to secure well-being and further mental development for the few, is needed no more: well-being can be secured for all, without placing on anyone the burden of oppressive, degrading toil, and humanity can at last rebuild its entire social life on the bases of justice. Whether the modern civilized nations will find in their midst the social constructive capacities, the creative powers and the daring required for utilising the conquests of the human intellect in the interest of all,—it is difficult to say beforehand.

Whether our present civilization is vigorous and youthful enough to undertake so great a task, and to bring it to the desired end, we cannot foretell. But this is certain:—that the recent revival of science has created the intellectual atmosphere required for calling such forces into existence, and it has already given us the knowledge necessary for the realisation of this great task.

Reverting to the sound philosophy of Nature which remained in neglect from the time of Ancient Greece until Bacon woke scientific research from its long slumber, modern science has now worked out the elements of a philosophy of the universe, free of supernatural hypotheses and the metaphysical "mythology of ideas," and at the same time so grand, so poetical and inspiring, and so expressive of freedom, that it certainly is capable of calling into existence the new forces. Man no longer needs to clothe his ideals of moral beauty, and of a society based on justice, with the garb of superstition: he does not have to wait for the Supreme Wisdom to remodel society. He can derive his ideals from Nature and he can draw the necessary strength from the study of its life.

One of the greatest achievements of modern science was, that it proved the *indestructibility of energy* through all the ceaseless transformations which it undergoes in the universe. For the physicist and the mathematician this idea became a most fruitful source of discovery. It inspires, in fact, all modern research. But its philosophical import is equally great. It accustoms man to conceive the life of the universe as a never-ending series of transformations of energy: mechanical energy may become converted into sound, light, electricity; and conversely, each of these forms of energy may be converted into others. And among all these transformations, the birth of our planet, its evolution, and its final, unavoidable destruction and reabsorption in the great Cosmos are but an infinitesimally small episode—a mere moment in the life of the stellar worlds.

The same with the researches concerning organic life. The recent studies in the wide borderland dividing the inorganic world from the organic, where the simplest life-processes in the lowest fungi are hardly distinguishable—if distinguishable at all—from the chemical redistribution of atoms which is always going on in the more complex molecules of matter, have divested life of its mystical character. At the same time, our conception of life has been so widened that we grow accustomed now to conceive all the agglomerations of matter in the universe—solid, liquid, and gaseous (such are some nebulæ of the astral world)—as something *living* and going through the same cycles of evolution and decay as do living beings. Then, reverting to ideas which were budding once in Ancient Greece, modern science has retraced step by step that marvelous evolution of living matter, which, after having started with the simplest forms, hardly deserving the name of organism, has gradually produced the infinite variety of beings which now people and enliven our planet. And, by making us familiar with the thought that every organism is to an immense extent the product of its own environment, biology has solved one of the greatest riddles of Nature—it explained the adaptations to the conditions of life which we meet at every step.

Even in the most puzzling of all manifestations of life,—the domain of feeling and thought, in which human intelligence has to catch the very processes by means of which it succeeds in retaining and co-ordinating the impressions received from without—even in this domain, the darkest of all, man has already succeeded in catching a glimpse of the mechanism of thought by following the lines of research indicated by physiology. And finally, in the vast field of human institutions, habits and laws, superstitions, beliefs, and ideals, such a flood of light has been thrown by the anthropological schools of history, law, and economics that we can already maintain positively that "the greatest happiness of the greatest number" is no longer a dream, a mere Utopia. *It is possible*, and it is also clear, that the prosperity and happiness of no nation or class could ever be based, even temporarily, upon the degradation of other classes, nations, or races.

Modern science has thus achieved a double aim. On the one side it has given to man a very valuable lesson of modesty. It has taught him to consider himself as but an infinitesimally small particle of the universe. It has driven him out of his narrow, egotistical seclusion, and has dissipated the self-conceit under which he considered himself the centre of the universe and the object of the special attention of the Creator. It has taught him that without the whole the "ego" is nothing; that our "I" cannot even come to a self-definition without the "thou." But at the same time science has taught man how powerful mankind is in its progressive march, if it skilfully utilizes the unlimited energies of Nature.

4

NEED OF DETERMINING BASES OF MORALITY

Thus science and philosophy have given us both the material strength and the freedom of thought which are required for calling into life the constructive forces that may lead mankind to a new era of progress. There is, however, one branch of knowledge which lags behind. It is ethics, the teaching of the fundamental principles of morality. A system of ethics worthy of the present scientific revival, which would take advantage of all the recent acquisitions for reconstituting the very foundations of morality on a wider philosophical basis, and which would give to the civilized nations the inspiration required for the great task that lies before them—such a system has not yet been produced. But the need of it is felt everywhere. A new, realistic moral science is the need of the day—a science as free from superstition, religious dogmatism, and metaphysical mythology as modern cosmogony and philosophy already are, and permeated at the same time with those higher feelings and brighter hopes which are inspired by the modern knowledge of man and his history,—this is what humanity is persistently demanding.

That such a science is possible lies beyond any reasonable doubt. If the study of Nature has yielded the elements of a philosophy which embraces the life of the Cosmos, the evolution of living beings, the laws of physical activity, and the development of society, it must also be able to give us the rational origin and the sources of the moral feelings. And it must be able to show us where lie the forces that are able to elevate the moral feeling to an always greater height and purity. If the contemplation of the Universe and a close acquaintance with Nature were able to infuse lofty inspiration into the minds of the great naturalists and poets of the nineteenth century,—if a look into Nature's breast quickened the pulse of life for Goethe, Shelley, Byron, Lermontov, in the face of the raging storm, the calm mountains, the dark forest and its inhabitants,— why should not a deeper penetration into the *life of man and his destinies* be able to inspire the poet in the same way? And when the poet has found the proper expression for his sense of communion with the Cosmos and his unity with his fellow-men, he becomes cap-

5

able of inspiring millions of men with his high enthusiasm. He makes them feel what is best in them, and awakens their desire to become better still. He produces in them those very ecstasies which were formerly considered as belonging exclusively to the province of religion. What are, indeed, the Psalms, which are often described as the highest expression of religious feeling, or the more poetical portions of the sacred books of the East, but attempts to express man's ecstasy at the contemplation of the universe—the first awakening of his sense of the poetry of Nature?

The need of realistic ethics was felt from the very dawn of the scientific revival, when Bacon, at the same time that he laid the foundations of the present advancement of sciences, indicated also the main outlines of empirical ethics, perhaps with less thoroughness than this was done by his followers, but with a width of conception which few have been able to attain since, and beyond which we have not advanced much further in our day.

The best thinkers of the seventeenth and eighteenth centuries continued on the same lines, endeavouring to work out systems of ethics independent of the imperatives of religion. In England Hobbes, Cudworth, Locke, Shaftesbury, Paley, Hutcheson, Hume, and Adam Smith boldly attacked the problem on all sides. They indicated the natural sources of the moral sense, and in their determinations of the moral ends they (except Paley) mostly stood on the same empirical ground. They endeavoured to combine in varied ways the "intellectualism" and utilitarianism of Locke with the "moral sense" and sense of beauty of Hutcheson, the "theory of association" of Hartley, and the ethics of feeling of Shaftesbury. Speaking of the ends of ethics, some of them already mentioned the "harmony" between self-love and regard for fellow-men, which acquired such an importance in the moral theories of the nineteenth century, and considered it in connection with Hutcheson's "emotion of approbation," or the "sympathy" of Hume and Adam Smith. And finally, if they found a difficulty in explaining the sense of duty on a rational basis, they resorted to the early influences of religion, or to some "inborn

6

sense," or to some variety of Hobbes's theory, which regards law as the principal cause of the formation of society, while considering the primitive savage as an unsocial animal.

The French Encyclopædists and materialists discussed the problem on the same lines, only insisting more on self-love, and trying to find the synthesis of the opposed tendencies of human nature: the narrow-egoistic and the social. Social life, they maintained, invariably favours the development of the better sides of human nature. Rousseau, with his rational religion, stood as a link between the materialists and the intuitionists, and by boldly attacking the social problems of the day he won a wider hearing than any one of them. On the other side, even the utmost idealists, like Descartes and his pantheist follower Spinoza, and at one time even the "transcendentalist-idealist" Kant, did not trust entirely to the revealed origin of the moral ideas, and tried to give to ethics a broader foundation, even though they would not part entirely with an extra-human origin of the moral law.

The same endeavour towards finding a realistic basis for ethics became even more pronounced in the nineteenth century, when quite a number of important ethical systems were worked out on the different bases of rational self-love, love of humanity (Auguste Comte, Littré, and a great number of minor followers), sympathy and intellectual identification of one's personality with mankind (Schopenhauer), utilitarianism (Bentham and Mill), and evolution (Darwin, Spencer, Guyau), to say nothing of the systems rejecting morality, originating in La Rochefoucauld and Mandeville and developed in the nineteenth century by Nietzsche and several others, who tried to establish a higher moral standard by their bold attacks against the current half-hearted moral conceptions, and by a vigorous assertion of the supreme rights of the individual.

Two of the nineteenth-century ethical systems—Comte's positivism and Bentham's utilitarianism—exercised, as is known, a deep influence upon the century's thought, and the former impressed with its own stamp all the scientific researches which make the glory of

7

modern science. They also gave origin to a variety of sub-systems, so that most modern writers of mark in psychology, evolution, or anthropology have enriched ethical literature with some more or less original researches, of a high standard, as is the case with Feuerbach, Bain, Leslie Stephen, Proudhon, Wundt, Sidgwick, Guyau, Jodl, and several others. Numbers of ethical societies were also started for a wider propaganda of empirical ethics (i. e., not based on religion). At the same time, an immense movement, chiefly economical in its origins, but deeply ethical in its substance, was born in the first half of the nineteenth century under the names of Fourierism, Saint-Simonism, and Owenism, and later on of international socialism and anarchism. This movement, which is spreading more and more, aims, with the support of the working men of all nations, not only to revise the very foundations of the current ethical conceptions, but also to remodel life in such a way that a new page in the ethical life of mankind may be opened.

It would seem, therefore, that since such a number of rationalist ethical systems have grown up in the course of the last two centuries, it is impossible to approach the subject once more without falling into a mere repetition or a mere recombination of fragments of already advocated schemes. However, the very fact that each of the main systems produced in the nineteenth century—the positivism of Comte, the utilitarianism of Bentham and Mill, and the altruistic evolutionism, i. e., the theory of the social development of morality, of Darwin, Spencer, and Guyau—has added something important to the conceptions worked out by its predecessors,—proves that the matter is far from being exhausted.

Even if we take the last three systems only, we cannot but see that Spencer failed to take advantage of some of the hints which are found in the remarkable sketch of ethics given by Darwin in "The Descent of Man;" while Guyau introduced into morals such an important element as that of an overflow of energy in feeling, thought, or will, which had not been taken into account by his predecessors. If every new system thus contributes some new and valuable element, this very fact proves that ethical science is not yet constituted. In fact, it never will be, because new factors and new tendencies will always have to be taken into account in proportion as mankind advances in its evolution.

That, at the same time, none of the ethical systems which were brought forward in the course of the nineteenth century has satisfied, be it only the educated fraction of the civilized nations, hardly need be insisted upon. To say nothing of the numerous philosophical works in which dissatisfaction with modern ethics has been expressed,[1] the best proof of it is the decided return to idealism which we see at the end of the nineteenth century. The absence of any poetical inspiration in the positivism of Littré and Herbert Spencer, and their incapacity to cope with the great problems of our present civilization; the narrowness which characterizes the chief philosopher of evolution, Spencer, in some of his views; nay, the repudiation by the latter-day positivists of the humanitarian theories which distinguished the eighteenth-century Encyclopædists—all these have helped to create a strong reaction in favour of a sort of mystico-religious idealism. As Fouillée very justly remarks, a one-sided interpretation of Darwinism, which was given to it by the most prominent representatives of the evolutionist school, (without a word of protest coming from Darwin himself for the first twelve years after the appearance of his "Origin of Species"), gave still more force to opponents of the natural interpretation of the moral nature of man, —so-called "naturism."

Beginning as a protest against some mistakes of the naturalist philosophy, the critique soon became a campaign against positive knowledge altogether. The "failure of science" was triumphantly announced. However, the scientists know that every exact science moves from one approximation to another, i. e., from a first approximate explanation of a whole series of phenomena to the next more

[1] Sufficient to name here the critical and historical works of Paulsen, Wundt, Leslie Stephen, Lichtenberger, Fouillée, De Roberty, and so many others.

accurate approximation. But this simple truth is completely ignored by the "believers," and in general by lovers of mysticism. Having learned that inaccuracies have been discovered in the first approximation, they hasten to proclaim the "bankruptcy of science" in general. Whereas, the scientists know that the most exact sciences, such as, for example, astronomy, follow just this road of successive approximations. It was a great discovery to find out that all the planets move around the sun, and it was the first "approximation" to suppose that they follow circular paths. Then it was discovered that they move along somewhat oblong circles, i. e., ellipses, and this was the second "approximation." This was followed by the third approximation when we learned that the planets follow a wavy course, always deviating to one or the other side of the ellipse, and never retracing exactly the same path; and now, at last, when we know that the sun is not motionless, but is itself flying through space, the astronomers are endeavouring to determine the nature and the position of the spirals along which the planets are travelling in describing slightly wavy ellipses around the sun.

Similar approximations from one near solution of the problem to the next, more accurate one, are practiced in all sciences. Thus, for example, the natural sciences are now revising the "first approximations" concerning life, physical activity, evolution of plant and animal forms, the structure of matter, and so on, which were arrived at in the years 1856–62, and which must be revised now in order to reach the next, deeper generalizations. And so this revision was taken advantage of by some people who know little, to convince others who know still less, that science, in general, has failed in its attempted solutions of all the great problems.

At present a great many endeavour to substitute for science "intuition," i. e., simply guess work and blind faith. Going back first to Kant, then to Schelling, and even to Lotze, numbers of writers have of late been preaching "spiritualism," "indeterminism," "apriorism," "personal idealism," "intuition," and so on—proving that faith, and not science, is the source of all true knowledge.

Religious faith itself is found insufficient. It is the mysticism of St. Bernard or of the Neo-Platonist which is now in demand. "Symbolism," "the subtle," "the incomprehensible" are sought for. Even the belief in the mediæval Satan was resuscitated.[2]

It is true that none of these currents of thought obtained a widespread hold upon the minds of our contemporaries; but we certainly see public opinion floating between the two extremes—between a desperate effort, on the one side, to force oneself to return to the obscure creeds of the Middle Ages, with their full accompaniment of superstition, idolatry, and even magic; and, on the opposite extreme, a glorification of "a-moralism" and a revival of that worship of "superior natures," now invested with the names of "supermen" or "superior individualizations," which Europe had lived through in the times of Byronism and early Romanticism.

It appears, therefore, more necessary than ever to see if the present scepticism as to the authority of science in ethical questions is well founded, and whether science does not contain already the elements of a system of ethics which, if it were properly formulated, would respond to the needs of the present day.

The limited success of the various ethical systems which were born in the course of the last hundred years shows that man cannot be satisfied with a mere naturalistic *explanation of the origins of the moral instinct*. He means to have a *justification* of it. Simply to trace the origin of our moral feelings, as we trace the pedigree of some structural feature in a flower, and to say that such-and-such causes have contributed to the growth and refinement of the moral sense, is not enough. Man wants to have a criterion for judging the moral instinct itself. Whereto does it lead us? Is it towards a desirable end, or towards something which, as some critics say, would only result in the weakening of the race and its ultimate decay?

If struggle for life and the extermination of the physically weak-

2 See A. Fouillée, *Le Mouvement idéaliste et la Réaction contre la Science positive*, 2nd edition; [Paris, 1896]. Paul Desjardins, *Le Devoir présent*, which has gone through five editions in a short time; [6th ed., Paris, 1896]; and many others.

11

est is the law of Nature, and represents a condition of progress, is not then the cessation of the struggle, and the "industrial state" which Comte and Spencer promise us, the very beginning of the decay of the human race—as Nietzsche has so forcibly concluded? And if such an end is undesirable, must we not proceed, indeed, to a revaluation of all those moral "values" which tend to reduce the struggle, or to render it less painful?

The main problem of modern realistic ethics is thus, as has been remarked by Wundt in his "Ethics," to determine, first of all, the *moral end* in view. But this end or ends, however ideal they may be, and however remote their full realization, must belong to the world of realities.

The end of morals cannot be "transcendental," as the idealists desire it to be: it must be real. We must find moral satisfaction *in life* and not in some form of extra-vital condition.

When Darwin threw into circulation the idea of "struggle for existence," and represented this struggle as the mainspring of progressive evolution, he agitated once more the great old question as to the moral or immoral aspects of Nature. The origin of the conceptions of good and evil, which had exercised the best minds since the times of the Zend-Avesta, was brought once more under discussion with a renewed vigour, and with a greater depth of conception than ever. Nature was represented by the Darwinists as an immense battlefield upon which one sees nothing but an incessant struggle for life and an extermination of the weak ones by the strongest, the swiftest, and the cunningest: evil was the only lesson which man could get from Nature.

These ideas, as is known, became very widely spread. But if they are true, the evolutionist philosopher has to solve a deep contradiction which he himself has introduced into his philosophy. He cannot deny that man is possessed of a higher conception of "good," and that a faith in the gradual triumph of the good principle is deeply seated in human nature, and he has to explain whence originates this conception of good and this faith in progress. He cannot be lulled into indifference by the Epicurean hope, expressed by Tennyson—that "somehow good will be the final goal of ill." Nor can he represent to himself Nature, "red in tooth and claw,"—as wrote the same Tennyson and the Darwinian Huxley,—at strife everywhere with the good principle—the very negation of it in every living being—and still maintain that the good principle will be triumphant "in the long run." He must explain this contradiction.

But if a scientist maintains that "the only lesson which Nature gives to man is one of evil," then he necessarily has to admit the existence of some other, extra-natural, or super-natural influence which inspires man with conceptions of "supreme good," and guides human development towards a higher goal. And in this way he nullifies his own attempt at explaining evolution by the action of natural forces only.[3]

In reality, however, things do not stand so badly as that, for the theory of evolution does not at all lead to the contradictions such as those to which Huxley was driven, because the study of nature does not in the least confirm the above-mentioned pessimistic view of its course, as Darwin himself indicated in his second work, "The Descent of Man." The conceptions of Tennyson and Huxley are incomplete, one-sided, and consequently wrong. The view is, moreover, unscientific, for Darwin himself pointed out the other aspect of Nature in a special chapter of "The Descent of Man." There is, he showed, in Nature itself, another set of facts, parallel to those of mutual struggle, but having a quite different meaning: the facts of mutual support within the species, which are even more important than the former, on account of their significance for the welfare of the species and its maintenance. This extremely important idea,—to

[3] Thus it actually happened with Huxley in the course of his lecture on *Evolution and Ethics*, where he at first denied the presence of any moral principle in the life of Nature, and by that very assertion was compelled to acknowledge the existence of the ethical principle outside of nature. Then he retracted also this point of view in a later remark, in which he *recognized* the presence of the ethical principle in the social life of animals. [Volume 9 of *Collected Essays*, N. Y., contains the essay on *Evolution and Ethics*, written in 1893.]—Trans. Note.

13

which, however, most Darwinists refuse to pay attention, and which Alfred Russel Wallace even denies,—I attempted to develop further, and to substantiate with a great number of facts in a series of essays in which I endeavoured to bring into evidence the immense importance of Mutual Aid for the preservation of both the animal species and the human race, and still more so for their *progressive evolution.*[4]

Without trying to minimize the fact that an immense number of animals live either upon species belonging to some lower division of the animal kingdom, or upon some smaller species of the same class as themselves, I indicated that warfare in Nature is chiefly *limited to struggle between different species,* but that *within each species,* and within the groups of different species which we find living together, the practice of *mutual aid is the rule,* and therefore this last aspect of animal life plays a far greater part than does warfare in the economy of Nature. It is also more general, not only on account of the immense numbers of sociable species, such as the ruminants, most rodents, many birds, the ants, the bees, and so on, which do not prey at all upon other animals, and the overwhelming numbers of individuals which all sociable species contain, but also because nearly all carnivorous and rapacious species, and especially those of them which are not in decay owing to a rapid extermination by man or to some other cause, also practise it to some extent. *Mutual aid is the predominant fact of nature.*

If mutual support is so general in Nature, it is because it offers such immense advantages to all those animals which practise it, that it entirely upsets the balance of power to the disadvantage of the *predatory* creatures. It represents the best weapon in the great struggle for life which continually has to be carried on in Nature against climate, inundations, storms, frost, and the like, and continually requires new adaptations to the ever-changing conditions of existence. Therefore, taken as a whole, Nature is by no means

4 *Nineteenth Century,* 1890, 1891, 1892, 1894, and 1896; and in the book, *Mutual Aid: A Factor of Evolution,* London (Heinemann), 2nd edition, 1904. [Many later editions, Lond. and N. Y.]—Trans. Note.

14

an illustration of the triumph of physical force, swiftness, cunning, or any other feature useful in warfare. It seems, on the contrary, that species decidedly weak, such as the ant, the bee, the pigeon, the duck, the marmot and other rodents, the gazelle, the deer, etc., having no protective armour, no strong beak or fang for self-defence,—and not at all warlike—nevertheless, succeed best in the struggle for life; and owing to their sociality and mutual protection, they even displace much more powerfully-built competitors and enemies. And, finally, we can take it as proved that while struggle for life leads indifferently to both progressive and regressive evolution, the practice of mutual aid is the agency which always leads to progressive development. It is the main factor in the progressive evolution of the animal kingdom, in the development of longevity, intelligence, and of that which we call the higher type in the chain of living creatures. No biologist has so far refuted this contention of mine.[5]

Being thus necessary for the *preservation*, the *welfare*, and the *progressive development* of every species, the mutual-aid instinct has become what Darwin described as *"a permanent instinct,"* which is *always at work* in all social animals, and especially in man. Having its origin at the very beginnings of the evolution of the animal world, it is certainly an instinct as deeply seated in animals, low and high, as the instinct of maternal love; perhaps even deeper, because it is present in such animals as the molluscs, some insects, and most fishes, which hardly possess the maternal instinct at all. Darwin was therefore quite right in considering that the instinct of "mutual sympathy" is *more permanently* at work in the social animals than even the purely egotistic instinct of direct self-preservation. He saw in it, as is known, the rudiments of the moral conscience, which consideration is, unfortunately, too often forgotten by the Darwinists.

[5] See remarks in this connection by Lloyd Morgan and my reply to them. [Conwy L. Morgan, *Animal Behaviour*, Lond. 1900, pp. 227 ff. The reply is found in one of the notes to *Mutual Aid*.]—Trans. Note.

15

But this is not all. In the same instinct we have the origin of those feelings of benevolence and of that partial identification of the individual with the group which are the starting-point of all the higher ethical feelings. It is upon this foundation that the higher sense of justice, or equity, is developed, as well as that which it is customary to call self-sacrifice. When we see that scores of thousands of different aquatic birds come in big flocks from the far South for nesting on the ledges of the "bird mountains" on the shores of the Arctic Ocean, and live here without fighting for the best positions; that several flocks of pelicans will live by the side of one another on the sea-shore, while each flock keeps to its assigned fishing ground; and that thousands of species of birds and mammals come in some way without fighting to a certain arrangement concerning their feeding areas, their nesting places, their night quarters, and their hunting grounds; or when we see that a young bird which has stolen some straw from another bird's nest is attacked by all the birds of the same colony, we catch on the spot the very origin and growth of the sense of equity and justice in animal societies. And finally, in proportion as we advance in every class of animals towards the higher representatives of that class (the ants, the wasps, and the bees amongst the insects, the cranes and the parrots amongst the birds, the higher ruminants, the apes, and then man amongst the mammals), we find that the identification of the individual with the interests of his group, and eventually even self-sacrifice for it, grow in proportion. In this circumstance we cannot but see the indication of the natural origin not only of the rudiments of ethics, but also of the higher ethical feelings.

It thus appears that not only does Nature fail to give us a lesson of a-moralism, i. e., of the indifferent attitude to morality which needs to be combated by some extra-natural influence, but we are bound to recognize that *the very ideas of bad and good*, and man's abstractions concerning "the supreme good" have been borrowed from Nature. They are reflections in the mind of man of what he saw in animal life and in the course of his social life, and due to it these impressions were developed into *general* conceptions of right and wrong. And it should be noted that we do not mean here the personal judgments of exceptional individuals, but the judgment of the majority. They contain the fundamental principles of equity and mutual sympathy, which apply to all sentient beings, just as principles of mechanics derived from observation on the surface of the earth apply to matter in the stellar spaces.

A similar conception must also apply to the evolution of human character and human institutions. The development of man came about in the same natural environment, and was guided by it in the same direction, while the very institutions for mutual aid and support, formed in human societies, more and more clearly demonstrated to man to what an extent he was indebted to these institutions for his strength. In such a social environment the moral aspect of man was more and more developed. On the basis of new investigations in the field of history it is already possible to conceive the history of mankind as the evolution of an ethical factor, as the evolution of an inherent tendency of man to organize his life on the basis of mutual aid, first within the tribe, then in the village community, and in the republics of the free cities,—these forms of social organization becoming in turn the bases of further progress, periods of retrogression notwithstanding. We certainly must abandon the idea of representing human history as an uninterrupted chain of development from the pre-historic Stone Age to the present time. The development of human societies was not continuous. It was started several times anew—in India, Egypt, Mesopotamia, Greece, Rome, Scandinavia, and in Western Europe, beginning each time with the primitive tribe and then the village community. But if we consider each of these lines separately, we certainly find in each of them, and especially in the development of Europe since the fall of the Roman Empire, a continual widening of the conception of mutual support and mutual protection, from the clan to the tribe, the nation, and finally to the international union of nations. On the other hand, notwithstanding the temporary regressive movements which occasionally take place, even in the most civilized nations, there is—at least among the representatives of advanced thought in the civilized world and in the progressive popular movements—the tendency of always widening the current conception of human solidarity and justice, and of constantly improving the character of our mutual relations. We also mark the appearance, in the form of an ideal, of the conceptions of what is desirable in further development.

The very fact that the backward movements which take place from time to time are considered by the enlightened portion of the population as mere temporary illnesses of the social organism, the return of which must be prevented in the future, proves that the average ethical standard is now higher than it was in the past. And in proportion as the means of satisfying the needs of all the members of the civilized communities are improved, and the way is prepared for a still higher conception of justice for all, the ethical standard is bound to become more and more refined. Taking this viewpoint of scientific ethics, man is in a position not only to reaffirm his faith in moral progress, all pessimistic lessons to the contrary notwithstanding, but he can also put it on a scientific basis. He sees that this belief, although it originated only in one of those intuitions which always precede science, was quite correct, and is now confirmed by positive knowledge.

CHAPTER II

IF the empirical philosophers have hitherto failed to prove the existence of a steady progress of moral conceptions (which may be called the leading principle of evolution), the fault lies to a great extent with the speculative, i. e., the non-scientific philosophers. They have so strongly denied the empirical origin of man's moral feelings; they have gone to such subtle reasoning in order to assign a supernatural origin to the moral sense; and they have spoken so much about "the destination of man," the "way of his existence," and "the aim of Nature," that a reaction against the mythological and metaphysical conceptions which had risen round this question was unavoidable. Moreover, the modern evolutionists, having established the presence in the animal world of a keen struggle for life among different species, could not accept such a brutal process, which entails so much suffering upon sentient beings, as the expression of a Supreme Being; and they consequently denied that any ethical principle could be discovered in it. Only now that the evolution of species, races of men, human institutions, and of ethical ideas themselves, has been proved to be the result of natural forces, has it become possible to study all the factors of this evolution, including the ethical factor of mutual support and growing sympathy, without the risk of falling back into a supra-natural philosophy. But, this being so, we reach a point of considerable philosophical importance.

We are enabled to conclude that the lesson which man derives both from the study of Nature and his own history is the permanent presence of a *double tendency*—towards a greater development, on the one side, of *sociality,* and, on the other side, of a consequent increase of the intensity of life, which results in an increase of happiness for the *individuals,* and in progress,—physical, intellectual, and moral.

This double tendency is a distinctive characteristic of life in general. It is always present, and belongs to life, as one of its attributes, whatever aspects life may take on our planet or elsewhere. And this is not a metaphysical assertion of the "universality of the moral law," or a mere supposition. Without the continual growth of sociality, and consequently of the intensity and variety of sensations, life is impossible. Therein lies its essence. If that element is lacking life tends to ebb, to disintegrate, to cease. This may be recognized as an empirically discovered law of Nature.

It thus appears that science, far from destroying the foundations of ethics gives, on the contrary, a concrete content to the nebulous metaphysical presumptions which are current in transcendental extra-natural ethics. As science goes deeper into the life of Nature, it gives to evolutionist ethics a *philosophical certitude,* where the transcendental thinker had only a vague intuition to rely on.

There is still less foundation for another continually repeated reproach to empirical thought,—namely, that the study of Nature can only lead us to knowledge of some cold and mathematical truth, but that such truths have little effect upon our actions. The study of Nature, we are told, can at best inspire us with the love of truth; but the inspiration for higher emotions, such as that of "infinite goodness," can be given only by religion. It can be easily shown that this contention is not based on any facts and is, therefore, utterly fallacious. To begin with, love of truth is already one half—the better half—of all ethical teaching. Intelligent religious people understand this very well. As to the conception of "good" and striving for it, the "truth" which we have just mentioned, i. e., the recognition of mutual aid as the fundamental feature of life, is certainly an inspiring truth, which surely will some day find its expression in the poetry of Nature, for it imparts to our conception of Nature an additional humanitarian touch.

Goethe, with the insight of his pantheistic genius, at once understood all the philosophical significance of this truth, upon the very first hint of it that he heard from Eckermann, the zoölogist.[1] Moreover, the deeper we go into the study of primitive man, the more we realize that it was from the life of animals with whom he stood in close contact that he learned the first lessons of valorous defence of fellow-creatures, self-sacrifice for the welfare of the group, unlimited parental love, and the advantages of sociality in general. The conceptions of "virtue" and "wickedness" are zoölogical, not merely human conceptions.

As to the powers which ideas and intellectually conceived ideals exercise upon current moral conceptions, and how these conceptions influence in their turn the intellectual aspect of an epoch, this subject hardly need be insisted upon. The intellectual evolution of a given society may take at times, under the influence of all sorts of circumstances, a totally wrong turn, or it may take, on the contrary, a high flight. But in both cases the leading ideas of the time will never fail deeply to influence the ethical life. The same applies also to the individual.

Most certainly, *ideas* are *forces*, as Fouillée puts it;[2] and they are ethical forces, if the ideas are correct and wide enough to represent the real life of nature in its entirety,—not one of its sides only. The first step, therefore, towards the elaboration of a morality which should exercise a lasting influence upon society, is to base

---

[1] See Eckermann, *Gespräche mit Goethe,* Leipzig 1848, vol. III; 219, 221. When Eckermann told Goethe that a fledgling, which fell out of the nest after Eckermann had shot its mother, was picked up by a mother of another species, Goethe was deeply moved. "If," said he, "this will prove to be a widespread fact, it will explain the 'divine in nature.'" The zoölogists of the early nineteenth century, who studied animal life on the still-unpopulated parts of the American continent, and such a naturalist as Brehm, have shown that the fact noted by Eckermann is fairly common in the animal world. [There are several English translations of Eckermann's *Conversations with Goethe.* In his *Mutual Aid* Kropotkin gives a slightly different version of this "conversation."]—Trans. Note.

[2] [Alfred Fouillée, *La psychologie des idées-forces,* Paris, 1893, 2 vols.; 3d ed., enlarged, Paris, 1912.]—Trans. Note.

21

this morality upon firmly established truths. And indeed, one of the main obstacles to the working out of a complete ethical system, corresponding to the present needs, is the fact that the science of society is still in its infancy. Having just completed its storing of materials, sociology is only beginning to investigate them with the view to ascertaining the probable lines of a future development. But it continually meets in this field with a great number of deeply rooted prejudices.

The chief demand which is now addressed to ethics is to do its best to find through the philosophical study of the subject the common element in the two sets of diametrically opposed feelings which exist in man, and thus to help mankind find a synthesis, and not a compromise between the two. In one set are the feelings which induce man to subdue other men in order to utilize them for his individual ends, while those in the other set induce human beings to unite for attaining common ends by common effort: the first answering to that fundamental need of human nature—struggle, and the second representing another equally fundamental tendency— the desire of unity and mutual sympathy. These two sets of feelings must, of course, struggle between themselves, but it is absolutely essential to discover their synthesis, whatever form it takes. Such a synthesis is so much more necessary because the civilized man of to-day, having no settled conviction on this point, is paralyzed in his powers of action. He cannot admit that a struggle to the knife for supremacy, carried on between individuals and nations, should be the last word of science; he does not believe, at the same time, in solving the problem through the gospel of brotherhood and self-abnegation which Christianity has been preaching for so many centuries without ever being able to attain the brotherhood of men and nations nor even tolerance among the various Christian sects. As regards the teaching of the Communists, the vast majority of men, for the same reason, have no faith in communism.

Thus the principal problem of ethics at present is to help mankind to find the solution for this fundamental contradiction. For this purpose we must earnestly study what were the means resorted to by men at different periods of their evolution, in order so to direct the individual forces as to get from them the greatest benefit for the welfare of all, without at the same time paralyzing personal energies. And we have to study the tendencies in this direction which exist at the present moment—in the form of the timid attempts which are being made, as well as in the form of the potentialities concealed in modern society, which may be utilized for finding that synthesis. And then, as no new move in civilization has ever been made without a certain enthusiasm being evoked in order to overcome the first difficulties of inertia and opposition, it is the duty of the new ethics to infuse in men those *ideals* which would provoke their enthusiasm, and give them the necessary forces for building a form of life which would combine individual energy with work for the good of all.

The need of a realistic ideal brings us to the chief reproach which has always been made to all non-religious systems of ethics. Their conclusions, we are told, will never have the necessary authority for influencing the actions of men, because they cannot be invested with the sense of *duty*, of *obligation*. It is perfectly true that empirical ethics has never claimed to possess the imperative character, such as belongs, for example, to the Mosaic Decalogue. True, that when Kant advanced as the "categorical imperative" of all morality the rule: "So act that the maxim of thy will may serve at the same time as a principle of universal legislation," [3] it required no sanction whatever for being universally recognized as obligatory. It was, he maintained, a *necessary* form of reasoning, a "category" of our intellect, and it was deduced from no utilitarian considerations.

However, modern criticism, beginning with Schopenhauer, has shown that Kant was mistaken. He has certainly *failed to prove* why it should be a duty to act according to his "imperative." And, strange to say, it follows from Kant's own reasoning that the only

---

[3] [Kant's *Metaphysics of Morals.* See Abbott's trans., *Kant's Theory of Ethics*, page 39; also pp. 18, 41.]—Trans. Note.

ground upon which his "imperative" might recommend itself to general acceptance is its social *utility,* although some of the best pages which Kant wrote were precisely those in which he strongly objected to any considerations of utility being taken as the foundation of morality. After all, he produced a beautiful panegyric on the sense of duty, but he failed to give to this sense any other foundation than the inner conscience of man and his desire of retaining a harmony between his intellectual conceptions and his actions.[4]

Empirical morality does not in the least pretend to find a substitute for the religious imperative expressed in the words, "I am the Lord," but the painful discrepancy which exists between the ethical prescriptions of the Christian religion and the life of societies calling themselves Christian, deprives the above reproach of its value. However, even empirical morality is not entirely devoid of a sense of conditional obligation. The different feelings and actions which are usually described since the times of Auguste Comte as "altruistic" can easily be classed under two different headings. There are actions which may be considered as absolutely necessary, once we choose to live in society, and to which, therefore, the name of "altruistic" ought never to be applied: they bear the character of reciprocity, and they are as much in the interest of the individual as any act of self-preservation. And there are, on the other hand, those actions which bear no character of reciprocity. One who performs such acts gives his powers, his energy, his enthusiasm, expecting no compensation in return, and although such acts are the real mainsprings of moral progress, they certainly can have no character of

[4] Later, however, he went further. It follows from his *Philosophical Theory of Faith,* published in 1792, that if he began by setting rational ethics over against the anti-Christian teachings of that time, he ended by recognizing the "inconceivability of the moral faculty, pointing to its divine origin." (Kant's *Works,* Hartenstein's Edition, vol. VI, pp. 143–144). [Leipzig, 1867–8, 8 vols. Kropotkin refers here to Kant's *Vorlesungen über die philosophische Religionslehre,*—a series of articles, the first of which appeared in a German magazine in 1792. They were edited, Leipzig, 1817, by Pölitz. See also, J. W. Semple's *Kant's Theory of Religion,* Lond. 1838; 1848.]—Trans. Note.

obligation attached to them. And yet, these two classes of acts are continually confused by writers on morality, and as a result many contradictions arise in dealing with ethical questions.

This confusion, however, can be easily avoided. First of all it is evident that it is preferable to keep ethical problems distinct from the problems of law. Moral science does not even settle the question whether legislation is necessary or not. It stands above that. We know, indeed, ethical writers—and these were not the least influential in the early beginnings of the Reformation—who denied the necessity of any legislation and appealed directly to human conscience. The function of ethics is not even so much to insist upon the defects of man, and to reproach him with his "sins," as to act in the *positive* direction, by appealing to man's best instincts. It determines, and explains, the few fundamental principles without which neither animals nor men could live in societies; but then it appeals to something superior to that: to love, courage, fraternity, self-respect, accord with one's ideal. It tells man that if he desires to have a life in which all his forces, physical, intellectual, and emotional, may find a full exercise, he must once and for ever abandon the idea that such a life is attainable on the path of disregard for others.

It is only through establishing a certain harmony between the individual and all others that an approach to such complete life will be possible, says Ethics, and then adds: "Look at Nature itself! Study the past of mankind! They will prove to you that so it is in reality." And when the individual, for this or that reason, hesitates in some special case as to the best course to follow, ethics comes to his aid and indicates how he would like others to act with respect to him, in a similar case.[5] But even then true ethics does not trace a stiff line of conduct, because it is the individual himself who must weigh the relative value of the different mo-

[5] "Ethics will not tell him, 'This you must do,' but inquire with him, 'What is it that you will, in reality and definitively—not only in a momentary mood?'" (F. Paulsen, *System der Ethik*, 2 vols., Berlin, 1896, vol. I, p. 20.)

tives affecting him. There is no use to recommend risk to one who can stand no reverse, or to speak of an old man's prudence to the young man full of energy. He would give the reply—the profoundly true and beautiful reply which Egmont gives to old Count Oliva's advice in Goethe's drama—and he would be quite right: "As if spurred by unseen spirits, the sun-horses of time run with the light cart of our fate; and there remains to us only boldly to hold the reins and lead the wheels away—here, from a stone on our left, there from upsetting the cart on our right. Whereto does it run? Who knows? Can we only remember wherefrom we came?" "The flower must bloom," as Guyau says,[6] even though its blooming meant death.

And yet the main purpose of ethics is not to advise men separately. It is rather to set before them, as a whole, a higher purpose, an ideal which, better than any advice, would make them act instinctively in the proper direction. Just as the aim of mental training is to accustom us to perform an enormous number of mental operations almost unconsciously, so is the aim of ethics to create such an atmosphere in society as would produce in the great number, entirely by impulse, those actions which best lead to the welfare of all and the fullest happiness of every separate being.

Such is the final aim of morality; but to reach it we must free our moral teachings from the self-contradictions which they contain. A morality, for example, which preaches "charity," out of compassion and pity, necessarily contains a deadly contradiction. It starts with the assertion of full equity and justice, or of full brotherhood, but then it hastens to add that we need not worry our minds with either. The one is unattainable. As to the brotherhood of men, which is the fundamental principle of all religions, it must not be taken literally; that was a mere poetical phrase of enthusiastic preachers. "Inequality is the rule of Nature," we are told by religious preachers, who in this can call Nature to their aid; in this

[6] M. Guyau, *A Sketch of Morality independent of Obligation or Sanction,* trans. by Gertrude Kapteyn, London (Watts), 1898.

respect, they teach us, we should take lessons from Nature, not from religion, which has always quarreled with Nature. But when the inequalities in the modes of living of men become too striking, and the sum total of produced wealth is so divided as to result in the most abject misery for a very great number, then sharing with the poor "what can be shared" without parting with one's privileged position, becomes a holy duty.

Such a morality may certainly be prevalent in a society for a time, or even for a long time, if it has the sanction of religion interpreted by the reigning Church. But the moment man begins to consider the prescriptions of religion with a critical eye, and requires a reasoned conviction instead of mere obedience and fear, an inner contradiction of this sort cannot be retained much longer. It must be abandoned—the sooner the better. Inner contradiction is the death-sentence of all ethics and a worm undermining human energy.

A most important condition which a modern ethical system is bound to satisfy is that it must not fetter individual initiative, be it for so high a purpose as the welfare of the commonwealth or the species. Wundt, in his excellent review of the ethical systems, makes the remark that beginning with the eighteenth-century period of enlightenment, nearly all of them became individualistic. This, however, is only partly true, because the rights of the individual were asserted with great energy in one domain only—in economics. And even here individual freedom remained, both in theory and in practice, more illusory than real. As to the other domains—political, intellectual, artistic—it may be said that in proportion as economic individualism was asserted with more emphasis, the subjection of the individual—to the war machinery of the State, the system of education, the mental discipline required for the support of the existing institutions, and so on—was steadily growing. Even most of the advanced reformers of the present day, in their forecasts of the future, reason under the presumption of a still greater absorption of the individual by society.

27

This tendency necessarily provoked a protest, voiced by Godwin at the beginning of the nineteenth century, and by Spencer towards its end, and it brought Nietzsche to conclude that all morality must be thrown overboard if it can find no better foundation than the sacrifice of the individual in the interests of the human race. This critique of the current ethical systems is perhaps the most characteristic feature of our epoch, the more so as its mainspring is not so much in an egoistic striving after economical independence (as was the case with the eighteenth-century individualists, with the exception of Godwin) as in a passionate desire of *personal independence for working out a new, better form of society*, in which the welfare of all would become a groundwork for the fullest development of the personality.[7]

The want of development of the personality (leading to herd-psychology) and the lack of individual creative power and initiative are certainly one of the chief defects of our time. Economical individualism has not kept its promise: it did not result in any striking development of individuality. As of yore, creative work in the field of sociology is extremely slow, and imitation remains the chief means for spreading progressive innovations in mankind. Modern nations repeat the history of the barbarian tribes and the mediæval cities when they copied from one another the same political, religious, and economic movements, and the "charters of freedom." Whole nations have appropriated to themselves lately, with astounding rapidity, the results of the west European industrial and military civilization; and in these unrevised new editions of old types we see best how superficial is that which is called culture, how much of it is mere imitation.

[7] Wundt makes a very interesting remark:—"For, unless all signs fail, a revolution of opinion is at present going on, in which the extreme individualism of the enlightenment is giving place to a revival of the universalism of antiquity, supplemented by a better notion of the liberty of human personality—an improvement that we owe to individualism." (*Ethics*, III, p. 34 of the English translation; p. 459 of German original.) [Eng. tr. by Titchener, Julia Gulliver, and Margaret Washburn, N. Y. & Lond., 1897–1901, 3 vols. German original, *Ethik*, Stuttgart, 1903 (3rd ed.), 2 vols.]—Trans. Note.

GRADUALLY EVOLVING BASES OF NEW ETHICS

It is only natural, therefore, to ask ourselves whether the current moral teachings are not instrumental in maintaining that imitative submission. Did they not aim too much at converting man into the "ideational automaton" of Herbart, who is absorbed in contemplation, and fears above all the storms of passion? Is it not time to rise in defence of the rights of the real man, full of vigour, who is capable of really loving what is worth being loved and hating what deserves hatred,—the man who is always ready to fight for an ideal which ennobles his love and justifies his antipathies? From the times of the philosophers of antiquity there was a tendency to represent "virtue" as a sort of "wisdom" which induces man to "cultivate the beauty of his soul," rather than to join "the unwise" in their struggles against the evils of the day. Later on that virtue became "non-resistance to evil," and for many centuries in succession individual personal "salvation," coupled with resignation ai. d a passive attitude towards evil, was the essence of Christian ethics; the result being the culture of a monastic indifference to social good and evil, and the elaboration of an argumentation in defence of "virtuous individualism." Fortunately, a reaction against such egoistic virtue is already under way, and the question is asked whether a passive attitude in the presence of evil does not merely mean moral cowardice,—whether, as was taught by the Zend-Avesta, an active struggle against the evil Ahriman is not the first condition of virtue? [8] We need moral progress, but without moral courage no moral progress is possible.

Such are some of the demands presented to ethics which can be discerned amid the present confusion. All of them converge towards one leading idea. What is wanted now is a new conception of morality,—in its fundamental principles, which must be broad enough to infuse new life in our civilization, and in its applications, which must be freed both from the survivals of transcendental thinking, as

[8] C. P. Tiele, *Geschichte der Religion in Altertum,* German translation by G. Gehrich. Gotha, 1903, vol. II pp. 163 sq. [Trans. from the Dutch of Cornelius Petrus Tiele, Gotha, 3 vols., 1896–1903.]—Trans. Note.

well as from the narrow conceptions of philistine utilitarianism.

The elements for such a new conception of morality are already at hand. The importance of *sociality*, of *mutual aid*, in the evolution of the animal world and human history may be taken, I believe, as a positively established scientific truth, free of any hypothetical assumptions. We may also take next, as granted, that in proportion as mutual aid becomes an established custom in a human community, and so to say instinctive, it leads to a parallel development of the sense of *justice*, with its necessary accompaniment of the sense of *equity* and equalitarian self-restraint. The idea that the personal rights of every individual are as unassailable as the same rights of every other individual, grows in proportion as class distinctions fade away; and this thought becomes a current conception when the institutions of a given community have been altered permanently in this sense. A certain degree of identification of the individual with the interests of the group to which it belongs has necessarily existed since the very beginning of social life, and it manifests itself even among the lowest animals. But in proportion as relations of equity and justice are solidly established in the human community, the ground is prepared for the further and the more general development of more refined relations, under which man understands and feels so well the bearing of his action on the whole of society that he refrains from offending others, even though he may have to renounce on that account the gratification of some of his own desires, and when he so fully identifies his feelings with those of others that he is ready to sacrifice his powers for their benefit without expecting anything in return. These unselfish feelings and habits, usually called by the somewhat inaccurate names of *altruism* and *self-sacrifice*, alone deserve, in my opinion, the name of morality, properly speaking, although most writers confound them, under the name of altruism, with the mere sense of justice.

Mutual Aid—Justice—Morality are thus the consecutive steps of an ascending series, revealed to us by the study of the animal world and man. They constitute an *organic necessity* which carries in itself its own justification, confirmed by the whole of the evolution of the animal kingdom, beginning with its earliest stages, (in the form of colonies of the most primitive organisms), and gradually rising to our civilized human communities. Figuratively speaking, it is a *universal law of organic evolution,* and this is why the sense of Mutual Aid, Justice, and Morality are rooted in man's mind with all the force of an inborn instinct—the first instinct, that of Mutual Aid, being evidently the strongest, while the third, developed later than the others, is an unstable feeling and the least imperative of the three.

Like the need of food, shelter, or sleep, these instincts are self-preservation instincts. Of course, they may sometimes be weakened under the influence of certain circumstances, and we know many cases when the power of these instincts is relaxed, for one reason or another, in some animal group, or in a human community; but then the group necessarily begins to fail in the struggle for life; it moves towards its decay. And if this group does not revert to the necessary conditions of survival and of progressive development: Mutual Aid, Justice, and Morality—then the group, the race, or the species dies out and disappears. Since it did not fulfil the necessary condition of evolution—it must inevitably decline and disappear.

Such is the solid foundation which science gives us for the elaboration of a new system of ethics and its justification; and, therefore, instead of proclaiming "the bankruptcy of science," what we have now to do is to examine how scientific ethics can be built from the materials which modern research, stimulated by the idea of evolution, has accumulated for that purpose.

CHAPTER III

THE MORAL PRINCIPLE IN NATURE

THE work of Darwin was not limited to biology only. Already in 1837, when he had just written a rough outline of his theory of the origin of species, he entered in his notebook this significant remark: "My theory will lead to a new philosophy." And so it did in reality. By introducing the idea of evolution into the study of organic life he opened a new era in philosophy,[1] and his later sketch of the development of the moral sense, turned a new page in ethics. In this sketch Darwin presented in a new light the true origin of the moral sense, and placed the whole subject on such a firm scientific basis, that although his leading ideas may be considered as a further development of those of Shaftesbury and Hutcheson, he must be, nevertheless, credited with opening a new path for science in the direction faintly indicated by Bacon. He thus became one of the founders of the ethical schools, together with such men as Hume, Hobbes, or Kant.

The leading ideas of Darwin's ethics may easily be summed up. In the very first sentence of his essay he states his object in quite definite terms. He begins with a praise of the sense of duty, which he characterises in the well-known poetical words,—"Duty! Wondrous thought that workest neither by fond insinuation, flattery, nor by any threat . . ." etc. And he undertakes to explain this sense of duty, or moral conscience, "exclusively from the viewpoint of

[1] In his *History of Modern Philosophy*, the Danish professor, Harald Höffding, gives an admirable sketch of the philosophical importance of Darwin's work. *Geschichte der neueren Philosophie*, German translation by F. Bendixen (Leipzig, 1896), vol. II, pp. 487 sq. [Eng. tr., Lond., 1900, by B. E. Meyer, 2 vols.]—Trans. Note.

natural history"—an explanation, he adds, which no English writer had hitherto attempted to give.[2]

That the moral sense should be acquired by each individual separately, during his lifetime, he naturally considers "at least extremely improbable in the light of the general theory of evolution;" and he derives this sense from the social feeling which is instinctive or innate in the lower animals, and probably in man as well (pp. 150–151). The true foundation of all moral feelings Darwin sees "in the social instincts which lead the animal to take pleasure in the society of its fellows, to feel a certain amount of sympathy with them, and to perform various services for them"; sympathy being understood here in its exact sense—not as a feeling of commiseration or "love," but as a "feeling of comradeship" or "mutual sensibility," in the meaning of capability to be influenced by another's feelings.

This being Darwin's first proposition, his second is that as soon as the mental faculties of a species become highly developed, as they are in man, the social instinct will also necessarily be developed. To leave this instinct ungratified will assuredly bring the individual to a sense of dissatisfaction, or even misery, whenever the individual, reasoning about his past actions, sees that in some of them "the enduring and always present social instinct had yielded to some other instinct, at the time stronger, but neither enduring nor leaving behind it a very vivid impression."

For Darwin the moral sense is thus not the mysterious gift of unknown origin which it was for Kant. "Any animal whatever," he says, "endowed with well-marked social instincts, the parental and filial affections being here included, would inevitably acquire a moral sense, or conscience (Kant's 'knowledge of duty'), as soon as its intellectual powers had become as well, or nearly as well, developed as in man" (ch. iv. pp. 149–150).

To these two fundamental propositions Darwin adds two second-

[2] *The Descent of Man*, chap. iv. pp. 148 sq. All quotations are from the last (cheap) edition of Mr. Murray, 1901. [First edition, 1871, Lond. & N. Y.; 2nd, N. Y., 1917].—Trans. Note.

ary ones. After the spoken language had been acquired, so that the wishes of the community could be expressed, "the common opinion how each member ought to act for the public good would naturally become, in a paramount degree, the guide of action." However, the effect of public approbation and disapprobation depends entirely upon the development of mutual sympathy. It is because we feel in sympathy with others that we appreciate their opinions; and public opinion acts in a moral direction only where the social instinct is sufficiently strongly developed. The truth of this remark is obvious. It refutes those theories of Mandeville (the author of "The Fable of the Bees") and his more or less outspoken eighteenth-century followers, which attempted to represent morality as nothing but a set of conventional customs. Finally, Darwin mentions also *habit* as a potent factor for framing our attitude toward others. It strengthens the social instinct and mutual sympathy, as well as obedience to the judgment of the community.

Having thus stated the substance of his views in these four propositions, Darwin develops them further. He examines, first, sociality in animals, their love of society, and the misery which every one of them feels if it is left alone; their continual social intercourse; their mutual warnings, and the services they render each other in hunting and for self-defence. "It is certain," he says, "that associated animals have a feeling of love for each other which is not felt by non-social adult animals." They may not sympathize much with one another's pleasures; but cases of sympathy with one another's distress or danger are quite common, and Darwin quotes a few of the most striking instances. Some of them, such as Stansbury's blind pelican [3] or the blind rat, both of which were fed by their congeners,

[3] [The reference is to Captain Stansbury, who, on a trip to Utah, saw a blind pelican being fed by other pelicans,—on fish brought a distance of thirty miles. Kropotkin quotes this from Darwin's *Descent of Man*, Chapter iv. See also, L. H. Morgan's *The American Beaver*, 1868, p. 272, to which Kropotkin refers in his *Mutual Aid*, page 51. Howard Stansbury, *Exploration and Survey of the Valley of the Great Salt Lake*, Phil., 1852; 1855. The case of the blind rat is taken from M. Perty's *Ueber das Seelenleben der Thiere*, pp. 64 ff., Leipzig, 1876.]—Trans. Note.

have become classical by this time. "Moreover, besides love and sympathy," Darwin continues, "animals exhibit other qualities connected with social instincts which in us would be called moral," and he gives a few examples of the moral sense in dogs and elephants.[4]

Generally speaking, it is evident that every action in common— (and with certain animals such actions are quite common: all their life consists of such actions)—requires restraint of some sort. However, it must be said that Darwin did not analyse the subject of sociality in animals and their incipient moral feelings to the extent which it deserved in view of the central position which it occupies in his theory of morality.

Considering next human morality, Darwin remarks that although man, such as he now exists, has but few social instincts, he nevertheless is a sociable being who must have retained from an extremely remote period some degree of instinctive love and sympathy for his fellows. These feelings act as an impulsive instinct, which is assisted by reason, experience, and the desire of approbation. "Thus," he concluded, "the social instincts, which must have been acquired by man in a very rude state, and probably even by his ape-like progenitors, still give the impulse for some of his best actions." The remainder is the result of a steadily growing intelligence and collective education.

It is evident that these views are correct only if we are ready to recognize that the intellectual faculties of animals differ from those of man in degree, but not in their essence. But this is admitted now by most students of comparative psychology; and the attempts which have been made lately to establish "a gulf" between the instincts and the intellectual faculties of man and those of animals have not attained their end.[5] However, it does not follow from

[4] Not long after, Herbert Spencer, who at first took a negative attitude toward morality in animals, cited a few similar facts in James Knowles' magazine, *Nineteenth Century*. These facts are reproduced in his *Principles of Ethics*, vol. II, Appendix 1. [vol. X of the *Synthetic Philosophy*.]

[5] The incapacity of an ant, a dog, or a cat to make a discovery, or to hit upon the correct solution of a difficulty, which is so often pointed out by

this resemblance that the moral instincts developed in different species, and so much more in species belonging to two different classes of animals, should be identical. If we compare insects with mammals we must never forget that the lines of their development have diverged at a very early period of animal evolution. The consequence was that a deep physiological differentiation between separate divisions of the same species (workers, drones, queens) took place with the ants, the bees, the wasps, etc., corresponding to a permanent physiological division of labour in their societies, (or more accurately, division of labour and a physiological division in structure). There is no such division among mammals. Therefore it is hardly possible for men to judge the "morality" of the worker-bees when they kill the drones in their hive; and this is why the illustration of Darwin to this effect met with so much hostile criticism from the religious camp. Societies of bees, wasps, and ants, and the societies of mammals have so long ago entered upon their independent paths of development, that they have lost mutual understanding in many respects. A similar, though not so pronounced lack of mutual understanding is observed also between human societies in different stages of development. And yet the moral conceptions of man and the actions of social insects have so much in common that the greatest ethical teachers of mankind did not hesitate to recommend certain

some writers on this subject, is not a proof of an essential difference between the intelligence of man and that of these animals, because the same want of inventiveness is continually met with in men as well. Like the ant in one of John Lubbock's experiments, thousands of men in an unfamiliar region, similarly attempt to ford a river, and perish in the attempt, before trying to span the river with some primitive bridge—a trunk of a fallen tree, for example. And, on the other hand, we find in animals the collective intelligence of an ant's nest or a beehive. And if one ant or one bee in a thousand happens to hit upon the correct solution, the others imitate it. And thus they solve problems much more difficult than those in which the individual ant, or bee, or cat has so ludicrously failed in the experiments of some naturalists, and, I venture to add, as the naturalists themselves fail in the arrangement of their experiments and in their conclusions. The bees at the Paris Exhibition, and their devices to prevent being continually disturbed in their work—they plastered the peep-window with wax (see *Mutual Aid*, Ch. 1)—or any one of the well-known facts of inventiveness among the bees, the ant, the wolves hunting together, are instances in point.

features of the life of the ants and the bees for imitation by man. Their devotion to the group is certainly not surpassed by ours; and, on the other hand,—to say nothing of our wars, or of the occasional exterminations of religious dissenters and political adversaries—the human code of morality has been subjected in the course of time to deepest variations and perversions. It is sufficient to mention human sacrifices to deity, the "wound-for-wound and life-for-life" principle of the Decalogue, the tortures and executions,—and to compare this "morality" with the profound respect for everything that lives preached by the Bodhisattvas, and the forgiveness of all injuries taught by the early Christians, in order to realize that moral principles, like everything else, are subject to "development" and at times to perversion. We are thus bound to conclude that while the differences between the morality of the bee and that of man are due to a deep physiological divergence, the striking similarities between the two *in other essential features* point to a community of origin.

Thus Darwin came to the conclusion that the social instinct is the common source out of which all morality originates; and he attempts to give a scientific definition of instinct. Unfortunately, scientific animal psychology is still in its infancy, and therefore it is extremely difficult to disentangle the complex relations which exist between the social instinct proper, and the parental, filial, brotherly instincts, as well as several other instincts and faculties, such as mutual sympathy, on one side, and reason, experience, and a tendency to imitation on the other. Darwin finally realized this difficulty, and therefore he expressed himself very guardedly. The parental and filial instincts, he suggested, "apparently lie at the base of the social instincts"; and in another place he wrote:—"The feeling of pleasure in society is probably an extension of the parental or filial affections, since the social instinct seems to be developed by the young remaining for a long time with their parents."

This caution was fully justified, because in other places Darwin pointed out that the *social instinct is a separate instinct,* different from the others—an instinct which has been developed by natural

37

selection *for its own sake,* as it was useful for the well-being and the preservation of the species. It is so fundamental that when it runs counter to another instinct, even one so strong as the attachment of the parents to their offspring, it often takes the upper hand. Birds, for example, when the time has come for their autumn migration, will leave behind their tender young (from the second hatching) which are not yet strong enough for a prolonged flight, and will follow their comrades.

To this very important fact I may also add that the social instinct is strongly developed also in many lower animals, such as the land-crabs, and in certain fishes with whom it could hardly be considered as an extension of the filial or parental feelings. In these cases it appears rather as an extension of the brotherly or sisterly relations, or feelings of comradeship, which probably develop each time that a considerable number of young creatures, having been hatched at a given place and at a given moment, (insects, or even birds of different species) continue to live together—whether they are with their parents or not. It would seem, therefore, more correct to consider the social, the parental, and the comradely instinct as closely connected instincts, of which the social is perhaps the earlier, and therefore the stronger, but they have all been developing together in the evolution of the animal world. Their growth was, of course, aided by natural selection, which, as soon as they come into conflict, keeps the balance between them for the ultimate good of the species.[6]

The most important point in the ethical theory of Darwin is, of course, his explanation of the moral conscience of man and his sense of duty and remorse of conscience. This point has always been the

[6] In an excellent analysis of the social instinct (*Animal Behaviour*, London, 1900, pp. 231–232) Professor Lloyd Morgan says: "And this question Prince Kropotkin, in common with Darwin and Espinas, would probably answer without hesitation that the primeval germ of the social community lay in the prolonged coherence of the group of parents and offspring." Perfectly true,—I should only add the words: "or of the offspring without the parents," because this addition would better agree with the facts stated above, while it also renders more correctly Darwin's idea.

stumbling block of all ethical theories. Kant, as is known, utterly failed, in his otherwise excellent work on morality, to explain why his "categorical imperative" should be obeyed at all, unless such be the will of a supreme power. We may admit that Kant's "moral law," if we slightly alter its formula while maintaining its spirit, is a *necessary conclusion of the human reason.* We certainly object to the metaphysical form which Kant gave it; but, after all, its substance, which Kant, unfortunately, did not express, is equity, justice. And, if we translate the metaphysical language of Kant into the language of inductive science, we may find points of contact between his conception of the origin of the moral law and the naturalist's view concerning the origin of the moral sense. But this is only one-half of the problem. Supposing, for the sake of argument, that Kantian "pure reason," independent of all observation, all feeling, and all instinct, but by virtue of its inherent properties,—must inevitably come to formulate a law of justice similar to Kant's "imperative," and even granting that no reasoning being could ever come to any other conclusion, because such are the inherent properties of reason—granting all this, and fully recognizing the elevating character of Kant's moral philosophy, the great question of all ethics remains, nevertheless, in full: "Why should man obey the moral law, or principle, formulated by his reason?" Or, at least, "Whence comes that feeling of obligation of which men are conscious?"

Several critics of Kant's ethical philosophy have already pointed out that it left this great fundamental question unsolved. But they might have added also that Kant himself recognized his inability to solve it. After having thought intensely upon this subject, and written about it for four years, he acknowledged in his book,—for some reason generally neglected—"Philosophical Theory of Religion" (Part I., "Of the Radical Evil of Human Nature," published in 1792) that *he was unable to find the explanation of the origin of the moral law.* In fact, he gave up the whole problem by recognizing "the incomprehensibility of this capacity, *a capacity which points to a divine origin."* This very incomprehensibility, he wrote, must rouse man's spirit to enthusiasm and give him strength for any sacrifices which regard for his duty may impose upon him.[7] Such a decision, after four years of meditation, is equivalent to a complete abandoning of this problem by philosophy, and the delivering of it into the hands of religion.

Intuitive philosophy having thus acknowledged its incapacity to solve the problem, let us see how Darwin solved it from the point of view of the naturalist. Here is, he said, a man who has yielded to the sense of self-preservation, and has not risked his life to save that of a fellow-creature; or, he has stolen food from hunger. In both cases he has obeyed a quite natural instinct, and the question is —Why does he feel ill at ease? Why does he now think that he ought to have obeyed some other instinct, and acted differently? Because, Darwin replies, in human nature "the more enduring social instincts conquer the less persistent instincts." Moral conscience, continues Darwin, has always a retrospective character; it speaks in us when we think of our past actions; and it is the result of a struggle in which the less persistent, the less permanent *individual* instinct yields before the more enduring *social* instinct. With those animals which always live in societies "the social instincts are ever present and persistent." Such animals are always ready to join in the defence of the group and to aid each other in different ways. They feel miserable if they are separated from the others. And it is the same with man. "A man who possessed no trace of such instincts would be a monster."

On the other hand, the man's desire to satisfy his hunger or let loose his anger, or to escape danger, or to appropriate somebody's possessions, is in its very nature temporary. *Its satisfaction is always weaker than the desire itself.* And when we think of it in the past, we cannot revive it with the same intensity that it had before its satisfaction. Consequently, if a man, with a view of satisfying

---

[7] Hartenstein's edition of Kant's works, vol. VI. pp. 143–144 [Leipzig, 1867–87]. English translation by Th. K. Abbott: Kant's *Critique of Practical Reason and Other Works*, London, 1879, pp. 425–427. [Lond., 1889].

such a desire, has acted contrary to his social instinct, and afterwards reflects upon his action—which we do continually—he will be driven "to make a comparison between the impressions of past hunger, vengeance satisfied, or danger shunned at other men's cost, with the almost ever-present instinct of sympathy, and with his early knowledge of what others consider as praiseworthy or blamable." And once he has made this comparison he will feel "as if he had been baulked in following a present instinct or habit, and this with all animals causes dissatisfaction, and in the case of man, even misery."

And then Darwin shows how the promptings of such a conscience, which always "looks backwards, and serves as a guide for the future," may in the case of man take the aspect of shame, regret, repentance, or even violent remorse, if the feeling be strengthened by reflection about the judgment of those with whom man feels in sympathy. Gradually, habit will inevitably increase the power of this conscience upon man's actions, while at the same time it will tend to harmonize more and more the desires and passions of the individual with his social sympathies and instincts.[8] The principal difficulty, common to all systems of ethical philosophy, is to interpret the first germs of the sense of duty, and to explain why the human mind must inevitably come to the conception of duty. With this explained, the accumulated experience of the community and its collective intelligence, account for the rest.

We have thus, in Darwin for the first time, an explanation of the sense of duty on a naturalistic basis. True that it runs counter to

[8] In a footnote, Darwin, with his usual deep insight, makes, however, one exception. "Enmity, or hatred," he remarks, "seems also to be a highly persistent feeling perhaps more so than any other that can be named. . . . This feeling would thus seem to be innate, and is certainly a most persistent one. It seems to be the complement and converse of the true social instinct." (Footnote 27) [of chap. iv, p. 114, 2nd ed. N. Y., 1917]. This feeling, so deeply seated in animal nature, evidently explains the bitter wars that are fought between different tribes, or groups, in several animal species and among men. It explains also the simultaneous existence of two different codes of morality among civilized nations. But this important and yet neglected subject can better be treated in connection with the discussion of the idea of justice.

the ideas that are current about animal and human nature; but it is correct. Nearly all ethical writers have hitherto started with the unproved postulate that the strongest of all the instincts of man, and more so of animals, is the *self-preservation instinct*, which, owing to a certain looseness of their terminology, they have identified with self-assertion, or egoism properly speaking. They conceived this instinct as including, on the one hand, such primary impulses as self-defence, self-preservation, and the very act of satisfying hunger, and, on the other hand, such derivative feelings as the passion for domination, greed, hatred, the desire for revenge, and so on. This mixture, this hodge-podge of instincts and feelings among animals and modern civilized men, they represented as an all-pervading and all-powerful force, which finds no opposition in animal and human nature, excepting in a certain feeling of benevolence or pity. *But once the nature of all animals and of man was recognized as such,* the only obvious course was to lay a special stress upon the softening influence of those moral teachers who appealed to mercy, and who borrowed the spirit of their teachings from a world that lies *outside nature*—outside and above the world which is accessible to our senses. And they endeavoured to strengthen the influences of their teachings by the support of a supernatural power. If one refused to accept this view, as did Hobbes, for example, the only alternative was to attribute a special importance to the coercive action of the State, inspired by lawgivers of extraordinary genius— which meant, of course, merely to credit with the possession of the "truth" not the religious preacher but the lawmaker.

Beginning with the Middle Ages, the founders of ethical schools, for the most part ignorant of Nature—to the study of which they preferred metaphysics,—had represented the self-assertive instincts of the individual as the primary condition of the existence of animals, as well as of man. To obey the promptings of these instincts was considered as the fundamental law of nature; to disobey—would lead to sure defeat and to the ultimate disappearance of the species. Therefore, to combat these egotistic promptings was possible only if man called to his aid the supernatural forces. The triumph of moral principles was thus represented as a *triumph of man over nature,* which he may hope to achieve only with an aid from without, coming as a reward for his good intentions.

We were told, for instance, that there is no greater *virtue,* no greater triumph of the spiritual over the physical than self-sacrifice for the welfare of our fellow-men. But the fact is that self-sacrifice in the interest of an ants' nest, or for the safety of a group of birds, a herd of antelopes, or a band of monkeys, is a *zoölogical fact of everyday occurrence in Nature*—a fact for which hundreds upon hundreds of animal species require nothing else but naturally evolved sympathy with their fellow-creatures, the constant practice of mutual aid and the consciousness of vital energy. Darwin, who knew nature, had the courage boldly to assert that of the two instincts—the social and the individual—it is *the social instinct which is the stronger, the more persistent, and the more permanently present.* And he was unquestionably right. All naturalists who have studied animal life in nature, especially on the still sparsely populated continents, would range themselves unconditionally on Darwin's side. The instinct of mutual aid pervades the animal world, because natural selection works for maintaining and further developing it, and pitilessly destroys those species in which it becomes for some reason weakened. In the great struggle for life which every animal species carries on against the hostile agencies of climate, surroundings, and natural enemies, big and small, those species which most consistently carry out the principle of mutual support have the best chance to survive, while the others die out. And the same principle is confirmed by the history of mankind.

It is most remarkable that in representing the social instinct under this aspect we return, in fact, to what Bacon, the great founder of inductive science, had already perceived. In his great work, "Instauratio Magna" (The Great Revival of the Sciences), he wrote:—

"All things are endued with an appetite for two kinds of good—

43

the one as a thing is a whole in itself, the other as it is a part of some greater whole; and this latter is more worthy and more powerful than the other, as it tends to the conservation of a more ample form. The first may be called individual, or self-good, and the latter, good of communion. . . . And thus it generally happens that the conservation of the more general form regulates the appetites." [9]

In another place he returns to the same idea. He speaks of "Two appetites (instincts) of the creatures": (1) that of self-preservation and defence, and (2) that of multiplying and propagating, and he adds: "The latter, which is active, and seems *stronger* and more worthy than the former, which is passive." It may be asked, of course, whether such a conception is consistent with the theory of natural selection, according to which *struggle for life, within the species,* was considered a necessary condition for the appearance of new species, and for evolution in general.

Having already discussed this question in detail in my "Mutual Aid," I will not enter into the matter here, and will only add the following remark. The first few years after the appearance of Darwin's "Origin of Species", we were all inclined to believe that an acute struggle for the means of existence between the members of the same species was necessary for *accentuating the variations,* and for the bringing into existence of the new sub-species and species. My observations of nature in Siberia, however, first engendered in me a doubt as to the existence of such a keen struggle *within the species;* they showed, on the contrary, the tremendous importance of mutual aid in times of migrations of animals and for the preservation of the species in general. But as Biology went deeper and deeper into the species of living

[9] *On the Dignity and Advancement of Learning,* Book VII, chap. i. (p. 270 of J. Devey's edition in Bohn's Library). Bacon's arguments in favor of this idea are of course insufficient; but it must be borne in mind that he was only establishing the outlines of a science which had to be worked out by his followers. The same idea was later expressed by Hugo Grotius, and by some other thinkers.

nature, and grew acquainted with the phenomenon of *the direct influence of the surroundings for producing variation in a definite direction,* especially in cases when portions of the species become separated from the main body in consequence of their migrations, it was possible to understand "struggle for life" in a much wider and deeper sense. Biologists had to acknowledge that groups of animals frequently act as a whole, carrying on the struggle against adverse conditions, or against some such enemy as a kindred species, *by means of mutual support within the group.* In this manner habits are acquired which reduce the struggle within the species while they lead at the same time to a higher development of intelligence amongst those who practise mutual aid. Nature abounds in such examples, and in each class of animals the species on the highest stage of development are those that are most social. *Mutual Aid within the species thus represents* (as was already briefly indicated by Kessler)[10] *the principal factor, the principal active agency in that which we may call evolution.*

Nature has thus to be recognized as the *first ethical teacher of man.* The social instinct, innate in men as well as in all the social animals,—this is the origin of all ethical conceptions and all the subsequent development of morality.

The starting point for a study of ethics was set by Darwin, three hundred years after the first attempts in this direction were made by Bacon, and partly by Spinoza and Goethe.[11] With the social instinct as a basis for the further development of moral feelings, it became possible, after having further strengthened that basis with facts, to build upon it the whole structure of ethics. Such a work, however, has not yet been carried out. Those evolutionists

[10] [Professor Kessler, one time Dean of the University of St. Petersburg, delivered a lecture on "The Law of Mutual Aid" before a meeting of the Russian Congress of Naturalists, Jan. 1880. It appears in the *Trudi (Memoirs)* of the St. Pet. Society of Naturalists, vol. II, 1880. See *Mutual Aid,* page x, and pp. 6–8.]—Trans. Note.

[11] See *Conversations between Eckermann and Goethe.* [Cf. Note, page 21 *supra.*]

who touched upon the question of morality mostly followed, for one reason or another, the lines of pre-Darwinian and pre-Lamarckian ethical thought, but not those which were indicated—perhaps too briefly—in "The Descent of Man."

This applies also to Herbert Spencer. Without going into a discussion of his ethics, (this will be done elsewhere), I shall simply remark that the ethical philosophy of Spencer was constructed on a different plan. The ethical and sociological portions of his "Synthetic Philosophy" were written long before Darwin's essay on the moral sense, under the influence, partly of Auguste Comte, and partly of Bentham's utilitarianism and the eighteenth-century sensualists.[12]

It is only in the first chapters of "Justice," (published in the "Nineteenth Century" in March and April 1890), that we find in Spencer's work a reference to "Animal Ethics" and "sub-human justice," to which Darwin has attributed such importance for the development of the moral sense in man. It is interesting to note that this reference has no connection with the rest of Spencer's ethics, because he does not consider primitive men as social beings whose societies are a continuation of the animal clans and tribes. Remaining true to Hobbes, he considers them loose aggregations of individuals who are strangers to one another, continually fight-

[12] Spencer's *Data of Ethics* appeared in 1879, and his *Justice* in 1891; that is, long after Darwin's *Descent of Man,* which was published in 1871. But his *Social Statics* had already appeared in 1850. Spencer was, of course, quite right in insisting upon the differences between his philosophical conceptions and those of Auguste Comte; but the influence upon him of the founder of Positivism is undeniable, notwithstanding the deep contrast between the minds of the two philosophers. To realize the influence of Comte it would be sufficient to compare Spencer's views on biology with those of the French philosopher, especially as they are expressed in chap. iii. of the *Discours préliminaire,* in vol. 1, of *Politique positive.* [*Système de politique positive,* Paris, 1851-4, 4 vols. Eng. tr., Lond., 1875-7, 4 vols.]—Trans. Note.

In Spencer's ethics, the influence of Comte is especially apparent in the importance attributed by Spencer to the distinction between the "militant" and the "industrial" stages of mankind, and also in the apposition of "egoism" to "altruism." This last word is used in the too wide, and therefore indefinite, sense in which it was used by Comte when he first coined it.

ing and quarrelling, and emerging from this chaotic state only after some superior man, taking power into his hands, organizes social life.

The chapter on animal ethics, added later by Spencer, is thus a superstructure on his general ethical system, and he did not explain why he deemed it necessary to modify his former views on this point. At any rate, he does not represent the moral sense of man as a further development of the feelings of sociality which existed amongst his remotest pre-human ancestors. According to Spencer, it made its appearance at a much later epoch, originating from those restraints which were imposed upon men by their political, social, and religious authorities ("Data of Ethics," § 45). The sense of duty, as Bain had suggested after Hobbes, is a product, or rather "a reminiscence," of the coercion which was exercised at the early stages of mankind by the first, temporary chiefs.

This supposition—which, by the way, it would be difficult to support by modern investigation—puts its stamp upon all the further developments of Spencer's ethics. He divides the history of mankind into two stages: the "militant," which is still prevalent, and the "industrial," which is being slowly ushered in at the present time, and each of them requires its own special morality. In the militant stage, coercion was more than necessary: it was the very condition of progress. It was also necessary during this stage that the individual should be sacrificed to the community, and that a corresponding moral code should be elaborated. And this necessity of coercion and sacrifice of the individual must continue to exist so long as the industrial State has not entirely taken the place of the militant State. Two different kinds of ethics, adapted to these two different States, are thus admitted ("Data," § 48–50), and such an admission leads Spencer to various other conclusions which stand or fall with the original premise.

Moral science appears, therefore, as the search for a compromise between a code of enmity and a code of amity—between equality and inequality (§ 85). And as there is no way out of that conflict— because the coming of the industrial state will only be possible after the cessation of its conflict with the militant state,—nothing can be done for the time being save to introduce into human relations a certain amount of "benevolence" which can alleviate somewhat the modern system based on individualistic principles. Therefore all his attempts to establish scientifically the fundamental principles of morality fail, and he finally comes to the unexpected conclusion that all the moral systems, philosophical and religious, complete each other. But Darwin's idea was quite the contrary: he maintained that the common stock out of which all systems and teachings of morality, including the ethical portions of the different religions, have originated, was the sociality, the power of the social instinct, that manifests itself even in the animal world and much more certainly among the most primitive savages. Spencer, like Huxley, vacillates between the theories of coercion, utilitarianism, and religion, unable to find outside of them the source of morality.

It may be added, in conclusion, that although Spencer's conception of the struggle between egoism and altruism bears a great resemblance to Comte's treatment of this subject, the views of the Positivist philosopher concerning the social instinct—notwithstanding all his opposition to the transmutation of the species—were nearer to the views of Darwin than to those of Spencer. Discussing the relative importance of the two sets of instincts, social and individual, Comte did not hesitate to recognize the preponderance of the former. He even saw in the recognition of this preponderance of the social instinct the distinctive feature of a moral philosophy which had broken with theology and metaphysics, but he did not carry this assertion to its logical conclusion.[13]

---

[13] "Positive morality thus differs, not only from metaphysical, but also from theological morality, in taking for a universal principle the direct preponderance of the social feelings" (*Politique positive, Discours préliminaire*, 2nd part, p. 93, and in several other places). Unfortunately, the flashes of genius which one finds scattered throughout the *Discours préliminaire* are often obscured by Comte's later ideas, which can scarcely be described as a development of the positive method.

48

THE MORAL PRINCIPLE IN NATURE

As already said, none of the immediate followers of Darwin attempted to develop further his ethical philosophy. George Romanes probably would have made an exception, because he proposed, after he had studied animal intelligence, to discuss animal ethics and the probable genesis of the moral sense; for which purpose he collected much material.[14] Unfortunately, we lost him before he had sufficiently advanced in his work.

As to the other evolutionists, they either adopted views in ethics very different from those of Darwin—as did Huxley in his lecture, "Evolution and Ethics,"—or they worked on quite independent lines, after having taken the central idea of evolution as a basis. Such is the moral philosophy of Guyau,[15] which deals mainly with the higher aspects of morality without discussing the ethics of animals.[16] This is why I thought it necessary to discuss the subject anew in a work, "Mutual Aid: a Factor of Evolution," in which the effect of the instincts and habits of mutual aid was analysed as one of the factors of progressive evolution. Now the same social habits have to be analysed from the two-fold point of view: of the inherited *ethical tendencies*, and the *ethical lessons* which our primitive ancestors gained from the observation of nature; I must, therefore, ask the reader's indulgence if I briefly allude here to some facts already mentioned in my previous work, "Mutual Aid," with the object of showing their ethical significance. Having discussed mutual aid as the weapon which the species uses in its struggle

[14] He mentions it in his *Mental Evolution in Animals* (London, 1883, p. 352.)

[15] *Esquisse d'une morale sans obligation ni sanction.* [Paris, 1896, 4th ed. Eng. tr., *A Sketch of Morality*, by Mrs. G. Kapteyn, London, 1898].—Trans. Note.

[16] The work of Professor Lloyd Morgan, who has lately rewritten his earlier book on animal intelligence under the new title of *Animal Behaviour* (London, 1900), is not yet terminated, and can only be mentioned as promising to give us a full treatment of the subject, especially from the point of view of comparative psychology. Other works dealing with the same subject, or having a bearing upon it, and of which *Des Sociétés animales*, Paris, 1877, by Espinas, deserves special mention, are enumerated in the preface to my *Mutual Aid*.

for existence, i. e., "in the aspect which is of special interest to the naturalist," I shall now briefly consider it as a primary source of the moral sense in man, i. e., in the aspect which is of special interest to ethical philosophy.

Primitive man lived in close intimacy with the animals. With some of them he probably shared his shelter under the overhanging rocks, in crevices, and occasionally in the caves; very often he shared with them food also. Not more than about one hundred and fifty years ago the natives of Siberia and America astonished our naturalists by their thorough knowledge of the habits of the most retiring beasts and birds; but primitive man stood in still closer relations to the animals, and knew them still better. The wholesale extermination of life by means of forest and prairie fires, poisoned arrows, and the like, had not yet begun; and from the bewildering abundance of animal life which was found by the white settlers when they first took possession of the American continent, and which was so well described by the most prominent naturalists, such as Audubon, Azara, Wied, and others, we may judge of the density of the animal population during the post-glacial period.

Palæolithic and neolithic man lived closely surrounded by his dumb brothers—just as Behring and his shipwrecked crew, forced to spend the winter on an island near Alaska, lived amidst the *multitudes* of polar foxes that prowled among the campers, devouring their food and gnawing at night at the very furs upon which the men were sleeping. Our primitive ancestors lived *with the animals, in the midst of them*. And as soon as they began to bring some order into their observations of nature, and to transmit them to posterity, the animals and their life supplied them with the chief materials for their unwritten encyclopædia of knowledge, as well as for their wisdom, which they expressed in proverbs and sayings. Animal psychology was the first psychology studied by man—it is still a favourite subject of talk at the camp fires; and animal life, closely interwoven with that of man, was the subject of the very first rudiments of art, inspiring the first engravers and sculptors, and entering into the composition of the most ancient and epical legends and cosmogonic myths.

The first thing our children learn in zoölogy is something about the beasts of prey—the lions and the tigers. But the first thing which primitive savages must have learned about nature was that it represents a vast agglomeration of animal clans and tribes: the ape tribe, so nearly related to man, the ever-prowling wolf tribe, the knowing, chattering bird tribe, the ever-busy ant tribe, and so on.[17] For them the animals were an extension of their own kin— only so much wiser than themselves. And the first vague generalization which men must have made about nature—so vague as to be almost a mere impression—was .that the *living being and its clan or tribe are inseparable.* We can separate them—they could not; and it seems very doubtful whether they could think of life otherwise than within a clan or a tribe.

At that time, such an impression of nature was inevitable. Among his nearest congeners—the monkeys and the apes—man saw hundreds of species [18] living in large societies, united together within each group by the closest bonds. He saw how they supported one another during their foraging expeditions; how carefully they moved from place to place, how they combined against their common enemies, and rendered one another all sorts of small services, such as picking thorns from one another's fur, nestling together in cold weather, and so on. Of course, they often quarreled; but then, as now, there was more noise in these quarrels than serious harm, and at times, in case of danger, they displayed the most striking mutual attachment; to say nothing of the strong devotion of the mothers to their young ones, and of the old males to their group. Sociality was thus the rule with the monkey tribe; and if there are now two species of big apes, the gorilla and the orang-utang, which are not sociable and keep in small families only, the

[17] Kipling realized this very well in his "Mowgli."
[18] The learned geologists assert that during the Tertiary period there existed nearly a thousand different species of monkeys.

very limited extent of the areas they inhabit is a proof of their being now a decaying species—decaying, perhaps, on account of the merciless war which men have waged against them in consequence of the very resemblance between the two species.

Primitive man saw, next, that even among the carnivorous beasts there is one general rule: *they never kill one another.* Some of them are very sociable—such are all the dog tribe: the jackals, the dholes or kholsun dogs of India, the hyænas. Some others live in small families; but even among these last the more intelligent ones—such as the lions and the leopards—join together for hunting, like the dog tribe. And as to those few which lead—nowadays, at least—a quite solitary life, like the tigers, or keep in small families, they adhere to the same general rule: they do not kill one another. Even now, when the countless herds of ruminants which formerly peopled the prairies have been exterminated, and the tigers subsist mainly on domesticated herds, and are compelled, therefore, to keep close to the villages, even now the natives of India will tell us that somehow the tigers manage to keep to their separate domains without fighting bloody internecine wars to secure them. Besides, it appears extremely probable that even those few animals that now lead a solitary existence—such as the tigers, the smaller species of the cat tribe (nearly all nocturnal), the bears, the martens, the foxes, the hedgehogs, and a few others—were not always solitary creatures. For some of them (foxes, bears) I found positive evidence that they remained social until their extermination by man began, and others even now lead a social life in unpopulated regions, so that we have reason to believe that nearly all once lived in societies.[19] But even if there always existed a few unsociable species, we can positively assert that they were the exception to the general rule.

The lesson of nature was, thus, that even the strongest beasts are bound to combine. And the man who has witnessed, once in his life, an attack of wild dogs, or dholes, upon the largest beasts of

[19] See *Mutual Aid,* chaps. i. and ii., and Appendix. I have gathered many new facts in confirmation of the same idea, since the appearance of that work.

prey, certainly realized, once and for ever, the irresistible force of the tribal unions, and the confidence and courage with which they inspire each individual.

In the prairies and the woods our earliest ancestors saw myriads of animals, all living in large societies—clans and tribes. Countless herds of roe-deer, reindeer, antelopes, thousands of droves of buffaloes, and legions of wild horses, wild donkeys, quaggas, zebras, and so on, were moving over the boundless plains, peacefully grazing together. Only recently this was witnessed by travellers through Central Africa, where giraffes, gazelles and antelopes were seen grazing side by side. Even the dry plateaus of Asia and America had their herds of llamas, of wild camels, and whole tribes of black bears lived together in the mountains of Thibet. And as man became more familiar with the life of these animals, he soon realized how closely united were all these beings. Even when they seemed fully absorbed in grazing, and apparently took no notice of the others, they closely watched one another's movements, always ready to join in some common action. Man saw that all the deer and the goat tribe, whether they graze or merely gambol, always post sentries, which never cease their watchfulness and are never late in signaling the approach of a beast of prey; he knew how, in case of a sudden attack, the males and the females would encircle their young ones and face the enemy, exposing their lives for the safety of the feeble ones. He also knew that animal herds follow similar tactics in retreat.

Primitive man knew all these things, which we ignore or easily forget, and he repeated these exploits of animals in his tales, embellishing the acts of courage and self-sacrifice with his primitive poetry, and *mimicking* them in his religious rites, now improperly called dances. Still less could the primitive savage ignore the great migrations of animals, for he even followed them at times—just as the Chukchi still follows the herds of the wild reindeer, when the clouds of mosquitoes drive them from one place of the Chukchi peninsula to another, or as the Lapp follows the herds of his half-domesticated reindeer in their wanderings, over which he has no control. And if we, with all our book-learning, and our ignorance of nature, feel unable to understand how animals scattered over a wide territory manage to gather in thousands at a given spot to cross a river (as I witnessed on the river Amur), or to begin their march north, south, or west, our ancestors, who considered the animals wiser than themselves, were not in the least astonished by such concerted actions, just as the savages of our own time are not astonished by these things. For them, all the animals— beasts, birds, and fishes alike—were in continual communication, warning each other by means of hardly perceptible signs or sounds, informing one another about all sorts of events, and thus constituting one vast community, which had its own rules of propriety and good neighbourly relations. Even to-day deep traces of that conception of nature survive in the folklore of all nations.

From the populous, animated and gay villages of the marmots, the prairie dogs, the jerboas, and so on, and from the colonies of beavers with which the Post-glacial rivers were thickly studded, primitive man, who himself was still in the nomadic stage, could learn the advantages of settled life, permanent dwelling, and common work. Even now we see (as I saw half a century ago at Transbaikalia) that the nomad cattle-breeders of Mongolia, whose improvidence is phenomenal, learn from the striped rodent (*Tamias striatus*) the advantages of agriculture and foresight, for every autumn they plunder the underground store-rooms of this rodent, and seize its provisions of eatable bulbs. Darwin tells us that during a famine-year, the savages learned from the baboon-monkeys what fruits and berries could serve for food. There is no doubt that the granaries of small rodents, full of all sorts of eatable seeds, must have given man the first suggestions as to the culture of cereals. In fact, the sacred books of the East contain many an allusion to the foresight and industry of animals, which are set up as an example to man.

The birds, in their turn—almost every one of their species—gave our ancestors a lesson in the most intimate sociability, of the joys of social life, and its enormous advantages. The nesting associations of aquatic birds and their unanimity in defending their young broods and eggs, were well known to man. And in the autumn, men who themselves lived in the woods and by the side of the forest brooks, had every opportunity to observe the life of the fledglings who gather in great flocks, and having spent a small part of the day for common feeding, give the rest of the time to merry chirping and playing about.[20] Who knows if the very idea of great autumn gatherings of entire tribes for joint tribal hunts (*Abà* with the Mongols, *Kadà* with the Tunguses), was not suggested by such autumn gatherings of the birds? These tribal gatherings last a month or two, and are a festive season for the whole tribe, strengthening, at the same time, tribal kinship and federated unions among different tribes.

Man observed also the play of animals, in which some species take such delight, their sports, concerts, and dances (see "Mutual Aid," appendix), and the group-flights of some birds in the evenings. He was familiar with the noisy meetings of the swallows and other migrating birds, which are held in the fall, on the same spot, for years in succession, before they start on their long journeys south. And how often man must have stood in bewilderment as he saw the immense migrating columns of birds passing over his head for many hours in succession, or the countless thousands of buffaloes, or deer, or marmots, that blocked his way and sometimes detained him for a few days by their tightly closed ranks, hurrying northward or southward. The "brute savage" knew all these beauties of nature, which we have forgotten in our towns and universities, and which we do not even find in our dead text books on "natural history"; while the narratives of the great ex-

[20] These gatherings are also mentioned by Professor Kessler. References to these gatherings are found in all the *field* zoölogists. [For comment on Professor Kessler, see note page 45. Kropotkin uses the term field zoölogist in contradistinction to desk, or book zoölogist]—Trans. Note.

plorers—such as Humboldt, Audubon, Azara, Brehm, Syevertsev,[21] and so many others, are mouldering in our libraries.

In those times the wide world of the running waters and lakes was not a sealed book for man. He was quite familiar with its inhabitants. Even now, for example, many semi-savage natives of Africa profess a deep reverence for the crocodile. They consider him a near relative to man—a sort of ancestor. They even avoid naming him in their conversations, and if they must mention him they will say "the old grandfather," or use some other word expressing kinship and veneration. The crocodile, they maintain, acts exactly as they do. He will never swallow his prey without having invited his relatives and friends to share the food; and if one of his tribe has been killed by man, otherwise than in due and just blood revenge, he will take vengeance upon some one of the murderer's skin. Therefore, if a negro has been eaten by a crocodile, his tribe will take the greatest care to kill the very same crocodile who had eaten their kinsman, because they fear that by killing an innocent crocodile they will bring upon themselves the vengeance of the kin of the slaughtered animal, such vengeance being required by the law of the clan vendetta. This is why the negroes, having killed the presumably guilty crocodile, will carefully examine his intestines in order to find the remnants of their kinsman, and to make sure thereby that no mistake has been made and that it is this particular crocodile that deserved death. But if no proof of the beast's guilt is forthcoming, they will make all sorts of expiatory amends to the crocodile tribe in order to appease the relatives of the innocently slaughtered animal; and they continue to search for the real culprit. The same belief exists among the Red Indians concerning the rattlesnake and the wolf, and among the Ostiaks about the bear, etc. The connection of such beliefs with the subsequent development of the idea of justice, is self evident.[22]

[21] [Spelled also, Syevertsov, Syevertsoff, and Syevertzov,—Nikolai A., a Russian naturalist. See *Mutual Aid*]—Trans. Note.

[22] Is it possible that the eloquent facts about animal morality collected by Romanes will remain unpublished?

THE MORAL PRINCIPLE IN NATURE

The shoals of fishes, and their movements in the transparent waters, the reconnoitering by their scouts before the whole herd moves in a given direction, must have deeply impressed man at a very early period. Traces of this impression are found in the folklore of savages in many parts of the globe. Thus, for instance, Dekanawideh, the legendary lawgiver of the Red Indians, who is supposed to have given them the clan organization, is represented as having retired from the people to meditate in contact with nature. He "reached the side of a smooth, clear, running stream, transparent and full of fishes. He sat down, reclining on the sloping bank, gazing intent into the waters, watching the fishes playing about in complete harmony. . . . " Thereupon he conceived the scheme of dividing his people into gentes and classes, or totems.[23] In other legends the wise man of the tribe learns wisdom from the beaver, or the squirrel, or some bird.

Generally speaking, for the primitive savage, animals are mysterious, enigmatic beings, possessed of a wide knowledge of the things of nature. They know much more than they are ready to tell us. In one way or another, by the aid of senses much more refined than ours, and by telling one another all that they notice in their rambles and flights, they know everything, for miles around. And if man has been "just" towards them, they will warn him of a coming danger as they warn one another; but they will take no heed of him if he has not been straightforward in his actions. Snakes and birds (the owl is considered the leader of the snakes), mammals and insects, lizards and fishes—all understand one another, and continually communicate their observations among themselves. They all belong to one brotherhood, into which they may, in some cases, admit man.

Inside this vast brotherhood there are, of course, the still closer brotherhoods of being "of one blood." The monkeys, the bears, the

[23] J. Brant-Sero, *Dekanawideh*, in the magazine *Man*, 1901, p. 166. [*Dekananawideh: the Law-giver of the Camengahakas.* By (Ra-onha) John O. Brant-Sero (Canadian Mohawk). In *Man*, Lon., 1901, vol. 1, no. 134.]—Trans. Note.

wolves, the elephants and the rhinoceroses, most ruminants, the hares and most of the rodents, the crocodiles, and so on, know perfectly their own kin, and they will not abide the slaughter by man of one of their relatives without taking, in one way or another, "honest" revenge. This conception must have had an extremely remote origin. It must have grown at a time when man had not yet become omnivorous and had not yet begun to hunt birds and animals for food. Man became omnivorous, most probably, during the Glacial period, when vegetation was perishing in the path of the advancing cold. However, the same conception has been retained down to the present time. Even now, when a savage is hunting, he is bound to respect certain rules of propriety towards the animals, and he must perform certain expiatory ceremonies after his hunt. Some of these ceremonies are rigorously enacted, even to-day, in the savage clans, especially in connection with those animals which are considered the allies of man, such as the bear, for example (among the Orochons on the Amur River).

It is a known custom that two men belonging to two different clans can fraternize by mixing the blood of the two, obtained from small incisions made for that purpose. To enter into such a union was quite common in olden times, and we learn from the folklore of all nations, and especially from the Scandinavian sagas, how religiously such a brotherhood was maintained. But it was also customary for man to enter into brotherhood with some animal. The tales frequently mention this. An animal asks a hunter to spare it, and if the hunter accedes to the demand the two become brothers. And then the monkey, the bear, the doe, the bird, the crocodile, or even the bee—(anyone of the social animals)—will take all possible care of the man-brother in the critical circumstances of his life, sending their animal brothers from their own or from a different tribe, to warn him or help him. And if the warning comes too late, or is misunderstood, and he loses his life, all these animals will try to bring him back to life, and if they fail, they will take due revenge, just as if the man were one of their own kin.

THE MORAL PRINCIPLE IN NATURE

When I journeyed in Siberia I often noticed the care with which my Tungus or Mongol guide would take not to kill any animal uselessly. The fact is that every life is respected by a savage, or rather was, before he came in contact with Europeans. If he kills an animal it is for food or clothing, but he does not destroy life for mere amusement or out of a passion for destruction. True, the Red Indians have done that very thing with the buffaloes; but it was only after they had been for a long time in contact with the whites, and had got from them the rifle and the quick-firing revolver. Of course, there are also some animals that are considered enemies of man—the hyæna, for instance, or the tiger; but, in general, the savage treats with respect the great animal world as a whole, and trains his children in the same spirit.

The idea of "justice," conceived at its origin as revenge, is thus connected with observations made on animals. But it appears extremely probable that the idea of return for "just" and "unjust" treatment must also have originated, with primitive mankind, in the idea that animals take revenge if they have not been properly treated by man. This idea is so deeply rooted in the minds of the savages all over the world that it may be considered as one of the fundamental conceptions of mankind. Gradually it grew to be a conception of the great whole, bound together by certain links of mutual support; this great whole watches over all the actions of living beings, and, owing to the mutuality of relation in the universe, undertakes retribution for wrong deeds. This idea evolved into the conception of the Eumenides and the Moirai of the Greeks, the Parcæ of the Romans, and of Karma among the Hindus. The Greek legend of the cranes of Ibycus which links together man and birds, and countless Eastern legends, are poetical embodiments of the same conception. Later this conception was extended over the region of the sky. The clouds, according to the most ancient books of India, the Vedas, were considered as living beings similar to animals.

This is what primitive man saw in nature and learned from it.

ETHICS: ORIGIN AND DEVELOPMENT

With our scholastic education, which has consistently ignored nature and has tried to explain its most common facts by superstitions or by metaphysical subtleties, we began to forget that great lesson. But for our Stone-Age ancestors sociality and mutual aid *within the tribe* must have been a fact so general in nature, so habitual, that they certainly could not imagine life under another aspect.

The conception of Man as an isolated being is a later product of civilization—the product of Eastern legends about men who withdrew from society. To a primitive man isolated life seems so strange, so much out of the usual course of nature, that when he sees a tiger, a badger, a shrew-mouse leading a solitary existence, or even when he notices a tree that stands alone, far from the forest, he creates a legend to explain this strange occurrence. He makes no legends to explain life in societies, but he has one for every case of solitude. The hermit, if he is not a sage who has temporarily withdrawn from the world to ponder over its destinies, or a wizard, is in most cases an outcast banished for some grave transgression against the code of social life. He has done something so contrary to the ordinary run of life that they have thrown him out of society. Very often he is a sorcerer, who has the command of all sorts of evil powers, and has something to do with the pestilential corpses which spread contagion in the world. This is why he prowls about at night, pursuing his wicked designs under the cover of darkness. All other beings live in societies, and human thought runs in this channel. Social life—that is, *we,* not *I*—is the normal form of life. *It is life itself.* Therefore, "We" must have been the habitual trend of thought with the primitive man, a "category" of his mind, as Kant might have said.

Here, in that identification, or, we might even say, in this absorption of the "I" by the clan or tribe, lies the root of all ethical thought. The self-assertion of "personality" came much later on. Even now, the psychology of the lower savages scarcely knows any "individual" or "personality." The dominant conception in their minds is the tribe, with its hard-and-fast rules, superstitions, taboos, habits, and interests.   In that constant, everpresent identification of the unit with the whole, lies the origin of all ethics, the germ out of which all the subsequent conceptions of *justice,* and the still higher conceptions of *morality,* evolved.

These consecutive steps in the evolution of ethics will be considered in the following chapters.

CHAPTER IV

THE progress made by the natural sciences in the nineteenth century awakened in modern thinkers the desire to work out a new system of ethics on positive bases. After having established the fundamental principles of a universal philosophy free from postulates of supernatural forces, and at the same time, majestic, poetical, and capable of stimulating in men the highest motives,—modern science no longer needs to resort to supernatural inspiration to justify its ideals of moral beauty. Besides, science foresees that in the not-distant future, human society, liberated, through the progress of science, from the poverty of former ages, and organized on the principles of justice and mutual aid, will be able to secure for man free expression of his intellectual, technical, and artistic creative impulses. And this prevision opens up such broad moral possibilities for the future, that for their realization there is no longer any need either of the influence of the supernatural world, or of fear of punishment in an existence after death. There is, consequently, the need of a new ethics on a new basis. The first chapter of this inquiry was devoted to demonstrating the present necessity of the new ethics.

Having awakened from a period of temporary stagnation, modern science, at the end of the fifties of the last century, began to prepare the materials for working out this new, rational ethics. In the works of Jodl, Wundt, Paulsen and of many others, we have excellent surveys of all previous attempts to base ethics on various foundations: religious, metaphysical, and physical. Throughout the entire nineteenth century a series of attempts was made to find the bases of the moral nature of man in rational self-love, in love of humanity (Auguste Comte and his followers), in mutual sympathy and intellectual identification of one's personality with mankind, (Schopenhauer), in usefulness (utilitarianism of Bentham and Mill) and in a theory of development, i. e., in evolution (Darwin, Spencer and Guyau).

The foundation of this last ethics was laid by Darwin; he attempted to derive the primary supports of the moral sentiment from the social instinct, which is deeply ingrained in all social animals. Since most writers on ethics pay no attention to this attempt, and since it was passed over in silence by most Darwinians, I have dwelt on it in detail in the third chapter, "The Moral Principle in Nature." In my book, "Mutual Aid," I already pointed out the widespread occurrence of the social instinct among the majority of animals of all species and subdivisions, while in the third chapter of the present treatise we have seen how the most primitive men of the Glacial and of the early Post-glacial period, had to learn the ways of social life, and its ethics, from the animals, with whom they lived then in close communication. And we have discovered how, in the earliest fairy tales and legends, man transmitted from generation to generation the practical instruction acquired from this knowledge of animal life.

Thus the first moral teacher of man was Nature. Not the nature described by the desk philosophers unfamiliar with it, or by naturalists who have studied nature only among the dead samples in the museums. It was the Nature in the midst of which lived and worked on the American continent, then sparsely populated, and also in Africa and Asia, the great founders of descriptive zoölogy: Audubon, Azara, Brehm, and others. It was, in short, that Nature which Darwin had in mind when he gave in his book, "The Descent of Man," a brief survey of the origin of the moral sentiment among mankind.

There is no doubt that the social instinct, inherited by man and therefore deeply rooted in him, had in it the germs of later development and strengthening, nothwithstanding even the hard struggle for existence. I also showed in the same work on Mutual Aid—again on the basis of works of competent investigators,—how far social life is developed among savages, and also how the sentiment of equity is developed in the most primitive representatives of the human race. I also showed how, due to sociality, the development of human societies was made possible, in spite of their hard life amidst wild nature.

Therefore, referring the reader to "Mutual Aid," I will now attempt to analyse how further moral conceptions were developed among the societies of primitive savages, and what influence those conceptions had on the later development of morality.

We know nothing about the life of the earliest primitive human beings of the Glacial Period and of the end of the Tertiary Period beyond the fact that they lived in small groups, eking out with difficulty meager means of support from the lakes and the forests, and making for that purpose implements of bone and stone.

But already in that form of life primitive man had to become accustomed to identifying his "I" with the social "We." In this manner he was working out the primary foundations of morality. He was growing accustomed to thinking of his tribe as of something of which he formed only a part, and not at all a principal part, for he saw how insignificant each one of his fellows would prove face to face with stern, threatening nature, if he should cease to be a member of the tribe. Owing to these considerations he was acquiring the habit of limiting his will by the will of others, which constitutes the primary source of all morality. And, really, we know that the earliest primitive men of the Glacial and of the early Post-glacial period were already living in groups—in caves, fissures in the rocks, or under overhanging rocks, and that they hunted and fished jointly with their primeval implements. Such living together and coöperation already presupposes the working out of certain rules of social morality.

This "bringing up" of primitive man continued for tens of thousands of years and, in this manner, the social instinct kept on developing and became in the course of time stronger than any selfish consideration. Man was learning to think of his ego in no other way than through the conception of his group. The high educational value of this way of thinking will be shown further on in our discussion.[1]

Already in the animal world we see how the personal will of individuals blends with the common will. The social animals learn this at a very early age—in their play,[2] where it is necessary to submit to certain rules of the game: it is not permitted to gore with the horns in earnest, to bite in earnest, or even to stand in the way of another's turn. And when they attain adult age the absorbing of the personal will by the social will is clearly seen in many cases. The preparations of the birds for their migrations from the North to the South and back; their "practice" flights in the evenings, during the few days preceding the migrations; co-ordination of actions of the wild beasts and birds of prey during hunting; the common defence against the beasts of prey of all the animals that live in herds; migrations of animals, and, also, the whole social life of the bees, wasps, ants, termites, almost all the wading birds, parrots, beavers, monkeys, etc.,—all these facts are prominent examples of such subordination of the personal will. They clearly show *the co-ordination of the individual will* with the will and the purpose of the whole, and this co-ordination has already become an hereditary habit, i. e., an instinct.[3]

[1] All thinking, as Fouillée justly remarked, has a tendency to become more and more objective, i. e., to renounce personal considerations and to pass gradually to general considerations. (Fouillée, *Critique des systèmes de morale contemporaine*, Paris, 1883, p. 18). In this manner the social ideal is gradually formed, i. e., a conception of a possibly better system.

[2] See on this subject, *Play of Animals*, by Karl Groos. [English trans. by Elizabeth L. Baldwin, N. Y. 1898.]—Trans. Note.

[3] The reader will find many facts in connection with the rudiments of ethics among the social animals, in the excellent works of Espinas, who analyzed various stages of sociality among animals in his book, *Des sociétés animales* (Paris, 1877). See also, *Animal Intelligence*, by Romanes; Huber's and Forel's books on ants, and Büchner's *Liebe und Liebesleben in der Thierwelt* (1879; enlarged edition, 1886). [Alfred Victor Espinas, 2d enlarged ed., 1878. Geo. John Romanes, N. Y., 1883; latest ed., 1912. Pierre Huber, *Recherches sur les moeurs des fourmis indigènes*, Genève, Paris, 1810 and 1861; English trans., *The Natural History of the Ants*, Lond., 1820, by J. R. Johnson. Auguste Forel, *Ants and some other Insects*, translated from the German by

ETHICS: ORIGIN AND DEVELOPMENT

As early as 1625 Hugo Grotius clearly understood that such an instinct contains the rudiments of *law*. But there is no doubt that the men of the Quaternary Period stood at least on the same step of social development, and, most likely, even on a considerably higher level. Once co-habitation is established, it unavoidably leads to certain forms of life, certain customs and traditions, which, being acknowledged useful and becoming habitual ways of thinking, evolve first into instinctive habits and then into rules of life. Thus each group evolves its own morality, its own ethics, which the elders— the preservers of the tribal customs—place under the protection of superstitions and religion, i. e., in substance, under the protection of the dead ancestors.[4]

Some prominent naturalists recently made various observations and experiments for the purpose of determining whether dogs, horses, and other animals living in close proximity to man, have conscious moral conceptions. The results gave a fairly definite affirmative answer. Thus, for example, the facts related by Spencer in the appendix to the second volume of his "Principles of Ethics" are particularly convincing and lead to conclusions that are by no means unimportant. Similarly, there are several quite convincing facts in the above-mentioned work by Romanes. We will not dwell on these facts, however. It is sufficient to establish that already in animal societies, and so much more in human societies owing to the social habit itself, conceptions are unavoidably developed which identify the personal "I" with the social "We," and as these conceptions

W. M. Whaler, Chic., 1904; the German work is *Die Psychischen fähigkeiten der Ameisen*, etc., München, 1901. Forel is the author of a vast work, *Le monde social des fourmis du globe, comparé à celui de l'homme*, Genève, 1921–23, 5 vols. Kropotkin had in mind, most likely, Forel's *Recherches sur les fourmis de la Suisse*, Zurich, 1874, which he quotes in his *Mutual Aid*. The last author named is Ludwig Büchner.]—Trans. Note.

[4] Élie Reclus (brother of the geographer Élisée Reclus), wrote brilliantly on the significance of the "great multitude" of dead ancestors in his *Les Primitifs*,—a book of few pages, but rich in ideas and facts. [Paris, 1885. The English trans., *Primitive Folk*, appeared in the Contemporary Scientific Series, Lond., 1896.]—Trans. Note.

evolve into hereditary instinct, the personal "I" even submits to the social "We." [5]

But once we have established that such identification of the individual with society was present even to a slight degree among men, it follows that if this attitude were useful to humanity it would unavoidably tend to become stronger and to develop, especially since Man had the gift of speech, which leads to the establishment of tradition. And finally, this attitude would lead to the creation of a permanent moral instinct.

This assertion, however, will probably give rise to some doubts, and many will probably ask: "Is it possible that, without the interference of any supernatural power, a semi-animal sociality could evolve into such high moral teachings as those of Socrates, Plato, Confucius, Buddha, and Christ?" Ethics must answer this question. It would not suffice simply to point to biology, which shows how microscopical unicellular organisms evolve in the course of tens of thousands of years into more highly developed organisms, up to higher mammals and Man. Ethics, therefore, will have to perform a task similar to that accomplished by Auguste Comte and Spencer in Biology, and by many research workers in the History of Law. Ethics must demonstrate how moral conceptions were able to develop from the sociality inherent in higher animals and primitive savages, to highly idealistic moral teachings.

The rules governing the mode of life of the various savage tribes of our time are different. In different climates, among tribes surrounded by different neighbours, varying customs and traditions were developed. Besides, the very descriptions of these customs and traditions by various travellers differ materially from one another, depending on the nature of the historian and on his general attitude toward his "lower brethren." It is wrong, therefore, to combine into a unit the descriptions of all kinds of primitive tribes, without giving consideration to the level of development of each particular tribe, and

[5] Spencer analyses these facts in detail in his *Principles of Ethics.* [Vols. IX, X of *A System of Synthetic Philosophy*, N. Y., 1898.]—Trans. Note.

without weighing critically the authors of these descriptions. This error was made by some beginners in anthropology, and even Spencer did not escape this fallacy in his ponderous compilation of anthropological data,[6] or even in his later work, "Ethics." On the other hand, Waitz, in his "Anthropology of Primitive Peoples," and a whole series of anthropologists such as Morgan, Maine, M. Kovalevsky, Post, and many others, did not fall into this error. In general, among the various accounts of savage life, only those can be utilized which were written by travellers and missionaries who spent a fairly long time among the savages they describe; the length of sojourn is in itself, to a certain extent, an indication of mutual understanding. And then, if we wish to learn something about the first beginnings of moral conceptions, we must study those savages who were able to preserve better than others some features of the tribal mode of life, from the time of the earliest Post-glacial period.

There are, of course, no tribes who have preserved completely the mode of life of that period. It is, however, best preserved by the savages of the extreme North—the Aleuts, the Chukchi, and the Eskimos, who are to this day living in the same physical environment in which they lived at the very beginning of the melting of the huge ice sheet,[7] and also by some tribes of the extreme South, i. e., of Patagonia and New Guinea, and by small remnants of tribes that survived in some mountain regions, especially in the Himalayas.

We have reliable information about these very tribes of the far North from men who lived among them; particularly, about the

---

[6] *Descriptive Sociology*, classified and arranged by Herbert Spencer, compiled and abstracted by Davis Duncan, Richard Schappig, and James Collier, 8 volumes in folio. [Amer. ed., 9 vols., N. Y., 1873–1910.]—Trans. Note.

[7] It is very likely that with the gradual melting of the ice sheet, which at the time of its greatest development in the Northern hemisphere extended approximately to 50° North Latitude, these tribes were continually moving northward under pressure of the increasing population of the more southern parts of the Earth (India, North Africa, etc.), unreached by the glacial layer.

MORAL CONCEPTIONS OF PRIMITIVE PEOPLES

Aleuts of North Alaska from a remarkable social historian, the missionary Venyaminov: and about the Eskimos from various expeditions that spent the winter in Greenland. The description of the Aleuts by Venyaminov is particularly instructive.

First of all, it must be noted that there are two divisions in Aleutian ethics, as well as in the ethics of other primitive peoples. Observance of one kind of custom, and consequently of the ethical regulations, is absolutely obligatory; observance of the other kind is merely recommended as desirable, and the transgressors are subjected only to ridicule or to a reminder. The Aleuts, for example, say that it is "shameful" to do certain things.[8]

"Thus, for example," wrote Venyaminov, "it is 'shameful' to fear unavoidable death; it is shameful to beg an enemy for mercy; it is shameful to be detected in theft; also to have one's boat capsized in the harbour. It is shameful to be afraid to put to sea during a storm; to be the first to weaken in a long voyage, or to show greed in dividing the spoils (in such a case all the rest give the greedy one their share, so as to shame him); it is shameful to babble to one's wife about the secrets of the tribe; it is shameful, while hunting with another, not to offer the best part of the game to one's companion; it is shameful to brag of one's deeds, especially the imaginary ones, or to call another derogatory names. It is also shameful to beg alms; to caress one's wife in the presence of others, or to dance with her; or to bargain personally with a purchaser, since the price for goods offered is to be fixed by a third party. For a woman it is shameful to be unable to sew or to dance, or, in general, not to know how to do things within the scope of woman's

[8] *Memoirs from the Unalashkinsky District*, Petrograd, 1840; [3 vols., in Russian]. Excerpts from this work are given in Dall's *Alaska*. Very similar remarks about the Eskimo tribes of Greenland, and also about the Australian savages of New Guinea, are found in the works of Mikhlucho-Maklay, and some others. [Ivan Yevseyevich Venyaminov (1797–1879), who later became Innokenti, Metropolitan of Moscow. For Mikhlucho-Maklay see note, page 72. Wm. Healey Dall, *Alaska and its Resources*. Boston, 1870.]—Trans. Note.

69

duties: shameful to caress her husband or even to converse with him in the presence of others." [9]

Venyaminov gives no information as to how these features of the Aleutian ethics are maintained. But one of the expeditions which spent a winter in Greenland gives a description of how the Eskimos live,—several families in one dwelling. Each family is divided from the others by a curtain made of hides. These corridor-like dwellings are sometimes made in the shape of a cross in the centre of which is located the hearth. On long winter nights the women sing songs in which they not infrequently ridicule those who are in some way guilty of transgressing the customs of good behaviour. But there are also regulations that are absolutely obligatory: in the first place stands, of course, the absolute insufferance of fratricide, i. e., of a murder within the tribe. It is equally insufferable that a murder, or a wound inflicted by a member of some other tribe, should pass without clan vengeance.

Then there is a whole series of actions that are so strictly obligatory that failure to observe them brings upon the offender the contempt of the whole tribe, and he runs the risk of becoming an outcast and of being banished from his clan. Otherwise, the offender against these rules might bring upon the whole tribe the displeasure of the wronged animals, such, for example, as the crocodiles, the bears, or of the invisible spirits of the ancestors who protect the tribe.

[9] In enumerating the principles of Aleutian ethics, Venyaminov includes also: "It is shameful to die without having killed a single enemy." I took the liberty of omitting this statement, because I think that it is based on a misunderstanding. By enemy cannot be meant a man of one's own tribe, for Venyaminov himself states that out of the population of 60,000 there occurred only one murder in the course of forty years, and it had unavoidably to be followed by vendetta, or by reconciliation after the payment of compensation. Therefore, an enemy whom it was absolutely necessary to kill could be only a man from some other tribe. But Venyaminov does not speak of any continual feuds among the clans or tribes. He probably meant to say "it is shameful to die without having killed the enemy who ought to be killed, as a requirement of clan-vendetta." This viewpoint is, unfortunately, still held even among the so-called "civilized" societies, by the advocates of capital punishment.

Thus, for instance, Venyaminov tells of the following case. Once when he was embarking for a voyage, the natives assisting him forgot to take a mess of dried fish which had been given to him as a present. Half a year later, when he returned to this place, he learned that in his absence the tribe had lived through a period of utter famine. But the fish presented to him were, of course, left untouched, and were brought to him intact. To have acted differently would have meant to precipitate various troubles upon the tribe. Similarly, Middendorf wrote that in the swampy plains of Northern Siberia no one will remove anything from a sleigh left by others in the marshes, even if it contains provisions. It is well known that the inhabitants of the far North are frequently on the verge of starvation, but to use any of the supplies left behind would be what we call a crime, and such a crime might bring all sorts of evil upon the tribe. The individual is in this case identified with the tribe.

Furthermore, the Aleuts, like all other primitive savages, have also a group of regulations that are absolutely obligatory,—one may say, sacred. They include all that pertains to the conservation of the tribal mode of life: the division into classes, the marriage regulations, the conceptions of the tribal and the family property, the regulations to be observed in hunting or fishing (jointly or singly), the migrations, etc.; and finally, there is a series of tribal rites of a purely religious character. Here we have a strict law the violation of which would bring misfortune upon the whole clan, or even upon the whole tribe, and therefore non-compliance with such a law is unthinkable or even impossible. And if once in a great while a violation of such a law does occur, it is punished like treason, by banishment from the tribe, or even by death. It must be said, however, that the violation of such laws is so rare that it is even considered unthinkable, just as the Roman Law considered parricide unthinkable and, accordingly, had no law providing punishment for this crime.

Generally speaking, all the primitive peoples known to us have developed a very complicated mode of tribal life. They have, consequently, their own morality, their own ethics. And in all these unwritten "statutes" protected by tradition, three main categories of tribal regulations are to be found.

Some of them preserved the usages established for procuring means of livelihood for each individual and for the whole tribe. These regulations set down the principles of using what belongs to the whole tribe: the water expanses, the forests, sometimes the fruit-trees wild or cultivated, the hunting regions, and also the boats. There are also strict rules for hunting, for migrations, for preservation of fire, etc.[10]

Then the individual rights and relations are determined: the subdivision of the tribe into clans, and the system of permissible marital relations,—another very complicated division, where the institutions become almost religious. To the same category belong the rules for bringing up the youth, sometimes in the special "long huts," as is done by the savages of the Pacific Islands; the relations to the old people and to the newly born; and, finally, the ways of preventing acute personal collisions, i.e., what is to be done when the multiplication of separate families makes violence possible within the tribe, and also in case of an individual's dispute with a neighbouring tribe, especially if the dispute might lead to war. An array of rules is here established which, as was shown by the Belgian professor, Ernest Nys, later developed into the beginnings of international law. And, finally, there is the third category of regulations, which are held sacred and pertain to religious superstitions, and

[10] Preservation of fire is a very important thing. Mikhlucho-Maklay writes that the inhabitants of New Guinea, among whom he lived, still retain a legend describing how their ancestors once suffered from scurvy because they let the fire go out, and remained without fire for a considerable time, until they were able to get some from the neighbouring islands. [Nikolai N. Mikhlucho-Maklay, a Russian traveller and naturalist (1846–88). His notes on New Guinea were contributed to *Petermann's Mitteilungen*, 1874, 1878. A part of New Guinea bears the name of Maclay Coast. See the article on M.-M. by Finsch in *Deutsche Geographische Blättern*, vol. xi, pts. 3–4, Bremen, 1888. Excerpts from his note-books appear, in Russian, in the *Izvestia* of the Russian Geographical Society, 1880, pp. 161 ff.]—Trans. Note.

the rights connected with the season of the year, hunting, migrations, etc.

All these questions can be definitely answered by the old men of each tribe. Of course, these answers are not the same for different clans and tribes, just as the rites are different. What is important here, however, is the fact that every clan or tribe, no matter how low its stage of development, already *has its own very complicated ethics, its own system of the moral and the immoral.*

The origin of this morality lies, as we have seen, in the feeling of sociality, in the herd instinct, and in the need of mutual aid, which became developed among all social animals and which was still further developed by primitive human societies. It is natural that Man, owing to the gift of speech which helps the development of memory and creates tradition, worked out much more complicated rules of life than the animals. Moreover, with the appearance of religion, even in its crudest form, human ethics was enriched by a new element, which gave to that ethics a certain stability, and later contributed to it inspiration and a measure of idealism.

Then, with further development of social life, the conception of *justice* in mutual relations had to become more and more prominent. The first signs of justice in the sense of equity, can be observed among animals, especially the mammals, in cases where the mother feeds a few sucklings, or in the play of many animals, where there is always adherence to certain rules of play. But the unavoidable transition from the social instinct, i. e., from the simple desire or need to live among similar creatures, to the conclusion that justice is necessary in mutual relations, had to be made by Man for the sake of the preservation of social life itself. And truly, in any society the desires and the passions of individuals inevitably collide with the desires of the other members of the same society. Such collisions would inevitably lead to endless feuds and to disintegration of the society, if it were not that human beings develop, at the same time,—(just as it is already developing in some gregarious animals)—a conception of the equality of rights of all the members

73

of the society. The same conception had to evolve gradually into the conception of *justice*, as is suggested by the very origin of the word—*Æquitas, Équité*, which denotes the conception of justice, equality. It is for this reason that the ancients represented justice as a blindfold woman holding a pair of scales.

Let us take a case from actual life. There are, for example, two men who have quarreled. Word follows word, and one of them accuses the other of having insulted him. The other tries to prove that he was right, that he was justified in saying what he said. It is true he had thereby insulted the other, but his insult was but a retaliation for the insult offered him, and it was equal, equivalent to the latter, and by no means greater.

If such a dispute leads to a quarrel and finally results in a fight, both will try to prove that the first blow was a retaliation for a grave insult, and that each subsequent blow was a retaliation for the exactly equivalent blow of the adversary. Then, if the case goes as far as injury and a trial, the judges will consider the extent of the injuries, and he who has inflicted the greater injury will have to pay the fine, to re-establish the equality of injuries. This had been the practice for many centuries, whenever the case was laid before the communal judgment.

It is clearly seen from this example, which is not imaginary but is taken from actual life, what the most primitive savages understood by "justice," and what the more enlightened peoples understand to this day by the words *fairness, justice, Æquitas, Équité, Rechtigkeit*, etc. They see in these conceptions the *re-establishment of the disturbed equality*. No one is to disturb the equality of two members of society; and once it is disturbed it has to be re-established by the interference of society. Thus proclaimed the Mosaic Pentateuch, saying: "Eye for eye, tooth for tooth, wound for wound," but no more. Thus acted Roman justice, thus act to this day all the savages,—and many of these notions are still preserved in modern jurisprudence.

Of course, in any society, regardless of its stage of develop-

74

ment, there will always be individuals aiming to take advantage of their strength, adroitness, cleverness, daring, in order to subjugate the will of others to their own will, and some of these individuals attain their aim. Such individuals were found, of course, also among the most primitive peoples, and we meet them among all tribes and peoples in all stages of social development. But to counterbalance such tendencies customs were evolved, among peoples in all stages of development, which tended to resist the aggrandizement of an individual at the expense of the whole society. All the institutions developed at various times by the human race—the tribal code of life, the village commune, the city, the republics with their common councils, self-government of the parishes and districts, representative government, etc.,—all these were really meant to protect societies from the arbitrary acts of such individuals and from their rising power.

Even the most primitive savages, as we have just seen, have groups of customs that are evolved for this purpose. On the one side, custom establishes the equality of rights. Thus, for example, Darwin, while observing the Patagonian savages, was astonished to note that whenever any of the whites gave to a savage a bit of food, the savage immediately shared the morsel equally among all those present. The same circumstance is mentioned by many observers in connection with various primitive tribes, and I, too, had occasion to observe the same thing even among people in a more advanced stage of development—among the Bouriats, who live in remote parts of Siberia.[11]

There is a great number of such facts in all the serious descriptions of primitive peoples.[12] Wherever they are studied, the ob-

[11] According to the customs of the Bouriats, who live in Sayany, near the Okinski Outpost, when a ram is killed, the whole village comes to the fire where the feast is being prepared, and all take part in the meal. The same custom existed also among the Bouriats of the Verkholensky district.

[12] Those who desire further information on this subject are referred to such monumental works as Waitz, *Anthropologie der Naturvölker;* Post, *Afrikanische Jurisprudenz,* and *Die Geschlechtsgenossenschaft der Urzeit;* M. Kovalevsky, *Primitive Law. Tableau des origines de la famille et de la propriété;*

servers always find the same sociable tendencies, the same social spirit, the same readiness to curb wilfulness for the sake of supporting the social life. And when we attempt to penetrate into the life of Man at the most primitive stages of his development, we find the same tribal life, the same alliances of men for mutual aid. And we are forced to acknowledge that the social qualities of Man constitute the principal factor in his past development and in his future progress.

In the eighteenth century, under the influence of the first acquaintance with the savages of the Pacific Ocean, a tendency developed to idealize the savages, who lived "in a natural state,"— perhaps to counterbalance the philosophy of Hobbes and his followers, who pictured primitive men as a crowd of wild beasts ready to devour one another. Both these conceptions, however, proved erroneous, as we now know from many conscientious observers. The primitive man is not at all a paragon of virtue, and not at all a tiger-like beast. But he always lived and still lives in societies, like thousands of other creatures. In those societies he has developed not only those social qualities that are inherent to all social animals, but, owing to the gift of speech and, consequently, to a more developed intelligence, he has still further developed his sociality, and with it he has evolved the rules of social life, which we call morality.

In the tribal stage Man first of all learned the fundamental rule of all social life: do not unto others what you do not wish to have done unto you; he learned to restrain in various ways those who did not desire to submit to this rule. And then he developed the ability *to identify his personal life with the life of his tribe.* In

Morgan, *Ancient Society;* Dr. H. Rink, *The Eskimo Tribes,* and many scattered researches mentioned in the above works, and also in my treatise on *Mutual Aid.* [Theodor Waitz, Leipzig, 1859–1872, 6 vols. Albert Hermann Post, *Afrik. Juris.,* Oldenburg, 1887, 2 vols. in 1; second work, Oldenburg, 1875. Maxim M. Kovalevsky. *Primitive Law* (in Russian), 1876; *Tableau, etc.,* Stockholm, 1890. Lewis Henry Morgan, N. Y., 1878. Hinrich J. Rink, Copenhagen, 1887–91, 2 vols. in 1. Peter A. Kropotkin, *Mutual Aid,* Lond. and N. Y., 1919.]—Trans. Note.

studying primitive men, beginning with those who still preserve the mode of life of the Glacial and of the early Post-glacial period, and ending with those who are in the latest stages of development of the tribal system—we are most impressed by this feature: the *identification* of the individual man with his tribe. This principle can be traced throughout the early history of the development of the human race, and it is particularly well preserved by those who still retain the primitive forms of the tribal system and the most primitive devices for fighting the stepmother, Nature. Such are the Eskimos, the Aleuts, the inhabitants of Terra del Fuego, and some mountain tribes. And the more we study primitive man, the more we are convinced that, even in his insignificant acts, he identified and still identifies his life with the life of his tribe.

The conceptions of good and evil were thus evolving not on the basis of what represented good or evil for a separate individual, but on what represented good and evil for the whole tribe. These conceptions, of course, varied with time and locality, and some of the rules, such, for example, as human sacrifices for the purpose of placating the formidable forces of nature—volcanoes, seas, earthquakes,—were simply preposterous. But once this or that rule was established by the tribe, the individual submitted to it, no matter how hard it was to abide by it.

Generally speaking, the primitive savage identified himself with his tribe. He became truly unhappy if he committed an act that might bring upon his tribe the curse of the wronged one, or the vengeance of the "great multitude" of ancestors, or of some animal tribe: crocodiles, bears, tigers, etc. The "code of custom" means more to a savage man than religion to the modern man—it forms the foundation of his life, and therefore, self-restraint in the interests of the tribe,—and in separate individuals, self-sacrifice for the same reason,—is a most common occurrence.[13]

[13] Bastian, *Der Mensch in der Geschichte,* vol. 3; Grey, *Journals of two Expeditions,* 1841; and all reliable accounts of the life of savages. On the part played by intimidation through the "curse," see the famous work by Professor Westermarck. [*Marriage Ceremonies in Morocco,* London, 1914; and

ETHICS: ORIGIN AND DEVELOPMENT

In short, the nearer the primitive society is to its most ancient forms, the more strictly is the rule, "everyone for all," observed. And it is only due to their total lack of knowledge of the actual life of primitive man, that such thinkers as Hobbes and Rousseau and their followers, asserted that morality originated from an imaginary "moral covenant," and others explained its appearance by the "inspiration from above," coming to a mythical lawgiver. In reality, the source of morality lies in a sociality inherent in all the higher animals, and so much more in Man.

Unfortunately, in the tribal system, the rule "everyone for all" does not extend further than the individual's own tribe. A tribe is not obliged to share its food with other tribes. Moreover, the territory is divided among various tribes, as it is in the cases of some mammals and some birds, and each tribe has its own district for hunting or fishing. Thus from the most ancient times Man was developing two kinds of relations: within his own tribe, and with the other tribes where an atmosphere was created for disputes and wars. It is true that already in the tribal stage attempts were made, and are still being made, to improve the mutual relations of neighbouring tribes. When a man enters a dwelling all weapons are to be left outside, at the entrance; and even in case of war between two tribes there are certain rules to be observed, relating to the wells and the paths which women use for drawing and carrying water. But, generally speaking, inter-tribal relations (unless a federation between neighbouring tribes was arranged) are entirely different from relations within the tribe. And in the subsequent development of the human race no religion could eradicate the conception of a "stranger." Actually, religions most frequently became a source of ferocious enmity, which grew still more acute with the development of the State. And as a result a double stand-

see his *L'âr: the transference of conditional oaths in Morocco.* (In *Anthropological essays presented to Edward Burnett Tylor.* Oxford, 1907. pp. 361–374.) Adolf Bastian, Leipzig, 3 vols. in 1, 1860. Sir Geo. Grey, *Journals of two expeditions of discovery in North-west and western Australia.* Lond. 1841, 2 vols.]—Trans. Note.

ard of ethics was being developed, which still exists in our own time and leads to such horrors as the recent war.

In the beginning the whole tribe was made up of one family, and, as it has been proved in modern times, separate families within the tribe began to appear only gradually, while the wives in these families had to be taken from some other tribe.

It is to be noted that the system of separate families led to the disintegration of the communistic system, for it gave opportunities for amassing family wealth. Nevertheless, the need for sociality, which had been developed during the previous system, began to assume new forms. In the villages, the village commune was evolved, and in the cities—the guilds of the craftsmen and the merchants, from which sprang the mediæval free cities. With the help of these institutions the masses were creating a new system of life, where a new type of unity was being born, to take the place of the tribal unity.

On the other hand, the great transmigration of peoples and the continual raids by neighbouring tribes and races led unavoidably to the formation of the military class, which kept on gaining in power in proportion as the peaceable rural and urban population came to forget more and more the military art. Simultaneously, the elders, the keepers of the tribal traditions as well as the observers of Nature who were accumulating the rudiments of knowledge, and the performers of the religious rituals, were beginning to form secret societies for the purpose of strengthening their power among the peasant communities and in the free cities. Later, with the establishment of the State, the military and the ecclesiastical powers formed an alliance, owing to their common subjection to the power of the king.

It must be added, however, that in spite of all the developments described above, there was never a period in the life of the human race when wars constituted a normal condition of life. While the combatants were exterminating each other, and the priests were glorifying the mutual massacres,—the great masses in villages and in towns continued to live their ordinary life. They kept on with their habitual work, and at the same time endeavoured to strengthen the organizations based on mutual aid and mutual support, i. e., on their code deriving from custom. This process continued even later, after the people fell under the power of the clergy and of the kings.

After all, the whole history of the human race may be regarded as a striving, on the one side, for seizure of power by separate individuals or groups, for the purpose of subjugating the largest possible masses, and on the other hand, the striving, at least by the males, to preserve the equality of rights and to resist the seizure of power, or at least to limit it. In other words: *the striving to preserve justice within the tribe, or the federation of tribes.*

The same striving strongly manifested itself in the mediæval free cities, especially during the few centuries immediately following the liberation of these cities from their feudal lords. In fact, the free cities were the defensive alliances of the enfranchised burghers against the surrounding feudal lords.

But little by little division of the population into classes began to manifest itself in the free cities as well. At the beginning trading was conducted by the entire city. The products of city manufacture or the goods purchased in the villages, were exported by the city as a whole, through its trusted men, and the profits belonged to the entire city community. But by slow steps trading began to be transformed from communal to private, and began to enrich not only the cities themselves but also private individuals, and independent merchants—"mercatori libri"—especially from the time of the crusades, which brought about lively trading with the Levant. A class of bankers began to be formed. In time of need these bankers were appealed to for loans, at first by the noblemen-knights, and later by the cities as well.

Thus, in each of the once free cities there began to develop a merchant aristocracy, which held the cities in the hollow of their hands, supporting alternately the Pope and the Emperor when they were striving for possession of a certain city, or lending aid to a king or prince who was about to seize one of the cities, sometimes with the support of the rich merchants, and sometimes of the poor townsfolk. Thus the ground was prepared for the modern centralized State. The work of centralization was completed when Europe had to defend itself against the invasions of the Moors into Spain in the ninth, tenth, and eleventh centuries, of the Mongolians into Russia in the thirteenth century, and of the Turks in the fifteenth. The cities and the small principalities, which had been continually quarrelling among themselves, proved powerless against such mass invasions, and so the process of the subjugation of the small units by the larger ones, and also the process of the centralization of power, culminated in the formation of large political states.

Needless to say, such fundamental changes in social life, as also the religious uprisings and wars, put their stamp on the entire structure of the moral conceptions in the various countries at different times. At some future day an extensive research will probably be undertaken in which the evolution of morality will be studied in connection with the changes in the mode of social life. We are here entering a field where the science of the moral conceptions and teachings, i. e., Ethics, frequently coincides with another science—*Sociology*, i. e., the science of the life and the development of societies. Therefore, to avoid changing from one field to the other, it will be better to point out beforehand to what subjects the realm of Ethics is to be restricted.

We have seen that in all human beings, even at the lowest stages of development, and also in some gregarious animals, there are certain marked features which we call moral. In all stages of human development we find sociality and the herd instinct, and separate individuals manifest also the readiness to help others, sometimes even at the risk of their own lives. And since such features assist in maintaining and developing social life, which in turn insures the life and well-being of all, such qualities, accord-

81

ingly, were considered by human societies from the most ancient times not only as desirable, but even as obligatory. The elders, the wizards, the sorcerers of the primitive tribes, and later the priests and the clergy, claimed these qualities of human nature as commandments from above, issuing from the mysterious forces of nature, i. e., from the gods, or from one Creator of the universe. But even in the very distant past, and especially from the time of the revival of the sciences,—which began in Ancient Greece more than 2500 years ago,—the thinkers began to consider the question of the natural origin of the moral feelings and conceptions, —those feelings which restrain men from evil acts against their kinsmen and, in general, from acts tending to weaken the social fabric. In other words, they endeavoured to find a natural explanation for that element in human nature which it is customary to call moral, and which is considered unquestionably desirable in any society.

Such attempts had been made, it would appear, even in remote antiquity, for traces of them are seen in China and in India. But in a scientific form they reached us only from Ancient Greece. Here a succession of thinkers, in the course of four centuries,— Socrates, Plato, Aristotle, Epicurus, and later the Stoics, gave thoughtful and philosophical consideration to the following questions:

"Whence originate in a human being the moral principles, which contradict his passions and which frequently serve to check them?

"Whence originates the feeling of the obligatory nature of the moral principles, which manifests itself even in men who deny the moral principles of life?

"Is it merely the outcome of our up-bringing,—an outcome that we dare not renounce,—as is now maintained by some writers, and as, in the past, was proclaimed from time to time by certain negators of morality?

"Or is the moral conscience of Man the outcome of his very nature? In such a case, might it not be the quality that developed from the very fact of his social life in the course of many thousands of years?

"Finally, if the surmise be true, should that moral conscience be encouraged and developed, or would it be better to eradicate it and to encourage the development of the opposite sentiment of self-love (egoism), which considers as desirable the negation of all morality? And would it be well to hold this negation as the ideal of the developed human being?"

These are the problems over the solution of which the thinkers of the human race have been working for more than two thousand years, alternately supplying answers leaning now toward one, now toward the other decision. These investigations led to the formation of a special science—Ethics, which is closely allied on one side to Sociology, and on the other side to Psychology, i. e., the science of the emotional and the intellectual qualities of Man.

After all, in Ethics, all the aforementioned questions reduce themselves to two fundamental problems. Ethics aims: 1) To establish the origin of the moral conceptions and sentiments; 2) To determine the fundamental principles of morality and to work out in this manner a proper (i. e., one that answers its purpose) moral ideal.

The thinkers of all nations worked and are still working over this problem. Therefore, prior to expounding my own conclusions on these questions, I shall endeavour to make a survey of the conclusions at which the thinkers of various schools have arrived.

We will now take up that task, and I will give special attention to the development of the conceptions of justice, which, if I am not mistaken, lies at the root of all morality and constitutes the starting point in all the conclusions of moral philosophy,—although this circumstance is far from being acknowledged by the majority of thinkers who have written on Ethics.

CHAPTER V

WE have seen in the previous chapter that the most primitive peoples develop their own mode of social life and evolve their own carefully preserved customs and traditions,—their own conceptions of what is good and what is bad, what is not to be done, and what is proper in different situations. In short, they evolve their own morality, their own Ethics.

Part of such rules of conduct is placed under the protection of custom. Certain acts are to be avoided because they are "wrong" or "shameful"; they would indicate a physical weakness or a weakness of character. But there are also more serious offences and sterner rules. He who breaks these rules not only displays undesirable traits of character, but also does hurt to his tribe. But the welfare of the tribe is being watched over by the "great multitude" of the dead ancestors, and if anyone breaks the rules of conduct established from generation to generation, the dead ancestors take revenge not only on the offender against the rules laid down by them, but also on the entire tribe that permitted the violation of the ancient traditions.[1] The animal kingdom, as we have seen in the second chapter, assists the good and the just man, and in all possible ways interferes with the evil and the unjust one. But in cases where the entire tribe takes part in a deed of evil, then the forces of nature interfere, these forces being personified by benevolent or evil creatures, with whom the dead ancestors of men are in communication. In general, among the primitive peoples much more than among the civilized, each member of the tribe is identified with his tribe. In clan vengeance, which exists at present, and existed,

[1] See note 3, page 65.

as is known from history, among all the primitive peoples, each is responsible for all, and all for each of their kinsmen.

Custom, i. e., the habit of living according to established traditions, the fear of change, and inertia of thought, plays, accordingly, the principal rôle in the preservation of the established rules of social life. But accidental deviations are always possible, and in order to preserve intact the established mode of life the elders, the prophets, the sorcerers resort to intimidation. They threaten violators of custom with the vengeance of the ancestors and of various spirits populating the aerial region. The mountain, the forest-spirits, avalanches, snow-storms, floods, sickness, etc., all rise to the defence of violated custom. And in order to maintain this fear of retribution for the desecration of rules and customs, sacred rites signifying the worship of the forces of nature are established, sacrifices to these forces are made, and various semi-theatrical ceremonies are conducted.[2]

Morality is thus placed under the protection of the deified powers, and the worship of these powers evolves into religion, which sanctifies and strengthens the moral conceptions.[3]

In such an atmosphere the moral element in Man is so intimately interwoven with mythology and religion, that it becomes extremely difficult to separate the moral element from mystical commands handed down from above, and from religion in general. Owing to this circumstance, the linking of morality with religion has endured to the present time.

[2] Some American investigators call these rites "dances"; in reality they have a much deeper significance than mere amusement. They serve to maintain all the established customs of hunting and fishing, and also the entire tribal mode of life.

[3] In his extensive work, based on familiarity with the inhabitants of Morocco as well as on study of the voluminous literature on the primitive peoples, Professor Westermarck showed what an important part the "curse" played and still plays in the establishment of the obligatory customs and traditions. A man cursed by his father or mother, or by the whole clan, or even by some individual not connected with him (for refusal of aid, or for an injury) is subject to the vengeance of the invisible spirits, of the shades of the ancestors, and of the forces of nature.

ETHICS: ORIGIN AND DEVELOPMENT

Like all the primitive peoples, the ancient Greeks for a long time pictured to themselves the celestial bodies and the formidable phenomena of nature in the form of mighty beings in human likeness, who continually interfered with the life of men. A splendid monument of those times has come down to us in the "Iliad." It is clear from this work that the moral conceptions of its time were of the same nature as are now found among many savage peoples.

The violation of what was then considered moral, was punished by the gods, each of the gods personifying in human likeness this or that force of nature.

But, while many peoples remained for a long time in this stage of development, in Ancient Greece, as early as a few hundred years after the time depicted in the "Iliad" (i. e., about the seventh and the sixth century, B. C.) thinkers began to appear who strove to base the moral conceptions of Man not merely on fear of the gods, but also on an understanding of man's own nature: on self-respect, on the sense of dignity, and on the comprehension of the higher intellectual and moral aims.

In those early days, the thinkers were already divided into several schools. Some attempted to explain the whole of nature, and consequently the moral element in Man, in a naturalistic way, i. e., through study of nature and through experiment,—as is now done in the natural sciences. Others, however, maintained that the origin of the universe and its life cannot be explained in the naturalistic way, because the visible world is the creation of supernatural powers. It constitutes the embodiment of something, of some forces or "essences," that lie outside the regions accessible to human observation. Hence Man can come to know the Universe not through the impressions which he receives from the external world, but only by means of abstract speculation—"metaphysics." [4]

[4] "Metaphysics" in Greek means "outside of physics," i. e., beyond the domain of the physical laws. Aristotle gave this name to one of the divisions of his works.

Nevertheless, in all these essences hidden from our eye or understanding, the thinkers of that time saw the personification of the "Supreme Intelligence," "The Word" (or Reason), "The Supreme Will," or "The Universal Soul," which man could conceive only through knowledge of himself. No matter how the abstract thinker, the metaphysician, tried to spiritualize these qualities and to ascribe to them a superhuman or even a supernatural existence, he always pictured them to himself, like the gods of antiquity, in the image and the likeness of human reason and human feelings, and whatever he learned about these qualities and feelings came about solely through self-observation and the observation of others. The conception of the spiritual supernatural world thus continued to bear the traces of the most primitive anthropomorphism of nature. The Homeric gods were returning, only in more spiritualized form.

It must be said, however, that from the time of Ancient Greece, and up to the present day, the metaphysical philosophy found highly gifted followers. They were not content with descriptions of the celestial bodies and of their movements, of thunder, lightning, falling stars, or of planets and animals, but they strove to undertand surrounding nature as a *cosmic whole*. For this reason they succeeded in making a considerable contribution to the development of general knowledge. Even the first thinkers of the metaphysical school understood—and therein lies their great merit —that whatever be the explanation given to natural phenomena, they cannot be regarded as *arbitrary* acts of certain rulers of the universe. Neither arbitrariness, nor the passions of the gods, nor blind accident can explain the life of nature. We are compelled to acknowledge that every natural phenomenon—the fall of any particular stone, the flow of a brook, or the life of any one tree or animal, constitutes the necessary manifestation of the properties of the *whole*, of the sum total of animate and inanimate nature. They are the unavoidable and logical consequences of the development of fundamental properties in nature and its entire antecedent life. And these laws can be discovered by human intellect. In view of these facts the "metaphysicians" often anticipated the discoveries of science, expressing them in a poetical form. And indeed, owing to such interpretation of the universal life, as early as the fifth century B. C., some Greek thinkers expressed, in spite of their metaphysics, such suppositions about natural phenomena that they may be called the forerunners of modern scientific physics and chemistry. Similarly, in the Middle Ages, and later, up to the eighteenth century, some important discoveries were made by investigators who, while keeping to the metaphysical or even purely religious explanations in interpreting the intellectual and especially the moral life of man, adopted, nevertheless, the scientific method when they undertook the study of the physical sciences.

At the same time religion began to acquire a more spiritual character. Instead of the conception of separate, man-like gods, there appeared in Greece, especially among the Pythagoreans, conceptions of some sort of general forces creating the life of the universe. Such was the conception of "fire" (i. e., "caloric") permeating the whole world, of "numbers," i. e., the mathematical laws of motion, of "harmony," i. e., a rational essence in the life of nature; while on the other hand, there was originating a conception of a Single Being, ruling the universe. There were also hints of "Universal Truth," and "Justice."

However, Greek philosophy could not content itself for a long time with such abstract conceptions. More than four centuries B. C. there appeared, on the one hand, the *Sophists* and the *amoralists* (hedonists, etc., who did not recognize the obligatory nature of moral principles) and, on the other hand, thinkers like Socrates and Plato (in the fifth century B. C.), Aristotle (in the fourth), and Epicurus (in the third), who laid the foundations of Ethics, i. e., the science of the moral, and these foundations have not lost their importance to the present day.

The writings of the Sophist Protagoras (born about 480 B. C.) have reached us only in fragments and we cannot, therefore, form a complete idea of his philosophy. We only know that he adopted a negative attitude toward religions, and as for morality, he considered it an institution of human social origin. This morality, in his opinion, was determined by the development in all respects of each people at a particular period. This accounts for the differences in moral principles among different peoples. Hence follows the conclusion that "good" and "evil" are relative conceptions.

Such ideas were advocated not only by Protagoras, but there soon formed in Greece a whole *school of Sophists,* who held to these notions.

In general, we find in Ancient Greece no leaning toward the idealistic philosophy; the predominating element in Greece was the striving for *action* and for the training of *will,* for active participation in the life of society, and for the development of men intellectually strong, and energetic. Faith in gods as governing the acts of men, was on the wane. The whole mode of life of Ancient Greece,—which then consisted of small independent republics,—the thirst for an understanding of nature, the growing acquaintance with the surrounding world owing to travel and colonization—all these factors urged Man toward the assertion of his individuality, toward the negation of the power of custom and faith, toward the liberation of the intellect. And side by side with this process came the rapid development of the sciences. This development was so much the more remarkable because, only a few centuries later, during the existence of the Roman Empire, and especially after the invasion of the Barbarians, who moved upon Europe from Asia, scientific progress came to a halt throughout the entire human race. For many centuries science was at a standstill.

The intellectual movement originated by the Sophists could not remain long in the same form. It unavoidably led to a deeper study of man—his thinking, his feeling, his will, and his social institutions, and also of the whole life of the Cosmos-Universe, i. e., of Nature in general. And with such study the superficial attitude of the Sophists toward moral questions soon ceased to satisfy thoughtful men. And on the other hand, the development of the sciences, liberating man from slavish obedience to religion and custom, led to cultivation of the moral principles through experimental knowledge and in a manner much more thorough than the Sophists could attain by means of their dialectics.

All this taken together undermined the philosophy of mere negation.

Socrates (born 469, died 399 B. C.) came out against the Sophists in the name of true knowledge. He shared their revolutionary tendencies, but he sought a more solid support for the foundation of morality than the superficial critique of the Sophists. While remaining a revolutionary in religion and in philosophy, he hung everything upon the supreme reason of Man, and upon the attaining by man of the inner harmony between reason and the various feelings and passions. Besides, Socrates did not, of course, "negate virtue," but merely interpreted it very broadly, as the ability to attain proficiency in intellectual development, in the arts, and in creative work. To reach this goal, first of all *knowledge* is necessary; not so much scientific knowledge, as the understanding of social life and of the inter-relations among men. *Virtue*, he taught, *is not a revelation from the gods, but a rational innate knowledge of what is truly good, and of what makes man capable of living without oppressing others but treating them justly; makes him capable of serving society, and not himself alone.* Without this, society is inconceivable.

A disciple of Socrates, Plato (428–348 B. C.) expounded these ideas more completely and spiritualized them with an idealistic conception of morality. He enquired even more deeply into the essence of morality, although his mode of thinking was metaphysical. Without attempting to present Plato's principal ideas in their abstract form, but merely dwelling on their essence, his teaching may be formulated as follows: the principles of good and justice are contained in Nature itself. There is an abundance of evil and injustice in the cosmic life, but side by side with them are laid the foundations of all good. It was this element of Good and Justice that Plato endeavoured to reveal and to set forth in all its power, so that it should become the guiding principle in human life.

Unfortunately, instead of following the path which was then already being marked out in Greece, instead of showing in what form the fundamental principles of morality result from the life of Nature itself, from the sociality of men, and from the nature of man's intelligence, from innate intelligence as well as from that developed by social life—Plato sought the foundations of morality outside of the universe, *in the "idea" which underlies the structure of cosmic life, but which is not expressed in it quite definitely.*

In spite of the unending number of interpretations of Plato's abstract thought, it is difficult to get at the essence of his philosophy. But we will hardly make a mistake in saying that the great Greek thinker, with his deep understanding of the intimate connection between human life and the life of Nature as a whole, found it impossible to explain the moral element in Man by mere striving for what is individually acceptable, as was done by the Sophists. He was still less capable of considering morality an accidental product of social life simply because morality assumed different forms in different places and at different times. He might have asked himself the question,—as perhaps he did: how does it happen that though man is led by a striving for what is acceptable to him personally, he nevertheless arrives at moral conceptions that are, after all, similar among different peoples and at different times, since they all hold as desirable *the happiness of all?* Why is it that, in the final analysis, the happiness of the *individual* is identified with the happiness of the *majority of men?* Why is not the former possible without the other? And what transforms man from a self-loving creature into a being capable of considering the

91

interests of others, and not infrequently of sacrificing for them his personal happiness and even his life?

As a disciple of Socrates, Plato could no longer ascribe the origin of the conception of the good to the revelation of gods: Thunder, Sun, Moon, etc., i. e., to the forces of Nature endowed with human attributes. On the other hand, owing to the rudimentary state of knowledge about human societies, he could not look for the explanation of the good,—as we are seeking it now and finding it, —in the gradual development of sociality and of the consciousness of equity. He found, therefore, the explanation of the good in the *Idea*, in something abstract which pervades the whole universe, and consequently, Man as well. "Nothing can manifest itself in this world, which is not already implied in the life of the whole," such was his fundamental thought,—a perfectly true philosophic thought. He did not carry it, however, to its ultimate conclusion. It would seem that he should have arrived at the conclusion that if the human reason seeks good, justice, order, in the form of the "laws of life," it does it because *all these elements are contained in the life of Nature;* he should have concluded that the mind of man draws from Nature its conceptions of the principles of good, justice, social life. Instead of that, although he tried to free himself from the error of his predecessors, Plato came to the conclusion that man's search for something higher than the everyday life, i. e., his search for Good and Justice, has its explanation and its basis not in Nature, but in something which is beyond the limits of our knowledge, of our senses, and of our experience,—namely, in the Universal Idea.

It can be easily understood how, in after times, the "Neo-Platonists," and later Christianity, took advantage of this conclusion of the brilliant and stimulating Greek thinker,—first for the purpose of Mysticism, and then for the justification of monotheism, and for the explanation of all the moral elements in man as coming by no means through the natural development of the social sentiments and of reason, but through revelation, i. e., inspiration from above originating in a Supreme Being.

92

It can also be readily understood how, not having considered the necessity of establishing morality on the very fact of social life, which would probably have led him to recognize the equality of men,—not being permeated with the idea that all moral teachings will be impotent if the system of social life is in contradiction with them, Plato, like his predecessors, pictured in his "Republic" as an ideal social system, a class republic, based on the subjugation of some classes by others, and even on slavery, and even on the death penalty.

This also explains why, later, throughout the entire history of Ethics as a science of the development of moral conceptions in Man, beginning with ancient Greece and up to the time of Bacon and Spinoza, there prevails the same fundamental idea of the extra-human and extra-natural origin of morality.

It is true that certain Sophists, predecessors of Plato, arrived at a natural explanation of phenomena. Already in those early times they tried to explain the life of Nature by mechanical causes, just as it is now being explained by the "positivist" philosophy; and some Sophists even regarded moral conceptions as the necessary consequence of the physical structure of man. But the scientific knowledge of mankind of that epoch was not sufficient to render such interpretations of morality acceptable, and for many centuries Ethics remained under the guardianship of religion. Only now is it beginning to be built up on the basis of the natural sciences.

Owing to the fact that the study of Nature had made but small progress in those days, the teaching of Plato was, naturally, the most accessible to the majority of educated men. Probably it also harmonized with the new religious influences coming from the East, where Buddhism was already being developed. These circumstances alone, however, do not suffice to explain the influence of Plato,—an influence that has lasted to our own era. The point is that Plato introduced into Ethics the *idealistic interpretations of morality*. A "soul" was to him a blending of reason, feeling and will, from which come wisdom, courage, and moderation in passion. His ideal was

—Love, Friendship; but the word Love (Eros) had at that time a broader meaning than it bears now, and Plato understood by Eros not only a mutual attachment of two beings, but also the sociality based on the accord between the desires of the individual and the desires of all the other members of society. His Eros was also what we now call *sociability, mutual sympathy,* the feeling which, as can be seen from the previously mentioned facts taken from the life of animals and of human beings, *permeates the whole world of living creatures and which is just as necessary a condition of their lives as is the instinct of self-preservation.* Plato did not know this, but he already felt the importance of this fundamental factor of all progressive development, i. e., of that which we now call *Evolution.*

Furthermore, though Plato did not realize the importance of justice in the development of morality, he nevertheless presented justice in such a form that one really wonders why subsequent thinkers did not put it at the basis of Ethics. Thus, in the dialogue "Alcibiades (I)," which is ascribed to a still youthful Plato, Socrates makes Alcibiades acknowledge that although men are capable of waging desperate wars, presumably for the sake of justice, they are, nevertheless, really fighting for what they consider most useful for themselves. The just, however, is always beautiful; it is always good, i. e., always expedient; so that there cannot be "any matters greater than the just, the honourable, the good, and the expedient." [5]

It is interesting to note that when Plato, in the same Dialogue, speaks through the mouth of Socrates about the soul and its divine aspect, he considers "divine" that part of the soul "which has to do with wisdom and knowledge," i. e., not the feelings, but the reason. And he concludes the Dialogue with the following words, spoken by Socrates: "You and the State, if you act wisely and justly, will act according to the will of God,"—and "you will look only at what is bright and divine," (i. e., at the reason which gives strength

---

[5] *Alcibiades I,* 118. [*The Dialogues of Plato,* translated by Benj. Jowett, Lond., and N. Y., 1892, 3rd Edition, p. 484. All further references will be to this edition]—Trans. Note.

to the soul) and "in that mirror you will see and know your-selves and your own good." [*Alcibiades I* § 134; p 507].

Plato wrote still more definitely about justice, and morality in general, in his dialogue, "The Symposium," where the participants in the feast extol the god of love, Eros. Of course, not in the first part of this discourse, where commonplaces are being said about the god, but in the second part, where the conversation is between the poet-dramatist Agathon, and Socrates.

The virtues of Eros, says the poet, are his Justice, his Temperance, and his Courage; then his love of beauty; he tolerates no ugliness. He is the god "who empties men of disaffection and fills them with affection . . . who sends courtesy and sends away discourtesy; who gives kindness ever, and never gives unkindness," etc. [*Symposium* § 197; p. 567.]

In the same work Plato asserts, and proves through the words of Socrates, that Love is inseparable from goodness and beauty. Love, says Socrates in the "Symposium," is "birth in beauty, whether of body or soul." Love strives to cleave to the good and the beautiful, and thus, in the final analysis, love comes to be the search for the good and the beautiful. " . . . The beauty of one form is akin to the beauty of another. . . ." When a man perceives this he "will become a lover of all beautiful forms; in the next stage he will consider that the beauty of the mind is more honourable than the beauty of the outward form" and in this manner he will come to the contemplation of beauty which consists in performing his duty, and then he will understand that "the beauty in every form is one and the same," and beauty of form will no longer be to him so important. Having attained this stage of interpreting beauty, says Plato, a man "will perceive a nature of wondrous beauty . . . which is everlasting, not growing and decaying, or waxing and waning," but which is "absolute without diminution, and without increase, or any change" in all its parts, at all times, in all respects, in all places, and for all men. Plato reaches the highest degree of idealism when he adds: this beauty will not appear as something contained in anything else, something "existing for example in an animal, or in heaven, or in earth, or in any other place;" but as something "absolute, separate, simple," which exists independently and is self contained." [*Symposium*, § 211; p. 581.]

Such was Plato's idealism, and it is no wonder, therefore, that it has followers to the present day. On one side, it prepared the path for the populous school of the "Eudemonists" who are still in the majority in Ethics and who assert (just as the Sophists asserted before Plato, and after him Epicurus and his followers) that whatever man does, he does "for his own pleasure." Needless to say, Plato understood this "pleasure" not in the narrow sense of the enjoyments of a half-man, half-beast, but in that higher sense which he defined in the Dialogues "Laches" and the "Symposium." But on the other hand, introducing at the same time the conceptions of "soul" and "beauty," as of something which is, in a sense, contained in Nature, and yet stands above it, he prepared the ground for religious ethics, and he remains, therefore, to our time the favourite of religious thinkers. He was their predecessor. It is remarkable, however, that his high conception of Nature and of moral beauty in Nature—which remains insufficiently appreciated to this time by both the religious and the non-religious ethics—separates him from the former, as well as from the latter.

In the second half of his life, when Plato fell under the influence of the Pythagoreans, he attempted, with the assistance of the Tyrant of Syracuse, Dionysius, to establish a state according to the plan which he expounded in his works, "Statesman" and "Laws" (a product of a mind already falling into decrepitude). At that time he was no longer the same idealist as at the first period of his life and teaching. In his "State," as one of his great admirers, Vladimir Solovyev, points out with bitterness, Plato not only retained slavery, but also the death sentence for slaves for not reporting another's offence, and for the citizens in general when guilty of disrespect toward the established religion. He thus called upon men to commit the very crime which so strongly aroused his indignation when his teacher Socrates was executed owing to the same religious intolerance. "Eros," i. e. Love, which Plato preached in such wondrous form, did not prevent him from approving these crimes. Later they were perpetrated also by the Christian Church, in spite of the love-gospel of its founder.

The middle position between the natural-scientific and the metaphysical understanding of morality is occupied by the teaching of Aristotle, who lived in the fourth century B. C. (384–322 B. C.).

Aristotle sought the explanation of our moral conceptions not in the Supreme Reason or in the Universal Idea, as Plato did, but in the actual life of men: *in their striving for happiness and for what is useful to them,—and in human reason.* In this striving, he taught, two principal social virtues were evolved: friendship, i. e., love for our fellowman (we should now call it sociality) and Justice. But he understood Justice, as we shall see later, not in the sense of equality of rights.

Thus in Aristotle's philosophy we find for the first time the doctrine of the self-sufficiency of human reason. Like Plato, he thought that the source of reason is the Divinity, but this divinity, though it is the source of "reason and movement in the universe," does not interfere with the universal life. In general, while Plato strove to establish the existence of two separate worlds: the sensible world which we know through our senses, and the super-sensible world which is inaccessible to them, Aristotle strove to unite them. There was no room for faith in his teaching, and he did not recognize personal immortality. We can attain the true understanding of our life, taught Aristotle, only through the understanding of the universe.

He saw the foundation of the moral conceptions of man in the facts of actual life. All are striving for the greatest happiness. Happiness is what makes life "eligible and in want of nothing."

ETHICS: ORIGIN AND DEVELOPMENT

The crude mob seeks happiness in enjoyment, while the enlightened people seek it in something higher, not in the "idea," as Plato taught, but in "an energy [6] of the soul and actions performed with reason," or, at least, not contrary to reason. "Man's chief good is "an energy of the soul according to virtue," and, it must be added, in the course of the man's entire life,—an active virtue combined with energy. Happiness is attained through a life which is in accordance with the requirements of justice, and such a life is more beautiful than anything else: It combines with the above benefits also health and "the obtaining what we love." (*Ethica*, book I, ch. vii.–viii., pp. 17–20.) "Nevertheless," adds Aristotle, "it appears to stand in need of the addition of external goods," among which he includes "friends, money, political influence, noble birth, good children, and beauty." Without this "external prosperity," happiness is not complete. (ch. viii, 12, pp. 20–21.) Chance plays a part in apportioning happiness, but "it is possible, that by means of some teaching and care, it should exist in every person who is not incapacitated for virtue" (ch. ix, 3, p. 21), for even the irrational part of man's soul (i. e., our passions) "in some sense partakes of reason." (ch. xiii, 13; p. 31.) In general, Aristotle ascribed tremendous importance to reason in the development of an individual; it is the function of reason to restrain the passions; it is owing to reason that we are able to understand that striving for the good of society gives a much higher, much more "beautiful happiness" than striving for the satisfaction of one's own impulses.

It may be seen from these extracts that instead of looking for the basis of the moral conceptions in man in revelations from

[6] [The quotations are from *The Nichomachean Ethics* of Aristotle. The translators have used the version of R. W. Browne, Bohn's Library, Lond., 1853. Mr. Browne gives the following note, in part, in connection with the word "energy": "Energy implies an activity, an active state" as contrasted with the potential. (Page 2, note b). Other translations of the *Ethics* are, by Chase, Everyman series, Lond. and N. Y., 1911; by F. H. Peters, Lond., 1909, 11th ed.; by J. E. C. Welldon, Lond. and N. Y., 1920.]—Trans. Note.

above, Aristotle reduced these conceptions to the decision of reason, seeking for the highest satisfaction and happiness, and he understood that the happiness of an individual is intimately connected with the happiness of society ("state," he said, meaning by it an organized community). Thus Aristotle is the predecessor of the large school of "Eudemonists," who later explained the moral instincts, feelings, and acts of man as a striving for personal happiness, and also of the modern school of the "utilitarians," beginning with Bentham and Mill and reaching to Herbert Spencer.

Aristotle's "Ethics," in its form and in its careful development of each separate thought, is unquestionably just as remarkable a monument of the development of Ancient Greece, as is the rest of his works, scientific and political. But in his "Ethics," as well as in the "Politics," he pays full tribute to what we now call opportunism. Such is his famous definition of virtue as "a habit, accompanied with deliberate preference, in the *relative mean*, defined by reason, and as the prudent man would define it. It is *a mean state between two vices, one in excess, the other in defect."* (Book II, ch. vi, 10; p. 45; also Book I, ch. viii.)

The same can be said of his conception of Justice.[7] Although Aristotle devoted to it a separate chapter in his "Ethics," he defined it in the same spirit as he defined virtue in general, i. e., as the middle between two extremes, and he understood it not as a principle of equality of men, but in a very limited sense.[8]

[7] "But we must inquire into the subject of justice and injustice, and see what kind of actions they are concerned with, what kind of mean state justice is, and between what things 'the just', that is, the abstract principle of justice, is a mean"—thus he begins the book *Of Justice and Injustice.* (Book V, ch. i, i; p. 116.)

[8] "Now the transgressor of law appears to be unjust, and the man who takes more than his share, and the unequal man." Thus the conception of justice means at the same time both the lawful and the equitable (attitude toward men). Then he continues: "But laws make mention of all subjects, with a view either to the common advantage of all, or of men in power, or of the best citizens" (Book V, ch. i, 6, 10, pp. 118, 119). Thus, as is to be expected in a society based on slavery, Aristotle's interpretation of Justice, as obedience to the law, leads him to a recognition of inequality among men.

99

Such an interpretation of justice is worthy of particular note, because he considered justice the greatest of all the virtues, "and neither the evening nor the morning star is so admirable."

"In justice all virtue is comprehended," says a proverb of that time. Aristotle undoubtedly understood the moral importance of justice, because he taught that "justice alone of all the virtues seems to be *a good to another person*" (Book V, ch. i, 13; p. 120); in other words, it is a "virtue" which is not egotistical.[9] Moreover, Aristotle very justly concluded that "in all other acts of injustice it is possible always to refer the action to some specific vice." [Book V, ch. ii, 3; p. 121.] From this it can be surmised that he also understood that any act which we consider evil, almost invariably turns out to be an act of injustice against someone.

At the same time, while distinguishing between two different types of injustice—the universal, which consisted in breaking the law, and the "particular injustice," which consisted in an inequitable attitude toward men,—and while distinguishing between the two corresponding types of justice,—Aristotle recognized two other species of "particular justice" ("distributive" and "corrective"). "One species is that which is concerned in the *distributions* of honour, equal or unequal, or of wealth or of any of those other things which can possibly be distributed among the members of a political community" . . . " the other is that which is *corrective* in transactions between man and man" (Book V, ch. iii, 8, 9; pp. 122–123). And to this the great thinker of the ancient world immediately adds, that in equity, consequently also in justice, there should be the "mean." And since the "mean" is a purely relative conception, he destroyed thereby the very conception of justice as the *true* solution of complex, doubtful moral questions, where a man hesitates between two possible decisions. And, actually, Aristotle did

9 ". . . justice, therefore, is not a division of virtue, but the whole of virtue; nor is the contrary injustice a part of vice, but the whole of vice." (Book V, ch. i, 14; p. 120).

not recognize equality in "distribution," but merely demanded "corrective" justice.[10]

Thus it is clear that, living in a society where slavery existed, Aristotle did not venture to acknowledge that justice consists in equity among men. He limited himself to commercial justice, and did not even proclaim equity the ideal of social life. Mankind had to live for nearly two thousand years longer in organized communities, before, in one country—France—equality was proclaimed as the idea of social life, together with liberty and fraternity.

Generally speaking, in questions of morality and in politics, Aristotle was not in advance of his time. But in his definitions of science, wisdom and art, (Book VI, ch, iii, iv, vii) he was a forerunner of Bacon's philosophy. In his discussion of the various types of the "good," and in his classification of pleasures, he anticipated Bentham. Moreover, he understood the importance of mere sociality, which, however, he confused with friendship and mutual love (Book VIII, ch. vi), and, on the other hand, he was the first to realize what has been so frequently overlooked by the majority

---

[10] He added: "This is clear from the expression 'according to worth'; for, in distributions all agree that justice ought to be according to some standard of worth, yet all do not make that standard the same; for those who are inclined to democracy consider liberty as the standard; those who are inclined to oligarchy, wealth; [others nobility of birth;] and those who are inclined to aristocracy, virtue." (Book V., ch. iv., 3; p. 124). And in summarizing all that he had said in support of this idea, he concludes with the following words: "Now we have said what the just and what the unjust are. But this being decided, it is clear that just acting is a mean between acting and suffering injustice; for one is having too much, and the other too little. But justice is a mean state," etc. (Book V, ch. vi, 13; p. 132). Aristotle returns again and again to this subject; thus, in Book VIII, ch. vii, 3 (p. 216) he wrote: "equality in proportion to merit holds the first place in justice, and equality as to quantity, the second." In the book Of Justice and Injustice he even defends slavery in the following words:

"But the just in the case of master and slave, and father and child, is not the same . . . for there is not injustice, abstractedly, towards one's own; a possession and a child, [as long as he be of a certain age,] and be not separated from his father, being as it were a part of him; and no man deliberately chooses to hurt himself; and therefore there is no injustice towards one's self" (Book V, ch. vi, 7; p. 134).

of thinkers of our time, namely,—that in speaking of morality, distinction should be made between that which we have the right to demand from all, and that heroic virtue which exceeds the powers of the ordinary man (Book VII, ch. i). And it is just this quality (which we now call self-sacrifice or generosity)—that moves humanity forward and develops striving for the beautiful,—which Aristotle's Ethics aims to develop. (The whole of ch. viii of Book IX.) [11] But, of course, we have no right to demand it from everybody.

Such was the moral philosophy of a great, but not a profound scientist, who stood out in the civilization of his time and who has exercised for the last three centuries (from the time of the Renaissance in the sixteenth century) a strong influence on science in general, and also on ethical philosophy.

The teaching of Plato and the teaching of Aristotle thus represented two schools which differed somewhat radically in the interpretation of morality. Disputes between the two did not cease even long after the death of their founders. Little by little, however, these disputes lost their interest because both schools were already agreed that the moral element in man is not an accidental phenomenon, but that it has its deep foundation in human nature, and that there are moral conceptions that are common to all human societies.

In the third century B. C. appeared two new schools— the *Stoics* and the *Epicureans*. The Stoics taught, in agreement with their predecessors, Plato and Aristotle, that man must live *in accordance with his nature*, i. e., with his intelligence and his abilities, because only such a life can give the highest happiness. But, as is known, they particularly insisted that man finds happiness, "eudemonia," not in the pursuit of external benefits: wealth, honors, etc., but in striving for something higher, something ideal; in the development of a spiritual life for the good of the man himself, his family, and

[11] [The author refers the reader, by mistake apparently, to Book VIII, ch. vi–vii, which deal with some other subject.]—Trans. Note.

society; and most of all, in the attainment of *inner freedom.* The teaching of the Stoics will be discussed further on in this chapter. I shall only remark at this point that although the Stoics rejected in their teachings the Socratic metaphysics of morality, they nevertheless continued his work, for they introduced the conception of *knowledge,* which enables man to distinguish between different types of enjoying life and to seek for happiness in its *more perfect* and spiritual form. The influence of the Stoics, as we shall see, was tremendous, especially later, in the Roman world; it prepared minds for the acceptance of Christianity, and we feel it to our time. This is especially true of the teaching of Epictetus (end of the second and beginning of the first century B. C.), the essence of which was absorbed by positivism and the modern natural-scientific school of ethics.

In contrast with the Stoics, the Sophists, especially Democritus, (470–380 B. C.) founder of molecular physics, and the school of the Cyrenaics in general, held as the fundamental trait of man or of any living creature the search for pleasure, for delight, for happiness ("hedonism," from the Greek word "hedone"). However, they did not sufficiently emphasize the thought that there may be different forms of striving for happiness, ranging from purely animal self-gratification to the most altruistic self-sacrifice; from narrow-personal aspirations to aspirations of a broadly social nature. But that is just the problem of Ethics,—namely, to analyse these different forms of striving for happiness, and to show where they lead and what degree of satisfaction each one of them gives. This was very conscientiously done by Epicurus, who lived in the third century B. C. and who acquired wide popularity in the Greco-Roman world of that time, owing to his carefully worked out *Eudemonism,* i. e., a moral teaching which is also based on the striving for happiness, but with careful choice of means to that happiness.

"The aim of life toward which all living beings are unconsciously striving is happiness," taught Epicurus: (one might call it "the pleasant") "because, as soon as they are born, they already desire gratification and resist suffering." Reason has nothing to do with it: nature itself guides them in that direction. Reason and feeling blend in this case, and reason is subjected to feeling. In short, "pleasure is the essence and the aim of a happy life—the primary and natural good." Virtue is desirable only if it leads to that good, while philosophy [12] is energy which, through reasoning, gives a happy life.

Then Epicurus expresses his fundamental thought and, probably with intention, in a rather blunt form. "The origin and the root of all good is the pleasure of the belly." His opponents freely took advantage of this saying, thus bringing Epicureanism into disrepute. Whereas Epicurus, obviously, merely meant to say that the pleasure of nourishment is the starting point of all pleasant sensations, from which later evolve all the base, as well as all the sublime sensations. Little by little this fundamental pleasure assumes thousands of variations, transforms itself into pleasures of taste, sight, imagination,—but the starting point of all pleasurable sensations in man or in animal is the pleasant sensation experienced while taking nourishment. Those modern biologists who are investigating the first steps of conscious life, will readily agree with this idea, especially if further explanations of the Epicureans are taken into account.

"Wise and beautiful things," wrote Epicurus, "are connected with this pleasure." This pleasure, of course, does not constitute the final aim of happiness, but can be taken as the starting point, because life is impossible without nourishment. Happiness, however, results from the sum total of pleasures; and while other hedonists (Aristippus the Younger, for example), did not make sufficient distinction between various pleasures, Epicurus introduced

[12] In this exposition of the teaching of Epicurus, I follow, principally, M. Guyau, in his remarkable work, *La Morale d'Épicure et ses rapports avec les doctrines contemporaines.* (Paris, 3d enlarged ed., 1917), where he made a thorough study not only of the few writings of Epicurus that have come down to us, but also of the writings of those who expounded his teachings after his death. Good analyses of Epicurus's teachings are given also by Jodl, Wundt, Paulsen, and others.

a valuation of pleasures, depending on their influence on our life as a whole. Our very sufferings—he taught—may be useful, and may lead to good. Thus the Epicurean Ethics rises much higher than the Ethics of mere pleasure: [13] it came upon the path which was followed in the nineteenth century by Bentham and John Stuart Mill.

Putting as man's aim the happy life in its entirety, and not the gratification of momentary whims and passions, Epicurus pointed the way to achieving such happiness. First of all a man must limit his desires and be contented with little. Epicurus, who in his own life was ready to be content with a barley millcake and water, speaks here as a most rigorous Stoic.[14] And then one must live without inner conflicts, with a *whole life*, in harmony with oneself, and must feel that one lives independently, and not in enslavement to external influences.[15]

At the basis of human conduct should be that which gives man highest satisfaction. But aspirations for personal gain cannot serve as such a basis, because the highest happiness is attained by *concord between personal aspirations and the aspirations of others.* Happiness is freedom from evil; but this freedom cannot be attained unless the life of each individual is in accord with the interests of all. Life teaches us this lesson, and Man, as a reasoning creature, capable of utilizing the lessons of experience, chooses between the acts that lead to this accord, and the acts that lead away from it. Thus the moral structure of society, its Ethics, is developed.

Now it is easy to understand how, starting with the assertion that virtue in itself, or disinterestedness in the exact meaning of the word, does not exist, and that the whole of morality is nothing but a rationalized egoism (self-love), Epicurus arrived at a moral teaching which is in no wise inferior in its conclusions to the teach-

[13] This is very well shown by many scholars, and among them by Guyau (ch. iii, § 1 and ch. iv, introduction).
[14] *Ibid.,* ch. iv § 1.
[15] *Ibid.,* Book I, ch. iv, § 2.

ings of Socrates or even of the Stoics. Purely physical pleasure does not embrace the whole life of man; such pleasure is fleeting. But there is a life of *mind and heart,* a life of *reminiscence and hopes,* of *memory and foresight,* which opens to man a whole paradise of new delights.

Epicurus also endeavoured to free men from the fears instilled in them by faith in gods endowed with all kinds of evil qualities; he tried to free them from dread of the horrors of life beyond the grave, and from faith in the influence of "fate,"—a faith supported even by the teachings of Democritus. To free men from all these fears it was necessary, first of all, to free them from fear of death, or rather from fear of life after death. This fear was very strong in antiquity, for life after death was then pictured as a sleep in subterranean darkness, during which man retained something like conscience, to torture him.[16] At the same time Epicurus combated the pessimism that was preached by Hegesias (his pessimism was akin to the modern pessimism of Schopenhauer) i. e., the desirability of death, in view of the abundant presence of evil and suffering in the world.

Generally speaking, the whole of Epicurus's teaching strove for intellectual and moral liberation of men. But it contained one important omission: it supplied no high moral aims, not even the one of self-sacrifice for the good of society. Epicurus did not foresee such aims as the equality of rights of all the members of society, or even the abolition of slavery. Courage, for example, consisted for him not in seeking perils, but in the ability to avoid them. The same with regard to love: a wise man must avoid passionate love, for it contains nothing natural and rational; it reduces love to a psychological illusion, and is a form of religious adoration,—which is not to be tolerated. He was against marriage, because marriage, and later children, give too much trouble

[16] By promising men that the chosen ones of them will not remain in the subterranean darkness, but will ascend to the luminous regions of Heaven, Christianity, remarks Guyau, effected a complete revolution in the mind. Everyone might cherish the hope of being chosen.

(nevertheless he loved children). But friendship he valued very highly. In friendship man forgets his self-interest; in doing an act pleasing to our friend, we give pleasure to ourselves. Epicurus was always surrounded with friends, and his disciples attracted so many followers by the spirit of good fellowship in their common life, that, as one of their contemporaries, Diogenes Laertius, put it, "entire cities would not provide room for them all." Contemporary writers could not praise enough the Epicurean fidelity in friendship.

In his analysis of the teachings of the Epicureans, Guyau pointed out an interesting peculiarity in them. At the first glance friendship and self-sacrifice for the friend's sake seem to contradict the principle of self-interest, by which, according to Epicurean theory, a rationally thinking man should be guided. And in order to avoid this contradiction, the followers of Epicurus explained friendship as a tacit understanding based on justice, (i. e., reciprocity, or equity—we will add). This understanding is maintained through habit. At first, the relation arises through a personal pleasure that is mutual, but little by little such relations change into a habit; love springs up, and then we love our friends without considering whether they are useful to us. Thus the Epicureans justified friendship, proving that it does not contradict their fundamental principle—the striving for personal happiness.

But the question presented itself: "What position is an Epicurean to take with reference to the whole of society?" Plato had already expressed the thought (in the dialogue "Gorgias"), says Guyau, that the only law of nature is the right of the strong. After Plato, the skeptics and Democritus denied "natural justice," and many thinkers of that time acknowledged that the rules of civic life were established by force, and then became firmly implanted through habit.

Epicurus was the first, Guyau asserts, to express the thought that was later developed by Hobbes, and after him by many others, that the so-called "natural law" was nothing but a "mutual agreement not to inflict harm nor to suffer harm at the hands of another" . . . "Justice has no value in itself: it exists only in mutual agreements and is established wherever a mutual obligation is assumed not to do harm to others, nor to suffer harm from them." *Such covenants are introduced by wise men,"* says Epicurus. "And not in order to avoid doing an injustice, but in order not to suffer it from others." It is owing to reciprocity that it turns out that in protecting ourselves from others we also protect others from ourselves. Without such covenants and laws, society would be impossible; people would devour each other, says Metrodorus, a follower of Epicurus.[17]

Consequently, the conclusion from the entire Epicurean teaching was, that what we call duty and virtue is identical with the interests of the individual. Virtue is the surest means of attaining happiness, and in case of doubt as to how to act, it is best always to follow the path of virtue.

But that virtue did not contain even the rudiments of human equality. Slavery roused no indignation in Epicurus. He himself treated his slaves well, but he did not recognize that they had any rights: the equality of men, apparently, did not even occur to him. And it took many hundreds of years before those thinkers who devoted themselves to moral problems ventured to proclaim as the watchword of morality—equal rights, the equality of all human beings.

It must be noted, however, for the sake of completeness in characterizing the Epicurean teaching, that in the writings of one of Epicurus's followers, where we find the most complete exposition of his teachings, i. e., in the work of the Roman writer Lucretius (first century B. C.), in his celebrated poem "On the Nature of Things," we find already the expression of the idea of progressive development, i. e., of evolution, which now lies at the base of modern philosophy. He also expounds the scientific, materialistic understanding of the life of Nature, as it is interpreted by modern science. Generally speaking, Epicurus's conception of Nature and

[17] Guyau, Book III, ch. ii.

the universe was built, like his ethics, without any recognition of faith, while the Stoics, as pantheists, continued to believe in the constant interference of super-natural forces in our life. And the followers of Plato, especially the philosophers of the Alexandrian school, who believed in miracles and magic, had to succumb of necessity before the Christian faith. Only the Epicureans continued to remain non-believers, and their teaching endured very long. i. e., over five hundred years. Until the appearance of Christianity it was the most widely spread teaching in the ancient world, and thereafter it remained popular for about four hundred years. And when in the twelfth century, and later in the epoch of the Renaissance, the rationalistic movements began in Europe, their first steps in Italy were directed by the teachings of Epicurus.[18]

The Epicurean teaching exercised strong influence upon the rationalist, (seventeenth-century) Gassendi (1592–1655) and also upon his disciple, Hobbes, and even upon Locke, who prepared the ground for the Encyclopædists and for modern naturalistic philosophy. His influence was also strong on the philosophy of "negationists" like La Rochefoucauld and Mandeville, and in the nineteenth century upon Stirner, Nietzsche, and their imitators.

Finally, the fourth school, which was also developing in ancient Greece, and later came to Rome, and which has left to this day deep traces on ethical thinking, was the school of the Stoics. The founding of this school is ascribed to Zeno (340–265 B. C.) and Chrysippus (281 or 276, to 208 or 204 B. C.); and later in the Roman Empire the same teachings were developed by Seneca (54 B. C – 36 A. D.) and especially by Epictetus (end of the first and beginning of the second century A. D.) and by Marcus Aurelius (121–180 A. D.).

The Stoics aimed to lead men to happiness through cultivating in them virtue, which consisted in a life that is in accord with nature, and through developing reason, and the knowledge of the life of the universe. They did not seek the origin of the moral conceptions and aspirations of man in any supernatural power: on

[18] Guyau, Book IV, ch. i.

the contrary, they asserted that nature itself contains moral laws, and consequently also the example of morality. That which men call moral law is the sequence of the universal laws that govern the life of nature, they said. Their point of view, accordingly, is in line with the ideas that are apparent in the modern ethics of Bacon, Spinoza, Auguste Comte, and Darwin. Only, it should be noted that when the Stoics spoke of the primary foundations of morality and of the life of Nature in general, they often clothed their ideas in words natural to metaphysicians. Thus they taught that Reason or the "Word" (from the Greek "logos") permeates the universe as the General Universal Reason, and that the thing which men call moral law is the sequence of the universal laws that govern the life of Nature.[19] Human reason, said the Stoics, and consequently our conceptions of morality, are nothing but one of the manifestations of the forces of nature: this view, of course, did not prevent the Stoics from holding that the evil in nature and in man, physical as well as moral, is just as natural a consequence of the life of nature as is the good. Accordingly, all their teachings were directed toward helping man to develop the good in himself and to combat evil, thus attaining the greatest happiness.

Opponents of the Stoics pointed out that their teachings annihilate the distinction between the good and the evil, and it must be admitted that, though in actual life most of the Stoics did not confuse these conceptions, they nevertheless failed to point out a definite criterion for distinguishing between the good and the evil, as was done, for example, in the nineteenth century by the utilitarians, who held as the ethical aim the greatest happiness of the greatest number of people (Bentham),—or by those who refer to the natural preponderance of the social instinct over the personal (Bacon, Darwin),—or by those who introduce into ethics the idea of justice, i. e., equality.

[19] Epictetus did not think it necessary to study nature in order to know the essence of its laws. Our soul, he said, knows them directly, because it is in intimate connection with Divinity.

In general, it has been well said that in their reasoning the Stoics did not go so far as actually to construct the theory of morality on the natural basis. It is true that when the Stoics asserted that man should live in accordance with the laws of Nature, some of them had in view the fact that man is a social animal, and should therefore subordinate his impulses to reason and to the aims of society as a whole, and Cicero (106–143 A. D.) even referred to justice as to a foundation for morality. Man can attain wisdom, virtue, and happiness, said the Stoics, only by living in accordance with universal reason, and Nature itself ingrains in us healthy moral instincts. "But how badly the Stoics knew how to find the moral in the natural, and the natural in the moral," Jodl justly observed in his "History of Ethics." [20] And on account of this deficiency in their teaching, a deficiency which was, after all, unavoidable in those days, some of the Stoics, such as Epictetus, came to Christian ethics, which recognizes the necessity of divine revelation for knowing the moral; while others, like Cicero, vacillated between the natural and the divine origin of morality; and Marcus Aurelius, who had written such beautiful moral Maxims, permitted the cruel persecution of Christians (in defence of the officially recognized gods). His Stoicism had already become transformed into religious fanaticism.

Generally speaking, the teachings of the Stoics contained much that was fragmentary, and even many contradictions. Regardless of this fact, however, they left deep traces on the philosophy of morality. Some of them attained the height of the gospel of universal brotherhood; but, at the same time, they did not reject individualism, passionlessness, and renunciation of the world. Seneca, the tutor of Nero (who later executed him) combined stoicism with the metaphysics of Plato, and also mingled with it the teachings of Epicurus and of the Pythagoreans. On the other hand, Cicero had a definite leaning toward the religious interpretation of morality,

[20] [Friedrich Jodl, *Geschichte der Ethik als philosophischer Wissenschaft,* Stuttgart, Berlin, 2 vols. 1912.]—Trans. Note.

seeing in the latter the expression of natural and divine laws.[21] But the fundamental thought of the Stoics was the finding of the foundation of morality *in the reason of man*. The striving for the social good they considered an inborn quality, which developed in man as his intellectual broadening progressed. That form of conduct is wise, they added, which is in accordance with human nature and with the nature of "all things," i. e., with Nature in general. Man must base all his philosophy and all his morality on knowledge: on knowledge of himself and of the whole of Nature. To live in accordance with Nature first of all, means, for Cicero, to know Nature and to cultivate the social impulse in oneself, i. e., the ability to check the impulses leading to injustice, in other words, to develop in oneself justice, courage, and the so-called civic virtues in general. It is easy to understand now why Cicero became the favourite writer beginning with the Renaissance, and later also among the writers of the seventeenth century, and why he exercised so marked an influence upon Locke, Hobbes, Shaftesbury, and upon the forerunners of the French Revolution,—Montesquieu, Mably, and Rousseau.

Thus Eucken is perfectly right when he says that the fundamental idea of Stoicism, i. e., the interpretation of morality from a scientific viewpoint, and the uplifting of morality to its full height and independence in connection with the realization of the universe as a unit, is preserved to our own time.[22] To live in the world and to submit to it unconsciously is not worthy of man. One must attain the understanding of the universal life and interpret it as a continuous development (evolution), and one must live in accordance with the laws of this development. Thus did the best among the Stoics understand morality, and by this interpretation Stoicism greatly assisted the progress of the science of morality.

[21] The naturalistic pantheism of the first Stoics, became transformed in his teachings into naturalistic theism, wrote Jodl. Seneca also assisted this transformation of Stoicism. [*Geschichte der Ethik*, vol. 1, p. 27.]—Trans. Note.

[22] Eucken. *Die Lebensanschauungen der grossen Denker*, seventh ed., 1907, p. 90. [Leipzig.]

Furthermore, the watchword of the Stoics was, to assume not an indifferent but an active attitude toward the social life. For this purpose strength of character was developed, and this principle was very forcibly developed by Epictetus. Paulsen writes in his "System of Ethics," "nowhere shall we find more forcibly exhortations to make ourselves independent of the things which are not in our power, and to depend upon ourselves with inner freedom, than in Epictetus' little *Manual*." [23]

Life demands rigorism, wrote the Stoics, i. e., a stern attitude toward one's weakness. *Life is a struggle,* and not the Epicurean enjoyment of various pleasures. The absence of a higher aim is the bitterest enemy of man. A happy life requires inner courage, loftiness of soul, heroism. And such ideas led them to the thought of universal brotherhood, of "humanity," i. e., to a thought which had not occurred to their predecessors.

But side by side with these beautiful aspirations, we find in all the prominent Stoics indecision, antinomy. In the governing of the universe they saw not only the laws of nature, but also the will of the Supreme Reason, and such a confession unavoidably paralyzed the scientific study of Nature. Their philosophy contained an antinomy, and this contradiction led to compromises that were contrary to the fundamental principles of their morality— to reconciliation with that which they rejected in their ideal: The fundamental antinomy led such a thinker as Marcus Aurelius to cruel persecutions of the Christians. The attempt to merge personal life with the surrounding life led to pitiable compromises, to reconciliation with the crude, miserable reality, and as a result, we already find in the writing of the Stoics the first cries of despair,—pessimism. Regardless of all these considerations, however, the influence exercised by the Stoics was very great. It prepared many minds for the acceptance of Christianity, and we feel its influence even now among the rationalists.

[23] [*A System of Ethics,* by Friedrich Paulsen. Translated by Frank Thilly, N. Y., 1899.]—Trans. Note.

CHAPTER VI

SUMMING up the pre-Christian ethics of ancient Greece, we see that in spite of the different interpretations of morality by the Greek thinkers they all agreed on one point: they saw the source of morality in Man, in his natural tendencies and in his reason. They were far from having a clear idea as to the true nature of these tendencies. But they taught that, owing to his reason and owing to his social mode of life, Man naturally develops and strengthens his moral tendencies, which are useful for the maintenance of the sociality essential to him. For this reason the Greek thinkers did not look for any external, supernatural forces to come to the aid of Man.

Such was the essence of the teaching of Socrates, Aristotle, and partly even of Plato and of the early Stoics, though Aristotle already attempted to base morality on a natural-scientific basis. Only Plato introduced into morality a semi-religious element. On the other hand, Epicurus, possibly in opposition to Plato, advanced a new doctrine: a rational striving of Man toward happiness, toward pleasure, and he tried to present this search for happiness as the principal source of the moral in a thinking man.

Epicurus was unquestionably right in asserting that man's striving, correctly understood, for personal happiness, for fullness of life, is a moral motive force. And indeed, a man who fully realizes how very much sociability, justice, and a kind, equitable attitude toward one's fellow-men contribute to the happiness of each individual as well as to the happiness of society as a whole—such a man will not be unmoral. In other words, a man who has recognized the principle of equality and who has been taught by experience

114

to identify his interests with the interests of all, unquestionably *must* find in such an interpretation of personal happiness a support for his morality. But Epicurus needlessly narrowed the actual foundations of morality in asserting that the rational search for happiness will by itself lead man to the moral attitude toward others. Epicurus forgot that no matter how great the tribute that Man pays to egoism, he still retains the habits of sociality; he also has a conception of justice which leads to a recognition, to some extent of the equality of men, and that there is, even in men who have fallen to a very low moral level, a vague conception of the ideal and of moral beauty.

Epicurus thus minimized the importance of the social instincts in man and helped man to put practical "reasonableness" in the place of Reason based on justice, which is the necessary condition for the progressive development of society. At the same time, he overlooked the influence of the environment and of the division into classes, which is inimical to morality when a pyramidal structure of society permits to some what is forbidden to others.

And indeed, the followers of Epicurus, who were fairly numerous in the empire of Alexander the Great and later in the Roman Empire, found a justification for their indifference to the ulcers of the social system in this absence of a moral ideal which would uphold justice and the equality of men as the aim of morality.[1]

A protest against the social horrors of that time and against the decline of sociality was inevitable. And, as we have seen, this pro-

[1] Guyau pointed out in his excellent treatise on the philosophy of Epicurus, that this philosophy in the course of a few centuries united many excellent men; and this is perfectly true. In the mass of humanity there is always a nucleus composed of men whom no amount of philosophizing, be it religious or utterly sceptical, can make better or worse in the social sense. But side by side with these there are masses of average people who are forever vacillating and forever fall in with the predominant teaching of the time. For this majority, weak in character, the philosophy of Epicurus served as the justification of their social indifference. The others, however, who sought for an ideal, turned to religion to find it. [For the reference to Guyau's work on Epicurus, see foot-note, page 104].—Trans Note.

test manifested itself first in the teachings of the Stoics, and later in Christianity.

In the fifth century B. C. there began the wars between Greece and Persia, and these wars gradually led to a complete decline of the system of free City-Republics of Ancient Greece, under which science, art, and philosophy reached a high stage of development. Then, in the fourth century B. C., the Macedonian Realm was created and the military expeditions of Alexander the Great into inner Asia began. Flourishing, independent democracies of Greece were then being converted into provinces subjected to the new, vanquishing Empire. The conquerors were bringing the slaves and the plundered riches from the East and at the same time introduced centralization and its inevitable consequences: political despotism and the spirit of plundering greed. And what is more, the riches imported into Greece attracted to it the plunderers from the West, and already in the third century B. C. there began the conquest of Greece by Rome.

Ancient Hellas, once a conservatory of knowledge and art, now became a province of a Roman Empire lusting for conquest. The beacon of science that had shone in Greece was extinguished for many centuries, while Rome spread in all directions its centralized, plundering state, where luxury of the upper classes was based on the slave-labour of the conquered peoples, and where the vices of the upper, the ruling classes, reached extreme limits.

Under such circumstances a protest was inevitable, and it came first in the form of echoes of the new religion—Buddhism, which originated in India where a social disintegration similar to that of the Roman Empire was taking place,—and then, about four hundred years later, in the form of Christianity, rising in Judea, whence it soon spread to Asia Minor, where Greek colonies abounded, and thence to the very centre of Roman domination—to Italy.

It is easy to imagine how deep an impression, especially among the poor classes, was produced by the appearance of these two teachings that have so much in common. Tidings of the new religion began to penetrate from India, its land of origin, into Judea and Asia Minor during the last two centuries before our era. There was a rumour that the King's son, Gautama, spurred by the need of a new faith, had parted with his young wife and with his palace, had thrown off his royal garments, renounced wealth and power, and become a servant of his people. Subsisting on alms, he taught contempt for wealth and power, love for all men, friends and enemies alike; he taught sympathy for all living creatures, he preached kindness, and recognized the equality of all classes, including the lowest.

The teaching of Buddha Gautama [2] speedily found numerous followers among the peoples wearied by wars and extortions and offended in their best feelings by the ruling classes. Gradually this teaching spread from North India to the south and eastward over the whole of Asia. Tens of millions of people embraced Buddhism.

A like situation arose about four hundred years later, when a similar, but a still higher teaching, Christianity, began to spread from Judea to the Greek colonies in Asia Minor, and then penetrated into Greece, and thence to Sicily and Italy.

The soil was well prepared for the new religion of the poor, who rose against the depravity of the rich. And then the vast, elemental migrations of entire peoples from Asia to Europe, which began about the same time and lasted for fully twelve centuries, cast such a horror over the minds of people that the need of a new religion became acute.[3]

[2] The word "Buddha" means "teacher."

[3] With the end of the Glacial Period, and then of the Lake Epoch which followed during the melting of the ice sheet, there began a rapid drying-up of the high table-lands of Central Asia. These lands are now unpeopled deserts, with the remnants of once populous cities now buried in sand. This drying-up compelled the inhabitants of the table-lands to descend to the south,—to India, and to the north,—to the low-lands of Jungaria and Siberia, whence they moved westward to the fertile plains of South Russia and western Europe. Entire peoples migrated in this manner, and it is easy to imagine what horror these migrations inspired in the other peoples who were already settled on the plains of Europe. The newcomers either plundered

117

ETHICS: ORIGIN AND DEVELOPMENT

Amid the horrors that were then experienced, even sober thinkers lost their faith in a better future for humanity, while the masses regarded these invasions as the work of an Evil Power. The idea of "the end of the world" arose involuntarily in people's minds, and men the more willingly sought salvation in religion.

The principal point wherein Christianity and Buddhism differed from all preceding religions was in the fact that instead of the cruel, revengeful gods to whose will men had to submit, these two religions brought forward—as an example for men and not to intimidate them—an *ideal man-god*. In the case of Christianity the love of the divine teacher for men,—for all men without distinction of nation or condition, and especially for the lowest,—led to the highest heroic sacrifice—to death on the cross for the salvation of humanity from the power of evil.

Instead of fear of a revengeful Jehova, or of gods personifying the evil forces of nature, Christianity advocated *love for the victims of oppression*. The moral teacher in Christianity was not a revengeful deity, not a priest, not a man of the priestly cast, and not even a thinker from among the sages, but a simple man from the people. While the founder of Buddhism, Gautama, was a king's son who voluntarily became a pauper, the founder of Christianity was a carpenter who left his house and his kin, and lived as "the birds of heaven" live, in expectation of the approaching "Day of Judgment." The life of these two teachers was passed, not in temples, not in academies, but among the poor, and from among these poor and not from among the temple-priests came Christ's apostles. And

the native peoples or annihilated the population of entire regions where resistance was offered. What the Russian people lived through in the thirteenth century, at the time of the Mongol invasion, Europe experienced during the first seven or eight centuries of our era, on account of the migrations of the hordes that advanced, one after the other, from Central Asia. Spain and South France suffered similarly from the invasion of the Arabs, who advanced upon Europe from North Africa, due to the same causes of drying-up. [Of the lakes. Kropotkin's reference to the "Lake" Epoch—a name not found in several standard works on geology—seems to refer to a subdivision of the late-Glacial (Pleistocene) Epoch, when lakes were drying up in parts of the "old" and the "new" world.]—Trans. Note.

118

if at a later date Christianity as well as Buddhism evolved into the "Church," i. e., the government of the "chosen," with the inevitable vices of all governments—such development constituted a flagrant deviation from the will of the two founders of religion, notwithstanding all the attempts that were later made to justify this deviation by citing the books written many years after the death of the teachers themselves.

Another fundamental feature of Christianity which was the chief source of its strength was the fact that it advanced as the leading principle of man's life not his personal happiness, but the *happiness of society*,—and consequently an ideal, a *social ideal*, for which a man would be ready to sacrifice his life (see, for example, the tenth and the thirteenth chapter of the Gospel of St. Mark). The ideal of Christianity was not the retired life of a Greek sage, and not the military or the civic exploits of the heroes of ancient Greece or Rome, but a preacher who rose against the abuses of contemporary society and who was ready to face death for the gospel of his faith, which consisted in justice for all, in recognition of the equality of all men, in love for all, friends and strangers alike, and finally, *in forgiveness of injuries*, contrary to the general rule of those times of the obligatory revenge for injuries.

Unfortunately, just these fundamental features of Christianity,— especially equality and forgiveness of injuries—very soon began to be toned down and altered in the preaching of the new religion, and then were forgotten altogether. Christianity, like all other moral teachings, very soon, in the time of the apostles in fact, became contaminated by opportunism, i. e., by the teaching of the "happy mean." And this process was made easier by the formation in Christianity, as in all other religions, of a group of men who asserted that they whose duty it was to perform the rites and the sacraments, are the ones who preserve the teaching of Christ in all its purity and must wage war on the continually arising faulty interpretations of this teaching.

There is no doubt that this compliance on the part of the apostles

119

has its explanation, in a measure, in the cruel persecutions to which the first Christians were subjected in the Roman Empire,— until Christianity became the state religion; and it is also likely that the concessions were made only for appearance' sake, while the inner nucleus of the Christian communes adhered to the teaching in all its purity. And indeed, it has now been established through a long series of careful investigations that the four gospels that were recognized by the Church as the most truthful accounts of the life and of the teaching of Christ, as well as the "Acts" and the "Epistles" of the Apostles in those versions that have reached us, were all written not earlier than between 60–90 A. D., and probably even later, between 90–120 A. D. But even at that time the Gospels and the Epistles were already copies of more ancient records, which the copyists usually supplemented with legends that reached them.[4] But it was just during those years that there took place the most relentless persecution of the Christians by the Roman State. Executions in Galilee commenced only after the rebellion of Judah the Galilean against the Roman rule, 9 A. D., and later even more cruel persecutions against the Jews began after their uprising, that lasted from 66 to 71 A. D., and the executions were numbered in hundreds.[5]

In view of these persecutions, the Christian preachers who themselves were ready to perish on the cross or in the fire, naturally made some minor concessions in their epistles to the faithful, perhaps in order not to subject to persecution the still youthful Christian communes. Thus, for example, the words, so glibly cited by the ruling classes: "Render unto Cæsar the things that are Cæsar's, and unto God the things that are God's" (St. Mark, xii, 17), may have gotten into the gospels as an unimportant concession, that did not affect the essence of the teaching, all the more since Chris-

[4] The evangelist St. Luke testifies to the existence of many such records in the opening passage of his gospel, (ch. i, 1-4) where he compiles and extends previous records.

[5] Disturbances in Judea began, apparently, in the very years when Christ was preaching. (See St. Luke, xiii, 1, and St. Mark, xv, 7).

tianity advocated renunciation of worldly goods. Furthermore, having originated in the East, Christianity was influenced by Eastern beliefs in one very important direction. The religions of Egypt, Persia, and India were not content with simple humanization of the forces of Nature, as was conceived by the Greek and the Roman heathendom. They saw in the universe a struggle of two equally powerful essences—the Good and the Evil, Light and Darkness,—and they transferred this struggle to the heart of man. And this conception of two antagonistic forces battling for supremacy in the world, gradually penetrated Christianity and became its fundamental principle. And then, for many centuries, the Christian Church, in order to annihilate with unspeakable cruelty all those who dared to criticize its henchmen, utilized to the full this conception of the powerful devil who obtains possession of the human soul.

Thus the Church directly rejected the kindness and all-forgivingness which were advocated by the founder of Christianity and which constituted its difference from all other religions, with the exception of Buddhism. And more than that: in its persecution of its antagonists it knew no limit of cruelty.

Later, the followers of Christ, even the nearest, went even further on the road of deviation. More and more alienated from the original teaching, they came to the point where the Christian Church made a complete alliance with the rulers, so that in the eyes of the "princes of the Church" the true teachings of Christ even came to be considered as dangerous, so dangerous, indeed, that the Western Church forbade the publication of the New Testament in any other than the Latin language, utterly incomprehensible to the people, and in Russia, in the slightly more comprehensible old-Slavonic tongue.[6]

[6] In Russia this prohibition remained in force up to 1859 or 1860. I vividly remember the impression produced in Petersburg by the first appearance of the New Testament in the Russian language, and I remember how we all hastened to buy this unusual edition at the Synod Typography, the only place where it could be obtained.

But worst of all was the fact that on becoming transformed into the State Church, official Christianity forgot the fundamental difference distinguishing it from all the preceding religions except Buddhism. It forgot the *forgiveness of injuries,* and it avenged every injury in the spirit of Eastern despotism. Finally, the representatives of the Church soon became the owners of serfs equally with the lay nobility, and they gradually acquired the same profitable judicial power as the counts, the dukes, and the kings; and in using this power the princes of the Church proved to be just as vengeful and greedy as the lay rulers. And later, in the fifteenth and sixteenth centuries, when the centralized power of the kings and the tsars began to extend over the states that were then forming, the Church never failed to help with its influence and its wealth the creation and expansion of this power, and shielded with its cross such beast-like rulers as Louis XI., Phillip II., and Ivan the Terrible. The Church punished any show of opposition to its power with purely Eastern cruelty—with torture and fire, and the Western Church even created for this purpose a special institution—the "Holy" Inquisition.

Thus, concessions to secular powers made by the early followers of Christ led Christianity far afield from the teaching of its Founder. Forgiveness of personal injuries was thrown overboard, like unnecessary ballast, and in this way was discarded that which constituted the fundamental difference between Christianity and all preceding religions except Buddhism.[7]

And really, if we examine without prejudice not only the earlier religions but even the usages and customs of the earliest tribal mode of life among the savages, we shall find that in all the primitive religions and in the most primitive groups it was already con-

[7] There exists voluminous literature on the subject of the preparing of the ground for Christianity by the teaching of Plato, especially by his doctrines as to the soul; also by the teachings of the Stoics, and by some adaptations from earlier teachings. One may mention especially the work by Harnack, *Die Mission und Ausbreitung des Christenthums in den ersten drei Jahrhunderten,* 1902. [Leipzig, 2 vols. Trans., N. Y., 1908, 2 vols. (Theological Trans. Library, vols. 19, 20.)]—Trans. Note.

sidered, and is now considered, a rule not to do unto others, i. e., to men of the same tribe, that which you do not want done unto yourself. For thousands of years all human societies have been built on this rule, so that in advocating an equitable attitude to one's own people Christianity introduced nothing new.[8]

As a matter of fact, in such an old monument of the tribal system as the Old Testament, we find a rule: "Thou shalt not avenge, nor bear any grudge against the children of thy people, but thou shalt love thy neighbour as thyself." This is said in the name of God in the third book of the Pentateuch (Leviticus, xix, 18). And the same rule was applied to the stranger: "The stranger that dwelleth with you shall be unto you as one born among you, and thou shalt love him as thyself: for ye were strangers in the land of Egypt." (Leviticus, xix, 34). Similarly, the assertion of the Evangelists, so poetically expressed in the gospel of St. Mark (ch. xiii),[9] that there is no higher merit than to lay down one's soul for one's people, even this appeal cannot be considered as a distinguishing feature of Christianity, because self-sacrifice for one's own people was eulogized by all the heathen peoples, and the defence of near ones at the risk of one's life is a common phenomenon not only among the most savage tribes, but also among most of the social animals.

The same is true of charity, which is often represented as a distinguishing feature of Christianity as contrasted with pagan antiquity. The fact of the matter is that even in the tribal system

[8] See, for example, the description of the life of the Aleuts, who at that time were still making knives and arrows of stone. (The description given by the priest, Venyaminov, later Metropolitan of Moscow, in his *Memoirs of the Unalashkinsky District*, St. Petersburg, 1840). See also the exactly similar descriptions of the Eskimos of Greenland, recently furnished by a Danish Expedition. [*The Eskimo Tribes*, by Dr. Henry Rink, vol. 11 of *Denmark, Commissionen, for ledelsen af de geologiske og geografiske under-sogelser i Grønland. København.* (1887–1923).]—Trans. Note.

[9] [Chapter xiii of St. Mark does not make this assertion, but Chapter viii of his gospel and a similar section of Matthew's account, conveys the same idea in words somewhat different from those Kropotkin uses in his paraphrase.]—Trans. Note.

123

it was and still is considered a crime to refuse shelter to one of the same tribe—or even to an unknown wanderer,—or not to share a meal with them. I have already mentioned in the third chapter that an accidentally impoverished Buriat has a right to be fed in turn by each member of his tribe, and also that the Fuegians, the Hottentots, and all other "savages" divide among themselves equally every morsel of food given them as a present. Therefore, if in the Roman Empire, especially in the cities, such customs of the tribal system had actually disappeared, it was not the fault of Paganism but of the entire political system of the all-conquering Empire. I will remark, however, that in pagan Italy, in the times of Numa Pompilius, and then much later, in the days of the Empire, there were strongly developed the so-called "collegia," i. e., associations of craftsmen, known, in the Middle Ages, as the "guilds." These collegia practised the same compulsory mutual aid; on certain days they had meals in common, etc., which usage later became a distinguishing feature of every guild. Therefore, the question presents itself: was mutual aid truly alien to the Roman pre-Christian society, as is asserted by some writers, who point to the absence of *state* charity and of *religious* charity? Or was the need of charity brought about by the weakening of the crafts organizations of the collegia as state centralization increased?

We must, therefore, acknowledge, that in preaching fraternity and mutual aid among one's own people, Christianity did not introduce any new moral principle. But the point where Christianity and Buddhism did introduce a new principle into the life of humanity was in demanding of man *complete forgiveness for the harm inflicted upon him.* Up to that time the tribal morality of all peoples demanded revenge, personal or even tribal, for every injury: for murder, for wound, for insult. But the teaching of Christ, in its original form, rejected both revenge and legal prosecution, demanding from the wronged person a renunciation of all "retribution" and complete forgiveness for injury, and not merely once or twice, but always, in every case. In the words, "Do not take vengeance on your enemies," lies the true greatness of Christianity.[10]

But the principal commandment of Christ, directing the renunciation of all vengeance, was very soon rejected by the Christians. Even the Apostles adhered to it in a considerably modified form: "Be not rendering evil for evil, or railing for railing; but contrariwise, blessing," wrote Apostle Peter in his first "Epistle General" (iii, 9). But St. Paul merely hints feebly at the forgiveness of injuries, and even that hint is expressed in egoistic form: "Therefore thou art inexcusable, O man, whosoever thou art, that judgest (another): for wherein thou judgest another, thou condemnest thyself." (Epistle to the Romans, ii, 1). In general, instead of the definite commandments of Christ, rejecting vengeance, the apostles offer the timid advice to "postpone vengeance," and advise a general gospel of love. Thus, finally, vengeance through the courts, even in its most cruel forms, became a necessary essence of that which is known as justice in Christian states and in the Christian Church. It is significant that priest and executioner are together at the scaffold.

A similar fate befell another fundamental principle in Christ's teaching. His teaching was the teaching of equality. A slave and a free Roman citizen were for him equally brothers, children of God. "And whosoever of you will be the chiefest, shall be servant of all," taught Christ. (St. Mark, x, 44). But in the Apostles we already find different ideas. The slaves and the subjects are equal to their masters . . . "in Christ." But in reality the Apostles St.

[10] In the Mosaic Law, in the aforementioned passage from Leviticus (xix, 18), we already meet with the words, "Thou shalt not avenge nor bear any grudge against the children of thy people." This commandment, however, stands alone and there are no traces of it in the subsequent history of Israel. On the contrary, in another passage, namely in Exodus, xxi, 21, it is permitted to strike with impunity one's slave or maid-servant, provided only that they do not die within a day or two, and finally, as among all groups still living according to the tribal system, in case of a fight "if any mischief follow, then thou shalt give life for life, eye for eye, tooth for tooth, hand for hand, foot for foot, burning for burning, wound for wound, stripe for stripe" (vv. 23 to 25).

125

Peter and St. Paul present as a fundamental Christian virtue the obedience of subjects to the established authorities as to God's anointed with "fear and trepidation," and the obedience of slaves to their masters. These two Apostles merely recommend to the slaveholders a more kindly attitude toward their servants, and not at all the renunciation of the *right to own slaves,* even in cases where the slave-owners happen to be "faithful and beloved," i. e., those converted to Christianity.[11]

This advice of the Apostles could of course be explained by their desire not to subject their followers to the beastly cruelty of the Roman Emperors. But through preaching obedience to the beast-like Cæsars *as to God's anointed,* Christianity dealt itself a blow from which it has not recovered to this day. It became the religion of the State.

As a result, slavery and slavish obedience to the rulers, both supported by the Church, endured for eleven centuries, up to the first townsfolk and peasant uprisings of the eleventh and twelfth centuries.

John Chrysostom, Pope Gregory, whom the Church called the Great, and various people whom the Church included among the

---

[11] "Submit yourselves to every ordinance of man for the Lord's sake: whether it be to the king, as supreme; or unto governors, as unto them that are sent by him for the punishment of evildoers, and for the praise of them that do well," wrote St. Peter when such beasts as Caligula and Nero reigned in Rome. (*The First Epistle General of Peter,* ii, 13, 14). And further, "Servants, be subject to your masters with all fear; not only to the good and gentle, but also to the forward," etc. (*Ibid,* 18–25). And as regards the advices that St. Paul gave to his flock, it is really disgusting to speak of them; they were in direct contradiction to the teaching of Christ. "Let every soul be subject unto the higher powers. For there is no power but of God" . . . "He (the ruler) is the minister of God." (*Epistle to the Romans,* xiii, 1–5). He sacrilegiously ordered the slaves to obey their masters "like Christ"; at any rate, this is the statement made in his *Epistle to the Ephesians,* [vi, 5], which is recognized by the Christian Churches as the genuine Epistle of St. Paul. As to the masters, instead of urging them to renounce the labor of the slaves, he merely advised them to be moderate—"moderating their strictness". Moreover, St. Paul exhorts to special obedience those slaves who "have believing masters . . . because they are faithful and beloved." [*The first Epistle to Timothy,* vi, 2; *Colossians,* iii, 22]; *Titus,* ii, 9, and iii, 1. [The translators have corrected several faulty references of the original.]—Trans. Note.

126

saints, approved slavery, and St. Augustine even vindicated it, asserting that sinners became slaves in punishment for their sins. Even the comparatively liberal philosopher, Thomas Aquinas, asserted that slavery is a "divine law." Very few slave-owners set their slaves free, and some bishops collected money in order to buy the slaves their freedom. And only with the beginning of the Crusades could the slaves be liberated from their masters by sewing a cross to their sleeves and going to the East for the conquest of Jerusalem.

The Church was followed openly or tacitly by most philosophers. Only in the eighteenth century, on the eve of the French Revolution, were voices of the freethinkers raised against slavery. It was the Revolution and not the Church that abolished slavery in the French Colonies and serfdom in France itself. But during the first half of the nineteenth century, trading in negro-slaves flourished in Europe and in America and the Church was silent. In Russia the abolition of slavery, known as peasant serfdom, became an accomplished fact only in 1861. It was prepared for by the plots of the Decembrists in 1825 and of the Petrashevists in 1848, as well as by the peasant uprising of the 'fifties, reawakening in the nobility the fear of another Pugachev rebellion. In 1863 the abolition of slavery took place also in the "deeply religious" United States. After a bloody struggle with the slave-owners, the slaves were proclaimed free; they were given for their subsistence, however, not even an inch of the soil that they had cultivated.

Christianity proved impotent in the struggle against the greed of the slave-owners and the slave-dealers. Slavery endured until the slaves themselves began to revolt, and until the development of machine production offered the possibility of extracting more profits from hired labour than from the labour of the peasant serfs or the slaves.

Thus the two fundamental principles of Chrisianity—equality, and the forgiveness of injuries—were rejected by its followers and by its preachers. And fifteen centuries passed before some writers broke with religion and dared to recognize one of these principles, equality of rights, as the foundation of civic society.

Finally, it must be pointed out that Christianity had also confirmed the belief in the devil and his hosts as the powerful rivals of the Good. The belief in the might of the Evil Power became especially strengthened at the time of the great transmigrations of the peoples. Later the Church fully utilized this belief in order to annihilate those "servants of the devil" who dared to criticize its leaders. More than that:—the Roman Church even considered the Christian prohibition of vengeance as a mistake of a too kind Teacher, and it substituted for mercy its sword and its bonfires, to destroy those whom it considered heretics.[12]

In spite of all the persecutions of the Christians in the Roman Empire, and in spite of the small numbers of the early Christian communes during the first few centuries, Christianity continued to conquer minds, first in Asia Minor, and then in Greece, in Sicily, in Italy, and, in general, throughout Western Europe. Christianity

[12] Eugene Sue, in his remarkable novel *Les mystères du peuple: histoire d'une famille de prolétaires à travers les âges*, gives a deeply stirring scene where the Great Inquisitor reproaches Christ for his error in being too merciful to men. As is known, Dostoyevsky, a great admirer of Sue, introduced a similar scene into his novel, *The Brothers Karamazov*. In order to realize fully to what an extent the Church interfered with the free development of Ethics, and of all the natural sciences, it is sufficient to survey the rule of the Inquisition up to the nineteenth century. In Spain it was destroyed only in 1808 by the French army, after having subjected to its judgment, and almost invariably to its tortures, in the course of 320 years, more than 340,000 people, among whom 32,000 were burned "in person," 17,659 "in effigy," and 291,450 were subjected to various tortures. In France the Inquisition was abolished only in 1772. Its power was so great that it made even such a moderate writer as Buffon renounce publicly his geological conclusions as to the antiquity of the geological layers, which he had expressed in the first volume of his famous description of the animals populating the globe. In Italy, although the Inquisition was locally abolished at the end of the eighteenth century, it was soon re-established and continued to exist in Central Italy up to the middle of the nineteenth century. In Rome, i. e., in Papal Rome, its remnants still exist in the form of the Secret Tribunal, while certain groups of the Jesuits of Spain, Belgium, and Germany still advocate its re-establishment. [The novel referred to here is in fifteen volumes; many of these have appeared in English, N. Y., 1910, etc.]—Trans. Note.

was a protest against the entire mode of life in the Roman Empire of that time, and against the ideals of that life, where the opulence of the ruling classes was based on the desperate poverty of the peasants and of the town proletariat, and where the "culture" of the well-to-do was limited to the development of the comforts of life and to a certain external elegance, with total neglect of the higher spiritual needs, both mental and moral.[13] But already at that time many felt dissatisfied with the refinements of the pleasures of the higher classes, coupled with the general degradation; and therefore, not only the poor whom Christianity promised liberation, but also separate individuals from among the free and the wealthy classes sought in Christianity a way to a more spiritual life.

At the same time, mistrust of human nature was developing. It had begun to manifest itself already in the Greco-Roman world of the time of Plato and his followers. And now, under the influence of the harsh conditions of life at the time of the great transmigrations of the peoples, in the face of the iniquities of Roman society, and under the influence of the East, pessimism began to develop; faith in the possibility of attaining a better future through the efforts of Man himself, was waning. The assurance grew of the triumph of the Evil Power on earth, and people willingly sought consolation in the faith in life after death, where there is to be no earthly evil or suffering.

Under such circumstances Christianity acquired greater and greater power over the mind. It is remarkable, however, that it produced no substantial change in the general mode of life. And indeed, not only did it fail to originate any new forms of life at all widely distributed, but it even became reconciled, like pagan-

[13] In recent times, especially in Germany and in Russia, the conceptions of "culture" and civilization are often confused. They were, however, clearly distinguished in the 'sixties. The term "culture" was then applied to the development of the external conveniences of life: hygiene, means of communication, elegance of house-furnishing, etc., while the term "civilization," or enlightenment, was applied to the development of knowledge, thought, creative genius, and striving for a better social system.

ism formerly, to Roman slavery, to Norman serfdom, and to the abominations of Roman absolutism. The Christian priests soon became the supporters of the emperors. Property inequality and political oppression remained the same as before, and the mental development of society was considerably lower. Christianity did not develop any new social forms. And really, awaiting a speedy end of the world, it took little interest in such reforms, so that more than a thousand years elapsed before, from entirely different sources, new systems of life began to be developed in Europe in the cities that declared themselves independent, first along the shores of the Mediterranean, and later inland as well. In these new centres of free life, which resembled in this respect the free cities of Ancient Greece, there began also the revival of the sciences, which had suffered a decline from the time of the Macedonian and Roman Empires.

At the time of the Apostles, the followers of Christ, who lived in expectation of the speedy Second Advent, were chiefly concerned in spreading the teaching that promised men salvation. They hastened to spread the "happy tidings," and, if necessary, perished by the martyr's death. But as early as the second century of the Christian Era the Christian "Church" began to develop. It is well known how easily new religions split into numerous factions in the East. Every one interprets the new teaching in his own way and adheres fanatically to his interpretation. Christianity was also in danger of such a splitting into small parts, all the more because in Asia Minor and in Egypt, where it was rapidly spreading, it was being commingled with other religions: Buddhism and ancient paganism.[14] In view of this fact, from the earliest times the teach-

---

[14] Draper, in his treatise, *Conflicts of Science with Religion*, showed how many elements were admingled to Christianity from the heathen cults of Asia Minor, Egypt, etc. He did not, however, give sufficient attention to the much greater influence of Buddhism, which to this time remains insufficiently investigated. [John Williams Draper, *History of the conflict between religion and science*. N. Y., 1875.]—Trans. Note.

ers of Christianity aimed to create in accordance with the ancient tradition, a "church," i. e., a closely associated group of teachers who were to keep the teaching in all its purity, or, at least, in uniform condition.

But with the development of the churches as the guardians of the teaching and of its rites, there came into existence, as in Buddhism, on the one hand the monastic institution, i. e., the withdrawal of some of the teachers from society, and on the other hand, there was formed a special, powerful caste, the clergy, and the rapprochement of this caste with the secular power grew steadily. In guarding what it considered the purity of faith, and in persecuting what it considered perversion and criminal heresy, the Church soon reached the limit of cruelty in its persecutions of the "apostates." And for the sake of success in this struggle, it first sought and then demanded support from the secular powers, which in turn demanded from the Church a benevolent attitude toward them and a support by religion of their tyrannical power over the people.

Thus the fundamental thought of the Christian teaching, its modesty, its "spirit of meek wisdom" was being forgotten. The movement which began as a protest against the abominations of the ruling power, now became a tool of that power. The blessing of the Church not only forgave the rulers their crimes, —it actually even represented these crimes as the fulfilment of God's will.

At the same time the Christian Church used all its efforts to prevent the studying by the Christians of "pagan antiquity." The monuments and the manuscripts of ancient Greece, the only sources of knowledge at that time, were being destroyed, for the Church saw in them only "pride" and "faithlessness" suggested by the devil. This prohibition was so strict, and suited so well the general intolerant spirit of Christianity, that some of the writings of the Greek thinkers disappeared completely, and they reached Western Europe only because they were preserved by the Arabs in Arabian translations. Thus zealously, Christianity was stamping out the "Hellenic wisdom." [15]

In the meantime, however, the feudal system, with its serfdom, which established itself in Europe after the disruption of the Roman Empire, began to disintegrate, especially from the time of the Crusades and after a series of serious peasant uprisings and of revolts in towns.[16]

Owing to the intercourse with the East, and owing to the increasing commercial activity on sea and land, Europe gradually developed cities in which, side by side with the development of commerce, crafts, and arts, was developed also the spirit of freedom. Beginning with the tenth century these cities began to overthrow the power of their secular rulers and of the bishops. Such revolts spread rapidly. The citizens of the revolting cities drew up for themselves the "charters" or the "statutes" of their rights, and either forced the rulers to recognize and to sign these charters, or simply expelled their rulers and swore to observe among themselves these new statutes of freedom. The townsfolk first of all refused to recognize the courts of the bishops or of the princes, and elected their own judges; they created their own town militia for the defence of the city and appointed its commander, and finally, they entered into alliances and federations with other free cities. Many cities also liberated from the yoke of the secular and the ecclesiastical rulers the peasants of the neighbouring districts, by sending the town militia to the assistance of the villages. Genoa, for example, acted in this manner as early as the tenth century. And gradually the liberation of the cities and the formation of free communities spread throughout Europe: first in Italy and in Spain, then in the twelfth century in France, in the Netherlands, and in

[15] The works of the great founder of Natural Science, Aristotle, became known for the first time in mediæval Europe through the translation from the Arabian language into Latin.

[16] The Crusades caused vast movements of population. A peasant-serf who sewed a cross upon his sleeve and joined the crusaders became free from serfdom.

132

CHRISTIANITY—THE RENAISSANCE

England, and finally throughout the whole of Central Europe, as far as Bohemia, Poland, and even Northwestern Russia, where Novgorod and Pskov, with their colonies in Viatka, Vologda, etc., existed as free democracies for a period of a few centuries. In this manner the free cities were reviving the free political system, due to which, fifteen hundred years earlier, enlightenment had blossomed forth so splendidly in Ancient Greece. The same situation now repeated itself in the free cities of Western and Central Europe.[17]

And simultaneously with the birth of the new free life, there began also that revival of knowledge, art, and freedom of thought which has received in history the name of "The Renaissance."

I shall refrain here, however, from an analysis of the causes which brought Europe to "renascence" and then to the so-called "Epoch of Enlightenment." There are many splendid works about this reawakening of the human mind from a long sleep, and even a brief survey of them would lead us too far afield from our immediate purpose. Moreover, I should have to discuss much more fully than has hitherto been done, not only the influence exercised on the development of science and art by the discovery of the monuments of ancient Greek science, art, and philosophy, as well as the influence of the far voyages and travels undertaken in this period of trading with the East, the discovery of America, etc., but I should also have to consider the influence of the *new forms of social life* that developed in the free cities. Then it would also be necessary to show how these conditions of town life and the awakening of the peasant population led to a new understanding of Christianity and to the deep-rooted popular movements in which the protest against the power of the Church was blended with the striving to throw off the yoke of serfdom.

Such uprisings spread in a mighty wave over the whole of Europe.

[17] There are many excellent treatises covering this period of history, but they are passed over in silence by our state schools anu universities. The reader will find a list in my book, *Mutual Aid,* where there is also given a brief sketch of life in the mediæval free cities.

133

They began with the movement of the Albigenses in Southern France in the eleventh and twelfth centuries. Then, at the end of the fourteenth century, in England, there took place the peasant uprisings of John Ball, Wat Tyler, and of the Lollards, directed against the lords and against the state, in connection with the protestant movement of Wickliffe. In Bohemia there developed the teaching of the great reformer and martyr, John Huss (burned at the stake by the Church in 1415), whose numerous followers rose up against the Catholic Church as well as against the yoke of the feudal lords. Then began the communistic movement of the Moravian Brothers in Moravia and of the Anabaptists in Holland, Western Germany, and Switzerland. Both these movements aimed not only to purify Christianity from the evils that had come to it owing to the secular power of the clergy, but also to change the entire social system to one of equality and communism. Finally, it would be necessary to dwell on the great peasant wars of Germany in the sixteenth century, which began in connection with the Protestant movement,—as well as on the uprisings against the power of the Pope, the landlords, and the kings, which spread over England from 1639 to 1648 and which ended in the execution of the king and the abolition of the feudal system. Of course, none of these movements accomplished its political, economic, and moral aims. But at any rate they created in Europe two comparatively free federations—Switzerland and Holland,—and then two comparatively free countries—England and France,—where minds were already prepared to such an extent that the teachings of the free-thinking writers found numerous followers, and where thinkers could write, and sometimes even print their works, without the risk of being burned at the stake by the princes of the Christian Church, or of being imprisoned for life.

In order to explain fully the revival of philosophical thought which characterized the seventeenth century, it would be necessary, therefore, to trace the influence of these revolutionary popular movements together with the influence of the then newly discovered remains of ancient Greek literature,—those works that are so easily discussed in all the histories of the Renaissance, with no mention made of the popular movements. But such an investigation in the realm of the general philosophy of history would lead us too far afield from our immediate purpose. I will therefore limit myself to pointing out that all these causes *taken together* helped to develop a new and freer mode of life. And by giving a new direction to thought they helped gradually the development of the new science which was slowly liberating itself from the wardship of theology; they helped the development of the new philosophy which was striving to embrace the life of all of Nature and to explain it on a natural basis; and finally, they helped to awaken the *creative powers* of the human mind. At the same time I shall attempt to show the ever-increasing prominence assumed thereafter in the moral field by *free personality*, which proclaimed its independence of the Church, the State, and the established traditions.

In the course of the first ten centuries of our era the Christian Church saw in the study of Nature something unnecessary, or even harmful, leading to conceit and to "pride," and pride was persecuted as a source of faithlessness. The moral element in men, asserted the Church, originates not at all in his nature, which can only urge him toward evil, but exclusively in divine revelation. Every investigation of the natural sources of morality in man was rejected, and therefore Greek science, which attempted to base morality on a naturalistic foundation, was categorically rejected. Fortunately, the sciences originated in Greece found a refuge among the Arabs, who translated Greek writers into their language, and who themselves contributed to our knowledge, especially about the globe and the celestial bodies,—as well as mathematics in general and medicine. The knowledge of the moral was considered by Arabian science, as by Greek, a part of the knowledge of Nature. But the Christian Church rejected this knowledge as heretical. This situation lasted for over a thousand years and only in the eleventh century, when the town revolts began in Europe, did there begin also the free-thinking (rationalistic) movement. A diligent search was made for the scattered surviving monuments of ancient Greek science and philosophy; and from these sources geometry, physics, astronomy, and philosophy began to be studied. Amidst the deep darkness that had reigned over Europe for so many centuries, a discovery and a translation of a manuscript of Plato or Aristotle became an event of world importance; it opened new, unknown horizons, it awakened minds, it revived the feeling of delight in Nature, and it aroused at the same time faith in the power of human reason,— the faith which the Christian Church took such pains to discourage. From that time there started the revival, first of sciences and then of knowledge in general, as well as of the investigations into the essence and the foundations of morality. Abélard of the many sorrows, (1079–1142), early in the beginning of the twelfth century, dared to assert, in accordance with the thinkers of Ancient Greece, that man carries in himself the rudiments of moral conceptions. He did not find, however, any support for this heresy, and only in the next century did there appear in France the thinker, Thomas Aquinas (1225–1278), who tried to combine the teaching of the Christian Church with a part of Aristotle's teaching. About the same time, in England, Roger Bacon (1214–1294) attempted at last to reject supernatural forces in the interpretation of nature in general, as well as of the moral conceptions of man.

This tendency, however, was soon suppressed, and it took the already mentioned popular movements, (spreading through Bohemia, Moravia, the lands now forming Germany, Switzerland, France, —especially the Southern part,—the Netherlands and England),— it took hundreds of thousands of people who perished by fire and sword while their leaders were subjected to terrible tortures,—in short, it took the tremendous upheaval that gradually involved the whole of Europe from the twelfth to the sixteenth century, before the Church and the secular rulers guided by it, permitted thinkers to speak and to write about the *social instinct of man* as the source of moral conceptions, and about the significance of *human reason* in the working out of moral principles. But even then Thought, freeing itself from the yoke of the Church, preferred to ascribe to wise rulers and lawmakers that which was formerly ascribed to divine revelation,—until at last a new current of thought dared to acknowledge that the working out of the moral principles was the creative effort of all of humanity.

In the middle of the sixteenth century, shortly before the death of Copernicus (1473–1543), appeared his book on the structure of our planetary system. This book gave a powerful impetus to scientific thought. The book proved that the Earth is by no means situated in the centre of the Universe, and not even in the centre of our planetary system; that the sun and the stars do not revolve around the Earth as it seems to us; and that not only our Earth but also the Sun around which it revolves are mere grains of sand amidst the infinite number of worlds. These ideas differed fundamentally from the teachings of the Church, which asserted that the Earth is the centre of the Universe, and that Man is the object of special concern to the Creator of Nature. Of course the Church began to persecute cruelly this teaching, and many men fell victims of this persecution. Thus an Italian, Giordano Bruno (1548–1600), was burned by the Inquisition at Rome in 1600 for his work, "Spaccio della bestia trionfante," in which he gave support to the Copernican heresy. But the new tendency had already been set by astronomers, and in general there came a realization of the importance of accurate observation and of mathematical analysis, and of knowledge based on experiment, as contrasted with conclusions based on metaphysics. In Florence there was even organized an Academy "del Cimento," i. e., of experiment.

Soon afterwards, in 1609 and 1619, detailed investigations of the laws of planetary motion around the sun by Kepler (1571–1630) confirmed Copernicus's conclusions, and twenty years later the Italian scientist Galileo (1564–1642) published his principal works, which not only confirmed the teaching of Copernicus but demonstrated even further where physics based on experiment leads. For his adherence to the teaching of Copernicus the Church subjected

Galileo to torture in 1633, and he was forced under torture to renounce his "heresy." But thought was already being liberated from the yoke of the Christian and of the old Hebrew teachings, and in the English thinker and experimenter, Francis Bacon (of Verulam) science found, not only a continuator of the bold investigations of Copernicus, Kepler, and Galileo, but also the founder of a new method of scientific investigation—the *inductive method,* based on the careful study of the facts of nature and the drawing of conclusions from these facts, as against the deductive interpretation of nature, i. e., on the basis of previously assumed abstract principles. More than that,—Bacon outlined the essentials of the new science based in all its branches on observation and experiment. Already at that time there was serious unrest in England, which soon culminated in the revolution of the peasants and especially of the middle classes (1632–1648), ending in the proclamation of the Republic and in the execution of the king. And side by side with the economic and the political upheaval, i. e., with the abolition of the power of the feudal landlords and with the advent to power of the urban middle class, there was taking place the liberation of minds from the yoke of the Churches, and the development of a new philosophy, of a new interpretation of Nature, based not on mental speculations but on the serious study of nature and on the gradual development of life, i. e., evolution, which constitutes the essence of modern science.

Bacon and Galileo were the forerunners of this science which, in the second half of the seventeenth century, more and more came to feel its strength and the necessity of a complete liberation from the Catholic as well as from the new Protestant Church. For this purpose the scientists began to combine and to establish scientific "Academies," i. e., societies for the free study of Nature. The fundamental principle of these academies was *experimental investigation,* instead of the former logomachy. Such were the aims of the academies, that first originated in Italy, and also of the Royal Society which was established in England in the seventeenth century

138

and which became the stronghold of scientific knowledge and a model for similar societies, established in France, Holland, and Prussia, etc.

This trend in Science naturally reflected itself also in the science of morality. Francis Bacon, a few years before the English Revolution, made an attempt—a very cautious one, it is true—to free from religion the question of the origin and the essence of moral conceptions. He dared to express the idea that it is wrong to consider the absence of religious convictions as detrimental to morality; he maintained that even an atheist may be an honest citizen, whereas, on the other hand, superstitious religion is a real danger when it undertakes to guide man's moral conduct. Bacon expressed himself very guardedly—it was impossible to speak in any other way in his time,—but the essence of his thought was understood, and from that time on the same idea began to be more and more loudly and definitely expressed in England and in France. Then the philosophy of Epicurus and of the Stoics was recalled, and the development of *rationalistic ethics,* i. e., ethics based on science, was begun in the works of Hobbes, Locke, Shaftesbury, Cudworth, Hutcheson, Hume, Adam Smith, and others in England and Scotland, and of Gassendi, Helvétius, Holbach, and many others in France.[18]

It is interesting to note that the principal point in Bacon's interpretation of morality (which I have already pointed out in the second chapter) i. e., the fact that even among animals the *instinct of sociality may prove stronger and more stable than the instinct*

[18] The remarkable work of Giordano Bruno, *Spaccio della bestia trionfante,* published in 1584, passed almost unnoticed. Similarly, Charron's book *De la sagesse,* published in 1601 (in the edition of 1604 the bold passage about religion is omitted) where the attempt was made to base morality on plain common sense, was not widely known, it appears, outside of France. However, Montaigne's *Essais* (1588), where variety of forms in religion is vindicated, met with great success. [In Bruno's *Opere italiane,* Gottinga, 1888, two vols. in one. And see Vincenzo Spampanato, *Lo Spaccio de la bestia trionfante con alcuni antecedenti,* Portici, 1902. Charron's *De la Sagesse,* Bourdeaus, 1601, reprinted Paris, 1797, three vols. in two. English translation, *Of wisdome: three books . . . ,* by Samson Lennard, Lond., 1615; and by Geo. Stanhope, Lond., 1707, 2 vols.]—Trans. Note.

of self-preservation, was disregarded by his followers and even by the bold advocates of the naturalistic interpretation of morality.[19]

Only Darwin, toward the end of his life, ventured to repeat Bacon's thought on the basis of his own observations of nature, and he developed this idea in a few remarkable pages on the origin of the moral sentiments in his book, "The Descent of Man," (see above, Chap. II). But even now writers on ethics fail to stress this thought, which ought to be the foundation of rationalistic ethics, all the more because—though in a less definite form—it is suggested in the essence of all the teachings that sought the explanation of morality in the nature of man himself.

After Bacon, among the philosophers of the seventeenth century, the same idea was well understood and still more definitely expressed by Hugo Grotius in his work "De jure bellis," in 1625. After a few remarks on the Creator and his influence on the development of the moral conceptions,—not directly, but through the agency of Nature, "though created by Him, but unchangeable and *rational Nature,"*—Grotius did not hesitate to acknowledge that the sources of "law" and of the moral conceptions so intimately connected with it, were: *Nature, and Reason which interprets it.*

He excluded religious morality and ritual regulations from the realm of naturalistic morality, and he occupied himself only with the study of the latter. By nature he meant human nature, and he denied that it is unable to distinguish between the right and the wrong, because man as well as animals has the instinct of *sociality,* which inevitably urges man toward the establishing of a peaceful mode of life with his fellow creatures.

In addition to his strong social tendencies, continued Grotius, man, due to his language, has the ability to derive general rules

[19] It is remarkable that Jodl, the historian of Ethics, who is very keen to note all new influences in ethical philosophy, also fails to give due credit to the few words in which Bacon expressed his idea. Jodl saw in these words the echo of Greek philosophy, or of the so-called natural law, *lex naturalis* (1573); whereas Bacon, in deriving morality from sociality, which is inherent in man as well as in the majority of animals, gave a new, scientific explanation of the primary foundations of morality.

140

for the maintenance of social living, and the desire to act in accordance with these rules. This concern about society becomes the source of established customs and of the so-called *natural law* or the *law based on custom.* The development of these conceptions is also aided by the *conception of the common benefit,*—from which is derived the conception of *what is considered just.* But it is utterly wrong to assert, he wrote, that men were compelled by their rulers to be concerned about the law, or that they were concerned about it merely for the sake of benefit. Man's nature impelled him to act in this manner.

"Because," wrote Grotius, "even among the animals there are some who, for the sake of their children or their fellow creatures, will limit attention to their own wants, or even forget self. This, in our opinion, is due to a sort of knowledge coming from without, and constituting the principle of such acts, since in other, simpler acts this instinct is not noticeable." [20]

A similar tendency to do kind acts toward others is found to a certain extent among children. Sound reason also acts in the same direction (§ 9). "The natural law," wrote Grotius, "is a rule suggested to us by reason, by means of which we judge the moral necessity or the moral inacceptability of an act, depending on its agreement or disagreement with rational nature itself" (with the very nature of reason, § 10, I).[21]

"More than that," continues Grotius, "the natural law is so unchangeable that God himself cannot change it. For, though God's power is exceeding, it may be said there are things over which it does not extend." (Book I, chapter I, § 10, 5.)

---

[20] I quote from the French translation: *De jure bellis. Le Droit de guerre et de paix, traduit du latin par M. de Courtin,* La Haye, 1703. Préface, § 7. [The first edition of this French translation appeared in Amsterdam, 1688; the 1703 edition is credited to M. de Vourtin, 3 vols. English translations: *The rights of war and peace,* by A. C. Campbell, N. Y., and Lond., 1901; and *Selections,* by W. S. M. Knight, Lond., 1922.]—Trans. Note.

[21] [Kropotkin gives the two possible interpretations of the clause.]—Trans. Note.

In other words, on combining the teachings of Bacon and Grotius, the origin of the moral conceptions becomes clear, if we recognize the *instinct of sociality* as the fundamental trait of Man. This instinct leads to the development of social life, with some inevitable concessions to personal egoism. Social life, in its turn, aids the development of the conceptions of *tribal morality*, which we find among all primitive savages. Furthermore, in the field of life which shapes itself under the influence of the unquestionably strong instinct of sociality, there is a continual activity of reason, which leads man to evolve more and more complicated rules of life,—and these in turn serve to strengthen the dictates of the social instinct and the habits suggested by it. Thus occurs, in a natural way, the evolution of what we call law.

It is thus clear that the moral nature and conceptions of Man have no need of supernatural explanation. And indeed, during the second half of the eighteenth century, and in the nineteenth century, the majority of writers on morality pointed to its origin from a two-fold source: the inborn feeling, i. e., the instinct of sociality; and reason, which strengthens and develops that which is suggested to it by the hereditary emotion and by the habits that have evolved into instinct.

Those, on the other hand, who insisted on introducing into ethics a supernatural, "divine" element, explained the instinct of sociality and the social habits of man by divine suggestion, completely ignoring the fact that the instinct and the habits of sociality are common to the great majority of animals. I will add here that we have now learned that the habits of sociality are the surest weapon in the struggle for existence, and for this reason they are becoming more and more strengthened among the social species.

The interpretation of morality given by Bacon and Hugo Grotius, however, unavoidably led to the question: on what does reason base its conclusions in evolving the principles of morality?

There are suggestions of this question even in Ancient Greece, and at that time it was given various answers. Plato,—especially during the later period of his life,—and his followers, in explaining the moral conceptions of man as due to "love" suggested to man by supernatural powers, naturally ascribed to reason a very modest place. Man's reason served merely as the interpreter of the"Reason of Nature," i. e., of the suggestions of the supernatural power.

It is true that the sceptical schools of the Sophists, and later Epicurus and his school, helped the thinkers of Ancient Greece to rid themselves of this religious ethics. These two schools, however, as well as others that did not recognize the interference of the Supernatural Will (e. g., the Cyrenaics and the followers of Aristotle), while attributing great importance to reason, ascribed to it, however, a very limited rôle, namely,—only the evaluation of various acts and modes of life with the purpose of determining which of them are a surer road to man's happiness. The moral mode of life, they said, is that which gives the greatest personal happiness and the most contented condition, not only to a single individual, but also to all. Happiness is freedom from evil; and owing to our reason, by renouncing momentary pleasures for the sake of the more permanent, future joys, we can select in our life that which leads us most surely toward the state of mental equilibrium, to general contentment, to harmonious life in accord with oneself, and also to the development of our personality in accordance with its individual peculiarities.

This view of ethics, consequently, rejects the pursuit of justice, —of virtue so-called,—for their sole sake. It pays but slight attention to life guided by the ideal of love, as preached by Plato. To *Reason* is ascribed an especially great importance by Aristotle. But he sees the activity of reason in *sensibleness and prudence,* rather than in bold decision of free thought. His ideal is "correct" thinking, the curbing of acts that man is ready to commit under the influence of strong emotion, and a will that keeps to the "rational mean" as determined by the nature of each separate individual.

Aristotle rejected metaphysics and took his stand on a practical basis, naming as the starting point of all activity the striving for happiness, self-love (egoism). The same point of view,—even more pronounced—was held, as we have seen, by Epicurus and later by his followers throughout five or almost six centuries. And from the time of the Renaissance, i. e., from the sixteenth century, this point of view was shared by a succession of thinkers, including later the Encyclopædists of the eighteenth century, and our contemporary utilitarians (Bentham, Mill), and naturalists (Darwin and Spencer).

But no matter how great the success of these teachings may have been, especially at the time when humanity felt the necessity of being liberated from the yoke of the Church and was endeavouring to open new ways to develop new forms of social life, these teachings, nevertheless, failed to solve the problem of the origin of the moral conceptions of man.

To say that man always strives for happiness and for the greatest possible freedom from evil, is merely to utter the forever obvious, superficial truth, expressed even in proverbs. And indeed, it has been often remarked that if the moral life led man to unhappiness, all morality would have long ago vanished from the world. But such a generalization is insufficient. There is no doubt that a desire for the greatest happiness is inherent in every living creature; in the final analysis man is guided by this desire. But this is precisely the essence of the question that now concerns us. "Why,—due to what mental or sense process, combined with some considerations which we call 'moral,'—does man so often renounce that which would unquestionably give him pleasure? Why does he often suffer all kinds of privations in order not to violate his moral ideal?" But the answer offered by the aforementioned thinkers of Ancient Greece, and later also by a whole series of utilitarian thinkers, does not satisfy our mind; we feel that the case is not limited to mere prudent weighing of pleasures and to mere renunciation of personal pleasures for the sake of other stronger and more permanent joys. We feel that we have here to deal with

144

something more complicated, and at the same time something more general.

Aristotle partially understood this when he wrote that a man to whom two alternatives are open, acts wisely if he adopts that decision which *does not bring conflict into his inner self and gives him a greater satisfaction with himself.* We strive for joy, honor, respect, etc., he wrote, not only for their own sake, but chiefly *for the sake of the sense of satisfaction which they give to our reason.* As we have seen, the same idea was repeated in a still better form by Epicurus. But if the part played by reason is accepted in this form, the question arises: *"Just what is it in our reason that is satisfied in such cases?"* And if the question is put thus, then, as we shall see later, the answer will necessarily be: "the need of justice," i. e., of equity. However, admitting that Aristotle and Epicurus did put to themselves this question, they gave no such answer. The entire structure of the society of their time, based as it was on slavery for the majority,—the entire spirit of society were both so far removed from justice and from its inevitable consequence—equity (equality in rights) that it is quite probable that Aristotle and Epicurus had not even thought of asking themselves the question.

However, at present, when the day of the old philosophy is over, we can no longer be satisfied with the conclusions of these two thinkers, and we ask ourselves: *"Why is it that a more developed mind finds greatest satisfaction just in those decisions which turn out to be the best for the interests of all?* Is there not some deep-lying, physiological cause for this fact?"

We have already seen the answer given to this question by Bacon and then by Darwin (see Chap. II). In man, said they, as in all herding animals, the instinct of sociality is developed to such an extent as to be *stronger and more permanent* than those other instincts that can be grouped together under the common name of the instinct of self-preservation. Moreover, in man, as in a ra-

145

tional being that has been living the social life for tens of thousands of years, reason aided the development and the observance of such usages, customs, and rules of life, as led to a fuller development of social life,—and as a consequence came the development of each separate individual.

But even this answer cannot completely satisfy us. From our personal experience we know how often, in the struggle between clashing impulses, narrowly egoistic feelings are victorious over feelings of a social nature. We see this in individuals as well as in entire societies. And we come, therefore, to the conviction, that if human reason did not have an inherent tendency to introduce into its decisions a corrective social factor, then the narrowly egoistic decisions would always gain the mastery over the judgments of a social nature. And, as we shall see in later chapters, such a corrective factor is applied. It springs, on the one hand, from our deep-seated instinct of sociality, as well as from sympathy toward those with whom our lot is cast,—a sympathy developed in us as a result of social life. On the other hand, it derives from *the conception of justice* inherent in our reason.

The further history of moral teachings will confirm this conclusion.

CHAPTER VII

DEVELOPMENT OF MORAL TEACHINGS IN THE MODERN ERA
(17th and 18th Centuries)

THE same two currents in ethics which manifested themselves in Ancient Greece, continued to exist among the thinkers of later times up to the middle of the eighteenth century. A majority of philosophers and thinkers still sought the explanation of the origin of morality in something supernatural, revealed to man from above. The ideas of Plato, developed and strengthened by the Christian Church constituted, and still make up the essence of such teachings, save that they are considerably narrowed. Plato, as well as Socrates, considered the knowledge of good as the real motive force of all morality. But Plato did not present this knowledge as something acquired from without. At the base of Plato's teaching, and especially of the teaching of the Stoics, was the idea that the moral sense, which manifests itself in man, even if in imperfect form, is a part of some fundamental principle of the universe. If this element were not present in nature it would not manifest itself in man.

Thus there was a certain kinship between the philosophy of Ancient Greece and modern science, but the Christian Church and the teachings inspired by it spared no effort to eradicate this idea from our *Weltanschauung*. It is true, Christianity brought into ethics, or, more correctly, strengthened in it the ideal of self-sacrifice for the good of our fellow-men; and by embodying this ideal in the person of a man-Christ, Christianity, like Buddhism, gave man a lofty moral lesson. But the followers of this teaching, and especially the Church, soon began to preach that the virtues of those who attempt to realize this ideal of life, are not at all of human

147

origin. "The world is steeped in evil," they said, in contrast to the thinkers of Ancient Greece. Expressing the pessimistic spirit of their time, the leaders of the Christian Church asserted that man is so immoral a creature, and the world is so much subjected to the evil power, that the Creator of the world had to send his son to the earth in order to show men the road to goodness, and to "redeem the world" from evil through his sufferings and his death.

This teaching, as we have seen, became so firmly established that more than fifteen centuries elapsed before, amidst the new forms of life that sprang into existence in Europe, voices began to be raised asserting that the germs of morality are contained in Nature itself. They have been already mentioned in the preceding chapter. But even in our time such voices are silenced by those who continue to assert with great self-confidence, but contrary to patent facts, that nature can give us only lessons of evil. They hold that the function of reason in moral questions should be the evaluation of that which gives us the greatest satisfaction under the given social system, and, therefore, that when the moral element manifests itself in man, it has a supernatural origin.

Nevertheless, the new current in ethics, which saw the sources of the moral conceptions of man in man himself and in Nature encompassing him, steadily gained in momentum in the last three hundred years, despite all the obstacles put in its path by Church and State. And this movement put more and more emphasis on the assertion that all our moral conceptions have developed in a perfectly natural way out of the feeling of sociality inherent in man and in most animals.

We will now proceed to analyze these new teachings and we shall see how they have had to maintain a constant struggle against the opposed teaching, which forever assumes new, and at times skilfully disguised, forms. But since the natural-scientific interpretation of morality has been following somewhat different paths in England and in France, we will examine this development separately in each of these countries. We will begin with England, where Bacon was the originator of the new movement; after him Hobbes became for a long time its prominent representative.

We have seen that the Greek philosophers, in spite of the differences in their various schools, all recognized that the moral conceptions of man are something that evolves from his natural tendencies, and that these conceptions are applied to life through man's own efforts in proportion as the rational understanding of sociality develops. We have also seen how Bacon and his contemporary, Hugo Grotius, quite definitely derived the moral principle from the social instinct. Thus the idea of the Stoics, who asserted that the moral element in man is something inherent in his nature, was revived in the new natural-scientific philosophy.

Hobbes, however, took a diametrically opposite stand. His views were undoubtedly influenced by the ideas of his French friend, Gassendi.[1] But his contemptuous attitude toward man, whom he considered a wicked animal, knowing no restraint to his passions, was, doubtlessly, formulated in England during the turbulent years of the Revolution which began in 1639 and which culminated in the overthrow and execution of the king in 1649. Already at that time Hobbes regarded the revolutionists with hatred, and he was forced to flee to France, where he wrote his first work, "De Cive" (Of the State).[2]

Owing to the complete absence at that time of knowledge about the life of the primitive savage, Hobbes pictured to himself the life of primitive man as a state of "war of all men, against all

---

[1] Gassendi's moral teaching will be discussed in the next chapter.

[2] As is known, the English revolution began in 1639. Hobbes's first work, *De Cive* [*Elementa philosophica de cive*], appeared first in Paris in the Latin language in 1648; just five years later it appeared in England in the English language. Hobbes's second work, *Leviathan*, appeared in English in 1652, three years after the execution of the king. [The English translation of *De Cive,—Philosophical Rudiments concerning Government and Society*—was published in London, in 1651; hence, three years after the original Latin.]— Trans. Note.

men"[3] from which men emerged only after they united into a society and concluded for that purpose a "social covenant."[4] Therefore Hobbes begins his work on the State with the assertion that man is not at all the "social animal," born with the habits of sociality, about which Aristotle spoke; on the contrary, men are as wolves to one another—"homo homini lupus."

If men seek companionship it is not by virtue of inborn sociality, but for the sake of the benefits they expect from others, or through fear of one another. (Chaps. I and II).

"For if by nature one man should love another (that is) as man, there could no reason be returned why every man should not equally love every man, or why he should rather frequent those whose society affords him honour or profit." [II, 2.] When men meet "for pleasure and recreation of mind, every man is wont to please himself most with those things which stir up laughter, whence he may by comparison of another man's defects and infirmities, pass the more current in his own opinion." [II, 2.] "All society therefore is either for gain or for glory, (i. e.,) not so much for love of our fellows, as for love of ourselves." And he concludes this paragraph with the following words: "We must therefore resolve that the original of all great, and lasting societies, consisted not in the mutual good will men had towards each other, but in the mutual fear they had of each other." [I, 2.]

The entire ethical system of Hobbes is based on this superficial representation of human nature. He held these conceptions as fundamental, and he reaffirmed them in his later notes to the text,— the notes being apparently called forth by various objections raised to his definitions and conclusions. [5]

[3] [*Philosophical Rudiments*, etc. (Lond., 1651), chap. I, § 15,—with modernized spelling.]—Trans. Note.

[4] [*Idem*, chap. II, chiefly § 11.]

[5] Thus in the note to the paragraph cited above Hobbes wrote: "It is true indeed that to Men . . . solitude is an enemy; for infants have need of others to help them to live, and those of riper years to help them to live well, wherefore I deny not that men (nature compelling) desire to come to-

Group settlements of some animals and of savages, according to Hobbes, are not yet a state. The very mental make-up of man prevents him from combining into societies. It is due to this innate bent that men are enemies to one another, and even the sociality manifested by man is not his natural quality but has been engrafted on him by his upbringing. By nature every man considers himself the equal of every other, as long as his upbringing does not eradicate in him this idea, and he holds himself justified in doing evil unto others and in appropriating their property. Hence the state of continuous war of each against everyone. Man emerges from this state only when he becomes subject to others who are stronger or more cunning, or when a group of men, realizing the dangers of the mutual struggle, enters into an agreement and founds a society.[6]

The utter falsity of Hobbes's conception of primitive man has become fully apparent,—now that we have studied the life of the primitive savage as well as the life of the greater number of animals living on the still sparsely populated continents. We can now see clearly that sociality constitutes so powerful a weapon in the struggle against the hostile forces of nature and against other animals, that it was developed by many herd animals long before the appearance of man-like creatures on the earth. Therefore, to de-

gether. But civil societies are not mere meetings, but bonds to the making whereof faith and compacts are necessary." If an objection is raised that if men were such as Hobbes describes them, they would avoid each other,—to this Hobbes replies that such is really the case, for "they who go to sleep shut their doors, those who travel carry their swords with them," etc.

[6] "The cause of mutual fear consists partly in the natural equality of men, partly in their mutual will of hurting." And since it is an easy matter "even for the weakest man to kill the strongest" and since "they are equal who can do equal things one against the other," . . . "all men therefore among themselves are by nature equal; the inequality we now discern, hath its spring from the Civil Law." (1, 3.) Until then "by right of nature" everyone is himself the supreme judge of the means that he is to employ for his self-preservation. (1, 8, 9.) "By right of nature all men have equal right to all things." (1, 10.) But since this condition would lead to constant warfare, men entered into a social covenant establishing peace, and "by right of nature" all are bound to observe this covenant.

velop sociality, man had no need of either the "social covenant" or the "Leviathan-state."

It is clear that Hobbes again used his conception of the bases of human society for the derivation of the "laws of nature," on which he founded his idea of a social system. And since he was an ultra-conservative, with a mild tinge of popular sympathy (he stood for the monarchy and for the Pretender at the time of Cromwell's republic), he accordingly represented as the basis of the state the feudal aspirations of his party, on one side, and a few generally acceptable commonplaces on the other.

For those who are in any degree acquainted with the life of animals and of savages, Hobbes's views are obviously erroneous. Such ideas were possible in the middle of the seventeenth century, when so little was known of the life of the savage peoples, but it is difficult to understand how such views have survived to the present time in the face of the explanations and the discoveries of the eighteenth and nineteenth centuries. It may be still possible to account for Rousseau's adherence to similar views of the origin of human society, but it is utterly incomprehensible how the same ideas came to be shared by the modern naturalistic Huxley, whom I had to remind, when he began to develop ideas worthy of Hobbes, that the *appearance of societies on the earth preceded the appearance of man.*

Hobbes's error can be explained only by the fact that he wrote at a time when it was necessary to counteract the conception—widespread in those days—of the idyllic "primitive state" of man. His conception was connected with the legend of Paradise and of the fall of man, and it was adhered to by the Catholic Church as well as by the newly established Protestant Churches, which, even more firmly than the Catholics, considered redemption a fundamental dogma.

Under such circumstances, a writer who categorically denied the "primitive state" and who derived the moral conceptions of the primitive man-beast from the consideration that peaceful co-habitation is more advantageous than continual warfare,—such a writer was assured of success. Either the "social covenant" or subjugation by a conqueror who limits by force the unbridled license of individuals,—such was, according to Hobbes, the first stage in the development of morality and of law. Then Reason proceeded to limit the natural rights of the individuals in their own interest, and thus were developed in time all the "moral" virtues: compassion, honesty, gratitude, etc.

Moral conceptions, according to Hobbes, come about in many different ways, depending on time and place; and therefore moral rules contain *nothing general, nothing absolute.*[7] Moreover, they are to be observed only in cases where there is reciprocity, and Reason should be the sole guide in all decisions. But it is unreasonable to observe moral rules with respect to those who do not reciprocate. In general it is not safe to rely upon social reason for the establishment of morality. This object calls for a *governing power which creates social morality under fear of punishment,* and to this power of an individual or of a group of men everyone should render unconditional obedience. In the State, as in Nature,—might is right. The natural state of man is war of all men against all men. The State protects life and property of its subjects at the price of their absolute obedience. The will of the State is the supreme law. The submission to the power of the omnipotent "Leviathan-State" is the basis of sociality. This is the only way to attain the peaceful co-habitation, which our moral laws and regulations aim to establish. As regards the hereditary instinct of sociality —it is of no importance, for it is insufficiently developed in primitive man and cannot become the source of moral principles. Reason, likewise, is of no consequence in developing the rules of social

---

[7] Moral philosophy, according to Hobbes, is nothing but the science of what is good and what is evil, in the mutual relations of men and in human society. "*Good* and *Evil* are names given to things to signify the inclination, or aversion of them by whom they were given. But the inclinations of men are diverse, according to their diverse constitutions, customs, opinions"; accordingly, men differ also in their interpretation of good and evil. [(*Philosophical Rudiments*, III, 31). Page 55, Lond., 1651].—Trans. Note.

life: man has no inherent conception of justice; and human reason, like a true opportunist, establishes rules of social life in accordance with the requirements of the time. He who is victorious—is right, for his victory proves that he foresaw the requirements of his contemporaries. This was the way in which Hobbes interpreted morality; and this is how it is regarded by the vast majority of the ruling classes quite up to the present time.

On the other hand, the fact that Hobbes in his interpretation of morality definitely renounced religion and metaphysics, attracted many followers to his side. At the time when the struggle between the Catholic Church and the Protestants was raging in England with a ferocity bordering on frenzy, and when the liberation of personality and of thought had become an urgent necessity, the teaching that put on a rational basis so important a question as morality was especially valuable. Generally speaking, the liberation of ethics and philosophy from religion was a great step forward, and Hobbes's works exerted a considerable influence in this direction. Besides, Hobbes, following Epicurus, maintained that although the individual is always guided by personal interests, man nevertheless comes to the conclusion that his interests lie in the direction of the greatest possible development of sociality and of peaceful mutual relations. Thus it followed, that although moral conceptions originate in personal egoism, they nevertheless become the basis for an extension of better mutual relations and of sociality.

Owing to the causes already noted, the teaching of Hobbes met with a considerable and lasting success in England. But many were not satisfied by it, and soon several serious opponents came out against it; among them John Milton, the famous English poet of that time, a staunch republican and the advocate of freedom of conscience and of the press, and James Harrington, who in 1656 issued his Utopian "Oceanea" where, in opposition to Hobbes, he glorified the democratic republic. But the principal criticism of Hobbes's ethical teaching came from a group of scientists connected with Cambridge University. This group was equally hostile to

Cromwell's republican puritanism and to the natural-scientific trend of Hobbes's teachings. However, though these opponents of Hobbes did not share the narrow views then prevailing among English theologians, their philosophy, nevertheless, could under no circumstances reconcile itself either with rationalism in general or with Hobbes's views in particular, in which they saw a direct menace to all restraining moral force. It is impossible; held Cudworth, to derive our feeling of the obligatory nature of some of our moral judgments from considerations of personal gain. And what is more he maintained, morality is not a creation of men: its roots lie *in the very nature of things, which even the divine will is incapable of changing:* moral principles are as absolute as mathematical truths. Man discovers the properties of a triangle, but he does not create them: they are inherent in the changeless properties of things. Moral principles would remain true even if the present world should perish.

We find, accordingly, in these ideas of Cudworth, an approach to a conception of the equal importance of all men and the equality of rights of all men, which begins to manifest itself clearly in modern rationalistic ethics. But Cudworth was primarily a theologian, and for him philosophy remained empty of content without the inspiring power of religion and of the fear inculcated by it.

A much closer approach to modern ethical tendencies was effected by another representative of the Cambridge school, Richard Cumberland (1632–1718). In his work, "Philosophical Treatise on the Laws of Nature," [8] published in Latin in 1671, he states his views in the following words: "The good of society is the supreme moral law. All that leads to it is moral."

Man reaches this conclusion because all of nature impels him in that direction. Sociality is a quality inseparable from human nature—an inevitable consequence of man's organization and condition. As to the views of Hobbes, who attempted to prove the

---

[8] *De legibus naturae disquisitio philosophica*, London, 1672.

opposite, they are fallacious, because *sociality must have existed* from the very first origins of man.

It is true that Cumberland did not have at his disposal the proofs of this idea now in our hands, since extended voyages and the life of explorers among savages have given us an understanding of the mode of life among primitive peoples. Cumberland, accordingly, supported his divination only by general reasonings drawn from the structure of the world and of man, and his relation to other living beings endowed with reason. To this extent, he wrote, (evidently as a concession to the demands of his time) is the moral element a manifestation of the Divine Will; but it does not at all follow that it is arbitrary or changeable.

Thus, Cumberland's surmises as to the origin of the moral conceptions of man from the development of the sense of sociality were correct. Unfortunately, Cumberland did not trace any further the development of this sense. He merely pointed out that the feeling of general benevolence which evolves from the sense of sociality, strengthened and developed by reason, results in so much good for every rational being that man, without any interference on the part of divine authority, will consider moral rules obligatory for himself. Of course, in following the urge of sociality, man strives at the same time for his personal happiness: but under the influence of sociality his very striving for *personal* happiness leads to the common good. Therefore, obedience to the sense of sociality becomes in itself the source of joy and satisfaction, since it leads to a higher aim.

Cumberland stopped at this point. He did not attempt to explain *how and why,* starting from the instinct of sociality, man was able to develop his moral ideals to their present level and breadth, neither did he consider the conception of *justice,* leading to equity and the further conclusions based on this idea.

This was done on the one hand by John Locke and his followers, who attempted to base morality on utility, and on the other hand by Shaftesbury and his followers, who saw the source of morality in the inherent instincts and feelings. But before examining these systems we must dwell on the ethics of Spinoza, which exercised tremendous influence on the further development of ethical teachings.

Spinoza's ethics has a point in common with that of Hobbes, in denying the extra-natural origin of morality. At the same time it radically differs from it in its fundamental conceptions. For Spinoza, God is—Nature itself. "Besides God there is no substance, nor can any be conceived." [9]

Corporeal substance cannot be divided from divine substance, for God is the efficient cause of all things, but He acts from the laws of His own nature only. It is wrong to imagine that He can bring it about that those things that are in His power should not be. It would be equally wrong to assert that intellect of the highest order and "freedom of will" both pertain to the nature of God. (I, 17.) In Nature there is nothing contingent, but all things are determined from the necessity of the divine nature to exist and act in a certain manner. (I, 29.) *In short, that which men call God is Nature itself, misunderstood by man.* The will is only a certain mode of thought, like the intellect, and therefore no volition can exist or be determined to action unless it be determined by another cause, and this again by another, and so on *ad infinitum*. (I, 32.) From this it follows that "things could have been produced by God in no other manner and in no other order than that in which they have been produced." (I, 33.) The power which the common people ascribe to God is not only a human power (which shows that they look upon God as man, or as being like a man), but it also involves weakness. (II, 3.) In general, the causes that lead men to ascribe various events of their life to supreme power, are very well analyzed by Spinoza in Part I, prop 36.[10]

---

[9] *Ethics*, part I, proposition 15. W. Hale White's translation, fourth edition, Oxford University Press, 1910. For brevity, in further references the part will be indicated by Roman figures and the proposition by Arabic, thus: (I, 15).

[10] [Kropotkin refers here to the Appendix to Part I, which follows Proposition 36.]—Trans. Note.

Spinoza was, consequently, a follower of Descartes,[11] whose views on Nature he further developed; and in his denial of the divine origin of morality he approached Hobbes. But with his daring development of his scientific views and with his complete freedom from Christian mysticism, Spinoza understood man and nature too well to follow Hobbes in ethics. And he certainly could not conceive morality as something based on coercion exerted by the State. He showed, on the contrary, that without any influence of the feeling of fear of a Supreme Being or of government, human reason will freely and inevitably come to the moral attitude toward others, and that in doing this man finds supreme happiness, because such are the *demands of his freely and logically thinking reason.*

Spinoza thus created a truly ethical teaching, permeated with deep moral feeling. Such was also his personal life.

The mental process by way of which Spinoza arrived at his conclusions may be stated as follows: "The will and the intellect are one and the same. Both are but the individual *volitions* and *ideas*. Falsehood consists in the privation of knowledge which is involved by *inadequate knowledge* of things or by inadequate and confused ideas" (II, 35); wrong acts spring from the same source. Generally speaking, "In every human mind some ideas are adequate and others are mutilated and confused." In the first case idea is followed by *action*, while in the second case our mind suffers. Moreover, "the mind is subject to *passions* in proportion to the number of inadequate ideas which it has." (III, I.)

According to Spinoza "the mind and the body are one and the same thing, conceived at one time under the attribute of *thought*, and at another under that of *extension*." (III, 2.) Spinoza proves this proposition at length, refuting the current view which asserts that "this or that action of the body springs from the mind which has command over the body." When men say this, they simply confess that they are ignorant of the real cause of their actions.

[11] Descartes's teachings will be discussed in the next chapter.

(III, 2.) Decisions of the mind "arise in the mind by the same necessity as the ideas of things actually existing." (III, 2.) Moreover, "if anything increases and helps our body's power of action, the idea of that thing increases and helps our mind's power of thought." (III, 11.) Joy, merriment, cheerfulness lead our mind to greater perfection, while sorrow has the opposite effect. (III, 11.) In short, body and mind are inseparable from each other.

"Love is nothing but joy accompanied with the idea of an external cause, and hatred is nothing but sorrow with the accompanying idea of an external cause." (III, 13.) This explains to us the nature of hope, fear, confidence, despair, gladness ("joy arising from the image of a past thing whose issues we have doubted") and remorse ("the sorrow which is opposed to gladness"). (III, 18.)

From these definitions Spinoza derived all the fundamental principles of morality. Thus, for example, "we endeavour to affirm everything, both concerning ourselves and concerning the beloved object, which we imagine will affect us or the object with joy," and we endeavour to deny the contrary things.[12] And since the "mind's desire or power of thought is equal to and simultaneous with the body's desire and power of action, we endeavour to bring into existence everything which we imagine conduces to joy,"—ours, as well as the joy of those we love. From these fundamental propositions Spinoza derives the highest type of morality.

There is nothing in nature, wrote Spinoza, that is *obligatory:* there is only the *necessary.* "Knowledge of good or evil is nothing but an affect of joy or sorrow in so far as we are conscious of it." "We call a thing good or evil as it helps or hinders the preservation of our being, and as it increases or diminishes, helps or restrains, our power of action." (IV, 8.) But "no affect can be restrained by the true knowledge of good and evil in so far as it is true, but only in so far as it is considered an affect," i. e., when

[12] Spinoza used the word "thing" both for inanimate objects and for living beings.

it becomes a desire of *action*. In the latter case "it will restrain any other affect, provided that the latter be the weaker of the two." (IV, 14.)

It can be easily imagined what hatred Spinoza provoked in the theolological camp by these assertions. Spinoza denied the theologists' idea of antinomy, by virtue of which God is the bearer of the eternal truth, whereas the world created by Him is its negation.[13]

Spinoza built his ethics on the eudemonistic basis, i. e., on *man's striving for happiness*. Man, he taught, like all other creatures, strives for *greatest happiness*, and from this striving his reason derives moral rules of life: in doing this, however, man is *not free*, for he can do only that which is the necessary outcome of his nature.

There is no doubt that Spinoza was above all aiming to free our morality from the tyranny of the feelings incalculated by religion, and wished to prove that our passions and desires (affects) do not depend on our good or evil intentions. He aimed to represent the moral life of man as being completely governed by his reason, the power of which increases with the development of knowledge. Spinoza devotes to this subject many pages in the fourth part of his "Ethics," where he speaks "Of human bondage." The entire fifth part treats "of the power of the intellect, or of human liberty." In all this capital treatise Spinoza in every way urges man to action, proving that we attain the full gratification of our "ego" only when we *actively*, and not passively react to our surroundings. Unfortunately, he failed to consider the fact that *the ability to decide what is just and what is unjust is one of the expressions of the fundamental mode of our thinking, without which thinking is impossible.*

[13] The assertion that man is not free and can do only what is the outcome of his nature, in connection with the similar assertion about God, is found in several passages of Spinoza's *Ethics*. Thus, in the preface to the Fourth Part, "Of Human Bondage, or Of the Strength of the Affects," he wrote: "that eternal and infinite Being whom we call God or Nature acts by the same necessity by which He exists."

Spinoza's ethics is thoroughly scientific. It knows no metaphysical subtleties, nor revelations from above. Its conclusions are derived from the knowledge of man and of nature in general. But what does it see in nature? What does nature teach our reason, to which decision in moral questions belongs? In what direction does it lead us? It teaches, wrote Spinoza, not to be content with commiseration, not to look from afar at the joys and the sorrows of men, but to be *active*. But in what direction should this activity manifest itself? This question, unfortunately, Spinoza left unanswered. He wrote during the second half of the seventeenth century, and his "Ethics" first appeared in a posthumous edition in 1676. At that time two revolutions had already taken place: the Reformation, and the English Revolution. Both these revolutions went further than a mere struggle against theology and the Church. They both had a deeply social character, and human equality was the principal watchword of these popular movements. But these deeply significant phenomena found no response in Spinoza.

"Spinoza," as Jodl very justly remarks, "had looked deeper than anyone else into ethics. The moral, as he sees it, is at one and the same time the divine and the human, egoism and self-sacrifice, reason and affect (i. e., desire), freedom and necessity." At the same time, adds Jodl, in purposely building his ethics on egoism, Spinoza completely ignored the social propensities of man. Of course, he recognized the desires produced by social life and the fact that they are bound to overcome purely egoistic desires, but social union appeared to him as something of secondary importance, and he put the self-sufficiency of a personality perfect in itself, above the idea of work in common and of sociality.[14] Possibly, this defect may be explained by the fact that in the seventeenth century, when massacres in the name of the "true faith" were raging, the most urgent aim of ethics was to separate morality from any admixture of Christian virtues, and having done this, Spinoza,

[14] Friedrich Jodl, *Geschichte der Ethik als philosophischer Wissenschaft*, Stuttgart and Berlin, 1912.

161

it may be, hesitated to bring upon himself still heavier thunder of reproof by a defence of *social* justice, i. e., by a defence of the communistic ideas advanced at that time by the new religious movements. It was, above all, necessary to reestablish the rights of *personal, independent, autonomous reason.* Therefore, in basing morality on the principle of greatest happiness, which it affords without any reward in the form of "multiplying of herds" or "beatitude in heaven," it was necessary to break completely with theological ethics, without falling into "utilitarianism" or into the ethics of Hobbes and his followers. Whatever the case may be, the omission in Spinoza's ethics pointed out by Jodl, was an essential omission.

The inductive philosophy of Francis Bacon, the bold generalizations of Descartes, who aimed to reveal the natural life of the entire Universe, Spinoza's ethics, which explained the moral element in man without invoking any mysterious forces, and Grotius' attempt to explain the development of sociality, again without any interference on the part of a supernatural lawgiver,—all these teachings prepared the ground for a new philosophy, and it actually found its prominent representative in the English thinker Locke.

Locke did not write a special treatise on morality. But in his work, "An Essay Concerning Human Understanding," [15] he so deeply analyzed the foundations of our knowledge, that his analysis became for a whole generation the basis of a new philosophy. In discussing in another book [16] the practical application of his research to politics and to life in general, he voiced so many weighty thoughts on the origin of the moral conceptions that his views left their stamp on everything that was written on morality

[15] *An Essay Concerning Human Understanding* appeared in 1690, two years after the establishment of the constitutional monarchy in England. [All quotations are from Locke's *Philosophical Works*, 2 vols., Bohn's Standard Library, London, 1854.]—Trans. Note.
[16] *Two Treatises of Government,* 1689. *An Epistle on Tolerance,* 1690. *The Reasonableness of Christianity,* etc. [1697.]

during the eighteenth century. The very fact that Locke was not a founder of a new theory with strictly defined views, partly accounts for his influence. In giving his interpretation of human thought, of the so-called freedom of will, and of morality in general, he assumed a very tolerant attitude toward other teachings, trying to show in each one of them the element of truth, even if it was incorrectly expressed.

Locke, like Spinoza, was primarily a follower of Descartes in his interpretation of our knowledge, i. e., of our thinking processes and of the ways by which man arrives at his conclusions. Like Descartes, he rejected metaphysics and stood on a strictly scientific basis. But Locke disagrees with Descartes on the subject of the existence in man of *innate ideas,* in which Descartes and other predecessors of Locke saw the source of the moral conceptions of man. Locke asserted that there are no innate ideas either in morality or in reason in general. "Where is that practical truth," he asked, "that is universally received without doubt or question, as it must be if innate? Justice, and keeping of contracts, is that which most men seem to agree in. This is a principle which is thought to extend itself to the dens of thieves, and the confederacies of the greatest villains. . . . I grant that outlaws themselves do this one amongst another; but it is without receiving these as the innate laws of nature. They practise them as rules of convenience within their own communities. . . . Justice and truth are the common ties of society; and therefore even outlaws and robbers must keep faith and rules of equity amongst themselves, or else they cannot hold together. But will anyone say, that those that live by fraud or rapine have innate principles of truth and justice which they allow and assent to?" [17] And to those who would point out the usual divergence between thoughts and actions in men, Locke answers, not quite satisfactorily, that the actions of men

[17] *An Essay Concerning Human Understanding,* Book I, ch. iii, 2. [All further references are to the same essay. Books I–II are in vol. I, and books III–IV in vol. II of the Bohn edition.]—Trans. Note.

are the best interpreters of their thoughts. And since the principles of justice and morality are denied by many, and, though recognized by others, are not applied to life, "it is very strange and unreasonable to suppose innate practical principles, that terminate only in contemplation." (Ibid. 3.)

A modern reader, familiar with the theory of evolution, will probably notice that Locke's reasoning is superficial. Of course he was justified in denying the existence in man of inherent ideas or *conclusions*, including the moral, and he was justified in saying that in morality as well as in everything else *man arrives at his conclusions through experience*. But if he had known the laws of heredity, as we know them now, or even if he had simply given thought to the matter, he would hardly have denied that a social creature like man, or like other herd animals, *could and was bound to evolve through heredity not only a tendency to herd-life but also to equity and justice.*[18]

Nevertheless, in his time, i. e., in the seventeenth century, Locke's crusade against the "innate" moral conceptions was an important step forward, because this negation freed philosophy from subjection to the teachings of the Church about the fall of man and the lost Paradise.

After this introduction, which Locke needed to prove that moral

[18] Locke wrote: "But should that most unshaken rule of morality and foundation of all social virtue 'that one should do as he would be done unto,' be proposed to one who never heard of it before, might he not without any absurdity ask a reason why?" (Bk. I, ch. iii, § 4.) To this a Christian would reply: "Because God, who has the power of eternal life and death, requires it of us." But if a Hobbesist is asked why, he will answer: "Because the public requires it, and the 'Leviathan' will punish you if you do not'" (§ 5) "Virtue (is) generally approved, not because innate, but because profitable" (§ 6), "The great principle of morality, to do as one would be done to, is more recommended than practised." (§ 7.) Locke, therefore, completely followed Hobbes on this point, failing to notice that habits are inherited and evolve into instincts, and that the instincts, i. e., that which was then known as "appetites," are to a great extent hereditary. In his struggle against the doctrine of innate ideas, he failed to notice heredity, though its significance was already understood by Bacon, and partly by Spinoza.

conceptions cannot be regarded as inspired from above, he passed to the principal subject of his treatise: to the proof of the origin of our ideas and conclusions *from observation—from experience.* And in this field his research was so exhaustive that it was later accepted by all the principal thinkers of the eighteenth century, and up to our own time it is still adhered to by the positivists. Locke was very definitely proving that all our *ideas* (conceptions, thoughts) originate either directly from our *sensations,* received through our senses, or from the *perception of our sensations.* All material for the thinking process is supplied by experience, and *mind contains nothing that was not previously experienced by sensations.*

"This great source of most of the ideas we have, depending wholly upon our senses, and derived by them to the understanding, I call *sensation,*" wrote Locke (Book II, ch. 1, 3). But, of course, he did not deny that there are certain ways of thinking, inherent to our reason and that permit it to discover truths. Such are, for example, the identity and the difference of two things, discerned by reason, their equality or inequality; their adjacency in time and space, or their remoteness from each other; such is also the idea of cause and effect.

There are, according to Locke, two principal divisions in our simple ideas which we derive from sensations, and from our perceptions of sensations. Some are connected with pleasure, others with pain, some with joy, others with sorrow, and there is hardly a sensation or a perception of sensation which does not belong to the one or the other division. (Book II, ch. XX, 1.) "Things, then, are good or evil only in reference to pleasure or pain. That we call good, which is apt to cause or increase pleasure, or diminish pain in us." (§ 2.) The sensations produce in us the corresponding desires and passions, the nature of which we learn by observing them. In general, man seeks that which gives him pleasure, and avoids all that leads to suffering. (§ 3.) Furthermore, Locke pointed out that pleasure and pain may be not only physical but also mental, and thus he laid the foundation of the teaching which in the nineteenth century was brilliantly developed by John Stuart Mill, under the name of *Utilitarianism*.

Moreover, in observing the alterations in our simple ideas, (under the influence of broadening experience), we arrive at the conception of our power, i. e., our ability to act in one way or another; and from these observations springs the conception of the "free will." [19] (Book II, ch. XXI, 1–2.) "We find in ourselves," says Locke, "a power to begin or forbear, continue or end several actions of our minds, and motions of our bodies, barely by a thought or preference of the mind ordering, or, as it were, commanding the doing or not doing such or such a particular action." (§ 5.) From the consideration of the extent of the power of the mind over the actions of man, arises the idea of *free will*. (§ 7.) But, in fact, the question "Is our will free?" is incorrectly formulated. It would be more proper to ask "Is man free in his actions?" And the answer to this question would be that man can, of course, act *as he wills*. But is he free to will? (§ 22.) To this question, of course, Locke gives a negative answer, because *man's will is determined by a whole series of preceding influences*.

Further, in discussing how the mind determines the will, Locke pointed out that the anticipation of suffering, or even of mere uneasiness, influences our will more than the anticipation of the greatest joys in the life to come. In general, Locke so thoroughly discussed the relations of our mind to our actions that in this field he may be considered the progenitor of all subsequent philosophy.

However, it must be noted that although Locke's influence was felt mainly in the sceptical philosophy of the eighteenth century, its influence is apparent too in the conciliatory attitude of philosophy to religion, which later found expression in Kant and in German philosophy of the first half of the nineteenth century.

In freeing moral philosophy from the yoke of the Church, Locke at the same time put morality under the protection of the three

[19] [Locke uses the term "liberty" for the modern conception of "free will."]—Trans. Note.

types of law: the divine law, the civil law, and the law of opinion or reputation. (Book II, ch. XXVIII, § 7.) Thus he did not sever connection with the Church morality, based on the promise of bliss in the life to come. He only diminished the importance of this promise.

In conclusion, in the last part of the same essay Locke devoted a few chapters to the development of the idea which occurs frequently in writings on ethics, namely,—that moral truths, when they are freed from complications and are reduced to fundamental conceptions, can be proved in precisely the same manner as mathematical truths. *"Moral knowledge is as capable of real certainty as mathematics,"* wrote Locke, "our moral ideas, as well as mathematical, being archetypes themselves, and so adequate and complete ideas, all the agreement or disagreement which we shall find in them will produce real knowledge, as well as in mathematical figures." (Book IV, ch. iv, § 7.) All this part, and especially the section, "Morality capable of demonstration," (ch. III, § 18) are extremely interesting. They show clearly that Locke approached very closely the recognition of justice as the basis of moral conceptions. But when he attempted to define justice, he quite needlessly limited this conception, reducing it to the conception of property: "Where there is no property there is no injustice, is a proposition as certain as any demonstration in Euclid." (Book IV, ch. III, § 18.) And thus he deprived the conception of justice and equity of that prime importance, which, as we shall see in a later part of this work, it has in the development of moral ideas.

Locke's philosophy exerted a far-reaching influence upon the subsequent development of philosophy. Written in simple language, without the barbaric terminology of the German philosophers, it did not envelop its fundamental principles in the cloud of metaphysical phraseology which at times prevents the writer himself from forming a clear idea of what he aims to express. Locke clearly stated the fundamentals of the naturalistic, scientific interpretation of the Universe in the important field of morality. Therefore, all subsequent philosophy, from Kantian metaphysics to English "utilitarianism," to the "positivism" of Auguste Comte, and even up to modern "materialism"—consciously or unconsciously harks back to Locke and Descartes. This will be seen later, when we come to consider the philosophy of the Encyclopædists, and then the philosophy of the nineteenth century. And now let us examine what was the contribution of the English followers of Locke.

Among those who wrote on the resemblance of the moral rules to the mathematical, in the sense that both may be accurately derived from a few fundamental premises, was Samuel Clarke, a pupil of Descartes and Newton. In his "Discourse Concerning the Unchangeable Obligations of Natural Religion" [20] he ascribes to that idea very great importance, so much more that he vigorously asserted the independence of the moral principles from the will of the Supreme Being, and also that man assumes morality as obligatory regardless of all considerations as to the consequences of immoral acts. It might be expected, therefore, that Clarke would elaborate Bacon's idea of the hereditary nature of the moral instincts and would show how they develop. Recognizing the existence side by side with them of the anti-social instincts, frequently attractive to man, Clarke might have considered the rôle played by reason in choosing between the two, and he might have shown the gradually accumulating influence of the social instincts. He failed to do this, however. The time was not yet ripe for the theory of *evolution*, and although it was the last thing to be expected from an adversary of Locke, Clarke, like Locke, turned to divine revelation. Moreover, Clarke, like Locke and his followers, the utilitarians, resorted to the considerations of utility, whereby he still further weakened that part of his teaching in which he derives moral conceptions from hereditary instincts. As a result, his influence on ethical philosophy was much weaker than it might have been if he had limited himself to the thorough elaboration of the first part of his doctrine.

[20] [London, 1708]—Trans. Note.

MORAL TEACHINGS IN THE MODERN ERA

Much more complete was the moral philosophy of Shaftesbury. Of all those who wrote in the seventeenth century after Bacon, Shaftesbury came closer than any other to the idea of the great founder of inductive thinking. Shaftesbury expressed himself on the subject of the origin of moral conceptions in a much more daring and definite form than his predecessors, although he was, of course, compelled to cover his fundamental thoughts by concessions to religious teachings, for it was impossible at that time to make headway without concessions.

Shaftesbury first of all endeavoured to prove that the moral sense is not a derivative sense, but is inherent in human nature. It is by no means the outcome of our evaluation of the useful or harmful consequences of our actions; and "this primary and spontaneous character of our moral sense proves that morality is based on emotions and propensities the source of which lies in the nature of man, and which he can judge only secondarily, i. e., *after* they manifest themselves. In judging the manifestations of his feelings and instincts man calls them moral or immoral."

Thus the establishment of the bases of morality calls for reason; for understanding of what is right and what is wrong, in order to enable us to render correct judgments, so that "nothing horrid or unnatural, nothing unexemplary, nothing destructive of that natural affection by which the species or society is upheld, may on any account, or through any principle or notion of honour or religion, be at any time affected or prosecuted as a good and proper object of esteem." [21]

Shaftesbury ascribed no importance to religion in the strengthening of moral conceptions. A man who turned moral under the influence of religion, he wrote, possesses "no more of rectitude, piety, and sanctity, than there is meekness or gentleness in a tiger strongly

[21] *Characteristics of Men, Manners, Opinions, Times*, etc., by Anthony, Earl of Shaftesbury, 2 vols., Grant Richards, London, 1900. [The passage quoted is from Vol. I, Treatise IV, *An Inquiry Concerning Virtue or Merit*, Book I, Part II, Section III, p. 255.]—Trans. Note.

chained." [22] In general, Shaftesbury was quite outspoken in his discussion of religion and atheism.

Shaftesbury explained the origin of the moral conceptions exclusively by the inborn social instinct, controlled by reason. From them developed the conceptions of "Equity and Right," and their development was influenced by the following consideration: "To deserve the name of good or virtuous, a creature must have all his inclinations and affections, his dispositions of mind and temper, suitable and agreeing with the good of his kind, or of that system in which he is included, and of which he constitutes a part." [23]

Moreover, Shaftesbury proved that the social interests and the interests of the individual not only coincide, but are actually inseparable. Love of life and desire of life, when carried to the extreme, are not at all in the interests of the individual; they become a hindrance to his happiness.[24]

We also find in Shaftesbury the beginnings of the utilitarianist evaluation of pleasures, later developed by John Stuart Mill and other utilitarians, in the passage where he speaks of the preferability of the mental pleasures to the sensual.[25] And in his discourse, "The Moralists," published for the first time in 1709, where he defended his theories expounded in "An Inquiry Concerning Virtue or Merit," he ridiculed "the state of nature" in which, according to Hobbes's surmise, all men were enemies of one another.[26]

[22] *Ibid.*, Book I, Part III, Section III, p. 267; see also Book II, Part II, Section I.]—Trans. Note.

[23] *Ibid.*, Book II, Part I, Section I, p. 280.

[24] *Ibid.*, Book II, Part II, Section II, p. 318.

[25] *Ibid.*, Conclusion, p. 337. (See also Book II, Part II, Section I, p. 296.)

[26] *The Moralists: A Philosophical Rhapsody, being a recital of certain Conversations on Natural and Moral Subjects.* [In Vol. II of the *Characteristics*]:

"That it was their natural state to live thus separately can never without absurdity be allowed. For sooner may you divest the creature of any other feeling or affection than that towards society and his likeness." (Part II, Section IV, p. 80.) Further on he says, "If, on the other hand, their constitution be as ours . . . if they have *memory*, and senses, and *affections* . . . 'tis evident they can no more by their goodwill abstain from *society*

170

MORAL TEACHINGS IN THE MODERN ERA

It is remarkable that Shaftesbury, in refuting Hobbes's assertion that "man is a wolf to man," was the first to point out the existence of mutual aid among animals. "The learned," wrote Shaftesbury, "love to talk of this imaginary state of Nature" . . . but "to say in disparagement of man 'that he is to man a wolf' appears somewhat absurd, when one considers that wolves are to wolves very kind and loving creatures. The sexes strictly join in the care and nurture of the young, and this union is continued still between them. They howl to one another to bring company, whether to hunt, or invade their prey, or assemble on the discovery of a good carcass. Even the swinish kinds want not *common affection,* and run in herds to the assistance of their distressed fellows." [27]

Thus the words uttered by Bacon, Hugo Grotius, and Spinoza ("mutuam juventum," i. e., mutual aid) were apparently not lost, and through Shaftesbury they became incorporated into the system of Ethics. And now,—from serious observations of our best zoölogists, especially in the sparsely populated parts of America, and also from serious studies of the life of primitive tribes, conducted in the nineteenth century,—we know how right Shaftesbury was. Unfortunately, to this day there are many desk "naturalists" and "ethnologists," who keep on repeating the preposterous assertion of Hobbes.

Shaftesbury's views were so daring for his time, and in many points they approached so closely the conclusions of modern thinkers, that a few more words must be said about his teaching. Shaftesbury divided human tendencies into social, egoistical, and those that are, essentially, not "inherent." Such, he wrote, are hatred, malice,

than they can possibly preserve themselves without it." (Part II, Section IV, p. 82.) Moreover, Shaftesbury pointed to the weakness of human children, and their need for protection and better food. "Must not this [the human family, household] have grown soon into a *tribe?* and this tribe into a *nation?* Or though it remained a tribe only, was not this still a society for mutual defence and common interest?" Society, therefore, must be a *natural state* to man, and "out of society and community *he never did, nor ever can subsist."* (Part II, Section IV, p. 83.) This thought, as we shall see, was later reiterated by Hume.

[27] *Ibid.,* pp. 83–84.

passions. Morality is nothing but the proper relation between the social and the egoistic tendencies ("affections"). In general, Shaftesbury insisted on the independence of morality from religion, and from speculative motives, for its primary source lies not in reasoning about our actions, but in the very nature of man, in the sympathies which he developed in the course of the ages. Moreover, morality is independent also with regard to its *purposes*, for man is guided not by the ostensible utility of this or that way of acting, but by the feeling of *inner harmony within himself*, i. e., by the feeling of satisfaction or dissatisfaction after the act.

Thus Shaftesbury (as was already pointed out by Wundt) boldly proclaimed the independent origin of the moral sense. And he also understood how a moral code was inevitably developed from this primary source. Moreover, he categorically denied the origin of moral conceptions from the utilitarian considerations of the usefulness or harmfulness of a given way of acting. All the moral rules of religions and laws are the derivative, secondary forms, the primary basis of which is constituted by the hereditary moral instincts.

In this point the naturalistic moral philosophy of Shaftesbury completely diverges from the naturalistic philosophy of the French thinkers of the eighteenth century, including the Encyclopædists, who preferred to adhere in moral questions to the viewpoint of Epicurus and his followers. It is interesting to note that this divergence was already noticeable in the founders of the new philosophical movement in England and in France, i. e., in Bacon, who at once took the scientific, naturalistic standpoint, and in Descartes, who had not yet quite clearly defined his position.

At any rate, Shaftesbury's point of view was assumed also by Darwin (in his second fundamental work, "The Descent of Man"). And the same point of view must inevitably be adopted by every psychologist who is free from preconceived notions. We see in Shaftesbury, too, a predecessor of Guyau, in the ideas which the latter developed in his book, "Morality Without Obligation or

Sanction." The same conclusions are reached by modern Natural Science; so that after having studied mutual aid among animals and primitive savages, I was able to say that it would be easier for man to revert to walking on all fours, than to renounce his moral instincts, for these instincts had been developing in the animal world long before the appearance of man on the earth.[28]

Hutcheson, a pupil of Shaftesbury, more emphatically than any of his contemporaries, came out in favour of the inherent moral feeling. Shaftesbury did not explain sufficiently why disinterested striving for the good of others takes the upper hand of the manifestations of personal egoism,—and by this omission he left the road open for religion. Hutcheson, although he was much more believing and much more respectful toward religion than Shaftesbury, demonstrated more emphatically than any other thinker of his time the independent nature of our moral judgments.

In his works, "Philosophiae moralis institutio compendiaria" [29] and "System of moral philosophy," Hutcheson attempted to prove that we are not at all guided by considerations of the *utility* of the benevolent acts and of the *harmfulness* of the non-benevolent, but that we feel mental *satisfaction* after an act directed toward the good of others and that we call such an act "moral" before indulging in any speculations as to the utility or the harmfulness of our act. We feel mental dissatisfaction as the result of non-benevolent acts, just as we are pleased by harmony in the proportions of a building or in music, and are displeased by absence of harmony in architecture or in music. Reason, per se, would not be able to urge us to an act leading to the common good, if we had no natural bent to act in that manner. Therefore Hutcheson ascribes to reason a fairly modest, perhaps too modest a place. Reason, he held, only puts in order our sensations and impressions, and it plays only an educative part: it enables us to experience those highest delights which are of

[28] [See Appendix, page 339, below.]—Trans. Note.
[29] [Glasgow, 1742; Rotterdam, 1745. The *System of Moral Philosophy,* appeared in London, 1755; 2 vols.]—Trans. Note.

greatest importance for our happiness. Through reason, we know the Universal order and the ruling Spirit, but from reason also result those diversities in the interpretation of moral and immoral which lead peoples in different stages of development to establish most varied moral, and sometimes most immoral rules and customs. Shameful deeds committed at various times, originated in erroneous mental judgments, while moral sense, left to itself, was incapable of supplying a moral decision in a difficult case. [Book I, ch. V, § 7.]

However, it would be more correct to say, we may remark, that the moral feeling was always against these disgraceful deeds, and that at times separate individuals rebelled against them, but did not have on their side the necessary power to stamp them out. It should be also remembered to what extent religions are to be blamed for many moral disgraces. Denying the rights of reason in the development of morality, religions constantly urged upon men obsequiousness toward the rulers, and hatred of those following other religions, culminating in the brutalities of the Inquisition and the annihilation of entire cities due to religious disputes.

It is true Hutcheson saw the principal value of religion in the infinitely high qualities which we ascribe to God,—he saw, in fact, that by creating *social* worship it gratified the social needs of man. There is no doubt that religion, like any other social institution, aids the creation of an ideal. But as various writers on morality have pointed out, the principal part in social morality is played not so much by ideals, as by the daily habits of social life. Thus the Christian and the Buddhistic saints unquestionably serve as models and to a certain extent as stimuli to moral life, but we must not forget that the majority of people have a standing excuse for not imitating them in their lives: "Well, we are not saints." As regards the social influence of religion, other social institutions and the daily routine of life prove to be much stronger than the teachings of religion. The communistic mode of life of many primitive peoples maintains in them the feeling and the habits of solidarity much better than does the Christian religion. In the course of my conversations with the "savages" during my travels in Siberia and Manchuria, it used to be very difficult for me to explain how it was that in our Christian societies people frequently die from hunger, while side by side with them other people are living in affluence. To a Tungus, an Aleut, and to many others, such a situation is utterly incomprehensible: they are heathen, but they are men of a tribal mode of life.

Hutcheson's chief merit was in his endeavour to explain why disinterested propensities may, and do, get the upper hand of the narrowly personal aspirations. He explains this fact by the presence in us of the feeling of *inner* approval, which always makes its appearance when the social feeling attains preponderance over the self-directed aspirations. He thus freed ethics from the necessity of giving pre-eminence either to religion, or to considerations of the utility to the individual of a given act. His teaching, however, had a substantial defect: like his predecessors he made no distinction between that which morality holds *obligatory,* and that which it considers merely *desirable,* so that as a result he failed to notice that in all moral teachings and conceptions the *obligatory element is based on the recognition of equity by feeling and by reason.*

This defect, however, as we shall see later, is common also to the majority of modern thinkers.

I shall not consider in detail the teaching of the German contemporary of Shaftesbury and Hutcheson—Gottfried Wilhelm Leibnitz, —though there is a great deal of instructive matter in his critique of both Spinoza and Locke, and in his attempt to combine theology with philosophy and to reconcile the currents of thought that found expression in Catholicism and in various Protestant teachings, as well as in Scotch and English ethics. As is known, Leibnitz, simultaneously with Newton, introduced into mathematics a new and a very fruitful method of the investigation of phenomena through the study of infinitesimal changes. He also proposed a theory of the structure of matter similar to the modern atomic theory. But neither his all-embracing intellect, nor his brilliant exposition helped him to reconcile philosophical pantheism with the Christian faith, or to reconcile ethics based on the study of the fundamental properties of human nature, with the Christian ethics based on faith in a life after death.

But though Leibnitz failed in his attempt, he nevertheless aided the development of ethics by pointing out the importance of the instinct inherent in all men—socially—for the growth of the fundamental moral conceptions in man. He showed, too, the significance of the *development of will* in building the ideals, and also the moral character of the individual. Not enough attention had been paid to these factors.

There is no doubt that Leibnitz, in his mental make-up and his philosophy, could not part with the theological Christian ethics or with the thought that faith in life-after-death strengthens the moral powers of man. But at times he so closely approached the atheism of Bayle and Shaftesbury that he undoubtedly strengthened the influence of their doctrines. On the other hand, his very vacillation between the religious and the non-religious morality inevitably led to the thought that there is, in the very essence of morality, something besides the instincts, the passions, and the feelings; that in its judgments of the "moral" and "immoral" phenomena, our reason is guided not only by the considerations of personal or social *utility*, as was asserted by the school of the intellectualists—the followers of Epicurus; that there is in our reason something more general, more generally recognized. Leibnitz himself did not reach the conclusion that the supreme principle involved in reason is the conception of *justice*, but he prepared the way for it. On the other hand, he so beautifully expressed the need of a lofty mode of thought and of acts full of what is called self-sacrifice; he pictured so well the rôle of the *ideal* in the development of morality, that he prepared thereby the ground for an important modern differentiation in our moral conceptions. He led to the separation of that which must

176

serve as the indisputable basis of all of social life, i. e., justice, from that which man frequently gives to others in excess of *ordinary justice*, namely,— readiness for self-sacrifice.[30]

[30] The principal philosophical works of Leibnitz are: *Essais de theodicée sur la bonté de Dieu, la liberté de l'homme, et l'origine du mal*, 1710; *Nouveaux essais sur l'entendement humain* (a refutation of Locke, written in 1704, appeared only in 1760); *Système nouveau de la nature et de la communication des substances*. [The first work appeared in Amsterdam; the second, in Amsterdam and Leipzig, 1760 and 1765, (English translation by A. G. Langley, N. Y., 1896; and see John Dewey's critical exposition of the work in G. S. Morris, *German Philos. Classics*, Chicago, 1882); the *Système nouveau* is dated 1695,—see Leibnitz, *Œuvres philosophiques*, Ed. Janet, 1866, vol. 2, pp. 526 ff.]—Trans. Note.

CHAPTER VIII

DEVELOPMENT OF MORAL TEACHINGS IN THE MODERN ERA
(17th and 18th Centuries.—continued)

THE liberation of science from the Church's yoke—and consequently also of ethical teachings,—came about in France approximately at the same time as in England. The French thinker, René Descartes, took the same lead in this movement as did Francis Bacon in England, and their principal works appeared almost simultaneously.[1]

But due to various causes, the French movement took a somewhat different turn from the English; and in France, libertarian ideas penetrated to much wider circles and exercised a much deeper influence throughout Europe than the movement originated by Bacon, which created a revolution in science and in scientific speculation.

The liberating movement in France began at the end of the sixteenth century, but it followed a path different from that in England where it took the form of the Protestant movement and of the peasant and townsfolk revolution. In France the Revolution broke out only at the end of the eighteenth century, but libertarian ideas began to spread widely in French society long before the Revolution. Literature was the chief conductor of these ideas. The first to express libertarian ideas in French literature was Rabelais (1483(?)–1553), whom Michel Montaigne followed in spirit.

Montaigne was one of the most brilliant of French writers. He was the first to express in a light, easily readable form, precisely from the standpoint of "plain common sense," bold and most "heretical" views about religion.

[1] Bacon's *Novum Organum* appeared in 1620. Descartes's *Discours de la méthode* was published in 1637 [Paris; English translations, Lond., 1649; Edinburgh, 1850.]—Trans. Note.

MORAL TEACHINGS IN THE MODERN ERA

Montaigne's famous book, "Essais," which appeared in 1583, met with great success; it went through many editions and was read everywhere in Europe, and later even the prominent writers of the eighteenth and nineteenth centuries willingly recognized Montaigne as one of their teachers. Montaigne's book aided considerably in the liberation of ethics from the old scholastic dogmas.

In his "Essais" Montaigne gave nothing but a series of frank confessions about his own character and the motives of his judgments and acts, and also about the character of the people of his circle, for he was intimate with the best society. And he judged human actions as a refined, somewhat humanitarian Epicurean, whose egotism was softened by a slight tinge of philosophy; he exposed the religious hypocrisy behind which other epicurean egoists and their religious mentors are accustomed to hide. Thus, owing to his great literary talent, he prepared the soil for that critical, sarcastic tone with respect to religion, which later, in the eighteenth century, permeated the whole of French literature. Unfortunately, neither Montaigne, nor his followers up to the present time, have subjected to the same sort of popular, sarcastic critique from within, the machine of the state government, which has now taken the place of the hierarchy of the Church in ruling the social life of men.

A somewhat more serious inquiry, but still in the same style, was undertaken somewhat later by the theologian and father-confessor of Queen Margaret, Pierre Charron (1541–1603). His book "Traité de la Sagesse" (Treatise on Wisdom), appeared in 1601 and at once became popular. Although Charron remained a priest, he was in reality a true sceptic, and his scepticism was even sharper than that of Montaigne. In discussing similar doctrines in different religions—Christian and pagan—Charron showed how much they have in common and how little morality needs religion.[2]

[2] Jodl cites, in his *Geschichte, der Ethik als philos. Wissenschaft*, a passage from the first edition of the *Traité de la sagesse*, 1601, which was omitted in the later editions. In this passage Charron plainly states that he "would also

179

ETHICS: ORIGIN AND DEVELOPMENT

Generally speaking, this sceptical and at the same time realistic attitude toward religion later formed the distinguishing feature of French literature of the eighteenth century, and manifested itself with especial prominence in the writings of Voltaire and of the Encyclopædists, as well as in the novel, and particularly in the dramatic works, of the pre-revolutionary period, and finally in the Revolution itself.

Bacon gave science a new and a very fruitful method of studying natural phenomena,—the inductive method,—and thereby made possible the building up of a science about life on the globe and about the Universe, without the interference of religious and metaphysical explanations. Descartes, however, continued in some measure to use the deductive method. His thought preceded the discoveries to which the inductive investigation of nature was to lead, and he attempted to explain by means of physico-mathematical theorems such regions in the life of nature which had not yet yielded to scientific explanation,—the regions which we are only now beginning to penetrate. He always remained, however, on the firm ground of the physical interpretation of phenomena. Even in his boldest suppositions about the structure of matter he remained a physicist, and endeavoured to express his hypotheses in mathematical language.

Publishing his works in France, which had not yet freed itself from the yoke of the Catholic Church, as had England, Descartes was compelled to express his conclusions very guardedly.[3]

like to see devotion and religiousness, but not in order that they should implant in man morality, which is born with him and is given to him by nature, but in order to crown morality with completeness." [Vol. 1, page 189, Stuttgart; Berlin 1912.] This quotation shows that the interpretation of morality as an inherent faculty of man was far more widespread among thinkers than is apparent from their writings. [For a note on Charron's *Traité*, see *supra*, p. 139.]—Trans. Note.

[3] Thus, for example, from Descartes's letters to his friend Mersenne, in July, 1633 and January, 1634, cited by Lange in his *History of Materialism* (Note 69, Part II, vol. 1), it is seen that upon learning of the second arrest of Galileo by the Inquisition, and of the verdict against his book,—most likely because of his opinion about the rotation of the earth,—Descartes was ready to

MORAL TEACHINGS IN THE MODERN ERA

In 1628 he had to leave France and to settle in Holland, where he published his "Essais philosophiques" in 1637. This book included his fundamental work, "Discours de la méthode," which exercised a deep influence upon the development of philosophical thought and laid the foundation of the mechanistic interpretation of nature.

Descartes gave but little special attention to the question of morality and its relation to religion, and his views on moral matters can be learned only from his letters to the Swedish princess, Christina.

Even the relation of science to religion interested him but little, and his attitude toward the Church was very reserved, like that of all the French writers of his time. The burning of Giordano Bruno was still well remembered. But Descartes's attempt to explain the life of the Universe through physical phenomena which are subject to accurate mathematical investigation—(this method received the name of "Cartesianism")—so definitely set aside all the teachings of the Church, that the Cartesian philosophy soon became just as powerful a weapon for liberating knowledge from faith, as Bacon's "inductive method" had proved to be.

Descartes carefully avoided all attacks upon the teachings of the Church; he even advanced a series of proofs of the existence of God. These proofs, however, are based on such abstract reasoning that they produced the impression of being inserted only for the purpose of avoiding the accusation of atheism. But the scientific part of Descartes's teaching was so constructed that it contained no evidence of the interference of the Creator's will. Descartes's God, like Spinoza's God in later times, was the great Universe as a whole, Nature itself. When he wrote of the psychic life of man he endeavoured to give it a physiological interpretation despite the limited knowledge then available in the field of physiology.

renounce the same opinion, which he was about to express in his work. There are also indications of other concessions of this kind. [Friedrich Albert Lange, *Gesch. der Materialismus*, Iserlohn, two vols. in one: Eng. tr. by Ernest C. Thomas, Lond. & Bost., 1879-81, 3 vols.]—Trans. Note.

But in the world of the exact sciences, particularly in the field of the mathematical investigation of physical phenomena, Descartes's accomplishment was considerable. It is safe to say that he invented a new science through his methods of mathematical investigation, especially in analytical geometry, which he re-created. He not only discovered new methods but he also applied them to the investigation of some of the most difficult problems of universal physics, namely,—to the study of the vortex-motion of the infinitesimal particles of matter in cosmic space. Only now, in its study of the universal ether, has modern physics again approached these fundamental problems of cosmic life.

In giving science a new method of penetrating into the mysteries of nature, Descartes, like Bacon, demonstrated at the same time the power of science as compared to the impotence of superstitions and of intuitive, i. e., conjectural, explanations.

Shortly before, Copernicus had proved that our globe is but one of the satellites of the sun, and that the innumerable stars which we see are millions of worlds similar to our solar system. Thus the enigma of the Universe unfolded before man in all its grandeur, and the human mind began to seek the explanation of cosmic existence. Bacon was the first to assert that experiment and inductive method can help us understand this life, while Descartes endeavoured to penetrate into cosmic being and to divine at least some of its fundamental laws—the laws that are operative not only within the limits of our solar system, but also far beyond its borders, in the stellar world.

It is true, that in seeking the bases for a knowledge of nature in mathematical thinking, as was the dream of Pythagoras and his pupils, and later of Giordano Bruno, Descartes thereby increased the importance of metaphysics in the philosophy of the seventeenth and the eighteenth century; and he helped this philosophy to bear a semblance of science in its search for truth, not through observation and experiment, but through abstract thinking. But, on the other hand, Descartes put physics on a basis which enabled it, in the nineteenth century, to make the discovery that the essence of heat and electricity is in the vibrations of ponderable particles; and thus physics was able to discover towards the end of the century a series of invisible vibrations, among which the Roentgen rays were only an introduction to a vast region where several other discoveries are already germinating, just as astounding as these rays, or as wireless telephony.[4]

Bacon founded a new method of scientific research and foreshadowed the discoveries of Lamarck and Darwin, by pointing out that under the influence of changing conditions Nature continually evolves new species of animals and plants, while Descartes, by his "theory of vortices," foreshadowed in a sense the scientific discoveries of the nineteenth century.

In speaking of Epicurus I pointed out the great influence exercised by his teaching for five centuries in the Greek and then in the Roman world. The Stoics stubbornly opposed this teaching, but even such prominent representatives of Stoicism as Seneca and Epictetus were fascinated by Epicureanism. It was vanquished only by Christianity; but even among the Christians, as Guyau remarked, Lucian, and even St. Augustine, paid tribute to it.

When, in Renaissance times, there began the search for and the study of the monuments of Greco-Roman learning, the thinkers of various tendencies, who wished to be liberated from the yoke of the Church, began to turn with special affection to the writings of Epicurus and his followers: Diogenes Laertius, Cicero, and especially Lucretius, who was one of the earliest predecessors of the modern scientific interpretation of nature.

The chief strength of the Epicurean teaching, as we have seen, lay in the fact that in rejecting everything supernatural and miraculous, it rejected at the same time the supernatural origin of the moral sense in man. It explained this sense by the rational striving for

[4] See the article, *Unsuspected Radiations*, in the review of the scientific discoveries of the nineteenth century printed in *The Annual Report of the Smithsonian Institute*, for 1900, and in the magazine, *Nineteenth Century*, for December 1900,—[an article by Kropotkin.]—Trans. Note.

happiness. This happiness, according to Epicurus, consists not merely in the gratification of physical needs, but in the greatest possible fullness of life, i. e., in the gratification of the highest needs and feelings, including the need of friendship and sociality. It was in this form that "Epicureanism" began to be advocated by those who rejected theological morality.

Already in the second half of the sixteenth century Montaigne took an exactly similar stand. Somewhat later, in the seventeenth century, the Epicurean viewpoint of moral questions was adopted by the philosopher Pierre Gassendi, a learned priest, and a physicist, mathematician, and thinker.

In 1624, when he was a professor of philosophy in South France, he published in the Latin language a work openly opposed to the teachings of Aristotle, which then dominated the ecclesiastical schools.[5] In astronomy Gassendi pitted against Aristotle the views of Copernicus, who, as is known, proved that the Earth is not at all the centre of the Universe, but merely one of the lesser satellites of the Sun. Owing to these views Copernicus was considered by the

---

[5] *Exercitationes paradoxicae—adversus Aristotelae.* Upon the insistence of his friends, however, he had to omit five chapters from this work, because the Church, resting its case on the books which she recognized as sacred, staunchly supported Aristotle and Ptolemy, who taught that the earth is situated in the centre of the Universe, and that the sun, the planets, and the stars revolve around it; moreover, only five years previously [in 1619] Vanini was burned at the stake for a similar heretical work. In addition, Gassendi refuted the teaching of Descartes on the structure of matter, and expounded his own view closely approaching the modern atomic theory. Two of his works about Epicurus, Gassendi published himself at the time when he occupied a chair at the Collège de France; his fundamental work, however, *Syntagma philosophiae Epicuri* appeared only after his death. [Amsterdam, 1678. Gassendi's other works on Epicurus are: *Animadversiones,* etc., Lugdium, 1649, 3 vols.; *De Vita et moribus Epicuri,* Haggae—Comitum, 1656, (2nd. ed.). See G. S. Brett's *Philosophy of Gassendi,* Lond., 1908. According to Mr. Brett, the *Exercitationes adversus Aristotelae* was never finished. Book I was published in 1624, as Kropotkin says, and fragments of Book II were included in Gassendi's collected works. In 1624 Gassendi still held his professorship at Digne in Provence, in addition to a canonry at Grenoble. For Vanini (Lucilio, *called* Julius Cæsar) 1585-1619, see the French trans. of his works, *Œuvres philosophiques,* Paris, 1842; also Victor Cousin, *Vanini: Ses écrits, sa vie et sa mort,* ("Revue des deux mondes", Dec. 1843).]—Trans. Note.

Church a dangerous heretic. And in moral questions Gassendi took the exact position of Epicurus.

Man, asserted Gassendi, seeks in life, first of all, "happiness and pleasure," but both these conceptions, as was already pointed out by the Greek philosopher, are to be interpreted in a wide sense: not only in the sense of bodily pleasures, for the sake of which man is capable of harming others, but primarily in the sense of the inner peace of the soul which can be attained only when man sees in others not enemies but comrades. Thus the writings of Gassendi answered to the need of the educated classes of that time, who were already trying to throw off the yoke of the Church and of superstition, although they had not yet realized the need of the scientific interpretation of Nature in general. This tendency urged them so much more toward the new ideal of a social life based on equity among men. This ideal began to take form somewhat later, in the eighteenth century.

The time of Bacon and Descartes, i. e., the time of the revival of the scientific study of nature, marks also the turning point in ethics. The thinkers began to look for the natural sources of morality in human nature itself. Hobbes, who lived somewhat later than the two founders, already named, of modern natural science, (his principal works appeared in the middle of the seventeenth century, i. e., between 1642–1658), developed, as we have seen, a complete system of ethics freed from religion.

Unfortunately, as I have pointed out, Hobbes set out with an utterly erroneous conception of primitive man and of human nature in general, and consequently, he was led to conclusion entirely fallacious. But a new path in the study of morality was opened, and from that time a series of thinkers laboured to prove that the moral element in man is not the result of fear of punishment in this or a later life, but the result of the natural development of the really fundamental properties of human nature. Moreover, in proportion as modern humanity frees itself from fears inculcated by religions, there is an ever-increasing need to erect nobler and finer edifices of social life, and thus to raise the ideal of moral man to ever higher perfection.

We have seen already what the pantheist Spinoza,—the follower of Descartes,—and also his contemporary, Locke, thought in this connection. But even more definite were the pronouncements on this subject by the French contemporary of Locke,—Pierre Bayle.

Having been brought up on the philosophy of Descartes, Bayle, through his remarkable Encyclopædia,[6] laid the foundation of a scientific interpretation of nature that soon acquired tremendous importance in the intellectual development of mankind due to Hume, Voltaire, Diderot, and the Encyclopædists generally. He was the first to advocate openly the liberation of moral teachings from their religious motivation.

Starting with the definitions given by the Church itself, Bayle proceeded to prove that lack of faith might be considered a source or a support of the evil way of living only if we are to limit the meaning of faith to love of God, as the Supreme Moral Ideal. In reality, however, this is not the case. Faith, as is known, has a different character and is combined with numerous superstitions. Besides, mere adherence to certain formulæ, or even a sincere faith in the truth of religious dogmas, does not give the strength to follow them; and owing to this circumstance all religions add to their teachings threats of punishment for non-observance. On the other hand, morality, as is known, can very well exist side by side with atheism.

It becomes, therefore, necessary to investigate the possibility that

[6] *Dictionnaire historique et critique*, which appeared at Rotterdam in 1697, first in two volumes, and later, in 1820, in 16 volumes. [Paris]. Bayle expressed for the first time his anti-religious views in 1680 in connection with the appearance of a comet and the superstitions that it called forth, in a pamphlet entitled *Pensées diverses sur la comète*. This pamphlet was, of course, prohibited soon after its appearance. [*Pensées diverses écrites—à l'occasion de la Comète*, 1683; an earlier Letter on the appearance of the comet (in 1680),—insisting that there was nothing miraculous in the passing of comets—was written in 1680.]—Trans. Note.

human nature itself contains moral principles, resulting from the social life of men.

Guided by these considerations Bayle regarded the first principles of morality as an "eternal law,"—not of divine origin, but as a fundamental law of nature, or rather, its fundamental fact.

Unfortunately, Bayle's mind was pre-eminently that of a sceptic and a critic, and not of a builder of a new system. He did not develop, therefore, his idea of the natural origin of morality in man. But he was not permitted to carry his critique to its conclusions, for he aroused such animosity in the ecclesiastical camp and among the ruling classes, that he had to temper considerably the expression of his ideas. Nevertheless, his examination of both orthodox and moderate religiousness was so strong and witty, that he may be considered a direct predecessor of Helvétius, Voltaire, and the Encyclopædists of the eighteenth century.

La Rochefoucauld, a contemporary of Bayle's, though he was not a philosopher who created his own philosophical system, nevertheless did perhaps even more than Bayle to prepare in France the ground for the elaboration of a morality independent of religion. This he accomplished through the influence of his book, "Maximes." La Rochefoucauld was a man of the world, constantly moving in the highest society. As a keen psychologist and an attentive observer he clearly saw the emptiness of the upper layer of French society of his time, its hypocrisy and its vanity. He saw that in the final analysis the people of his circle were guided solely by the desire of personal gain or personal advantage. To La Rochefoucauld it was apparent that formal religion does not restrain men from immoral acts, and he painted in dark colours the life of his contemporaries. On the basis of his observations of this life he came to the conclusion that egoism is the sole motive power of human activity, and this thought underlies his book. Man, according to La Rochefoucauld, loves only himself; even in others he loves only himself. All human passions and attachments are merely variations of thinly disguised egoism. La Rochefoucauld explained by egoistic motives even the best feelings of man: in bravery and courage he saw a manifestation of vanity, in generosity the manifestation of pride, in largesse mere ambition, in modesty—hypocrisy, etc. However, in spite of his pessimism, La Rochefoucauld greatly aided the awakening of critical thought in France; and his book, "Maximes," and the work of his contemporary, La Bruyère, "Caractères," were the favourite and the most widely distributed books in France at the end of the seventeenth and the beginning of the eighteenth century.[7]

La Bruyère was less pessimistic than La Rochefoucauld, though he, too, depicts men as unjust and ungrateful,—pitiless egoists by nature. La Bruyère thought, however, that they deserve clemency, because they are made evil by the evil conditions of life; man is unfortunate rather than corrupt.

However, neither Bayle, nor La Rochefoucauld, nor La Bruyère, though they denied religious morality, was able to evolve an ethical system based on purely natural laws. This task was attempted somewhat later by La Mettrie, Helvétius, and Holbach.

La Mettrie was one of the most rebellious minds of the eighteenth century; in his writings he declared war upon all metaphysical, religious, and political traditions, and like Hobbes, he proceeded to elaborate a materialistic cosmology with the same daring that marked its development in our time, in the 'fifties and the 'sixties of the nineteenth century. In his works, "Histoire naturelle de l'âme humaine," "L'homme-plante," "L'homme machine," he denied the immortality of the soul and advocated materialistic ideas.[8] The very titles of his books, especially "Man-Machine," which appeared in Paris in 1748, show how he interpreted human nature. "Our

---

[7] [La Rochefoucauld, *Réflexions ou sentences et maximes morales*, The Hague, 1664. La Bruyère, *Caractères*, Paris, 1688.]—Trans. Note.

[8] [La Mettrie (Julian Offray de), *L'Homme machine*, Leyden 1748, is translated into English as *Man a Machine*, Lond., 1750. and, by G. S. Bussey, Chicago, 1912. The latter volume includes extracts from the *Essai sur l'origine de l'âme humaine* (1752); (La Haye 1745). *L'Homme-plante*, Potsdam, 1748.] —Trans. Note.

soul," wrote La Mettrie, "receives everything from feeling and sensations, and nature contains nothing beyond matter subjected to mechanical laws." For his ideas La Mettrie was exiled from France, and his book, "Man-Machine," was burned by an executioner in Paris. Simultaneously with La Mettrie, materialistic philosophy was expounded by Condillac (1715–1780), who developed his ideas in two works: "Treatise on the Origin of Human Knowledge" (1746), and "Treatise on Sensations" (1754).[9]

The eighteenth century was a remarkable period in the history of the development of mankind. A succession of thinkers, who became prominent in England and in France, rebuilt completely the very bases for our thinking,—for our outlook both on the external universe and in our understanding of ourselves and our moral conceptions. The French philosopher, Claude Helvétius, attempted, in the middle of the eighteenth century, to sum up these conquests of scientific thought in his famous book "On the Intellect." [10] In this book Helvétius expounded in a clearly understandable and vivid form all the scientific achievements of the eighteenth century and of the end of the seventeenth, especially in the field of morality.

At the request of the Parisian clergy, Helvétius' book was burned in 1759, which did not prevent it from enjoying a still greater success. The essential features of Helvétius' ideas are as follows: man is a "sensual" animal, and at the basis of human nature lie the sensations, from which result all the forms of human activity, directed by pleasure or suffering. Therefore, the highest moral law lies in following pleasure and avoiding pain; these two enable us to judge the properties of things and the actions of others. We call the pleasant and the useful—virtue, and its opposite we call vice. In his noblest and most disinterested acts man is but seeking pleas-

---

[9] [Condillac's *Essai sur l'origine des connaissances humaines*, Amsterdam 1746; *Traité des sensations*, 1754; Eng. trans., by Nugent, Lond., 1756.]—Trans. Note.

[10] [Helvétius' *De l'Esprit*, 2 vols., Paris, 1758. Eng. trans. Lond., 1810.]— Trans. Note.

ure, and he performs these acts when the pleasure which they afford exceeds the suffering which they may possibly entail. In the task of developing moral character Helvétius ascribed great importance to education, which must aim to make man realize the fact that our personal interests consist in their blending with the interests of others.

Helvétius' philosophy and his views met with great success, and exercised a strong influence upon French society by preparing the ground for the ideas of the Encyclopædists, who arose in France in the second half of the eighteenth century.

In his writings Holbach followed the trend of the philosophical views of La Mettrie and Helvétius. He expounded his ideas on morality in his book "The Social System," which appeared in 1773. This book was condemned by the French Parliament in 1776.

Holbach endeavoured to ground ethics on a purely naturalistic basis, without any metaphysical assumptions. He maintained that man is always striving for happiness: his very nature urges him to avoid suffering and to seek pleasure. In his search for happiness man is guided by Reason, i. e., by the knowledge of true happiness and of the means for its attainment.[11] Justice consists in permitting man to avail himself, or in not interfering with his availing himself, of his abilities, his rights, and of everything necessary for life and happiness.[12]

Holbach's ideas were shared by most of the French Encyclopædists, who were on very friendly terms with Holbach. His salon in Paris was the gathering place for the most prominent thinkers of that time: Diderot, d'Alembert, Grimm, Rousseau, Marmontel, and others. Through them Holbach's ideas received further development and became one of the fundamental elements in the philosophic system of the Encyclopædists.[13]

The Encyclopædists and their philosophy are the principal and

[11] *Système social*, Vol. 1, p. 17. [Lond. 1773, 3 vols. in 1.]—Trans. Note.
[12] [*Ibid*. Vol. 1, p. 104.]
[13] Holbach's ideas were to a great extent utilized also by the English Utilitarians.

the most characteristic expression of the spirit of the eighteenth century. The Encyclopædia sums up all the achievements of mankind in the realm of science and politics up to the end of that period. It constitutes a real monument of the scientific thought of the eighteenth century, for it was produced by the collaboration of all the liberally minded, notable men of France; and they evolved that spirit of destructive criticism which later served to inspire the best men of the Great Revolution.

As is known, the initiators and the inspirers of the Encyclopædia were the philosophers Diderot (1713–1784) and d'Alembert (1717–1783). The Encyclopædists aimed at the liberation of the human mind through knowledge; they took a hostile attitude toward the government and toward all the traditional ideas upon which the old social order rested. No wonder, therefore, that both the government and the clergy, from the very outset, declared war against the Encyclopædists and put many obstacles in the way of the Encyclopædia.

The ethics of the Encyclopædists was, of course, in accord with the ideas prevalent at that time in France. Its basic principles may be stated as follows: man strives for happiness, and for its attainment men combine into societies; all men have equal rights to happiness, and consequently to the means of reaching this happiness; therefore, the just is identified with the useful. Misunderstandings that arise from conflicts between various rights should be adjusted by the laws, which are the expression of the common will and which must sanctify only that which is useful for the happiness of all. The same general tendency was followed by Abbé Raynal (1713–1796), whose work, "History of the Settlements and Trade of the Europeans in the Indies," was written so much in the spirit of the Encyclopædia that by many it was ascribed to Diderot. It was written in such an attractive style that it went through several editions in a short time. In that book the "natural state" of the savages was depicted in true colours, and the truth was re-established as to the real nature of primitive men, whom Catholic missionaries had been in the habit of painting in the darkest colours as the imps of hell. Moreover, Raynal warmly advocated the necessity of the liberation of the negroes, so that his book was later nicknamed "The Bible of the Negroes." [14]

The same humanitarian and scientific spirit manifested itself also in the writings of the Italian, Beccaria (1738-1794). He came out against cruelty, and advocated the abolition of torture and executions. He preached in Italy the ideas of the French Encyclopædists, and in 1764 he wrote "Dei delitti e delle pene" (On Crimes and Punishment).[15] The book was at once translated into French by André Morellet; and Voltaire, Diderot, and Helvétius wrote additions to it. Beccaria proved in his book that the harsh punishments then practiced in Europe not only fail to eradicate crime, but, on the contrary, make the general mode of life more savage and cruel. He advocated the enlightenment of the masses as a way to prevent crime.

At the end of the seventeenth and the beginning of the eighteenth century there appeared in France numerous "Utopias," i. e., attempts to picture an ideal human society based on reason. All these Utopias were based on faith in the power of Reason, and on the faith that morality is the inherent property of human nature. The most remarkable of all the French writers who produced such Utopias was Abbé Morelly. In 1753 he published a communistic novel, "Naufrage des îles flottantes," [16] where he attempts to prove that peoples may attain the happy life not through political reforms but through conformity with the laws of nature. Morelly

[14] [Abbé G. T. F. Raynal, *Hist. philosophique et politique des établissemens et du commerce des Européens dans les deux Indes.* Amsterdam, 1773-74, 7 vols; Paris, 1820, 12 vols. Eng. tr., Lond. 1776, 5 vols., and 1778, 8 vols.; also later editions. Extracts from this work appeared in Philadelphia, (Pa.), in 1775.]—Trans. Note.

[15] [Cesara B. Beccaria's book appeared in a new edition, Edinburgh, 1801; Morellet's French translation was published at Lausanne, 1776; English versions came in 1767, London; 1777, Dublin; 1778, Edinburgh; 1793, Philadelphia: 1809, N. Y.; 1872, Albany; and in 1880, London, in James A. Farrer's *Crimes and Punishment,* pp. 109-251.]—Trans. Note.

[16] [*Naufrage des îles flottantes,* Messine, 1753.]—Trans. Note.

developed his communistic ideas more in detail in his work "Code de la Nature: ou le véritable esprit de ses loix" (Paris, 1755). In this work Morelly describes in detail the communistic structure of society, where nothing can be the property of an individual, except the objects of daily use.

Morelly's books exercised a mighty influence in the prerevolutionary period, and for a long time served as a model for all the plans of reorganization of society along communistic principles. These books, most likely, inspired Mably (1709–1785), who, in his works "Entretiens de Phocion sur le rapport de la morale avec la politique," (1763) and "Le Droit et les devoirs du citoyen," [17] advocated communism and community of property *(communité des biens)*. According to Mably, greed is the main obstacle in the road of mankind to a happy and moral life. It is necessary, therefore, to destroy first of all this "eternal enemy of equality" and to create a social system where no one would have a motive to seek happiness in augmenting his material welfare. Later these ideas inspired Gracchus Babeuf, who, together with his friends Buonarroti and Sylvain Maréchal, formed the "conspiracy of the Equals," for which Babeuf was executed in 1797.[18]

Side by side with the Utopian critique of the communists, in the middle of the eighteenth century, the physiocrats, headed by Quesnay [19] (1694–1774), undertook a purely scientific scrutiny of contemporary society, and for the first time pointed out the fundamental fault of the social system,—the division of society into

[17] [Mably's *Le Droit*, etc., Kell, 1789; Paris (?), 1789.]—Trans. Note.
[18] [Caius Gracchus (François Noël) Babeuf; Filippo Michele Buonarroti,— see his *Conspiration pour l'égalité dite de Babeuf*, Bruxelles, 2 vols. in 1, 1828; (Eng. tr., James B. O'Brien, Lond., 1836); Sylvian Maréchal, *Le Jugement dernier des rois* (a one-act play, in prose,) in L. E. D. Moland's *Théâtre de la Révolution*, Paris, 1877. On these men and their conspiracy, see Kropotkin's *French Revolution;* also, Victor Advielle, *Histoire de Gracchus Babeuf et du babouvisme*, Paris, 1884, 2 vols.; Ernest B. Bax, *The Episode of the French Revolution: being a history of Gracchus Babeuf and the conspiracy of the Equals*, Lond., 1911.]—Trans. Note.
[19] [Dr. François Quesnay, *Physiocratie*, Leyden, 1767-8, 2 vols.]—Trans. Note.

the producing class and into the parasitic proprietor class. They also raised for the first time the question of the nationalization of land. The need of social reorganization was being felt more and more urgently in France, and in the middle of the eighteenth century Baron Montesquieu, the greatest thinker of his time, came forth with his critique of the old order.

Montesquieu's first work, in which he subjected despotism and the social system in general to critical examination, was the "Persian Letters." In 1748 he published his principal work, "The Spirit of Laws," which is one of the remarkable productions of that epoch. In his book, "The Spirit of Laws," Montesquieu introduced a new interpretation of human society and its usages and laws, which he regarded as natural results of the development of social life under differing conditions.

This work of Montesquieu's exercised a vast influence upon all the thinkers of the second half of the eighteenth century and inspired many investigations in the same direction in the beginning of the nineteenth. Especially important in Montesquieu's remarkable work was the application of the inductive method to the question of the development of social institutions,—in the strict sense in which Bacon understood the method; some of his own findings were of no little importance for his time. His critique of the monarchical power, his prevision of the peaceful mode of life in proportion as the industrial form of the social system develops, his crusade against cruel punishment for civil crimes, etc., became the watchword of all the liberal movements of Europe.

The influence exerted by Montesquieu on the thought of his time was far-reaching,—but by its style and manner of presentation his book was accessible only to educated people. Montesquieu could not, or perhaps simply would not, write for the popular masses. Special qualities are necessary for this purpose: mainly a style that commands the attention of the mind and that makes clear all the ideas expounded. These qualities were possessed in a high degree by the two philosophers of that time: Voltaire and Jean Jacques

Rousseau, who thus became the two thinkers that prepared France for the Great Revolution and wielded a potent influence upon that revolution.

Voltaire was a man of exceptional gifts of intellect. He was not a philosopher in the narrow sense of the word, but he utilized philosophy as a strong weapon against prejudice and superstition. He was not a moralist in the true sense of the word; his ethical teachings are not deep, but they were, nevertheless, hostile to all ascetic and metaphysical exaggerations. Voltaire had no ethical system of his own, but by his works he aided considerably the strengthening in ethics of humanitarianism, of respect for human personality. In all his writings Voltaire bravely demanded freedom of conscience, the abolition of the Inquisition, of tortures, execution, etc. Voltaire spread widely ideas of civic equity and civic law, which the Revolution later endeavoured to apply to life.[20]

Simultaneously with Voltaire the philosopher, Jean-Jacques Rousseau, exerted a strong influence upon the French Revolution. Rousseau was a man of entirely different character from Voltaire's; he came forward with an attack on the contemporary social system, and called men to a simple and natural life. He taught that man is good and kind of nature, but that all evil comes from civilization. Rousseau explained moral tendencies by the desire for self-advancement, properly understood, but at the same time he held as the goal of development the highest social ideals. He saw the starting point of every rational social system in equity ("all men are born equal") and he upheld this principle so passionately, so alluringly, so convincingly that his writings exerted a tremendous influence not only in France, where the Revolution wrote on its

[20] Voltaire, of course, cannot be regarded either as a revolutionary or a democrat; he never demanded the overthrow of the social system of his time, and even when he spoke of equality among men he recognized this equality "in principle," but in society, said Voltaire, "men play different parts." "All men are equal as men, but they are not equal as members of society." (*Pensées sur l'Administration*, Works, vol. V. p. 351.) Voltaire's political ideal consisted in "enlightened despotism," directed for the good of the people. [*Works* (English trans.), N. Y., 1901, vol. 19, pt. 1, pp. 226-239.]—Trans. Note.

banner "Liberty, Equality, Fraternity," but throughout Europe as well. Generally speaking, Rousseau appears in all his works as the philosopher of feeling, in which he sees the vital force capable of correcting all defects and of doing great deeds. He is the enthusiast and the poet of high ideals, the inspirer of the rights of a citizen and of a man.

Speaking of the French philosophy of the second half of the eighteenth century we cannot fail to mention here two more thinkers, who were the first to formulate the idea of progress, the idea which has played a great part in the development of modern moral philosophy. These two thinkers are Turgot and Condorcet.

Turgot (1727–1781) was the first to develop the idea of human progress into a complete teaching in his work, "Discourse on Universal History." [21] Turgot formulated the law of progress as follows: "The human race, while gradually passing from quiescence to activity, slowly but unswervingly moves toward greater and greater perfection, which consists in sincerity in thought, kindliness in customs, and justice in laws."

Condorcet (1743–1794), who fell a victim of the Terror, in 1794, gave a further development of the idea of progress in his famous work, "Tableau des progrès de l'esprit humain." [22] He not only endeavoured to prove the existence of the law of progress, but he also attempted to derive the laws of future social development from the past history of mankind. Condorcet asserted that progress consists in striving for the abolition of social inequalities among citizens. He predicted that in the future men will learn to unite personal ends with the common interests, and that morality itself will become a natural need of man.

All these teachings and ideas influenced in one way or another the great social movement which it is customary to call the French Revolution. This revolution, as we have seen, had already taken

[21] [Turgot, *Plan de deux discours sur l'histoire universelle* (In *Œuvres*, Paris, 1844, vol. 2. pp. 626–675).]—Trans. Note.
[22] [*Esquisse d'un tableau historique des progrès*, etc., Paris, 1794.]—Trans. Note.

place in the minds of people toward the end of the eighteenth century; and new, daring ideas, inspired by the sense of human dignity, swept like a turbulent stream over society, destroying the antiquated institutions and prejudices. The Revolution broke up the last remnants of the feudal system, but the new institutions created by the Revolution were the fruit of the philosophical movement which began in England and found its consummation in France. The famous "Declaration of Rights of Man and Citizens," proclaimed by the French Revolution, is composed of the ideas developed in the writings of Montesquieu, Voltaire, Rousseau, and Condorcet. Its fundamental principles are: all men are born free and equal; all have equal right to enjoy life and liberty; all have equal right for the development of their natural powers and abilities; all have a right to religious freedom and freedom of conscience. In all these principles we see in a clear and concise form the ideas of Hobbes and Locke as developed by the French thinkers and philosophers. The French Revolution left to future generations the realization of this program.

The ideas of Bacon and Locke were brilliantly developed in England in the second half of the eighteenth century by a great thinker and philosopher, David Hume, who had the most independent mind of the eighteenth century. Hume gave the new philosophy a solid basis: he applied it to all regions of knowledge, as Bacon wished it, and thereby exerted strong influence upon all subsequent thinking. Hume began by strictly dividing morality from religion; he denied the influence, in the evolution of moral conceptions, that was ascribed to religion by his English and Scotch predecessors, except Shaftesbury. He himself took the same sceptical attitude as Bayle, although he made some concessions in his "Dialogues concerning Natural Religion." [23]

In developing the ideas of Bacon and Bayle, Hume wrote that

[23] Hume's principal works are: *Treatise Upon Human Nature*, London, 1738-40, 3 vols.; *Enquiry Concerning the Principles of Morals*, Edinburgh, 1751; *Enquiry Concerning Human Understanding*, London, 1748; *Natural History of Religion*, London, 1752.

men of independent type will evolve their own moral conceptions, but "in every religion, however sublime the verbal definition which it gives of its divinity, many of the votaries, perhaps the greatest number, will still seek the divine favour, not by virtue and good morals, which alone can be acceptable to a perfect being, but either by frivolous observances, by intemperate zeal, by rapturous ecstasies, or by the belief of mysterious and absurd opinions." [24]

Hume frequently speaks of the "Supreme Creator," but it was not to him that he ascribed the source of moral judgments in man: "Nothing can preserve untainted the genuine principles of morals in our judgment of human conduct, but the absolute necessity of these principles to the existence of society." (*Ibid.*, Sect. xiii, p. 443.)

The ethical part of Hume's philosophy represents, of course, only a special case of his general view on the origin of knowledge in man: "All the materials of thinking are derived either from our outward or inward sentiment," and all our conceptions originate from impressions and from ideas [25] that are the product of memory, imagination, and thought.[26] The bases of all knowledge rest on natural science, and its methods should be adopted in other sciences. Only, it must be remembered that in our study of the "laws" of the physical world we always proceed through successive "approximations."

As regards morality, Hume pointed out that there have been continual disputes as to where its bases are to be sought: in reason, or in sentiment? Do we arrive at morality through a chain of reasoning processes, or direct through feeling and intuition? Are the fundamental principles of morality identical for all thinking creatures, or, like judgments on beauty and ugliness, do they differ among different peoples, thus becoming the product of the historical development of man? The ancient philosophers, though they often

[24] *The Natural History of Religion*, Section xiv, pp. 443–444 in vol. II, *Essays and Treatises on Several Subjects*, Edinburgh, 1817.

[25] ["Sensations and perceptions," in modern terminology.]—Trans. Note.

[26] *An Inquiry Concerning the Human Understanding*, Sect. ii, vol. II, Edinburgh, 1817.

affirmed that morality is nothing but conformity to reason, still more often derived it from taste and sentiment. Modern thinkers, however, are more inclined to favour reason, and they derive morality from the most abstract principles. But it is very likely that our final judgment in moral questions,—that which makes morality an active factor in our life,—is determined by "some internal sense or feeling, which nature has made universal in the whole species." But in order to pave the way for such a sentiment, it must be preceded by much preliminary thinking, by correct conclusions, keen analysis of complex relations, and the establishment of general facts —in short, by the effort of reason.[27] In other words, our moral conceptions are the product of both our feelings and our reason,— and of their natural development in the life of human societies.

A striving for the general good is the distinguishing feature of every act which we call moral, and moral duty means being guided by the considerations of the general good. Hume did not deny the desire for personal happiness in this striving for the common welfare, but he also understood that moral feeling cannot be explained by egoistic motives alone, as, for example, Hobbes explained it. In addition to the desire for personal good he recognized as further sources of morality, sympathy, the conception of justice, and the feeling of benevolence. But he interpreted justice not as consciousness of something obligatory, evolving in our mind in the course of social life, but rather as virtue, as a form of charity. Then, following Shaftesbury, he pointed out the feeling of harmony and completeness inherent in moral character, the desire for self-improvement, the possibility of a full development of human nature, and the aesthetic emotion of beauty, resulting from the fullest development of personality,—the idea which, as is known, was long after developed so admirably by M. Guyau.

The second part of Hume's treatise is devoted to benevolence: in this he pointed out among other things that our language con-

[27] *An Enquiry Concerning the Principles of Morals*, Section I, in *Essays and Treatises on Several Subjects, Idem.*, vol. II.

tains very many words which prove that mutual benevolence has the general approval of mankind. Then, in discussing justice in the next part of his book, Hume makes an interesting remark concerning it. That justice is useful to society and is therefore respected—is clear. But such a consideration can not possibly be the sole source of this respect. *Justice has proved to be necessary.*

Every manner of social virtue would flourish in a society supplied abundantly with everything, without need of labour, but under such conditions there would be no thought of so cautious, jealous a virtue as justice. (*Ibid.*, Sect. iii, part I, p. 222.) Because of this fact, even now those things that are available in abundance are owned in common. Similarly, if our reason, friendship, generosity, were strongly developed—there would be no need of justice. "Why should I bind another by a deed or promise, when I know that he is already prompted by the strongest inclination to seek my happiness? . . . Why raise landmarks between my neighbour's field and mine?" etc. (p. 223.) In general, the more mutual benevolence, the less need of justice. But since human society in reality presents a middle state, far removed from the ideal, man needs the conception of property also needs justice. Whence it is clearly seen that the idea of justice presented itself to Hume chiefly under the guise of square dealing in order to protect the rights of property, and not at all in the broader sense of equity. He wrote: "Thus the rules of equity or justice depend entirely on the particular state and condition in which men are placed, and owe their origin and existence to that *Utility*, which results to the public from their strict and regular observance." (p. 226.)

Hume, of course, did not believe in the existence of the "Golden Age," nor in the likelihood of a period when man led a solitary existence. Society always existed, and if men had lived isolated lives, they would never have developed the conception of justice, or evolved rules of conduct. (pp. 227–228.)

According to Hume the sense of justice may have originated either from reflecting about the mutual relations of men, or from the natural instinct "which nature has implanted in us for salutary purposes." (p. 238.) But the second supposition must obviously be rejected. The universal character of the conception of justice shows that it was the inevitable outcome of social life itself. Society could not exist without this conception. We must, therefore, acknowledge that "the necessity of justice to the support of society is the *sole* foundation of that virtue." Its unquestionable usefulness explains its general distribution, and besides, it is "the source of a considerable part of the merit ascribed to humanity, benevolence, friendship, public spirit, and other social virtues. (*Ibid.*, Sect. iii, part ii, p. 241.)

Hume ascribed to self-love an important part in the evolution of moral usages and conceptions, and he understood why some philosophers found it convenient to regard all concern for the welfare of society simply as a modification of personal interest. But there are many cases in which the moral feeling is preserved even when personal interests do not coincide with the social; therefore, in citing a number of such examples, Hume definitely concludes: "we must renounce the theory which accounts for every moral sentiment by the principle of self-love." (Sect. v, part ii, p. 256.) "The sentiments which arise from humanity, are the same in all human creatures, and produce the same approbation or censure." (Sect. ix, part i, p. 310.)

And since there is no man who wishes to deserve the condemnation of others, Hume maintained that faith in God cannot be the source of morality, for religiousness does not make men moral. Many religious people, perhaps even the majority, aim to deserve "divine favour" not by virtue and by a moral life, but by performing meaningless rites, or by exalted faith in mystical sacraments.[28]

While not sharing the views of Hobbes that in ancient times men

[28] *Natural History of Religion*, Section xiv, pp. 443-444, vol. II. Edinburgh, 1817. " 'Those who undertake the most criminal and most dangerous enterprises are commonly the most superstitious'. . . . Their devotion and spiritual faith rise with their fears." (*Ibid.*, p. 447.) [Hume quotes the first sentence from Diodorus Siculus.]—Trans. Note.

lived in perpetual strife with one another, Hume was far from seeing in human nature nothing but elements of good. He recognized that man is guided in his actions by self-love, but he claimed that man also develops a sense of duty toward others.

When man reasons calmly about those of his acts that were prompted by various impressions, impulses, or passions, he feels a desire to be endowed with certain qualities, and thus the sense of duty comes to birth within him. On this point, therefore, Hume agreed with Spinoza. But in his analysis of the origin of the moral judgments of our actions, instead of recognizing their two-fold source—from feeling and from reason—Hume vacillated between them,—favouring now one and now the other. He even raised the question as to an intermediate faculty between reason and feeling, and finally expressed himself in favour of feeling. Like Shaftesbury and Hutcheson, he evidently assigned to reason only the preparation of judgments and the consideration of facts. But the decisive verdict belongs to feeling, after which the task of reason is to elaborate general rules.[29]

Hume ascribed a special importance to sympathy. It softens our

[29] The opinions of various writers on Hume's philosophy differ as to this point. Pfleiderer held that Hume merely prepared the ground for Kant's views "on practical reason," while Gizycki and Jodl hold different views, and in his *Gesch. der Ethik*, Jodl expressed a very true thought: "Morality can never become an active factor if moral development and education is to be deprived of its effective bases—this was conclusively proved by Hume; but he forgot one thing, namely, the capacity for formulating a moral ideal; he left no place for this capacity in his explanation of reason, which he presented as occupied solely with the synthesis and analysis of conceptions. This, of course, is not the starting point of morality; nor is it the starting point of human activity in the field of thinking or of creative effort. But the facts of moral life become intelligible only on the supposition that training and experience prepare the ground for the ideals, in which the intellectual and the practical elements are inextricably interwoven, and which contain an inner tendency toward realization." (*Gesch. der Ethik*, vol. 1, ch. vii, note 29.) In other words, feeling and reason are equally necessary for the development of moral conceptions and for their conversion into the motives of our actions. [Edmund Pfleiderer, *Empirik und Skepsis in David Hume's Philosophie*, Berlin 1874. Georg von Gizycki, *Die Ethik David Hume's*, Breslau, 1878.]—Trans. Note.

narrowly selfish tendencies, and, together with the general, natural benevolence of man, overcomes them. Thus, even if considerations of the utility of this or that way of acting exercise a certain influence, it is not upon them that the final decision in moral questions rests. Adam Smith, as is known, later developed this conception of sympathy and ascribed to it the primary importance in the evolution of moral principles.

Most interesting is Hume's attitude to the conception of justice. He certainly could not overlook its influence and he recognized the significance of justice in the development of moral conceptions. But either because he did not venture to ascribe a preponderance to reason in its struggle with feeling, or because he understood that in the final analysis justice is the recognition of the equality of all the members of society,—the very principle that was not recognized by the laws,—Hume forbore to break as sharply with the existing laws as he had already broken with religion.[30] Accordingly, he removed justice from the realm of ethics and pictured it as something that develops independently in society, as the result of regulations imposed by the State.

In this question Hume apparently followed Hobbes, who, after having pointed out that arbitrariness (or, more correctly, the interests of the ruling classes) has always prevailed in the realm of lawmaking, completely removed Law from the realm of morality as something entirely unconnected with it. However, on this point too, as on the question of the part played by feeling and reason in the evolution of moral principles, Hume did not arrive at a definite conclusion, so that those who have written on his philosophy differ in their interpretations.[31] In general, Hume did not offer a systematic explanation of the moral conceptions, and did not create

[30] He expounded in detail views nearly approaching atheism in his *Dialogues concerning Natural Religion* and in Section XV of his *Natural History of Religion.*

[31] See Jodl, *Geschichte der Ethik als philosophischer Wissenschaft*, vol. 1, ch. vii, Section ii.

a new, well-organized system of Ethics. But not content with stereotyped explanations, he so carefully and, in spots, so brilliantly analysed the motives of man in the infinite variety of his actions,— he ascribed so slight an influence both to religion and to egoism, as well as to considerations of the utility of our acts, that he compelled later writers to think these problems over more thoroughly than had hitherto been done. He prepared the ground for the scientific, naturalistic explanation of the moral element, but at the same time, as some of his interpreters have pointed out, he also prepared the ground for the opposite, non-rational, Kantian explanations. The influence Hume exercised upon the subsequent development of Ethics will be determined as we advance in our discussion.

One of the prominent continuators of Hume in England was Adam Smith, whose work, "The Theory of Moral Sentiment," appeared in 1759 and went through ten editions in the eighteenth century. Later Smith became particularly famous as the author of a serious scientific research in Economics,[32] and his work in the field of Ethics has been frequently overlooked. But his investigation of the moral sentiments was a new and a considerable step forward, for it explained morality on a purely natural basis, as an inherent quality of human nature and not as a revelation from above, and at the same time it did not regard morality as dependent on man's considerations of the utility of this or that attitude toward his fellow men.

The chief motive force in the development of moral conceptions Smith saw in Sympathy, i. e., in the feeling inherent in man as a social being. When we approve certain acts and disapprove of others we are guided not by considerations of the social benefit or harm, as the utilitarians asserted, but we are conscious of how these actions would react upon ourselves, and there arises in us, therefore, the agreement or disagreement of our own feelings with the

[32] [*An Inquiry into the Nature and Causes of the Wealth of Nations,* Lond., 1776, 2 vols.]—Trans. Note.

feelings that prompted these actions. When we witness the misery of others we are capable of living through it within ourselves, and we call this feeling *co*-miseration; not infrequently we rush to the aid of the suffering or of the wronged. And similarly, when witnessing the joy of others we ourselves experience a joyous emotion. We feel dissatisfied and displeased when we see evil being done to another, and we feel gratitude at the sight of good. This is a quality of human nature; it has developed from social life, and not at all from reasoning about the harm or the social utility of this or that act, as the utilitarians asserted, and Hume with them. We simply live through with others what they themselves experience, and in condemning one who has caused suffering to another, we later apply the same condemnation to ourselves if we bring sorrow to a fellow-man. Thus, little by little, our morality was evolved.[33]

Thus Adam Smith rejected the supernatural origin of morality and gave it a natural explanation, and at the same time he showed how the moral conceptions of man can develop aside from considerations of the utility of this or that type of mutual relations,— these considerations having been, hitherto, the only way to account for the moral element in man "without divine revelation." Moreover, Smith did not rest content with the general indication of this origin of the moral sentiments. On the contrary, he devoted the greatest part of his work to an analysis of the manner of development of various moral conceptions, taking in each case as the starting point the emotion of sympathy, regardless of all other considerations. At the end of his work he explained how all religions, from the very start, took upon themselves as a matter of course the protection and the support of useful manners and customs.

It would appear that having arrived at such an understanding of morality, Smith would have to recognize as the basis of the moral

[33] Smith ascribed such importance to this interpretation that he even included it in the title of his book, calling it *The Theory of Moral Sentiments; or an essay towards an analysis of the principles by which men naturally judge concerning the conduct and character first of their neighbours, and afterwards of themselves.*

not only the feeling of sympathy, which develops in social life and which actually leads to moral judgments, but also a certain mental make-up, which is the outcome of the same sociality and which takes the form of justice, i. e., the recognition of equity among all the members of society. But while admitting the participation of both reason and feeling in the elaboration of moral judgments, Smith did not draw any line of demarcation between them.

Besides, it is also possible that at the time Smith wrote his treatise, i. e., long before the French Revolution, the conception of equity was still alien to him. Therefore, though he ascribed great importance to the value of justice in our moral judgments, he nevertheless understood justice mainly in the judicial sense—in the sense of compensation to the wronged and punishment for the offender. The sense of indignation which we experience at seeing someone wronged he ascribed to what he called the natural desire for retribution and punishment; and he considered this desire one of the bases of sociality. He added, of course, that only hurtful acts, prompted by unworthy motives, deserve punishment.[34] But he did not utter a word about the equality of men,[35] and, in general, he wrote about judicial justice, and not about that justice which our mind seeks, regardless of courts and their verdicts.[36] But owing to this limitation we lose sight of social injustice,—class injustice which is upheld by the courts,—due to which fact society, by not protesting against it, gives it support.

As a rule, the pages devoted by Smith to the subject of Justice [37]

[34] *The Theory of Moral Sentiments,* part II, section II, ch. I, p. 112. G. Bell and Sons, London, 1911.

[35] [It is interesting to note that in the latter part of his work Smith does state the principle of equality of man in no uncertain terms: "We are but one of the multitude, in no respect better than any other in it." (Part III, ch. iii, p. 194). And yet he completely failed to draw the inevitable corollaries from this principle, and he did not assign to it a place of due prominence in his ethical system.]—Trans. Note.

[36] *Ibid.* pp. 114–115. In all that Smith wrote on justice (ch. i–iii, part II, sect. II, pp. 112–132) it is most difficult to distinguish his own opinion from that held by jurists.

[37] *Ibid.* Part II, Sections II and III.

produce the impression as of something left unsaid. It is equally impossible to determine what part in the development of morality Smith ascribed to feeling and what part to reason. But one thing stands out clearly: that Smith understood the moral element in man not as something mysterious, innate, or as a revelation from without, but as a product of sociality, slowly evolving in mankind, originating not in considerations of the utility or harmfulness of various traits of character, but as the inevitable consequence of every man's sympathy with the joys and sorrows of his fellow man.

Smith devoted a few admirable chapters [particularly Chap. iii, of part III,] which to this day have not lost their freshness and beauty, to the analysis of the natural development in man of conscience, the "impartial spectator" within us, and with it of love for dignity of character and for moral beauty. His examples are taken from actual life (sometimes from classical literature) and are full of interest to every one who thoughtfully considers the moral questions, and seeks strength, not in revelations from above, but in his own feelings and reason. In reading these pages, however, one regrets that Smith did not consider from the same point of view man's attitude to various problems of the social system, so much more that at the time when he wrote, these questions were already agitating society; and the day was approaching when these problems were to be brought forward in the form of a demand for social justice.[38]

[38] In giving an historical survey of earlier interpretations of morality Smith makes the following remark. He is speaking about the utilitarians and gives this explanation of the way by which they arrive at their conclusion that moral conceptions have originated in considerations of their utility:—"Human society," wrote Smith, "when we contemplate it in a certain abstract and philosophical light, appears like a great, an immense machine, whose regular and harmonious movements produce a thousand agreeable effects." The less unnecessary friction there is in the machine, the more graceful and beautiful will be its action. Similarly, in life, some acts tend to produce a life without friction and collisions, while others will have the opposite effect; but the fewer the reasons for collision, the easier and smoother will flow the course of social life. Therefore, when the Utilitarian authors describe to us the innumerable advantages of social life, and the new and broad vistas that sociality opens to man, the reader "is commonly so delighted with the discovery, that he

ETHICS: ORIGIN AND DEVELOPMENT

As we have seen, Smith offered only one explanation of our sympathetic attitude toward certain acts, and our attitude of condemnation toward others. It was his idea that we mentally apply these acts to ourselves and picture ourselves in the condition of the sufferer.

It would seem that in assuming this mental substitution of oneself for the one who is being wronged, Smith should have noticed that what really takes place in one's mind at the time is the recognition of equity. If I put myself mentally in the place of the wronged one, I thereby recognize our equality, and our equal capacity to feel the injury. But Smith conceives nothing of the kind. He failed to include in sympathy the element of equity and justice. In general, as Jodl remarked, he even avoided giving an objective basis to the moral judgment. Besides, Smith completely overlooked the necessity of pointing out the continuous development of the moral sentiment in man. Of course, he cannot be blamed for not having arrived at the idea of the gradual zoölogical evolution of man, to which we were brought in the nineteenth century by the study of evolution in nature. But he overlooked the lessons in goodness which primitive man was able to derive from nature, from the life of animal societies, and which were already hinted at by Grotius and Spinoza. We must fill in this omission and point out that so important a fact in the development of morality as sympathy, does not constitute a distinguishing feature of man: it is inherent in the vast majority of living creatures, and it had already been developed by all the gregarious and social

seldom takes time to reflect that this political view, having never occurred to him in his life before, cannot possibly be the ground of that approbation and disapprobation with which he has always been accustomed to consider those different qualities." [i. e., the vices and virtues of men.] Similarly, when we read in history of the good qualities of some hero, we sympathize with him not because these qualities may prove useful to us, but because we imagine what we would have felt had we lived in his times. Such sympathy with the men of the past cannot be regarded as manifestations of our egoism.

In general, Smith thought that the success of theories explaining morality by egoism is due to a faulty and insufficient understanding of morality. (Part VII, Section III, ch. I, pp. 163–165.)

animals. Sympathy is a fundamental fact of nature, and we meet it in all herd animals and in all birds nesting in common. In both cases the strongest individuals rush forward to drive away the enemy, be it beast or bird of prey. And among birds we have the instance of a bird of one species picking up the fledglings of some other species, when they fell out of the nest. This fact, as is known, greatly delighted old Goethe when he first learned of it from Eckermann.

Smith's entire work on morality aims to show that, as the result of man's very nature, morality *had* to develop in him. In showing how the development of character was influenced by the rules of mutuality and morality evolved by mankind, Smith spoke as a true naturalist in the realm of thought. In pointing out certain tendencies that may swerve man from the moral attitude toward others, he added that our nature contains in itself a corrective factor for this defect. Observing continually the conduct of others we arrive at certain rules as to what to do and what not to do. Thus there takes place the social education of characteristics, and thus the general rules of morality are formed. (Part III, ch. IV, pp. 221–228.) But immediately after, in the next chapter, he already asserts that the rules of life that were evolved in this manner are justly regarded as Divine Laws. "The regard to those general rules of conduct is what is properly called a sense of duty, a principle of the greatest consequence in human life, and the only principle by which the bulk of mankind are capable of directing their actions." And he adds,—"It cannot be doubted that they [the moral rules] were given us for the direction of our conduct in this life." (Part III, ch. V, p. 233.)

These remarks of Smith show to what an extent he was still bound by his time, and how difficult it was, even for a very brilliant and bold thinker, to analyze the subject of the origin of morality before men had become familiar with the fact of the revolution of social forms, as well as the judgments about these forms and the attitude of the individual toward them.

Smith did not limit himself to the explanation of the origin of morality. He analyzed many facts of everyday life in order to demonstrate the true nature of the moral attitude of men in their ordinary relations. And in this respect his attitude was the same as that of the Stoics of Ancient Greece and Rome, especially of Seneca and Epictetus. He regarded sympathy as the guiding and the deciding emotion in the evolution of morality, overlooking the importance of reason in questions of justice and equity. It is true he has a few excellent remarks on justice,[39] but he does not indicate anywhere its fundamental significance in the elaboration of moral conceptions. He concentrated attention on the sense of duty. And on this point he was in complete accord with the Stoics —especially Epictetus and Marcus Aurelius.

Generally speaking, Adam Smith placed ethics on a realistic basis and showed that the moral sentiments of man originated from sympathy with other men, unavoidable in social life, and that later, the education of society was carried on in this manner and the general rules of morality evolved. He demonstrated how these rules found support in the common agreement of men, and how at present we turn to them in case of doubt, as to the bases of our judgments.

By this view Smith undoubtedly prepared the ground for the understanding of morality as the natural product of social life: this morality developed slowly in man from the time of man's most primitive state, and has continued in the same direction up to the present,—always without need of external authority for its further progress. This was, indeed, the path followed by moral philosophy in the nineteenth century.

In summing up, we must note that in all the moral teachings that originated and developed in the seventeenth and the eighteenth cen-

---

[39] "There is, however, one virtue, of which the general rules determine, with the greatest exactness, every external action which it requires. This virtue is Justice . . . In the practice of the other virtues . . . we should consider the end and foundation of the rule more than the rule itself. But it is otherwise with regard to justice". . . . etc. (Part III, ch. VI, p. 249.)

tury, striving to explain the origin of morality in a purely scientific, naturalistic way, it is the influence of the Epicurean philosophy that stands out. Almost all the foremost representatives of philosophy, especially in the eighteenth century, were the followers of the Epicurean teaching. But, while resting on the philosophy of Epicurus, the ethical doctrines of the new time divided into two different currents. The currents were united only by the fact that they both rejected the religious as well as the metaphysical interpretations of morality. Representatives of both tendencies aimed to explain the origin of the moral in a natural way, and opposed the pretensions of the Church to connect morality with religion.

One of these groups in philosophy, while recognizing with Epicurus that man strives first of all for happiness, affirmed, however, that man finds greatest happiness not in exploiting other people for his personal benefit, but in friendly mutual relations with all around him; whereas the adherents of the other bent,—the chief representative of which was Hobbes,—continued to look upon morality as upon something forcibly engrafted upon man. Hobbes and his followers looked upon morality not as the outcome of human nature but as something prescribed to it by an external force. Only, in place of the Deity and the Church they put the State and the fear of this "Leviathan"—the implanter of morality in mankind.

One myth was thus replaced by another. It must be noted that in its time the substitution of the State, based on contract, for the Church, was of great importance for political purposes. The Church traced its origin to the Divine Will: she called herself the representative of God on earth. Whereas to the State, though it freely availed itself, from time immemorial, of the support of the Church, the advanced thinkers of the eighteenth century began at once to ascribe an earthly origin: they derived the inception of the state from the covenant of men. And there is no doubt that when, at the end of the eighteenth century, there began the struggle in Europe against the autocratic power of kings "by grace of God," the doctrine of the state as originating from the social contract, served a useful purpose.

The subdivision into two camps of the thinkers who explained morality in a purely scientific, naturalistic way, is observed throughout the period of the seventeenth and eighteenth centuries. In the course of time this division becomes wider and sharper. While one group of thinkers more and more comes to realize that morality is nothing but a gradual development of a sociality ingrained in man, other thinkers explain morality as the striving of man for personal happiness, rightly regarded. And two different conclusions are reached, depending on which of the two groups the thinker holds true. Some continue to affirm, like Hobbes, that man is "steeped in evil," and they see salvation only in a strictly organized central power, which restrains men from constant strife among themselves. Their ideal is a centralized State, governing the entire life of society,—and in this they go hand in hand with the Church. The others, however, maintain that only wide freedom of personality, and wide opportunity for men to enter into various agreements among themselves, will lead us to a new social system, based on just attainment of all needs.

These two views, with some intermediate steps, and also some doctrines that pay tribute more or less to the idea of the religious origin of morality, predominate at the present time. But from the moment that the theory of evolution, i. e., of the gradual development of beliefs, customs, and institutions, conquered for itself a place in science, the second view,—the one aiming at the free upbuilding of life,—gradually acquired the ascendancy.

In the next chapter we shall endeavour to trace the development of these two currents of ethical thought in the philosophy of modern times.

CHAPTER IX

As was pointed out in the preceding chapter, the teachings of the French philosophers of the eighteenth century—Helvétius, Montesquieu, Voltaire, of the Encyclopædists Diderot and d'Alembert, and of Holbach,—played an important part in the history of the evolution of Ethics. The bold denial by these thinkers of the importance of religion for the development of the moral conceptions, their assertions of *equity* (at least political), and, finally, the decisive influence in the elaboration of social forms of life credited by most of these philosophers to the rationally interpreted emotion of self-interest—all these factors were very important in forming correct conceptions of morality; and they helped to bring society to the realization of the fact that morality can be completely liberated from the sanction of religion.

However, the terror of the French Revolution, and the general upheaval that accompanied the abolition of feudal rights, and also the wars that followed the Revolution, compelled many thinkers to seek once more the basis of morality in some supernatural power, which they recognized in more or less disguised form. The political and the social reaction were paralleled in the realm of philosophy by a revival of metaphysics. This revival began in Germany, where at the end of the eighteenth century appeared the greatest German philosopher, Immanuel Kant (1724–1804). Kant's teaching is on the border line between the metaphysical philosophy of earlier times, and the scientific philosophy of the nineteenth century. We will now briefly survey Kant's moral philosophy.[1]

[1] Kant expounded his moral philosophy in three works: *Grundlegung zur*

213

ETHICS: ORIGIN AND DEVELOPMENT

Kant's aim was to create a *rational ethics,* i. e., a theory of moral conceptions entirely different from the *empirical ethics* advocated by most English and French thinkers of the eighteenth century. Kant's ethical system was to bear the same relation to preceding theories, as theoretical mechanics bears to applied mechanics.

The aim set by Kant was, of course, not new. Almost all thinkers preceding Kant made the endeavour to determine the rational bases of Ethics. But, contrary to the English and French thinkers of the seventeenth and eighteenth centuries, Kant intended to discover the fundamental laws of morality not through study of human nature and through observation of life and the actions of man, but through abstract thinking.

Reflecting on the basis of morality Kant came to the conclusion that it is found in our *sense of duty.* This sense of duty, according to Kant, originates neither from considerations of *utility* (whether individual or social) nor from a feeling of *sympathy* or *benevolence;* it is a property of human reason. According to Kant there are two kinds of rules of conduct that human reason can create; some of these rules are conditional, others are unconditional. For example: if you wish to be healthy—lead a moderate life:—this is a conditional rule. A man who does not want to lead a moderate life, may choose to neglect his health. Such prescriptions contain nothing absolute, and man may or may not carry them out. In this category of conditional rules are included all the rules of conduct

Metaphysik der Sitten, 1785 (*Fundamental Principles of the Metaphysic of Morals*); *Kritik der practischen Vernunft,* 1788 (*Critique of practical reason*); *Die Metaphysik der Sitten,* 1797 (*Metaphysics of Morals*). It is also necessary to include his articles on religion, especially *Religion innerhalb der Grenzen der blossen Vernunft.* (*Religion within the Bounds of Reason Alone*), otherwise named *Philosophische Religionslehre.* (*The Philosophical Theory of Religion.*)

A thorough analysis of Kant's moral philosophy may be found in the works of Jodl, Wundt, Paulsen, and others.

[All the above works, except *Die Metaphysik der Sitten,* appear in one volume in English translation:—*Kant's Critique of Practical Reason, and other works on the theory of Ethics,* translated by T. K. Abbott. All quotations, unless otherwise stated, are from the sixth edition of this book, London, 1909.]—Trans. Note.

based on interest,—and such conditional prescriptions cannot become the basis of morality. Moral rules should have the absolute character of a categorical imperative, and man's sense of *duty* constitutes such a categorical imperative.

Just as the axioms of pure mathematics are not acquired by man through experience, (so thought Kant), in the same way the sense of duty, with its intrinsic obligatory nature, partakes of the character of a natural law and is inherent in the mind of every rationally thinking creature. Such is the quality of "pure reason." It does not matter that in actual life man never obeys completely the moral categorical imperative. It is important that man came to recognize this imperative not through observation or through his feelings, but, as it were, discovered it in himself and acknowledged it as the supreme law in his actions.

What, then, is the nature of moral duty? Duty in its very essence is that which has absolute significance, and therefore it can never be merely a *means* toward some other end, but it is an *aim* in itself. What, then, has an absolute significance for man, and should, therefore, be his aim?

According to Kant, "Nothing can possibly be conceived in the world, or even out of it, which can be called good without qualification, except a goodwill," i. e., *free and rational will*. Everything in the world, says Kant, has relative value, and only a rational and free personality has an absolute value in itself. Therefore, free and rational will, possessing an absolute value, constitutes the object of the moral duty. *"Thou must be free and rational,"* such is the moral law.[2]

Having established this moral law Kant proceeds to derive the first formula of moral conduct: "So act as to treat humanity, whether in thine own person or in that of any other, in every case as an end withal, never as a means only." (*Ibid.*, p. 47.) All men, like ourselves, are endowed with free and rational will: therefore

[2] *Fundamental Principles of the Metaphysics of Morals*, Part I, page 9 of Abbott's translation.

they can never serve for us as means to an end. The ideal which morality is striving to approach is, according to Kant, a republic of free and rational human personalities; a republic in which every personality is the aim of all others. On this basis Kant formulated the moral law as follows: "Act as if the maxim of thy action were to become by thy will a universal law of nature." (p. 39.) Or, in another version,—"Act only on that maxim whereby thou canst at the same time will that it should become a universal law." (p. 38.) Or again,—"I am never to act otherwise than so that I could also will that my maxim should become a universal law." (p. 18.)

The short treatise in which Kant expounded these ideas is written in a simple and forcible style, appealing to the better instincts of man. It can easily be imagined, therefore, what an elevating influence Kant's teaching exerted, especially in Germany. In opposition to the eudemonistic and utilitarian theories of morality, which taught man to be moral because he would find in moral conduct either *happiness* (eudemonistic theory), or *utility* (utilitarian theory),— Kant asserted that we must lead a moral life because such is the demand of our reason. For example, you must respect your own freedom and the freedom of others, not only when you expect to derive from it pleasure or utility, but always and under all circumstances, because freedom is an absolute good, and only freedom constitutes aim in itself; everything else is but means. In other words, human personality constitutes, according to Kant, the ethical basis of morality and of law.

Thus Kant's ethics is particularly suited to those who, while doubting the obligatory nature of the prescriptions of Church or Bible, hesitate at the same time to adopt the viewpoint of natural science. Likewise, in the camp of the learned scientists, Kant's ethics finds adherents among those who like to believe that man performs on earth a mission predetermined by "Supreme Will," and who find in Kant's teaching the expression of "their own vague beliefs" that are a lingering survival of former faith.

The elevating character of Kant's ethics is indisputable. But, after all, it leaves us in complete ignorance with respect to the principal problem of ethics, i. e., *the origin of the sense of duty*. To say that man is conscious of so lofty a sense of duty that he holds himself *obliged* to obey it, does not advance us any further than we were with Hutcheson, who maintained that man possesses an inherent *moral feeling*, which urges him to act in this direction,—all the more that the development of feeling is undeniably influenced by reason. *Reason*, taught Kant, imposes upon us the moral law, reason independent of experience as well as of observations of nature. But, having proved this doctrine with so much fervour, and after teaching it for four years following the appearance of the "Critique of Practical Reason," he was finally forced to acknowledge that he was completely unable to find in man the source of respect for the moral law, and that he had to abandon the attempt to solve this fundamental problem of ethics,—hinting, at the same time, at a "divine origin" of this regard for the moral law.

Whether this change of viewpoint and this return to theological ethics was due to the influence of the aftermath of the French Revolution, or whether Kant expressed in 1792 the ideas which were already in his mind when he wrote his "Fundamental Principles of the Metaphysic of Morals" and his "Critique of Practical Reason," is a question difficult to answer. Whatever the case may be, here are his actual words (usually not cited by his interpreters): "There is, however, one thing in our soul which we cannot cease to regard with the highest astonishment, and in regard to which admiration is right or even elevating, and that is the original moral capacity in us generally. What is it in us (we may ask ourselves) by which we, who·are constantly dependent on nature by so many wants, are yet raised so far above it in the idea of an original capacity (in us) that we regard them all as nothing, and ourselves as unworthy of existence, if we were to indulge in their satisfaction in opposition to a law which our reason authoritatively prescribes; although it is this enjoyment alone that can make life desirable, while reason neither promises anything nor threatens. . . . The incomprehensibility of this capacity, a capacity which proclaims a Divine origin, must rouse man's spirit to enthusiasm, and strengthen it for any sacrifice which respect for this duty may impose on him.[3]

Having thus denied the significance, and almost the very existence in man of the feeling of sympathy and sociality, to which the moral teachings of Hutcheson and Adam Smith gave such prominence, and explaining the moral faculty of man by the fundamental property of reason, Kant could not, of course, find in nature anything that would point out to him the natural origin of morality. He had therefore to hint at the possibility of the divine origin of our sense of moral duty. And what is more, his repeated statement that the sense of moral duty is inherent in man as well as in all "rationally thinking beings" (while animals were excluded from that category) leads us to think, as was already pointed out by Schopenhauer, that in speaking thus Kant had in mind the "world of angels."

It must be acknowledged, however, that by his philosophy and by his moral teaching Kant aided considerably the destruction of traditional religious ethics and the preparation of the ground for a new, purely scientific ethics. It may be said without exaggeration that Kant helped to prepare the way for the evolutionary ethics of our time. It must also be remembered that, recognizing the elevating character of morality, Kant very justly pointed out that it cannot be based on considerations of *happiness* or *utility*, as the eudemonists and the utilitarians asserted. Moreover, Kant showed that morality cannot be based merely on the feeling of sympathy and commiseration. And indeed, no matter how completely the feeling of sympathy for others may be developed in a man, there are, nevertheless, moments in life when this highly moral feeling finds itself in contradiction with other tendencies of our nature: man is compelled to decide what course of action is to be taken in such a case,

---

[3] *The Philosophical Theory of Religion*, end of Part I, General Remark. Abbott's translation, pp. 357-358. [A similar passage on the "incomprehensibility of the moral imperative" is found in the concluding remark to the *Fundamental Principles of the Metaphysic of Morals*. (Abbott's translation, pp. 83-84).]—Trans. Note.

and at such times there is heard the strong voice of moral conscience. The fundamental problem of ethics lies in determining the faculty by means of which man is enabled to make a decision in such contradictory cases, and why the decision which we call moral gives him inner satisfaction and is approved by other men. This fundamental problem of ethics Kant left unanswered. He merely pointed out the inner struggle in man's soul, and he recognized that the decisive part in this struggle is played by reason and not by feeling. Such a statement is not a solution of the problem, because it immediately leads to another question: "Why does our reason reach this, and not some other decision?" Kant rightly refused to say that in the collision of two opposing tendencies our reason is guided by considerations of the usefulness of morality. Of course, considerations of the utility of moral acts for the human race exerted a very great influence on the development of our moral conceptions, but there still remains in moral acts something that cannot be explained either by habit or by considerations of utility or harm, and this something we are bound to explain. Similarly, the consideration of inner satisfaction which we feel on performing a moral act is also insufficient: it is necessary to explain why we feel such satisfaction, just as in considering the influence upon us of some combinations of sounds and chords, it was necessary to explain why certain combinations of sounds are physically pleasant to our ear, and why others are unpleasant, why certain combinations of lines and dimensions in architecture please our eye, while others "offend" it.

Thus Kant was unable to answer the fundamental question of ethics. But by his search of the deeper interpretation of the moral conceptions he paved the way for those who followed Bacon's suggestions and, like Darwin, sought the explanation of morality in the instinct of sociality which is inherent in all gregarious animals, constituting a *fundamental faculty* of man, and forever developing in the course of man's evolution.

A great deal has been written on Kant's moral philosophy and a great deal more might be added. I shall limit myself, however, to a few additional remarks.

In "The Fundamental Principles of the Metaphysic of Morals," —Kant's principal work on Ethics,—he frankly confesses that we do not see why we have to act in conformity with the moral law, "in other words, whence the moral law derives its obligation. . . . It must be freely admitted," he continued, "that there is a sort of circle here from which it seems impossible to escape. In the order of efficient causes we assume ourselves free, in order that in the order of ends we may conceive ourselves as subject to moral laws; and we afterwards conceive ourselves as subject to these laws, because we have attributed to ourselves freedom of will." [4] Kant attempted to rectify this seeming logical error by an explanation which constitutes the essence of his philosophy of knowledge. Reason, said Kant, stands not only above feeling but also above knowledge, for it contains something greater than that which our senses give us: "Reason shows so pure a spontaneity in the case of what I call ideas (Ideal Conceptions) that it thereby far transcends everything that the sensibility can give it, and exhibits its most important function in distinguishing the world of sense from that of understanding, and thereby prescribing the limits of the understanding itself." (*Ibid.*, p. 71.) "When we conceive ourselves as free we transfer ourselves into the world of understanding as members of it, and recognize the autonomy of the will with its consequence, morality; whereas if we conceive ourselves as under obligation, we consider ourselves as belonging to the world of sense, and at the same time to the world of understanding." (p. 72.) Freedom of will is merely an ideal conception of reason.[5]

It is obvious that Kant means by this that his "categorical imperative," his moral law which constitutes "the fundamental law of pure moral reason," is the necessary form of our thinking. But

[4] *The Fundamental Principles of the Metaphysic of Morals*, Abbott's translation, page 69.
[5] "Ideal" in the Kantian sense of the word.

Kant could not explain whence, due to what causes, our mind developed just this form of thinking. At present, however, if I am not mistaken, we can assert that it originates in the idea of justice, i. e., the recognition of equity among all men. Much has been written about the essence of the Kantian moral law. But what most of all prevented his formulation of this law from becoming generally accepted was his assertion that "moral decision must be such, that it could be accepted as the basis of universal law." But accepted by whom? By the reason of an individual, or by society? If by society, then there can be no other rule for the unanimous judgment about an act but the *common good,* and then we are inevitably led to the theory of *utilitarianism* or *eudemonism,* which Kant so persistently renounced. But if by the words "could be accepted" Kant meant that the principle guiding my act can and should be readily accepted by the reason of every man, not by the force of social utility but by the very nature of human thinking, then there must be some peculiar faculty in human reason which, unfortunately, Kant failed to point out. Such a peculiar faculty does actually exist, and there was no need to go through the entire system of Kantian metaphysics in order to comprehend it. It was very nearly approached by French materialists, and by English and Scotch thinkers. This fundamental faculty of human reason is, as I have already said, *the conception of justice, i. e., equity.* There is, and there can be, no other rule that may become the universal criterion for judging human acts. And what is more, this criterion is recognized, not fully, but to a considerable extent, by other thinking beings, not by the angels as Kant intimated, but by many social animals. It is impossible to explain this faculty of our reason in any other way than in connection with the progressive development, i. e., the *evolution,* of man and of the animal world in general. If this is true, it is impossible to deny that the principal endeavour of man is his striving for personal happiness in the broadest sense of that word. All the eudemonists and the utilitarians are right on this point. But it is equally unquestionable that the restraining

221

moral element manifests itself side by side with the striving for personal happiness, in the feelings of sociality, sympathy, and in the acts of mutual aid, which are observed even among the animals. Originating partly in fraternal feeling, and partly in reason, they develop together with the march of society.

Kantian critique unquestionably awakened the conscience of German society and helped it to live through a critical period. But it did not enable Kant to look deeper into the bases of German sociality.

After Goethe's pantheism, Kantian philosophy called society back to the supernatural explanation of the moral conscience, and urged it away, as from a dangerous path, from seeking the fundamental principle of morality in natural causes and in gradual development, —an explanation which the French thinkers of the eighteenth century were approaching.

Generally speaking, the modern admirers of Kant would do well to deepen and to extend the moral philosophy of their teacher. Of course it is desirable that "the maxim of our action should become a universal law." But did Kant discover this law? We saw, in all the moral teachings of the utilitarians and the eudemonists, that the common good is recognized as the basis of moral conduct. The whole question is, *what is to be regarded as the common good?* And Kant did not even look for an answer to this fundamental ethical question which so deeply concerned Rousseau and other French writers before the Great Revolution, and also some Scotch and English thinkers. Kant rested content with hinting at Divine Will and faith in a future life.

As regards Kant's second formula: "So act as to treat humanity whether in thine own person or in that of any other in every case *as an end withal, never as a means only,*"—putting it more simply one could say: "In all questions concerning society bear in mind not only your own, but also *social* interests."

But this element of disinterestedness, upon which Kant insisted so strongly, and in the exposition of which he saw his great philo-

222

sophical achievement,—this element is as old as ethics itself. It was already the object of dispute between the Stoics and the Epicureans in Ancient Greece, and in the seventeenth century between the intellectualists and Hobbes, Locke, Hume, etc. Moreover, Kant's formula is incorrect in itself. Man becomes truly moral not when he obeys the command of the law, which he considers divine, and not when his thinking is tinged with the mercenary element of "hope and fear,"—which is Kant's reference to the future life; [6] man is moral only when his moral acts have become second nature with him.

Kant, as was pointed out by Paulsen, thought well of the popular masses among which there manifests itself, at times more frequently than among the educated classes, strong and simple fidelity to duty. But he did not rise to a recognition of the social equality of the popular masses with the other classes. While speaking so alluringly about the sense of duty, and demanding, in effect, that everyone consider his action toward others as an act that is *desirable for all with respect to all*, he did not dare to utter the principle proclaimed by Rousseau and by the Encyclopædists, and which the Revolution had just written on its banners:—i. e., human equality. He lacked this brave consistency. He saw the value of Rousseau's teachings in their secondary consequences and not in their fundamental essence— the appeal to *justice*. Similarly, in ranking so high the conception of duty Kant did not ask himself: "whence this respect?" He failed to go beyond the words,—"universal law,"—without attempting to find some other cause for the regard for this law, except its possible universality. And finally, although the application of any rule to *all men without exception* leads unavoidably to the conception of the *equality of all men*, he never came to this inevitable

[6] [It is interesting to note that Shaftesbury, who used exactly the same expression in connection with this subject, took an intermediate position between that of Kant and the author. He wrote: "Principle of fear of future punishment and hope of future reward, how mercenary or servile soever it may be accounted, is yet in many circumstances, a great advantage, security and support to virtue." *An Inquiry concerning Virtue.* (Book 1, part 3, section 3).]—Trans. Note.

conclusion and placed his ethics under the protection of a Supreme Being.

All these considerations serve further to confirm our explanation of the origin of Kantian ethics. He saw in the moral looseness of societies at the end of the eighteenth century the pernicious influence of the Anglo-Scotch philosophers and of the French Encyclopædists. He wishes to re-establish respect for duty, which had been developing in the human race under the influence of religion, and he attempted to accomplish this in his ethics.

One need hardly dwell here on the extent to which Kantian philosophy, under the pretence of social good, aided the supression in Germany of the philosophy of *the development of personality*. This point has been sufficiently discussed by a majority of serious critics of Kant's philosophy,—viz., Wundt, Paulsen, Jodl, and many others.[7]

"Kant's immortal achievement," wrote Goethe, "was the fact that he led us out from the state of flabbiness into which we had sunk." And truly, his ethics undoubtedly introduced a more strict and rigorous attitude toward morality, in place of that looseness which, while not necessarily brought about by the philosophy of the eighteenth century, was in a measure being vindicated by it. But toward a further development of ethics and its better understanding—Kant's teaching contributed nothing. On the contrary, having satisfied to a certain extent the philosophical search for truth, Kant's teaching considerably retarded the development of Ethics in Germany. In vain did Schiller (owing to his familiarity with Ancient Greece) strive to direct ethical thought toward the realization that man becomes truly moral not when the dictates of duty struggle within him against the promptings of emotion, but when *the moral attitude has become his second nature*. In vain he strove to show that truly artistic development (of course, not that which is now

---

[7] About the relation of Kantian ethics to Christianity on the one side, and to egoistic utilitarianism on the other, see particularly, Wundt's *Ethics*, volume II, "Ethical Systems."

known as "æstheticism") aids the formation of personality, that the contemplation of artistic beauty and creative art helps man to rise to the level where he ceases to hear the voice of animal instinct, and where he is brought upon the road to reason and love for humanity. The German philosophers who wrote about morality after Kant, while contributing each his own peculiar point of view, continued, like their master, to occupy the intermediate position between the theological and the philosophical interpretation of morality. They blazed no new trails, but they gave thinkers certain social ideals, within the narrow limits of the semi-feudal system of their day. At the time when in the field of moral philosophy a school of the Utilitarians, headed by Bentham and Mill, was making headway, and when the birth of the Positivist school of Auguste Comte was preparing philosophy for the scientific ethics of Darwin and Spencer, German ethics continued to subsist on scraps of Kantism, or wandered in the mists of metaphysics, at times even reverting, more or less openly, to theological ethics.

We must say, however, that even if German philosophy of the first half of the nineteenth century, like German society of that time, did not dare throw off the fetters of the feudal system, still it aided the sadly needed moral revival of Germany, inspiring the young generation toward a higher and more idealistic service to society. In this respect Fichte, Schelling, and Hegel occupy an honourable place in the history of philosophy, and among them Fichte is of particular importance.

I shall not expound his teaching here, for that would necessitate the use of a metaphysical language that only obscures the thought, instead of clarifying it. Hence I refer those who wish to acquaint themselves with Fichte's teaching to the excellent exposition by Jodl, in his "History of Ethics," where he calls Fichte's teaching "Ethics of creative genius." I will only mention here one of the conclusions of this teaching in order to show how nearly Fichte approached some of the conclusions of rational, scientific ethics.

The philosophy of Ancient Greece strove to become a guide in human life. The same aim was pursued by the moral philosophy of Fichte. His demands with respect to morality itself were very high, i. e., he insisted upon complete disinterestedness of moral motives, rejecting all egoistic aims. He demanded complete and clear consciousness in human will, and he upheld the broadest and highest aims, which he defined as the supremacy of reason attained through human freedom and the eradication of human inertia.

In other words, it may be said that morality, according to Fichte, consists in the triumph of the very essence of man, of the very basis of his thinking, over that which he passively assimilates from the environment.

Furthermore, Fichte maintained that conscience should never be guided by authority. He whose actions are based on authority, acts in a conscienceless manner. It can easily be imagined how elevating an influence such principles were to the German youth in the twenties and thirties of the nineteenth century.

Fichte thus returned to the thought that was expressed in Ancient Greece. An inherent property of *human reason* lies at the bases of moral judgments, and in order to be moral, man has no need either of religious revelation from above, or of fear of punishment in this or in the after life. This idea, however, did not prevent Fichte from finally coming to the conclusion that no philosophy can subsist without divine revelation.

Krause went still further.[8] For him philosophy and theology merged into one. Baader built his philosophy on the dogmas of the Catholic Church, and his very exposition was permeated with the spirit of that Church.[9]

Schelling, Baader's friend, came straight to theism. His ideal is Plato, and his God—a personal God, whose revelation should take the place of all philosophy. Notwithstanding, the German theologists bitterly attacked Schelling, in spite of the fact that he made so

---

[8] [Karl Christian F. Krause (1781–1832). See Jodl's *Gesch. der Ethik*, vol. 2.]—Trans. Note.
[9] [Franz Xaver Baader (1765–1841)]—Trans. Note.

thoroughgoing a concession to them. They understood, of course, that his God was not the Christian God, but rather the God of Nature, with its struggle between good and evil. Besides, they saw what an elevating influence Schelling's philosophy exerted upon youth, an influence which their ecclesiastical teachings failed to attain.[10]

Hegel (1790–1831) did not devote a special work to ethics, but he considers moral problems in his "Philosophy óf Law." [11] In his philosophy, the law and its bases, and the teaching of the moral, merge into one,—a very characteristic feature of the German mind of the nineteenth century.

In analyzing the Kantian moral law, Hegel first of all pointed out that it is wrong to accept as the justification of the moral rule the fact that it may be generally acknowledged as desirable. He showed that it is possible to find some general basis for every act, or even to raise every act to the dignity of duty. And indeed, we all know that not only do the savages carry out from a sense of duty some actions against which our conscience revolts (killing of children, clan vendetta), but that even civilized societies accept as the general law such actions as many of us consider absolutely revolting (capital punishment, exploitation of labour, class inequalities, etc.).

With all due respect to Kant, those who reflect upon the foundation of the moral conceptions, feel that there is some general rule

[10]In Russia we know, for example, from the correspondence of the Bakunins, what an elevating influence Schelling's philosophy exerted, at first, upon the youth that grouped itself around Stankevich and Mikhail Bakunin. But in spite of some correct surmises, expressed but vaguely (about good and evil, for example) Schelling's philosophy, owing to its mystical elements, soon faded away, of course, under the influence of scientific thought. [See *Corréspondance de Michel Bakounine*, Paris 1896; Bakunin, *Soƶial-politischer Briefwechsel*, 1895. Also, Bakunin, *Œuvres*, 6 vols., Paris, 1895–1913. Nikolai V. Stankevich (1813–1840).]—Trans. Note.

[11] *Fundamental Principles of the Philosophy of Law (Grundlinien der Philosophie des Rechts*, 1821). *Also the Phenomenology of the Spirit*, and the *Encyclopædia of the Philosophical Sciences*,—on the scientific analysis of the Natural Law, 1802–1803. [See *Werke*, Berlin, 1832–45,—vol. 8 (*Grundlinien*); vol. 2 (*Phänomenologie des Geistes*); vols. 6 & 7 *Encyclopädie der philos. Wissenschaften*).]—Trans. Note.

hidden at the bottom of these conceptions. It is significant that from the time of Ancient Greece, thinkers have been searching for a suitable expression, in the form of a brief, generally acceptable formula, to denote that combination of judgment and feeling (or more correctly—judgment approved by feeling), which we find in our moral conceptions.

Hegel, too, felt this need, and he sought support for "morality" (*Moralität*) in the naturally developed institutions of the family, society, and especially the State. Owing to these three influences, wrote Hegel, man cultivates such a close bond with morality that it loses for him the character of an external compulsion; he sees in it the manifestation of his free will. Moral conceptions developed in this manner are, of course, not unalterable. They were first embodied in the family, then in the State,—but even here there were changes; new and higher forms of morality were constantly being developed, and greater and greater emphasis was being placed on the right of personality to independent development. But it should be remembered that the morality of a primitive shepherd has the same value as the morality of a highly developed individual.

In his interpretation of the development of moral conceptions Hegel unquestionably approached those French philosophers who, as early as the end of the eighteenth century, laid the foundations of the theory of evolution. Hegel was the first thinker in Germany (not counting Goethe) who built his philosophical system on the idea of evolution, although in his teaching this evolution took the form of the famous triad—thesis, antithesis, synthesis. In opposition to Kant, Hegel taught that absolute reason is not an unalterable truth, or immutable thinking; it is a living, constantly moving, and developing reason. This cosmic reason manifests itself in mankind, that finds its self-expression in the State. In Hegel's philosophy human personality is completely absorbed by the State, to which man must render obedience. The individual is only an instrument in the hands of the State, and is therefore but a means; under no circumstances can the individual serve as the aim for the State. The

State, governed by an intellectual aristocracy, takes, in Hegel's philosophy, an aspect of a superhuman, semi-divine institution.

Needless to say, such a conception of society inevitably rules out the idea of recognizing *justice* (i. e., equity) as the basis of moral judgments. It is also clear that so authoritarian an interpretation of the social structure leads back inevitably to religion, namely, to Christianity, which through its Church was one of the principal factors that created the modern State. Hegel, accordingly, saw the proper field for the creative activity of the human spirit not in the realm of the free building of social life, but in the realm of art, religion, and philosophy.

As Eucken justly remarked, we have in Hegel's philosophy a well-rounded system based on the laws of logic; at the same time intuition plays an important part in his philosophy. But if we were to ask: is Hegel's intuition consistent with his entire philosophy?— we should have to answer in the negative.

Hegel's philosophy exerted a vast influence not only in Germany, but also in other countries (especially in Russia). But it owes its influence not to its logical gradations, but to that vital sense of life which is so characteristic of Hegel's writings. Therefore, although Hegel's philosophy made for reconciliation with reality by insisting that "all that exists is rational," it served at the same time to reawaken thought, and brought a certain degree of revolutionary spirit into philosophy; it contained certain progressive elements, and these enabled the so-called "left" Hegelians to use Hegel's teaching as the basis of their revolutionary thought. But even for them the inconclusiveness of Hegelian philosophy proved to be a constant obstacle, especially its subservience to the State. Hence, in their critique of the social system, the "left" Hegelians always stopped short as soon as they came to consider the foundation of the State.

I shall not dwell in detail on the teaching of the German philosopher Schleiermacher (1768–1834), whose moral philosophy, as full of metaphysics as that of Fichte, was built (especially in his second period, 1819–1830) on the basis of theology, not even of religion;

229

it adds almost nothing to what was already said on the same subject by his predecessors. I will simply note that Schleiermacher indicated the three-fold nature of moral acts. Locke, and the eudemonist school in general, asserted that moral conduct is the supreme good; Christianity regarded it as virtue and the fulfilment of duty to the Creator; whereas Kant, while recognizing virtue, saw in moral conduct primarily the fulfilment of duty in general. For Schleiermacher's moral teaching these three elements are indivisible, and the place of justice as constituting the basic element of morality is taken by Christian love.

Generally speaking, Schleiermacher's philosophy constitutes an attempt on the part of a Protestant theologian to reconcile theology with philosophy. In pointing out that man feels his bond with the Universe, his dependence upon it, a desire to merge into the life of Nature, he endeavoured to represent this feeling as a purely religious emotion, forgetting (as Jodl justly remarked) "that this universal bond forges also cruel chains that bind the striving spirit to the base and the ignoble. The question 'Why am I such as I am?' was put to the mysterious cosmic forces as often with a bitter curse as with gratitude."

CHAPTER X

In the nineteenth century there appeared three new currents in ethics: 1) *Positivism,* which was developed by the French philosopher, Auguste Comte, and which found a prominent representative in Germany in the person of Feuerbach; 2) *Evolutionism,* i. e., the teaching about the gradual development of all living beings, social institutions, and beliefs, and also of the moral conceptions of man. This theory was created by Charles Darwin and was later elaborated in detail by Herbert Spencer in his famous "Synthetic Philosophy." 3) *Socialism,* i. e., a teaching of the political and social equality of men. This teaching derived from the Great French Revolution and from later economic doctrines originating under the influence of the rapid development of industry and capitalism in Europe. All three currents exerted a strong influence upon the development of morality in the nineteenth century. However, up to the present time, there has not been developed a complete system of ethics based on the data of all the three teachings. Some modern philosophers, such as, for example, Herbert Spencer, M. Guyau, and partly Wilhelm Wundt, Paulsen, Höffding, Gizycki, and Eucken, made attempts to create a system of ethics on the bases of positivism and evolutionism, but all of them more or less ignored socialism. And yet we have in socialism a great moral current, and from now on no new system of ethics can be built without in some way considering this teaching, which is the expression of the striving of the working masses for social justice and equity.

Before discussing the views on morality of the chief representatives of the three doctrinal currents, we shall briefly expound the ethical system of the English thinkers of the first half of the nineteenth century. The Scotch philosopher Mackintosh is the fore-runner of Positivism in England. By his convictions he was a radical and an ardent defender of the ideas of the French Revolution. He expounded his moral teaching in his book, "View of Ethical Philosophy," [1] where he systematized all the theories of the origin of morality advanced by Shaftesbury, Hutcheson, Hume, and Adam Smith. Like these thinkers Mackintosh recognized that man's moral actions are prompted by feeling and not by reason. Moral phenomena, he taught, are a special kind of *feelings:* sympathy and antipathy, approval and disapproval, with respect to all our propensities which give birth to all our actions; gradually these feelings combine and constitute a sort of unified whole, a special property of our psychic self, a faculty which can be called moral conscience.

We feel, thereby, that it depends upon our will whether we act with or against our conscience, and when we act against our conscience we blame upon it the weakness of our will or our will for evil.

Thus it is seen that Mackintosh reduced everything to feeling. There was no room whatsoever for the working of reason. Moreover, according to him the moral feeling is something innate, something inherent in the very nature of man, and not a product of reasoning or up-bringing.

This moral feeling, wrote Mackintosh, undoubtedly possesses an imperative character; it demands a certain attitude toward men, and this is because we feel conscious that our moral feelings, the condemnation or approval by them of our actions, operate within the bounds of our will.

Various moral motives merge little by little into a whole in our conception, and the combination of two groups of feelings, that have, in fact, nothing in common,—the egoistic feeling of self-preservation and the feeling of sympathy for others—determine the character of a man.

Such was, according to Mackintosh, the origin of morality, and such was its criterion. But these ethical bases are so beneficial to

[1] [*Dissertation on the Progress of Ethical Philosophy* (1830)]—Trans. Note.

232

man, they so closely bind each one of us to the good of the entire society, that they, inevitably, had to develop in mankind.

On this issue Mackintosh takes the viewpoint of the Utilitarians. And he particularly insisted that it is wrong to confuse (as is continually being done) the *criterion* of morality, i. e., that which serves us as the *standard* in evaluating the qualities and the actions of man, with that which urges us personally to desire certain actions and to act in a certain way. These two factors belong to different fields, and they should be always distinguished in a serious study. It is important for us to know what actions and what qualities we approve and disapprove from the moral point of view,—this is our criterion, our standard of moral evaluation. But we must also know whether our approval and disapproval are the product of a spontaneous feeling, or whether they come also from our mind, through reasoning. And, finally, it is important for us to know: if our approval and disapproval originate in a feeling, whether that feeling is a primary property of our organism, or has it been gradually developing in us under the influence of reason?

But if we are to formulate thus the problems of ethics, then, as Jodl justly remarked: "In certain respects this is the clearest and the truest observation ever made about the bases of morality. Then it really becomes clear that if there is anything innate in our moral feeling, this fact does not prevent reason from realizing afterwards that certain feelings and actions, developing through social education, are valuable for the common good." [2]

It also becomes clear, I will add, that *sociality*, and its necessary accompaniment—mutual aid, characteristic of the vast majority of animal species and so much more of man,—were the source of moral sentiments from the time of the very first appearance of man-like creatures on the earth, and that social sentiments were further strengthened by the realization and the understanding of the facts

---

[2] *Dissertation on the progress of ethical philosophy,* in the first volume of the *Encyclopædia Britannica,* (8th edition). Later this work was repeatedly reprinted as a separate edition. [Edinburgh, 1830.]

of social life, i. e., by the effort of reason. And in proportion to the development and increasing complexity of social life, reason acquired ever greater influence upon the moral make-up of man.

Finally, it is equally unquestionable that moral feeling can easily become dulled due to the stern struggle for existence, or to the development of instincts of robbery which at times acquire great intensity among certain tribes and nations. And this moral feeling might have withered altogether if the very nature of man, as well as of the majority of the more highly developed animals, did not involve, aside from the herd instinct, a certain mental bent which supports and strengthens the influence of sociality. This influence, I believe, consists in the conception of *justice*, which in the final analysis is nothing but the recognition of *equity* for all the members of a given society. To this property of our thinking, which we already find among the most primitive savages and to a certain extent among herd animals, we owe the growth in us of the moral conceptions in the form of a persistent, and at times even *unconsciously imperative* force. As regards magnanimity, bordering on self-sacrifice, which alone, perhaps, truly deserves the name "moral," I shall discuss this third member of the moral trilogy later, in connection with the ethical system of Guyau.

I shall not dwell upon the English philosophy of the end of the eighteenth and the beginning of the nineteenth century. It represents a reaction against the French Revolution and against the pre-revolutionary philosophy of the Encyclopædists, as well as against the daring ideas expressed by William Godwin in his book, "Inquiry Concerning Political Justice." This book is a complete and serious exposition of that which began to be advocated later under the name of *Anarchism*.[3] It is very instructive to become acquainted with the

---

[3] Godwin, *Enquiry concerning Political Justice and its Influence on General Virtue and Happiness*, 2 vols., London, 1793. Under fear of the persecutions to which Godwin's friends, the republicans, were subjected, the anarchistic and communistic assertions of Godwin were omitted from the second edition.

English philosophy of this period. I therefore refer all those interested to the excellent exposition by Jodl, in the second volume of his "Geschichte der Ethik."

I will only add on my part that, in general, the English thinkers of this period especially endeavoured to prove the insufficiency of mere feeling for the explanation of morality. Thus Stewart, a prominent representative of this epoch, maintains that morality cannot be sufficiently accounted for either by the "reflective affects" of Shaftesbury, or by Butler's "conscience," etc. Having pointed out the irreconcilability of various theories of morality, some of which are built on benevolence, others on justice, on rational self-love, or on the obedience to God's will, he did not wish to acknowledge, like Hume, that rational judgment alone is also incapable of giving us a conception of good, or of beauty; he showed, at the same time, how far moral phenomena are removed in man from a mere emotional impulse.

It would seem that, having arrived at the conclusion that in all moral conceptions reason binds our various perceptions together, and then develops new conceptions within itself (and he even mentioned the "mathematical idea of equality"), Stewart should have arrived at the idea of justice. But whether it was under the influence of the old ideas of the intuitive school, or of the new tendencies which, after the French Revolution, denied the very thought of the equality of rights of all men, Stewart did not develop his thoughts and failed to come to any definite conclusion.[4]

New ideas in the realm of ethics were introduced in England by a contemporary of Mackintosh, Jeremy Bentham. Bentham was not a philosopher in the strict sense of the word. He was a lawyer, and his specialty was the law and the practical legislation resulting from it. Taking a negative attitude to the law in the form in which it was expressed in legislation throughout thousands of years of historical absence of human rights, Bentham strove to find deep, strictly

---

[4] [Dugald Stewart, *Outlines of Moral Philosophy*, 1793; *Philosophy of the active and moral powers*, 1828.]—Trans. Note.

scientific, theoretical bases of law, such as could be approved by reason and conscience.

In Bentham's view law coincides with morality, and therefore he named his first book, where he expounded his theory, "An Introduction to the Principles of Morals and Legislation." [5]

Bentham, like Helvétius, sees the basic principle of all morality and law in the greatest happiness of the greatest number of men. The same principle, as we have seen, was adopted by Hobbes as the basis of his ethics. But Bentham and his followers (Mill and others) derived from this principle conclusions directly contrary to those of Hobbes. The reactionary Hobbes, under the influence of the Revolution of 1648, through which he had lived, maintained that the greatest happiness can be given to man only by a firm ruling power. On the other hand, Bentham, a "philanthropist" as he called himself, went so far as to recognize equality as a desirable aim. Although he rejected the socialistic teachings of Owen, he nevertheless acknowledged that "equality of wealth would help to attain the greatest happiness of the greatest number of men, provided only the realization of this equality does not lead to revolutionary outbreaks." As regards the law in general he even reached anarchistic conclusions, holding that the fewer laws, the better. "The laws," he wrote, "are a limitation of man's inherent ability to act, and therefore, from the absolute point of view, they represent an evil."

Bentham subjected to severe examination all the existing systems and all the current theories of morality. But, as I have already pointed out, while approaching socialistic and even anarchistic conclusions, Bentham did not venture to follow his ideas to their logical conclusion, and he directed his main efforts toward determining which pleasures are stronger, more lasting, and more fruitful. Since different people understand in different ways their own and the general human happiness, and are far from being able to determine what leads them to happiness and what to suffering, being even more apt to be mistaken as to what constitutes social good, Bentham, accord-

[5] [London, 1789; second edition, London, 1823.]—Trans. Note.

ingly, tried to determine what gives the individual as well as society the possibility of greatest happiness.

The search for happiness is a striving for personal pleasure,—therefore Bentham, like his predecessor in Ancient Greece, Epicurus, endeavoured to determine which of our pleasures are capable of giving us the greatest happiness,—not only a momentary happiness but a lasting one, even if it has to be linked with pain. For this purpose he tried to establish a sort of "scale of pleasures," and at the head of this scale he put the strongest and the deepest pleasures; those that are not accidental or momentary, but those that can last for life; those that are certain, and finally those whose realization is near and is not postponed to a distant and indefinite future.

The *intensity* of a pleasure, its *duration;* its *certainty or uncertainty;* its *propinquity or remoteness,*—these are the four criteria which Bentham endeavoured to establish in his "arithmetic of pleasures," and he also added *fecundity,* i. e., the capacity of a given pleasure to produce new pleasures, and also the *extent,* i. e., the capacity to give pleasure not only to me but also to others.[6] Parallel with his "scale of pleasures" Bentham also drew up "the scale of pains," where he distinguished between the troubles that harm individuals and those that harm all the members of society or a group of men, and finally, the sufferings and the calamities that undermine irreparably the strength of the individual or even of the whole of society.

In seeking the explanation of the moral feeling Bentham was not content with the previously given explanations of the origin of morality from an innate moral feeling (natural or inspired from above), sympathy and antipathy, "conscience," "moral duty," etc., —the very mention of "virtue," connected in history with the terrors of the Inquisition, aroused his indignation.

[6] [Bentham also includes a seventh criterion,—*"purity,* or the chance it has of *not* being followed by sensations of the opposite kind: that is, pain if it be pleasure; pleasure, if it be pain." (*Intro.,* etc., Ed. of 1907, Chapter IV, page 30).]—Trans. Note.

These thoughts of his are throughout sharply expressed and developed in detail in his "Deontology; or the Science of Morality," which was arranged and edited after Bentham's death by his friend, John Bowring.[7]

Morality must be built on different bases, taught Bentham. It is the duty of thinkers to prove that a "virtuous" act is a correct calculation, a temporary sacrifice which will give one the maximum of pleasure; whereas an immoral act is an incorrect calculation. Man should seek his personal pleasure, his personal interest.

Thus spoke Epicurus and many of his followers,—for example, Mandeville in his famous "Fable of the Bees." But as Guyau pointed out,[8] Bentham introduces here a considerable correction, whereby utilitarianism makes a great step forward. Virtue is not merely a calculation, wrote Bentham, it also implies a certain effort, a struggle,—man sacrifices immediate pleasure for the sake of a greater pleasure in the future. Bentham particularly insists upon this sacrifice, which is, in fact, a self-sacrifice, even if it is a temporary one. And indeed, not to see this would be refusing to recognize that which constitutes at least half of the entire life of the animal world, of the least developed savages, and even of the life of our industrial societies. Many who call themselves utilitarians actually fall into this error. But Bentham understood where utilitarianism would lead without this correction, and therefore he persistently called attention to it. So much more one would expect John Stuart Mill to insist upon this correction, for he wrote at the time when the communist teachings of Owen,—which also rejected all morality inspired from above,—had already become widespread in England.

These criteria of good and evil, Bentham proved, serve not alone as the basis of the moral evaluation of our own actions, but they must also serve as the basis of all legislation. They are the

[7] The first edition of *Deontology* appeared in 1834, in two volumes. [London; Edinburgh.]

[8] Guyau, *La Morale anglaise contemporaine* [Paris, 1879, 2nd. edition, rev. and aug., 1885.]—Trans. Note.

criterion of morality, its standard, its touchstone. But here enters also a series of other considerations which considerably influence and modify the conceptions of what is moral and desirable for individuals as well as for whole societies at different periods of their development. The intellectual development of man, his religion, his temperament, the state of his health, his up-bringing, his social position, and also the political system,—all these factors modify the moral conceptions of individuals and of societies, and Bentham, pursuing his legislative problems, carefully analyzed all these influences. With all that, though he was inspired by the highest motives and fully appreciated the moral beauty of self-sacrifice, he has not shown where, how, and why, instinct triumphs over the cold judgments of reason, what the relation is between reason and instinct, and where the vital connection is between them. We find in Bentham the instinctive power of sociality, but we cannot see how it keeps pace with his methodical reason, and hence we feel the incompleteness of his ethics and we understand why many, on becoming acquainted with it, were left unsatisfied, and continued to seek reinforcement for their ethical tendencies,—some in religion, and others in its offspring—the Kantian ethics of duty.

On the other hand, it is unquestionable that Bentham's critique is permeated with the desire to urge men toward creativeness, which would give them not only personal happiness, but also a broad understanding of social problems; he seeks also to inspire them with noble impulses. Bentham's aim is to have law and legislation inspired not by the current conceptions of human happiness under the firm hand of the ruling power, but by the higher considerations of the greatest happiness of the greatest number of the members of society.

Bearing in mind this feature of Bentham's ethics, and the general spirit of his work, his lofty aim, his concern for the preservation in society of the means for satisfying the personal enterprise of individual members, and his understanding of the æsthetic element

239

in the sense of duty, it is easy to grasp why, in spite of the arithmetical dryness of his starting point, Bentham's teaching exercised such potent influence upon the best men of his time. It is also clear why men who have thoroughly studied his teaching, such as Guyau, for example, in his excellent work on modern English ethics, consider Bentham the true founder of the entire English Utilitarian school,—to which Spencer partly belongs.

Bentham's ideas were further developed by a group of his followers, headed by James Mill and his son, John Stuart Mill (1806–1873). The latter's little book, "Utilitarianism," represents the best exposition of utilitarian ethics.[9]

Although John Stuart Mill wrote only this little book on the theory of morality, he nevertheless made a considerable contribution to moral science and carried the utilitarian teaching to a logical completeness. In his book, as well as in his writings on Economics, Mill is filled with the idea of the necessity of rebuilding social life on the new ethical bases.

To effect this rebuilding Mill saw no need either of the religious motivation of morality or of legislation derived from pure reason (Kant's attempt in this direction ended in complete failure);—he thought it possible to found the whole of moral teaching on one fundamental principle—the *striving for the greatest happiness*, correctly, i. e., rationally, understood. This interpretation of the origin of morality was already given by Hume. But Mill, as was to be expected of a thinker of the second half of the nineteenth century, completed this idea by pointing to the continuous development of the moral conceptions in mankind, owing to social life. The moral element is not innate in man but presents a *product of development*.

Humanity possesses some excellent propensities, but it has also evil ones; separate individuals are ready to work for the good of the whole, but others do not want to concern themselves with this.

[9] *Utilitarianism* appeared in 1861 in "Fraser's Magazine," and in 1863 in book form.

Conceptions of what is good for society, and consequently for the individual, are still very confused. But if we observe in this struggle a progress toward the better, it is due to the fact that *every human society* is interested in having in the ascendancy the elements of good, i. e., the common welfare, or, speaking in Kantian language, in having the altruistic elements triumph over the egoistic. In other words, we find in social life a synthesis of the moral tendencies based on the sense of duty, and those that originate in the principle of the greatest happiness (eudemonism), or of greatest utility (utilitarianism).

Morality, says Mill, is the product of the interaction between the psychic structure of the individual, and society; and if we regard morality in this light we open a series of broad and alluring vistas and a series of fruitful and lofty problems in the realm of reconstructing society. From this point of view we should see in morality the sum of demands that society makes on the character and the will of its members in the interest of their own welfare and further development. This, however, is not a dead formula, but on the contrary, something living, something not only legalizing changeability, but even requiring it; this is not the legalization of that which has been, and which has perhaps already outlived its time, but a vital principle for building the future. And if there is a clash of factions which interpret in different ways the problems of the future, if the striving for improvement collides with the habit of the old, there can be no other proofs, or any other criterion for checking them, than the welfare of mankind and its improvement.

It may be seen even from this brief outline, what vistas Mill opened by the application to life of the principle of utility. Owing to this circumstance he exerted a great influence upon his contemporaries, all the more that all his works were written in simple and clear language.

But the principle of justice, which was already pointed out by Hume, was absent from Mill's reasoning, and he makes allusion to justice only at the end of the book, where he speaks of a criterion by means of which could be checked the correctness of various conclusions reached by various movements striving for preponderance in the course of the progressive development of society.

As regards the question,—to what extent the principle of utility, i. e., *utilitarianism*, can be deemed sufficient for the explanation of the moral element in humanity,—we will consider it at a later time. Here it is important merely to note the forward step made by ethics, the desire to build it exclusively on a rational basis, without the covert or ostensible influence of religion.[10] Prior to passing to the exposition of the ethics of positivism and evolutionism it is necessary to dwell, even if briefly, on the moral teachings of some philosophers of the nineteenth century, who, though they took the metaphysical and spiritualistic viewpoint, still exerted a certain influence upon the development of modern ethics. In Germany such a thinker was Arthur Schopenhauer, and in France, Victor Cousin and his pupil, Théodore Jouffroy.

The ethical teaching of Schopenhauer is given a very different appreciation by various writers, as is, in fact, everything written by this pessimist-philosopher, whose pessimism originated not in his active sympathy for humanity, but in his extremely egoistic nature.

Our world, taught Schopenhauer, is an imperfect world; our life is suffering; our "will to live" begets in us desires, in trying to realize which we meet obstacles; and in struggle with these obstacles we experience suffering. But as soon as the obstacle is conquered

[10] It is necessary to add that in developing Bentham's ideas John Stuart Mill introduced a great deal of new matter. Bentham, for example, in expounding his utilitarian theory of morality, had in mind only the *quantity* of good, and accordingly he called his theory *"moral arithmetic,"* whereas Mill introduced into utilitarianism a new element—*quality*, and thereby laid the bases of *moral æsthetics*. Mill classified pleasures into higher and lower, into those worthy of preference, and unworthy of it. That is why he said that "a discontented (unhappy) Socrates, is higher in moral regard than a contented pig." To feel oneself a *man* is to be conscious of one's inner value, to feel one's dignity, and in judging various actions man should keep in mind the duty imposed upon him by *human dignity*. Here Mill already rises above narrow utilitarianism and indicates broader bases of morality than utility and pleasure. [Note by Lebedev, the Russian Editor.]

and the desire is fulfilled, dissatisfaction again arises. As active participants in life we become martyrs. Progress does not do away with suffering. On the contrary, with the development of culture our needs also increase; failure to satisfy them brings new sufferings, new disappointments.

With the development of progress and culture, the human mind becomes more sensitive to suffering and acquires the capacity of feeling not only its own pain and suffering, but also of living through the sufferings of other men and even of animals. As a result man develops the feeling of commiseration, which constitutes the basis of morality and the source of all moral acts.

Thus Schopenhauer refused to see anything moral in actions or in a mode of life based on the considerations of self-love and striving for happiness. But he also rejected the Kantian sense of duty as the basis of morality. Morality, according to Schopenhauer, begins only when man acts in a certain way out of sympathy for others, out of commiseration. The feeling of commiseration, wrote Schopenhauer, is a primary feeling, inherent in man, and it is in this feeling that the *basis of all moral tendencies* lies, and not in personal considerations of self-love or in the sense of duty.

Moreover, Schopenhauer pointed out two aspects of the feeling of sympathy: in certain cases something *restrains* me from inflicting suffering upon another, and in others something urges me to action when someone else is made to suffer. In the first case the result is simple *justice*, while in the second case we have a manifestation of love for one's neighbour.

The distinction drawn here by Schopenhauer is unquestionably a step forward. It is necessary. As I have already pointed out in the second chapter this distinction is made by the savages, who say that one *must* do certain things, while it is merely *shameful not to perform* others, and I am convinced that in time this distinction will be considered fundamental, for our moral conceptions are best of all expressed by the three-membered formula: *sociality, justice,* and *magnanimity,* or that which is to be considered *morality* proper.

ETHICS: ORIGIN AND DEVELOPMENT

Unfortunately, the postulate assumed by Schopenhauer for the purpose of dividing that which he called *justice* from the *love for fellow-men*, is hardly correct. Instead of showing that since commiseration has brought man to *justice* it is the recognition of *equity* for all men, a conclusion which was already reached by ethics at the end of the eighteenth and in the first part of the nineteenth century, he sought the explanation of this feeling in the metaphysical equality of all men in essence. Moreover, by identifying justice with commiseration, i. e., uniting a conception and a feeling that have different origins, he considerably diminished thereby the importance of so fundamental an element of morality as justice. After all he joined together that which is *just,* and has therefore an obligatory character, and that which is *desirable,* such as a generous impulse. Like most writers on ethics, therefore, he insufficiently distinguished between two motives, one of which says: "do not unto another what you do not want done unto yourself," and the second: "give freely to another, without considering what you will get in return."

Instead of showing that we have here a manifestation of two different conceptions of our attitude toward others, Schopenhauer saw the difference only in the degree to which they influence our *will.* In one case man remains inactive and abstains from hurting another, while in the second case he comes forward actively, urged by his love for his fellow-men. In reality the distinction goes much deeper, and it is impossible to discuss correctly the bases of ethics without recognizing as its first principle *justice* in the sense of *equity,* after which one can also recommend *magnanimity,* which Guyau so excellently characterized as the lavish spending of one's intellect, feelings, and will, for the good of others or of all.

Of course, since Schopenhauer saw in commiseration an act of justice, he could not altogether do without the conception of justice, interpreted in the sense of a recognition of equity. And indeed, the fact that we are capable of feeling sympathy for others, to be affected by their joys and sorrows, and to live through both of these with other men,—this fact would be inexplicable if we did not possess a conscious or subconscious ability to identify ourselves with others. And no one could possess such an ability if he considered himself as apart from others and unequal to them, at least in his susceptibility to joys and sorrows, to good and evil, to friendliness and hostility. The impulse of a man who plunges into a river (even though unable to swim) in order to save another, or who exposes himself to bullets in order to pick up the wounded on the battle-field, cannot be explained in any other way than by the recognition of one's equality with all others.[11]

But starting with the proposition that life is evil and that the lower levels of morality are characterized by a strong development of egoism, a passionate desire to live, Schopenhauer asserted that with the development of the feeling of commiseration man acquires the ability to realize and to feel the sufferings of others, and he therefore becomes even more unhappy. He maintained that only asceticism, retirement from the world, and æsthetic contemplation of nature can blunt in us the volitional impulses, free us from the yoke of our passions, and lead us to the highest goal of morality—"annihilation of the will to live." As the result of this annihilation of the will to live, the world will come to the state of infinite rest, Nirvana.

Of course, this pessimistic philosophy is a philosophy of death and not of life, and therefore pessimistic morality is incapable of creating a sound and active movement in society. I have dwelt on the ethical teaching of Schopenhauer only because, by his opposition to

[11] In former times, when peasant serfdom prevailed, i.e., when slavery existed, a large majority of landlords—really slave-owners, would not for a moment permit the thought that their serfs were endowed with just as "elevated and refined" feelings as their own. Hence it was considered a great merit in Turgeniev, Grigorovich, and others, that they succeeded in planting in the landlords' hearts the thought that the serfs were capable of feeling exactly like their owners. Before their time such an admission would have been regarded as a belittling, a debasement of the lofty "gentlemen's" feelings. In England, also, among a certain class of individuals, I met with a similar attitude toward the so-called "hands," i. e., the factory workers, miners, etc.—although the English "county," (administrative unit), and the church "parish" have already done much to eradicate such class arrogance.

245

Kant's ethics, especially to the Kantian theory of duty, Schopenhauer unquestionably helped to prepare the ground in Germany for the period when thinkers and philosophers began to seek the bases of morality in human nature itself and in the development of sociality. But, owing to his personal peculiarities, Schopenhauer was unable to give a new direction to ethics. As regards his excellent analysis of the problem of freedom of will and of the importance of will as the active force in social life, we will discuss these subjects in a later section of this work. Though the post-revolutionary period in France did not produce such pessimistic teachings as the doctrines of Schopenhauer, still the epoch of the restoration of the Bourbons, and the July Empire, are marked by the flourishing of spiritualistic philosophy. During this period the progressive ideas of the Encyclopædists, of Voltaire, Montesquieu, and Condorcet, were replaced by the theories of Victor de Bonald, Josephe de Maistre, Maine de Biran, Royer-Collard, Victor Cousin, and other representatives of reaction in the realm of philosophical thought.

We will not attempt an exposition of these teachings, and will only remark that the moral doctrine of the most prominent and influential of them, Victor Cousin, is the moral teaching of traditional spiritualism.

We must also note the attempt of Victor Cousin's pupil, Théodore Jouffroy, to point to the significance in ethics of that element of morality which I call in my ethical system *self-sacrifice* or *magnanimity*, i. e., of those moments when man gives to others his powers, and at times his life, without thought of what he will obtain in return.

Jouffroy failed duly to appreciate the significance of this element, but he understood that the thing which men call self-sacrifice is a true element of morality. But like all his predecessors, Jouffroy confused this element of morality with morality in general.[12] It

12 Jouffroy, *Cours de Droit Naturel*, Vol. 1, pp. 88–90. [3rd ed., Paris, 1858, 2 vols.; English tr. by Wm. H. Channing, *An Introduction to Ethics*, Boston, 1858, 2 vols.]—Trans. Note.

must be remarked, however, that the whole work of this school had the character of great indefiniteness and of eclecticism, and, perhaps for this very reason, of incompleteness. As we have seen, the second half of the eighteenth century was marked by a daring critique of the scientific, philosophical, political, and ethical conceptions current until that time, and this critique was not confined within the walls of academies. In France the new ideas gained a wide distribution in society and soon produced a radical change in the existing state institutions, and likewise in the entire mode of life of the French people,—economic, intellectual, and religious. After the Revolution, during a whole series of wars that lasted with short interruptions up to 1815, the new conceptions of social life, especially the idea of political equality, were spread at first by the Republican and then by the Napoleonic armies throughout the whole of Western and partly over Central Europe. Of course, the "Rights of Man" introduced by Frenchmen in the conquered territories, the proclamation of the personal equality of all citizens, and the abolition of serfdom, did not survive after the restoration of the Bourbons to the French throne. And what is more, there soon began in Europe the general intellectual reaction which was accompanied by a political reaction. Austria, Russia, and Prussia concluded among themselves a "Holy Alliance," whose object was to maintain in Europe the monarchical and the feudal system. Nevertheless, new political life began in Europe, especially in France, where after fifteen years of mad reaction the July Revolution of 1830 injected a stream of new life in all directions: political, economic, scientific, and philosophical.

Needless to say, the reaction against the Revolution and its innovations, that raged in Europe for thirty years, succeeded in doing a great deal to arrest the intellectual and the philosophical influence of the eighteenth century and of the Revolution, but with the very first breath of freedom that was wafted across Europe on the day of the July Revolution and the overthrow of the Bourbons, the rejuvenated intellectual movement again revived in France and in England.

Already in the thirties of the last century new industrial powers began to be developed in Europe: railroads began to be built, screw-driven steamships made distant ocean voyages possible, large factories applying improved machinery to raw products were established, a large metallurgical industry was being developed owing to the progress of chemistry, etc. The whole of economic life was being rebuilt on new bases, and the newly formed class of the urban proletariat came forth with its demands. Under the influence of the conditions of life itself, and of the teachings of the first founders of socialism—Fourier, Saint-Simon, and Robert Owen—the socialistic labour movement began steadily to grow in France and in England. At the same time a new science, based entirely on experiment and observation, and free from theological and metaphysical hypotheses, began to be formed. The bases of the new science had already been laid at the end of the eighteenth century by Laplace in astronomy, by Lavoisier in physics and chemistry, by Buffon and Lamarck in zoölogy and biology, by the Physiocrats and by Condorcet in the social sciences. Together with the development of the new science there arose in France, in the thirties of the nineteenth century, a fresh philosophy which received the name of *Positivism*. The founder of this philosophy was Auguste Comte.

While in Germany the philosophy of the followers of Kant, Fichte, and Schelling was still struggling in the fetters of a semi-religious metaphysics, i. e., of speculations that have no definite scientific basis, the positivist philosophy threw aside all metaphysical conceptions and strove to become positive knowledge, as Aristotle had attempted to make it two thousand years earlier. It set as its aim in science the recognition of only those conclusions that were derived experimentally; and in philosophy it sought to unite all the knowledge thus acquired by the various sciences into a unified conception of the universe. These teachings of the end of the eighteenth and the beginning of the nineteenth century (the theories of Laplace,

Lavoisier, Buffon, and Lamarck) opened up to man a new world of ever-active natural forces. The same was done in the realm of economics and history by Saint-Simon and his followers, especially the historian Augustin Thierry, and by a succession of other scientists who threw off the yoke of metaphysics.

Auguste Comte realized the necessity of unifying all these new acquisitions and conquests of scientific thought. He decided to unify all the sciences into a single orderly system and to demonstrate the close interdependence of all the phenomena of nature, their sequence, their common basis, and the laws of their development. At the same time Comte also laid the foundation of new sciences, such as *biology* (the science of the development of plant and animal life), *anthropology* (the science of the development of man), and *sociology* (the science of human societies). Recognizing that all creatures are subject to the same natural laws, Comte urged the study of animal societies for the purpose of understanding primitive human societies, and in explaining the origin of the moral feelings in man, Comte already spoke of social instincts.

The essence of positivism is concrete scientific knowledge,—and knowledge, taught Comte, is foresight—*savoir c'est prévoir*—(to know is to foresee), and foresight is necessary for extending the power of man over Nature and for increasing thereby the welfare of societies. Comte exhorted the scientists and the thinkers to come to earth from the realm of dreams and intellectual speculations, to come to human beings vainly struggling from century to century, to help them build a better life, a life more full, more varied, more powerful in its creativeness, to help them to *know* Nature, to enjoy its ever-throbbing life, to utilize its forces, to free man from exploitation by making his labour more productive. At the same time Comte's philosophy aimed to liberate man from the chains of the religious fear of Nature and its forces, and it sought the bases of life of a *free personality* in the social medium, not in compulsion, but in a freely-accepted social covenant.

All that the Encyclopædists vaguely foresaw in science and in philosophy, all that shone as an ideal before the intellectual gaze of the best men of the Great Revolution, all that Saint-Simon, Fourier, and Robert Owen began to express and to foretell, all that the best men of the end of the eighteenth and the beginning of the nineteenth century strove to attain,—all these elements Comte attempted to unite, to strengthen, and to affirm by his positivist philosophy. And from this "philosophy," i. e., from these generalizations and ideas, new sciences, new arts, new conceptions of the Universe, and a new ethics had to develop.

Of course, it would be naïve to consider that a system of philosophy, however thoroughgoing, can create new sciences, a new art, and a new ethics. Any philosophy is but a generalization, the result of intellectual movement in all the realms of life, whereas the elements for this generalization are to be supplied by the development of art, science, and social institutions. Philosophy can merely inspire science and art. A properly motivated system of thought, correlating that which has been already done in each of these realms separately, unavoidably imparts to each of them a new direction, gives them new powers, new creative impulse, and a new and better systematization.

This is what actually took place. The first half of the nineteenth century gave,—in philosophy—positivism; in science—the theory of evolution and a series of brilliant scientific discoveries that marked the few years from 1856 to 1862;[13] in sociology—the socialism of its three great founders: Fourier, Saint-Simon, and Robert Owen, together with their followers; and in ethics—a free morality, not forced upon us from without, but resulting from the innate endowments of human nature. Finally, under the influence of all these conquests of science there developed also a clearer understanding of the intimate connection between man and other sentient crea-

[13] Indestructibility of matter, mechanical theory of heat, homogeneity of physical forces, spectral analysis, and the convertibility of matter in the heavenly bodies, physiological psychology, physiological evolution of organs, etc.

tures, as well as between man's thinking processes and his outer life.

The philosophy of positivism endeavoured to bind into a unified whole all the results and the conquests of scientific thought, and all the higher aspirations of man, and it endeavoured to elevate man to a vivid realization of this unity. That which flashed through in sparks of genius in Spinoza and Goethe when they spoke of the life of Nature and of man, had to find its expression in the new philosophy as a logically inevitable, intellectual generalization.

Needless to say, with such an understanding of "philosophy" Comte ascribed prime importance to ethics. But he derived it not from the psychology of separate individuals, not in the form of moral preaching as was the method in Germany, but as something entirely natural, following logically from the entire *history of the development of human societies.* In urging the need of historical investigation in the realms of anthropology and ethics, Comte probably had in mind the work done in the field of comparative zoölogy by Buffon and then by Cuvier, which completely confirmed the opinions of Lamarck, on the slow, gradual development of the higher animals, although the reactionary Cuvier disputed this opinion. Comte compared the significance of historical investigation in these sciences with the significance of comparative zoölogy in the field of biology.

He regarded ethics as a great power capable of elevating man above the level of everyday interests. Comte endeavoured to base his system of ethics on a *positive foundation,* on the study of its actual development from the animal herd instinct and from simple sociality up to its highest manifestations. And though toward the end of his life,—whether due to decline of intellectual powers, or to the influence of Clotilde de Vaux,—he made concessions to religion, like many of his predecessors, even to the extent of founding his own Church, these concessions can under no circumstances be derived from his first work, "Positive Philosophy." These concessions were mere additions, and quite unnecessary additions, as was well understood by the best pupils of Comte—Littré and Vyroubov,[14] and by his followers in England, Germany, and Russia.[15]

Comte expounded his ethical views in his "Physique Sociale," [16] and he derived his principal ideas of the bases and the content of moral conceptions not from abstract speculations, but from the general facts of human sociality and human history. His main conclusion was that the social tendencies of man can be explained only by inherent quality, i. e., by instinct and by its urge toward the social life. As a contrast to egoism, Comte called this instinct *altruism,* and he regarded it as a fundamental property of human nature; moreover, he was the first to point out boldly that the same innate tendency exists in animals.

It is utterly impossible to divide this instinct from the influence of reason. With the help of reason we create out of our innate feelings and tendencies that which we call moral conceptions, so that the moral element in man is at once inherent and the product of evolution. We come into this world as beings already endowed with the rudiments of morality; but we can become moral men only through the development of our moral rudiments. Moral tendencies are observed also among social animals, but morality as the joint product of instinct, feeling, and reason, exists only in man. It developed gradually, it is developing now, and will continue to grow, —which circumstance accounts for the difference in moral conceptions among different peoples at different periods. This variation led some light-minded negators of morality to conclude that morality is something conditional, having no positive bases in human nature or human reason.

[14] [Grigoriev N. Vyroubov, a Russian mineralogist and positivist philosopher, born 1842.]—Trans. Note.

[15] Comte founded his own positivist church and his new religion where "Humanity" was the supreme deity. This religion of Humanity, in Comte's opinion, was to replace the outworn Christian creed. The religion of Humanity still survives among a small circle of Comte's followers, who do not like to part entirely with the rites, to which they ascribe an educational value.

[16] [Translated by Harriet Martineau, in vol. 2 of the *Phil. Positive,* Lond., 1853.]—Trans. Note.

MORAL TEACHINGS IN THE MODERN ERA

In studying various modifications of the moral conceptions, it is easy to be convinced, according to Comte, that there is in all of them a constant element,—namely, the understanding of what is due to others through the realization of our personal interest. Thus Comte recognized the utilitarian element in morality, i. e., the influence of the considerations of personal utility, of egoism, in the development of the moral conceptions that later evolve into rules of conduct. But he understood too well the importance in the development of morality of the three mighty forces: the feeling of sociality, mutual sympathy, and reason, to fall into the error of the Utilitarians who ascribed the predominating influence to *instinct* and to personal interest.

Morality, taught Comte, like human nature itself,—and like everything in Nature, we will add,—is something already developed and in process of developing at the same time. And in this process of the development of morality he ascribed a great influence to the family, as well as to society. The family, he taught, aids especially the growth of that element in morality which originates in reason. It is, however, difficult to agree with this demarcation, because with the social up-bringing of the youth, as in our boarding schools and residential colleges, for example, and among certain savages, especially in the islands of the Pacific, the herd instinct, the sense of honor and of tribal pride, the religious feeling, etc., develop even more strongly than in the family.

Finally, there is another feature in positivist ethics which must be pointed out. Comte particularly insisted on the great importance of the positivist interpretation of the Universe. It must lead men to the conviction of the close dependence of each individual life upon the life of humanity as a whole. It is therefore necessary to develop in each of us the understanding of the Universal life, of the universal order; and this understanding should serve as the basis for individual as well as for social life. There should also develop in each of us such consciousness of the righteousness of our lives that our every act and our every motive may be freely exposed to the

253

scrutiny of all. Every lie implies a debasement of the "ego," the admission of oneself as inferior to others. Hence Comte's rule, —"vivre au grand jour," to live so as to have nothing to conceal from others.

Comte pointed out three constituent factors in ethics: its essence, i. e., its fundamental principles and its origin; then its importance to society; and finally its evolution and the factors that govern this evolution. Ethics, taught Comte, develops on an historical basis. There is a natural evolution, and this evolution is progress, the triumph of human qualities over animal qualities, the triumph of man over the animal. The supreme moral law consists in leading the individual to assign a secondary place to his egoistic interests; the supreme duty is the social duty. Thus we should take as the basis of ethics the interest of mankind,—humanity—that great being of which each one of us constitutes merely an atom, living but a moment, and perishing in order to transmit life to other individuals. Morality consists in living for others.

Such is, briefly, the essence of Comte's ethical teaching. His scientific as well as his moral ideas continued to be developed in France by his pupils, especially by Emile Littré and G. N. Vyroubov, who published from 1867 to 1883 the magazine "Philosophie Positive," where articles appeared that threw light on various aspects of positivism. In a later part of this work we shall have occasion to refer to a fundamental explanation of the conception of justice offered by Littré.

In conclusion, it must be noted that positivism exerted a strong and a very fruitful influence on the development of the sciences: it can be safely stated that almost all the best modern scientists approach positivism very closely in their philosophical conclusions. In England the whole of Spencer's philosophy, with the fundamental principles of which most naturalists agree, is a positivist philosophy, —though Herbert Spencer, who apparently evolved this philosophy in part independently, even if later than Comte, repeatedly endeavoured to draw away from the French thinker.

MORAL TEACHINGS IN THE MODERN ERA

In the fifties of the nineteenth century, a teaching similar in many respects to the philosophy of Comte was promulgated in Germany by Ludwig Feuerbach. We will now consider this teaching in so far as it concerns ethics.

The philosophical teaching of Feuerbach (1804–1872) deserves a more detailed consideration, for it unquestionably exercised a great influence upon modern thought in Germany. But since the principal object of his philosophy was not so much the elaboration of the bases of morality, as the critique of religion, a more thorough discussion of Feuerbach's teaching would lead me too far afield. I will limit myself, therefore, to pointing out what new elements this teaching added to positivist ethics. Feuerbach did not at once come forward as a positivist who bases his philosophy on the exact data obtained by studying human nature. He began to write under the influence of Hegel, and only gradually, while subjecting to brilliant and daring criticism the metaphysical philosophy of Kant, Schelling, Hegel, and the "idealist" philosophy in general, did he become a philosopher with a "realist" viewpoint. He first expounded his principal thoughts in the form of aphorisms in 1842–1843,[17] in two articles, and only after 1858 did he devote his attention to ethics. In 1866, in his work, "Deity, Freedom, and Immortality from the Viewpoint of Anthropology," [18] he introduced a section on freedom of will, and after that he wrote a series of articles on moral philosophy dealing with the fundamental problems of ethics. But even here, as Jodl, from whom I take these data, remarks, there is no completeness; many matters are but faintly indicated. And yet these works taken together constitute a fairly complete exposition of scientific empiricism in ethics, to which Knapp supplied a good addition in his "System of the Philosophy of Law." [19] The thought-

[17] *Vorläufige Thesen zur Reform der Philosophie* (*Preliminary Theses for Reform in Philosophy*) and *Grundsätze der Philosophie der Zukunft* (*Bases of the Philosophy of the Future*). [The former appears in vol. 2 of Feuerbach's *Werke*, Leipzig, 1846. It was first published in 1842. The second work appeared in Zurich, 1843.]—Trans. Note.
[18] [*Gott, Freiheit und Unsterblichkeit.*]—Trans. Note.
[19] [Ludwig Knapp, *System der Rechtsphilosophie*, 1852.]—Trans. Note.

ful writings of Feuerbach, which, happily, were written in simple, readily understandable language, had a stimulating effect on German ethical thought.

It is true that Feuerbach did not succeed in avoiding certain very marked contradictions. While endeavouring to base his moral philosophy on the concrete facts of life, and taking the position of a defender of eudemonism, i. e., explaining the development of moral tendencies in mankind by the striving for a happier life,—he was at the same time lavish with praises of the ethics of Kant and Fichte, who were decidedly antagonistic to the Anglo-Scotch eudemonists, and who sought the explanation of morality in religious revelation.

The success of Feuerbach's philosophy is fully explained by the realistic, scientific trend of the public mind in the second half of the nineteenth century. Kantian metaphysics and the religiosity of Fichte and Schelling could not possibly dominate the mind during an epoch which was marked by a sudden blossoming forth of knowledge of nature and of cosmic life,—an epoch linked with the names of Darwin, Joule, Faraday, Helmholtz, Claude-Bernard, and others in science, and of Comte in philosophy. Positivism, or as they prefer to call it in Germany, Realism, was the natural outcome of this revival and of the success of natural science after half a century of accumulating of scientific data.

But Jodl points out in Feuerbach's philosophy a certain peculiarity in which he sees "the secret of the success of the realistic movement" in Germany. This was the "purified and deepened interpretation of will and its manifestations," as contrasted with the "abstract and pedantic interpretation of morality by the idealistic school."

This latter school theoretically explained the highest moral manifestations of will by something external, and the "eradication of these misconceptions, effected by Schopenhauer and Beneke, and secured by Feuerbach, constitutes an epoch in German ethics."

"If," says Feuerbach, "every ethics has for its object human will and its relations, it must be necessarily added that there can be no will where there is no urge; and where there is no urge toward happiness there can be no urge whatsoever. The impulse toward happiness is the urge of urges; wherever existence is bound up with will, desire and the desire for happiness are inseparable, in fact, even identical. I want, means that I do not want suffering, I do not want annihilation, but that I want to survive and to prosper. . . . Morality without happiness is like a word without meaning."

This interpretation of morality naturally produced a complete revolution in German thought. But, as Jodl remarks, "Feuerbach himself linked this revolution with the names of Locke, Malebranche, and Helvétius." For the thinkers of Western Europe this interpretation of the moral sense presented nothing new, although Feuerbach expressed it in a form that gained it wider currency than fell to the lot of earlier eudemonists.

As regards the question how the egoistic striving of an individual for personal happiness becomes converted into its "apparent opposite —into self-restraint and into activity for the good of others," the explanation offered by Feuerbach really explains nothing. It simply repeats the question, but in the form of an assertion. "Unquestionably," says Feuerbach, "the basic principle of morality is happiness, yet not happiness concentrated in one person, but extending to various persons, embracing me and thee, i. e., not a one-sided, but a two or many-sided happiness." This, however, is not a solution. The problem of moral philosophy consists of finding an explanation of *why* the feelings and thoughts of man take such a turn that he is capable of feeling and thinking in terms of the interests of others, or even of all men, as of his *own* interests. Is this an inherent instinct, or is it a judgment of our reason, which weighs its interests, identifies them with the interests of others, and which later becomes a habit? Or is it an unconscious feeling which, as the individualists assert, should be resisted? And finally, whence originated this strange sense—not exactly consciousness and not really emotion—of obligation, of duty, this identification of one's own interests with the interests of all?

These are the questions with which ethics has been concerned from the time of Ancient Greece, and to which it supplies most contradictory answers: viz:—revelation from above; egoism, rationally understood; the herd instinct; fear of punishment in the life to come; reasoning; rash impulse, etc. And Feuerbach could offer no new or satisfactory answer to these questions.

Jodl, who takes so sympathetic an attitude toward Feuerbach, points out that "there is obviously a gap in Feuerbach's exposition. He fails to show that the contraposition between me and thee is not a contraposition between two persons, but between the individual and society." [20] But even this remark still leaves the questions unanswered and they remain in all their force.

This omission, continues Jodl, was made good by Knapp's "System of the Philosophy of Law." Knapp definitely represented *the interests of the clan* as the logical starting point in the moral process.[21] *And the rational value of morality increases* in proportion as man identifies himself and his interests with an ever larger group of people, and finally with humanity as a whole. Knapp thus returned to the instinct of sociality, which was already understood by Bacon as a stronger and a more permanently active instinct than that of personal gratification.

Those who wish to gain a closer acquaintance with Feuerbach's ethics are referred to his easily readable works, based on observation of life and not on abstract assumptions, and full of valuable thoughts. Jodl's excellent exposition may be also recommended. I shall merely refer, by way of conclusion, to Feuerbach's explanation of the distinction between *tendencies* (egoistic as well as social) and *duty,* and to the significance of this distinction in ethics. The fact that native propensity and the sense of duty often contradict each other does not mean that they are inevitably antagonistic and must so remain. On the contrary, all moral education strives to

---

[20] Jodl, *Geschichte der Ethik.* Vol. II.

[21] Ludwig Knapp, *System der Rechtsphilosophie*, pp. 107–108, quoted by Jodl.

eliminate this contradiction, and even when a man risks his life for the sake of what he considers his duty, he feels that though action may lead to self-annihilation—*inaction* will unquestionably be a moral-annihilation. But here we are already leaving the realm of simple justice and are entering into the region of the third member of the moral trilogy, and of that I shall speak later. I will simply note one of Feuerbach's definitions which approaches very closely the conception of justice: "Moral will is a will that does not wish to inflict evil, because it does not wish to suffer evil."

The fundamental problem of Feuerbach's philosophy is the establishment of a proper attitude of philosophy towards religion. His negative attitude towards religion is well known. But while endeavouring to free humanity from the domination of religion, Feuerbach, like Comte, did not lose sight of the causes of its origin and its influence on the history of mankind,—the influence which should under no circumstances be forgotten by those who, assuming a scientific attitude, wage a battle against religion and superstition embodied in the Church and in its temporal alliance with the State. The revelation on which religion rests, taught Feuerbach, does not originate from a Deity, but is an expression of vague feelings of what is useful for the human race as a whole. Religious ideals and prescriptions express the ideals of mankind, and it is desirable that the individual should be guided by these ideals in his relations with his fellow-men. This thought is perfectly true, for otherwise no religion could have acquired the power that religions wield over men. But we must not forget that the wizards, the sorcerers, the shamans, and the clergy up to our own time, have been adding to the fundamental religious and ethical prescriptions a whole superstructure of intimidating and superstitious conceptions. Among these should be included the duty of submitting to the inequalities of class and caste, upon which the whole social structure was being erected, and which the representatives of the Church undertook to defend. Every State constitutes an alliance of the rich against the poor, and of the ruling classes, i. e., the military, the lawyers, the rulers, and the clergy, against those governed. And the clergy of all religions, as an active member of the State alliance, never failed to introduce into the "clan ideals" such recommendations and commands as best served the interest of the State alliance, i. e., of the privileged classes.

CHAPTER XI

(Continued)

IT may be seen from our brief survey of the various explanations of the origin of morality, that almost all who wrote on this subject came to the conclusion that we possess *an inherent feeling* that leads us to identify ourselves with others. Different thinkers gave different names to this feeling and offered varying explanations of its origin. Some spoke of the inherent moral feeling without going into any further explanations; others, who endeavoured to gain a deeper insight into the essence of this feeling, called it sympathy, i. e., the *co-miseration* of one individual with others, his equals; some, like Kant, making no distinction between the promptings of our feelings and the dictates of our reason, which most frequently and perhaps always *jointly* govern our actions, preferred to speak of *conscience* or the *imperative* of heart and reason, or of the sense of duty, or simply of the *consciousness* of duty, which is present in all of us. And they did not enter into a discussion of whence these things originate, and how they have been developing in man, as is now done by the writers of the anthropological and evolutionist school. Side by side with these explanations of the origin of morality, another group of thinkers, who did not deem instinct and feeling an adequate explanation of the moral tendencies in man, sought their solution in *reason*. This attitude was especially noticeable among the French writers of the second half of the eighteenth century, i. e., among the Encyclopædists and especially in Helvétius. But although they endeavoured to explain the moral propensities of man exclusively as the result of cold reason and egoism, they recognized at the same time another active force, that of *practical idealism*. This quite frequently makes man act by force of plain sympathy, by commiseration, by man's putting himself in the position of the wronged person and by identifying himself with another.

Remaining faithful to their fundamental point of view, the French thinkers explained these actions by "reason," which finds the gratification of one's selfishness" and of "one's higher needs" in acts directed toward the good of one's fellow-man.

As is known, the complete development of these views was given, after Bentham's manner, by his pupil, John Stuart Mill.

Parallel with these thinkers there were *at all times* two further groups of moral philosophers who attempted to place morality on an entirely different basis.

Some of them held that the moral instinct, feeling, tendency,—or whatever we choose to call it,—is implanted in man by the Creator of Nature, and thus they connected ethics with religion. And this group more or less directly influenced all of moral thought up to the most recent times. The other group of moral philosophers, which was represented in Ancient Greece by some of the Sophists, in the seventeenth century by Mandeville, and in the nineteenth by Nietzsche, took an utterly negative and mocking attitude toward all morality, representing it as a survival of religious environment and of superstitions. Their chief arguments were, on the one hand, the assumption of the *religious nature* of morality, and on the other, the *variety and changeability of moral conceptions.*

We shall have occasion to return to these two groups of interpreters of morality. For the present we will merely note that in all the writers on morality who assumed its origin from the inherent *instincts,* from the feeling of *sympathy,* etc., we already have in one form or another an indication of the consciousness that one of the bases of all morality lies in the mind's conception of *justice.*

We have already seen that many writers and thinkers,—Hume, Helvétius, and Rousseau among them, closely approached the conception of justice as a constituent and necessary part of morality;

they did not, however, express themselves clearly and definitively on the significance of justice in ethics.

At last the great French Revolution, most of whose leaders were under the influence of Rousseau's ideas, introduced into legislation and into life the idea of *political equality*, i. e., of the equality of rights of all the citizens of the State. In 1793–94 part of the revolutionists went still further and demanded "actual equality," i. e., economic equality. These new ideas were being developed during the Revolution in the People's Societies, Extremists' Clubs, by the "Enragés" ("The Incensed"), the "anarchists," etc. The advocates of these ideas were, as is known, defeated in the Thermidor reaction, (July 1794), when the Girondists returned to power. The latter were soon overthrown by the military dictatorship. But the demand for a revolutionary program—the abolition of all the vestiges of feudalism and of serfdom, and the demand for equality of rights, were spread by the Republican armies of France throughout Europe and to the very borders of Russia. And though in 1815 the victorious Allies, headed by Russia and Germany, succeeded in effecting a "restoration" of the Bourbons to the throne, nevertheless "political equality" and the abolition of all survivals of feudal inequality became the watchwords of the desired political system throughout Europe, and has so continued up to the present time.

Thus, at the end of the eighteenth century and the beginning of the nineteenth many thinkers began to see the basis of human morality in justice, and if this view did not become the generally accepted truth it was due to two causes, one of which is psychological and the other historical. As a matter of fact, side by side with the conception of justice and the striving for it, there exists in man equally the striving for personal *domination*, for *power over others*. Throughout the entire history of mankind, from the most primeval times, there is a conflict between these two elements: the striving for justice, i. e., equity, and the striving for individual domination over others, or over the many. The struggle between these two tendencies manifests itself in the most primitive societies.

263

ETHICS: ORIGIN AND DEVELOPMENT

The "elders," in their accumulated wisdom of experience, who saw what hardships were brought upon the entire tribe through changes in the tribal mode of life, or who had lived through periods of privation, were afraid of all innovations, and resisted all changes by force of their authority. In order to protect the established customs they founded the first institutions of the ruling power in society. They were gradually joined by the wizards, shamans, sorcerers, in combination with whom they organized secret societies for the purpose of keeping in obedience the other members of the tribe and for protecting the traditions and the established system of tribal life. At the beginning these societies undoubtedly supported equality of rights, preventing individual members from becoming excessively rich or from acquiring dominant power within the tribe. But these very secret societies were the first to oppose the acceptance of equity as the fundamental principle of social life.

But that which we find among the societies of primitive savages, and, in general, among the peoples leading a tribal mode of life, has been continued throughout the entire history of mankind up to the present time. The Magi of the East, the priests of Egypt, Greece, and Rome, who were the first investigators of nature and of its mysteries, and then the kings and the tyrants of the East, the emperors and the senators of Rome, the ecclesiastical princes in Western Europe, the military, the judges, etc.—all endeavoured in every possible way to prevent the ideas of equity, constantly seeking expression in society, from being realized in life and from threatening their right to inequality, to domination.

It is easy to understand to what an extent the recognition of equity as the fundamental principle of social life was retarded by this influence of the most experienced, the most developed, and frequently the most homogeneous part of society, supported by superstition and religion. It is also evident how difficult it was to abolish inequality, which developed historically in society in the form of slavery, serfdom, class distinctions, "tables of rank" etc., all the more that this inequality was sanctioned by religion and, alas, by science.

The philosophy of the eighteenth century and the popular movement in France ending in the Revolution, were a powerful attempt to throw off the age-long yoke, and to lay the foundations of the new social system on the principle of equity. But the terrible social struggle which developed in France during the Revolution, the cruel bloodshed, and the twenty years of European wars, considerably retarded the application to life of the ideas of equity. Only sixty years after the beginning of the Great Revolution, i. e., in 1848, there again began in Europe a new popular movement under the banner of equity, but in a few months this movement, too, was drowned in blood. And after these revolutionary attempts it was only in the second half of the 'fifties that there occurred a great revolution in the natural sciences, the result of which was the creation of a new generalizing theory—the theory of development, of evolution.

Already in the 'thirties the positivist philosopher, Auguste Comte, and the founders of socialism—Saint-Simon and Fourier (especially his followers) in France, and Robert Owen in England, endeavoured to apply to the life of human societies the theory of the gradual development of plant and animal life, promulgated by Buffon and Lamarck and partly by the Encyclopædists. In the second half of the nineteenth century the study of the development of the social institutions of man, made possible for the first time the full realization of the importance of the development in mankind of this fundamental conception of all social life—*equity*.

We have seen how closely Hume, and even more Adam Smith and Helvétius, especially in his second work ("De l'homme, de ses facultés individuelles et de son éducation")[1] approached the recognition of justice, and consequently also of equity, as the basis of morality in man.

[1] [Appeared posthumously, in 1793; his first work is *De l'Esprit*, 1758.]— Trans. Note.

ETHICS: ORIGIN AND DEVELOPMENT

The proclamation of equity by the "Declaration of the Rights of Man" at the time of the French Revolution (in 1791) put still greater emphasis on this fundamental principle of morality.

We must note here one extremely important and essential step forward that was made with respect to the conception of justice. At the end of the eighteenth century and at the beginning of the nineteenth many thinkers and philosophers began to understand by justice and equity not only political and civic equity, but primarily economic equality. We have already mentioned that Morelly, in his novel, "Basiliade," [2] and especially in his "Code de la Nature," openly and definitely demanded complete equality of possessions. Mably, in his "Traité de la Législation" (1776), very skillfully proved that political equality alone would be incomplete without economic equality, and that equality will be an empty sound if private property is to be preserved.[3] Even the moderate Condorcet declared, in his "Esquisse d'un tableau historique du progrès de l'esprit humain" (1794), that all wealth is usurpation. Finally, the passionate Brissot, who later fell a victim of the guillotine, and who was a Girondist, i. e., a moderate democrat, asserted in a series of pamphlets that private property is a crime against nature.[4]

All these hopes and strivings toward economic equality found expression at the end of the Revolution in the communistic teaching of Gracchus Babeuf.

After the Revolution, in the beginning of the nineteenth century, ideas of economic justice and economic equality were advanced in the teaching which received the name of *Socialism.* The fathers of this teaching in France were Saint-Simon and Charles Fourier, and in England, Robert Owen. Already among these early founders of socialism we find two different points of view as to the methods by

[2] [That is, *Naufrage des îles flottantes.*]—Trans. Note.

[3] [*De la législation; ou Principes des lois*, 2 vols., Amsterdam.]—Trans. Note.

[4] Extensive and valuable material on the subject of the socialistic tendencies in the eighteenth century is to be found in the monograph by André Lichtenberger, *Le Socialisme au XVIII siècle.*—[Paris, 1895.]

which they proposed to establish social and economic justice in society. Saint-Simon taught that a just social system can be organized only with the aid of the ruling power, whereas Fourier, and to some extent Robert Owen, held that social justice may be attained without the interference of the State. Thus Saint-Simon's interpretation of socialism is authoritarian, whereas that of Fourier is libertarian.

In the middle of the nineteenth century socialistic ideas began to be developed by numerous thinkers, among whom should be noted —in France: Considérant, Pierre Leroux, Louis Blanc, Cabet, Vidal, and Pecqueur, and later Proudhon; in Germany: Karl Marx, Engels, Rodbertus, and Schäffle; in Russia: Bakunin, Chernyshevsky, Lavrov, etc.[5] All these thinkers and their followers bent their efforts either to the spreading of the socialistic ideas in understandable form, or to putting them upon a scientific basis.

The ideas of the first theorists of socialism, as they began to take a more definite form, gave rise to the two principal socialistic movements: authoritarian communism, and anarchistic (non-authoritarian) communism, as well as to a few intermediate forms.   Such are the schools of State capitalism (State ownership of all the means of production), collectivism, co-operationism, municipal socialism (semi-socialistic institutions established by cities), and many others.

At the same time, these very thoughts of the founders of socialism, (especially of Robert Owen) helped to originate among the working masses themselves a vast labour movement, which is economic in form, but is, in fact, deeply ethical.   This movement aims to unite all the workingmen into unions according to trades, for the purpose of direct struggle with capitalism.   In 1864–1879 this movement gave origin to the International, or the International Workers Alli-

[5] [Most of these names are well-known. François Vidal was a French socialist of '48. Constantin Pecqueur (1801–87) author of *Économie sociale*. Albert E. F. Schäffle wrote his *Bau und Leben des Sozialen Körpers*, in 1875– 78, 4 vols. Chernyshevsky is the author of the novel, *What is to be done?* and of several fine works in economics, not found in English. Piotr L. Lavrov (1823–1900) wrote the *Historical Letters*, available in a French and a German translation.]—Trans. Note.

ance, which endeavoured to establish international co-operation among the united trades.

Three fundamental principles were established by this intellectual and revolutionary movement:

1) Abolition of the wage system, which is nothing but a modern form of the ancient slavery and serfdom.

2) Abolition of private ownership of all that is necessary for production and for social organization of the exchange of products.

3) The liberation of the individual and of society from that form of political enslavement—the State—which serves to support and to preserve economic slavery.

The realization of these three objects is necessary for the establishment of a social justice in consonance with the moral demands of our time. For the last thirty years the consciousness of this necessity has penetrated deeply into the minds not only of working-men, but also progressive men of all classes.

Among the socialists, Proudhon (1809–1865) approached nearer than any other the interpretation of justice as the basis of morality. Proudhon's importance in the history of the development of ethics passes unnoticed, like the importance of Darwin in the same field. However, the historian of Ethics, Jodl, did not hesitate to place this peasant-compositor,—a self-taught man who underwent great hardships to educate himself, and who was also a thinker, and an original one,—side by side with the profound and learned philosophers who had been elaborating the theory of morality.

Of course, in advancing justice as the fundamental principle of morality, Proudhon was influenced on one side by Hume, Adam Smith, Montesquieu, Voltaire and the Encyclopædists, and by the Great French Revolution, and on the other side by German philosophy, as well as by Auguste Comte and the entire socialistic movement of the 'forties. A few years later this movement took the form of the International Brotherhood of Workers, which put forward as one of its mottoes the masonic formula: *"There are no rights without obligations; there are no obligations without rights."*

268

But Proudhon's merit lies in his indicating clearly the fundamental principle following from the heritage of the Great Revolution—the *conception of equity*, and consequently of *justice*, and in showing that this conception has been always at the basis of social life, and consequently of all ethics, in spite of the fact that philosophers passed it by as if it were non-existent, or were simply unwilling to ascribe to it a predominating importance.

Already in his early work, "What is property?" Proudhon identified justice with equality (more correctly—equity), referring to the ancient definition of justice: "Justum aequale est, injustum inaequale" (The equitable is just, the inequitable—unjust). Later he repeatedly returned to this question in his works, "Contradictions économiques" and "Philosophie du Progrès"; but the complete elaboration of the great importance of this conception of justice he gave in his three-volume work, "De la Justice dans la Révolution et dans l'Église," which appeared in 1858.[6]

It is true that this work does not contain a strictly systematic exposition of Proudhon's ethical views, but such views are expressed with sufficient clearness in various passages of the work. An attempt to determine to what an extent these passages are Proudhon's own ideas, and how far they are adaptations from earlier thinkers, would be difficult and at the same time useless. I shall, therefore, simply outline their main contentions.

Proudhon regards moral teaching as a part of the general science of law; the problem of the investigator lies in determining the bases of this teaching: its essence, its origin, and its sanction, i. e., that which imparts to law and to morality an obligatory character, and that which has educational value. Moreover, Proudhon, like Comte and the Encyclopædists, categorically refuses to build his philosophy of law and of morality on a religious or a metaphysical basis. It is necessary, he says, to study the life of societies and

---

[6] [*Qu'est-ce que la Propriéte?*, Paris, 1840; *Contradictions économiques*, Eng. tr. by B. R. Tucker, Boston, 1888; *Philosophie du Progrès*, Bruxelles, 1853. The others are noted below.]—Trans. Note.

to learn from it what it is that serves society as a guiding principle.[7]

Up to this time all ethical systems were constructed more or less under the influence of religion, and not a single teaching dared to advance the *equity* of men and the *equality of economic rights* as the basis of ethics. Proudhon attempted to do this as far as was possible in the days of Napoleonic censorship, always on guard against socialism and atheism. Proudhon wished to create, as he expressed it, a *philosophy of the people*, based on knowledge. He regards his book, "On Justice in the Revolution and in the Church," as an attempt made in that direction. And the object of this philosophy, as of all knowledge, is foresight, so that the path of social life may be indicated before it is actually laid out.

Proudhon considers the *sense of personal dignity* as the true essence of justice and the fundamental principle of all morality. If this sense is developed in an individual it becomes with reference to all men—*regardless of whether they are friends or enemies*— a sense of human dignity. *The right* is an ability, inherent in all, to demand from all others that they respect human dignity in their own person; and *duty* is the demand that everyone should recognize this dignity in others. *We cannot love everybody,* but we must respect each man's personal dignity. We cannot demand the love of others, but we unquestionably have a right to demand respect for our personality. It is impossible to build a new society on mutual love, but it can and should be built on the demand of mutual respect.

"To feel and to assert human dignity first in all that pertains to us, and then in the personality of our fellow-men, without falling into egoism, as well as not paying attention either to deity or to society—this is right. To be ready under all circumstances to rise energetically in defence of this dignity—this is justice."

It would seem that at this point Proudhon should have declared quite definitely that a free society can be built only on equity. But

[7] *Qu'est-ce que la Propriété?* pp. 181 ff.; also 220-221. [Two English translations are available, of which the more recent was published in London, in 1902,—*What is Property; an inquiry into the principle of right and of Government.* 2 vols.]—Trans. Note.

he did not so declare, perhaps because of the Napoleonic censorship; in reading his "Justice" this conclusion (equity) seems almost inevitable, and in a few passages it is more than implied.

The question of the origin of the sense of justice was answered by Proudhon in the same manner as by Comte and by modern science, that it represents the *product of the development of human societies.*

In order to explain the origin of the moral element Proudhon endeavoured to find for morality, i. e., for justice,[8] an *organic base in the psychic structure of man.*[9] Justice, he says, *does not come from above* nor is it a product of the *calculation* of one's interests, for no social order can be built on such a basis. This faculty, moreover, is something different from the *natural kindness* in man, the *feeling of sympathy,* or the instinct of sociality upon which the Positivists endeavour to base ethics. A man is possessed of a special feeling, one that is higher than the feeling of sociality,—namely, the *sense* of *righteousness,* the consciousness of the equal right of all men to a mutual regard for personality.[10]

"Thus," Jodl remarks, "after his most vigorous protests against transcendentalism, Proudhon turns, after all, to the old heritage of intuitional ethics—conscience." ("Geschichte der Ethik," ch. 11, p. 267.) This remark, however, is not quite correct. Proudhon merely meant to say that the conception of justice cannot be a simple inborn tendency, because if it were it would be difficult to account for the preponderance it acquires in the struggle with other tendencies continually urging man to be unjust to others. The tendency to protect the interests of others at the expense of our own cannot be solely an *inborn feeling,* although its rudiments were always present in man, but these rudiments must be developed. And

---

[8] *De la Justice dans la Révolution et dans l'Église,* vol. 1, p. 216.

[9] At this point Jodl falls into the same error as Proudhon, by identifying Morality in general with Justice, which, in my opinion, constitutes but one of the elements of Morality.

[10] *Geschichte der Ethik,* 11, p. 266, references to Proudhon's *Justice, etc.,* Étude II.

this feeling could develop in society only through experience, and such was actually the case.

In considering the contradictions furnished by the history of human societies, between the conception of justice native to man and social injustice (supported by the ruling powers and even by the churches), Proudhon came to the conclusion that although the conception of justice is inborn in man, thousands of years had to elapse before the idea of justice entered as a fundamental conception into legislation,—at the time of the French Revolution in the "Declaration of the Rights of Man."

Like Comte, Proudhon very well realized the progress that was taking place in the development of mankind and he was convinced that further progressive development would occur. Of course, he had in mind not merely the development of *culture* (i. e., of the material conditions of life), but mainly of *civilization,* enlightenment, i. e., the development of the intellectual and the spiritual organization of society, the improvement in institutions and in mutual relations among men.[11]   In this progress he ascribed a great importance to idealization, to the ideals that in certain periods acquire the ascendancy over the petty daily cares, when the discrepancy between the law, understood as the highest expression of justice, and actual life as it is developed under the power of legislation, acquires the proportions of a glaring, unbearable contradiction.

In a later part of this work we shall have occasion to return to the significance of justice in the elaboration of the moral conceptions. For the present I will simply remark that no one prepared the ground for the correct understanding of this fundamental conception of all morality so well as Proudhon.[12]

[11] In recent time these two entirely different conceptions have begun to be confused in Russia.

[12] In addition to the work, *"De la Justice dans la Révolution et dans l'Église (Noueaux principes de philosophie pratique)*, 3 vols. Paris, 1858, very valuable thoughts on ethics and justice may be found in his *Système des contradictions économiques, ou, philosophie de la misère,* 2 vols. (A work which, of course, lost none of its considerable merit on account of Marx's malignant pamphlet, *La Misère de la Philosophie*); also *Idée générale sur la Révolu-*

MORAL TEACHINGS—XIX CENTURY

The highest moral aim of man is the attaining of justice. The entire history of mankind, says Proudhon, is the history of human endeavour to attain justice in this life. All the great revolutions are nothing but the attempt to realize justice by force; and since during the revolution *the means,* i. e., violence, temporarily prevailed over the old form of oppression, the actual result was always a substitution of one tyranny for another. Nevertheless, the impelling motive of every revolutionary movement was always justice, and every revolution, no matter into what it later degenerated, always introduced into social life a certain degree of justice. All these partial realizations of justice will finally lead to the complete triumph of justice on earth.

Why is it that in spite of all the revolutions that have taken place, not a single nation has yet arrived at the complete attainment of justice? The principal cause of this lies in the fact that the idea of justice has not as yet penetrated into the minds of the majority of men. Originating in the mind of a separate individual, the idea of justice must become a social idea, inspiring the revolution. The starting point of the idea of justice is the sense of personal dignity. In associating with others we find that this feeling becomes generalized and becomes the feeling of *human* dignity. A rational creature recognizes this feeling in another—friend or enemy alike—as in himself. In this, justice differs from love and from other sensations of sympathy; this is why justice is the antithesis of egoism, and why the influence which justice exerts upon us prevails over other feelings. For the same reason, in the case of a primitive man whose sense of personal dignity manifests itself in a crude way, and whose self-aimed tendencies prevail over the social, justice finds its expression in the form of supernatural prescription, and it rests upon

tion au XIX siècle, and *Qu'est-ce que la Propriéte?* An ethical system was shaping itself in Proudhon's mind from the time of his very first appearance as a writer, at the beginning of the 'forties. [Karl Marx's *Réponse à la Philosophie de la Misère de M. Proudhon,* Paris and Bruxelles, 1847; Eng. tr. by H. Quelch, Chicago, 1910. Proudhon's *Idée générale,* etc., Paris, 1851.] —Trans. Note.

religion. But little by little, under the influence of religion, the sense of justice (Proudhon writes simply "justice," without defining whether he considers it a *conception* or a *feeling*) deteriorates. Contrary to its essence this feeling becomes aristocratic, and in Christianity (and in some earlier religions) it reaches the point of humiliating mankind. Under the pretext of respect for God, respect for man is banished, and once this respect is destroyed justice succumbs, and with it society deteriorates.

Then a Revolution takes place which opens a new era for mankind. It enables justice, only vaguely apprehended before, to appear in all the purity and completeness of its fundamental idea. "Justice is absolute and unchangeable; it knows no 'more or less.' " [13] It is remarkable, adds Proudhon, that from the time of the fall of the Bastille, in 1789, there was not a single government in France which dared openly to deny justice and to declare itself frankly counter-revolutionary. However, all governments violated justice, even the government at the time of the Terror, even Robespierre,— especially Robespierre.[14]

Proudhon pointed out, however, that we should guard against tramping upon the interests of the individual for the sake of the interests of society. True justice consists in a harmonious combination of social interest with those of the individual. Justice, thus interpreted, contains nothing mysterious or mystical. Neither is it a desire for personal gain, since I consider it my duty to demand respect for my fellow-men, as well as for myself. Justice demands respect for personal dignity even in any enemy (hence the international military code).

Since man is a being capable of progressing, justice opens the path to progress for all alike. Therefore, wrote Proudhon, justice found expression in the earliest religions, in the Mosaic law, for example, which bade us love God with all our heart, with all our soul, with all our might, and to *love our neighbour as we love our-*

---

[13] *Justice*—etc., Ètude II, pp. 194–195, ed. of 1858.
[14] *Ibid.,* Étude II, p. 196.

selves (in the book of "Tobit," where we are told not to do unto others what we do not want done unto us).[15] Similar ideas were expressed by the Pythagoreans, by Epicurus, and Aristotle, and the same demand was made by non-religious philosophers like Gassendi, Hobbes, Bentham, Helvétius, etc.[16]

In short, we find that equity is everywhere considered the basis of morality, or, as Proudhon wrote: as regards the mutual personal relations—"without equality—there is no justice." [17]

Unfortunately, all the worshippers of the ruling power, even the State-socialists, fail to notice this fundamental principle of all morality and continue to support the necessity of the inequality and non-equity inherent in the State. Nevertheless, equity became in principle the basis of all the declarations of the Great French Revolution (just as it was accepted earlier in the Declaration of Rights in the North American Republic). Already the Declaration of 1789 proclaimed that "nature made all men free and equal." The same principle was reiterated in the Declaration of July 24, 1793.

The Revolution proclaimed individual equality, equality of political and civic rights, and also equality before the law and the courts. More than that, it created a new social economy by recognizing instead of private rights, the principle of the *equivalent value of mutual service.*[18]

---

[15] [*Tobit*, 4, 15]—Trans. Note.

[16] I will only add that we find the identical idea in the rules of conduct of all savages. (See my book, *Mutual Aid, a factor of Evolution.*)

[17] "En ce qui touche les personnes, hors de l'égalite point de Justice." (Étude III, beginning; vol. I, p. 206.)

[18] The formula of the communists, adds Proudhon,—"To each according to his needs, from each according to his abilities," can be applied only in a family. Saint-Simon's formula, "to each according to his abilities, to each ability according to its deeds" is a complete negation of actual equality and of equality of rights. In a Fourierist community the principle of mutuality is recognized, but in the application to an individual Fourier denied justice. On the other hand, the principle practiced by mankind from the remotest time is simpler, and, what is most important, more worthy; value is assigned only to the products of industry,—which does not offend personal dignity, and the economic organization reduces itself to a simple formula—*exchange.*

The essence of justice is respect for our fellow-men, Proudhon constantly insisted. We know the nature of justice, he wrote; its definition can be given in the following formula:

"Respect thy neighbour as thyself, even if thou canst not love him, and do not permit that he or thyself be treated with disrespect." "Without equality—there is no justice." (I. 204, 206).[19]

Unfortunately, this principle has not as yet been attained either in legislation or in the courts, and certainly not in the Church.

Economics suggested one way out—the subdivision of labour in order to increase production, which increase is, of course, necessary; but it has also shown, at least through the testimony of some economists, such as Rossi, for example, that this division of labor leads to apathy among the workers and to the creation of a slave-class. We thus see that the only possible way out of this situation is to be found in *mutuality of service,* instead of the *subordination* of one kind of service to another (I. 269),—and therefore in the *equality of rights and possessions.* This is just what was asserted by the declaration of the Convention of February 15, and July 24 of 1793, in which Freedom and the Equality of all before the law were proclaimed, and this declaration was reiterated in 1795, 1799, 1814, 1830, and 1848. (I. 270.) Justice, as Proudhon sees it, is not merely a *restraining* social force. He sees in it a *creative* force, like reason and work.[20] Then, having remarked, as Bacon had already done,

---

[19] Proudhon wrote these words in 1858. Since that time many economists have upheld the same principle.

[20] Man is a creature "rational and toiling, the most industrious and the most social creature, whose chief striving is not love, but a law higher than love. Hence the heroic self-sacrifice for science, unknown to the masses; martyrs of toil and industry are born, whom novels and the theatre pass over in silence; hence also the words: 'to die for one's country.'" "Let me bow before you, ye who knew how to arise and how to die in 1789, 1792, and 1830. You were consecrated to liberty, and you are more alive than we, who have lost it." "To originate an idea, to produce a book, a poem, a machine; in short, as those in trade say, to create one's chef d'œuvre; to render a service to one's country and to mankind, to save a human life, to do a good deed and to rectify an injustice,—all this is to reproduce oneself in social life, similar to reproduction in organic life." Man's life attains its fullness when it satisfies the following conditions: love—children, family; work—

276

that *thought is born of action,* and dedicating for this reason a series of excellent pages to the necessity of manual labour and of the study of trades in schools as a means of broadening our scientific education, —Proudhon proceeds to consider justice in its various applications: with respect to individuals, in the distribution of wealth, in the State, in education, and in mentality.

Proudhon had to acknowledge that the development of justice in human societies requires time: a high development of ideals and of the feeling of solidarity with all, is required, and this can be attained only through long individual and social evolution. We will return to this subject in another volume. I will only add here that all this part of Proudhon's book, and his conclusion in which he determines wherein lies the sanction of the conception of justice, contain very many ideas stimulating to human thought. This quality of mental stimulation is characteristic of all Proudhon's writings, and it was pointed out by Herzen and by many others.

However, in all his excellent words about justice, Proudhon did not indicate clearly enough the distinction between the two meanings given in the French language to the word "Justice." One meaning is equality, an equation in the mathematical sense,—while the other meaning is the *administering* of justice, i. e., the act of judging, the decision of the court, and even the *taking of the law into one's own hands.* Of course, when justice is mentioned in ethics it is interpreted only in the first sense, but Proudhon at times used the word Justice in its second sense, which circumstance leads to a certain indefiniteness. This is probably the reason why he did not try to trace the origin of this concept in man,—a problem with which, as we will see later, Littré dealt at some length.

At any rate, from the time of the appearance of Proudhon's work, "Justice in the Revolution and in the Church," it became impossible to build an ethical system without recognizing as its basis *equity,* the equality of all citizens in their rights. It is apparently for

industrial reproduction; and sociality, i. e., the participation in the life and progress of mankind. (Étude V, ch. v; vol. II. 128–130).

this reason that the attempt was made to subject this work of Proudhon's to a unanimous silence, so that only Jodl was unafraid of compromising himself and assigned to the French revolutionist a prominent place in his history of ethics. It is true that the three volumes which Proudhon devoted to justice contain a great deal of irrelevant matter, a vast amount of polemics against the Church (the title, "Justice in the Revolution and in the Church," justifies this, however, all the more because the subject under discussion is not justice in the Church, but in *Christianity* and in the religious moral teachings in general); they also contain two essays on woman, with which most modern writers will, of course, not agree; and finally they contain many digressions, which, though they serve a purpose, help to befog the main issue. But notwithstanding all this, we have at last in Proudhon's work an investigation in which justice (which had been already alluded to by many thinkers who occupied themselves with the problem of morality) was assigned a proper place; in this work, at last, it is stated that *justice is the recognition of equity* and of the striving of men for equality, and that this is the *basis of all our moral conceptions.*

Ethics had for a long time been moving toward this admission. But all along it had been so bound up with religion, and in recent times with Christianity, that this recognition was not fully expressed by any of Proudhon's predecessors.

Finally, I must point out that in Proudhon's work, "Justice in the Revolution and in the Church," there is already a hint of the *three-fold* nature of morality. He had shown in the first volume— though in a very cursory way, in a few lines,—the primary source of morality—sociality, which is observed even among the animals. And he dwelt later, toward the end of his work, on the third constituent element of all scientific, as well as of religious morality: the *ideal.* But he did not show where the dividing line comes between justice (which says: "give what is due," and is thus reduced to a mathematical equation), and that which man gives to another

278

or to all "above what is due," without weighing what he gives or what he receives—which, to my mind, constitutes a necessary, constituent part of morality. But he already finds it necessary to complete Justice by adding the *ideal*, i. e., the striving for idealistic actions, due to which, according to Proudhon, our very conceptions of justice are continually broadened and become more refined. And indeed, after all that mankind lived through from the time of the American and the two French Revolutions, our conceptions of justice are clearly not the same as they were at the end of the eighteenth century, when serfdom and slavery called forth no protest even from liberal moralists. We have now to consider a series of works on ethics by thinkers who take the evolutionist viewpoint and who accept Darwin's theory of the development of all organic life, as well as of the social life of man. Here ought to be included a succession of works by modern thinkers, because almost all who wrote on ethics in the second half of the nineteenth century show evidence of the influence of the evolutionist theory of gradual development—which rapidly conquered the mind, after it was so carefully elaborated by Darwin in its application to organic nature.

Even among those who did not write especially on the development of the moral sense in mankind, we find indications of the gradual growth of this sense parallel with the development of other conceptions—intellectual, scientific, religious, political, and of all the forms of social life in general. Thus, Darwin's theory had a tremendous and a decisive influence upon the progress of modern realistic ethics, or at least on some of its divisions. I will limit myself, however, to the discussion of only three chief representatives of evolutionist ethics: Herbert Spencer, Huxley, as a direct assistant of Darwin, and M. Guyau, although there is a group of very valuable works on ethics, carried out in the spirit of evolutionism, —viz., the great work of Westermarck, "The Origin and Development of the Moral Ideas"; by Bastian, "Der Mensch in der Geschichte"; by Gizicky, etc., not to mention non-original works like those of Kidd and Sutherland, or the popular works written for propaganda by socialists, social-democrats, and anarchists.[21]

I have already discussed Darwin's ethics in the third chapter of this book. In brief, it reduces itself to the following: we know that there is a moral sense in man, and the question naturally arises as to its origin. That each one of us acquires it separately is highly improbable, once we recognize the general theory of the gradual development of man. And, indeed, the origin of this sense is to be sought in the development of feelings of sociality—instinctive or innate—in all social animals and in man. Through the strength of this feeling an animal deserves to be in the society of its fellow-creatures, to know itself in sympathy with them; but this sympathy is not to be interpreted in the sense of commiseration or love, but in the narrow sense of the word, as the feeling of comradeship, feeling together, the ability to be affected by the emotions of others.

This feeling of social sympathy, which develops gradually with the increasing complexity of social life, becomes more and more varied, rational, and free in its manifestations. In man the feeling of social sympathy becomes the source of morality. But how are moral conceptions developed from it? Darwin answers this question as follows: man possesses memory and the ability to reason. And when a man does not hearken to the voice of the feeling of social sympathy, and follows some opposite feeling, as hatred for others, then after a brief sensation of pleasure or of gratification he experiences a feeling of inner dissatisfaction, and an oppressive emotion of *repentance*. At times, even at the very moment of man's inner struggle between the feeling of social sympathy and the opposite tendencies, reason imperatively points out the necessity of following the feeling of social sympathy, and pictures the consequences and the results of the act; in such a case, reflection, and

[21] [Edward A. Westermarck, Lond. & N. Y., 1906–8, 2 vols. Bastian's *Der Mensch*, etc., Leipzig, 1860, 3 vols. in 1. Alexander C. Sutherland, *Origin and Growth of the Moral Instinct*, Lond., 1895, 2 vols.]—Trans. Note.

the consciousness that the dictates of the promptings of social sympathy and not the opposite tendencies, are to be obeyed, becomes the consciousness of *duty*, the consciousness of the right way to act. Every animal in which the instincts of sociality, including the paternal and the filial instincts, are strongly developed, will inevitably acquire moral sense or conscience, provided its mental abilities become developed to the same extent as in man.[22]

Later, in a further stage of development, when the social life of men reaches a high level, moral feeling finds a strong support in *public opinion*, which points the way to acting for the common good. This public opinion is not at all an elaborate invention of a conventional up-bringing, as was rather flippantly asserted by Mandeville and his modern followers, but is the result of the development in society of mutual sympathy and a mutual bond. Little by little such acts for the common good become a habit.

I will not repeat here Darwin's further reasoning about the origin of morality in man, for I have already considered them in the third chapter of this work. I will merely point out that Darwin had thus returned to the idea expressed by Bacon in his "Great Instauration." I have already mentioned that Bacon was the first to point out that the social instinct is "more powerful" than the personal instinct. The same conclusion was reached, as we have seen, by Hugo Grotius.[23]

Bacon's and Darwin's ideas of the greater power, permanency, and

[22] Darwin, *Descent of Man*, chap. IV, pp. 149–150. Lond. 1859.

[23] Spinoza's writings also make mention of mutual aid among animals (*mutuum juventum*), as an important feature of their social life. And if such an instinct exists in animals it is clear that, in the struggle for existence, those species had the better opportunity to survive in difficult conditions of life and to multiply, which made most use of this instinct. This instinct, therefore, had to develop more and more, especially since the development of spoken language, and consequently of tradition, increased the influence in society of the more observant and more experienced man. Naturally, under such circumstances, among very many man-like species with which man was in conflict, that species survived in which the feeling of mutual aid was strongly developed, in which the feeling of social self-preservation held the ascendancy over the feeling of individual self-preservation,—for the latter could at times act against the interest of the clan or tribe.

preponderance of the instinct of social self-preservation over the instinct of personal self-preservation, shed such a bright light on the early periods of the progress of morality in the human race, that it would seem as if these ideas ought to become fundamental in all modern works on ethics. But in reality these views of Bacon and Darwin passed almost unnoticed. For instance, when I spoke to some English Darwinian naturalists about Darwin's ethical ideas, many of them asked "Did he write anything on Ethics?" While others thought that I had reference to the "merciless struggle for existence" as the fundamental principle of the life of human societies; and they were always greatly astonished when I pointed out to them that Darwin explained the origin of the sense of moral duty in man by the preponderance in man of the feeling of social sympathy over personal egoism. For them "Darwinism" consisted in the struggle for existence of everyone against all, and because of this they failed to take note of any other consideration.[24]

This interpretation of "Darwinism" strongly affected the work of Darwin's principal disciple—Huxley, whom Darwin selected for the popularization of his views in connection with the variability of species.

This brilliant evolutionist, who was so successful in confirming and spreading Darwin's teaching of the gradual development of organic forms on the earth, proved to be quite incapable of following his great teacher in the realm of moral thought. As is known, Huxley expounded his views on this subject, shortly before his death, in a lecture, "Evolution and Ethics," which he delivered at the University of Oxford in 1893.[25] It is also known from Huxley's

[24] In one of his letters, I do not remember to whom, Darwin wrote: "This subject remained unnoticed, probably because I wrote too briefly about it." This is just what actually happened with what he wrote on Ethics, and, I must add, with a great deal that he wrote in connection with "Lamarckism." In our age of capitalism and mercantilism, "struggle for existence" so well answered the needs of the majority that it overshadowed everything else.

[25] This lecture was published in the same year in pamphlet form with elaborate and very remarkable notes. Later Huxley wrote an explanatory introduction (*Prolegomena*) with which this lecture has since been reprinted

correspondence, published by his son, that he attributed great importance to this lecture, which he prepared with thorough care. The press took this lecture as a sort of agnostic manifesto,[26] and the majority of English readers looked upon it as the last word that modern science can say on the subject of the bases of morality, i. e., on the final goal of all philosophical systems. It is also necessary to say that to this study of evolution and ethics was ascribed such significance not only because it was the expression of views held by one of the leaders of scientific thought, who all his life fought for the recognition of evolutionist philosophy, and not only because it was written in so polished a form that it was acclaimed as one of the finest models of English prose, but chiefly because it expressed just those views on morality which are now predominant among the educated classes of all nations, which are so deep-rooted, and which are considered so irrefutable, that they may be called the religion of these classes.

The predominant thought of this research, the *leit*-motive pervading the entire exposition, consists of the following:

There is a "cosmic process," i. e., the universal life, and an "ethical process," i. e., the moral life, and these processes are diametrically opposed to each other, a negation of each other. The whole of nature, including plants, animals, and primitive man, is subject to the cosmic process: this process is crimsoned with blood, it stands for the triumph of the strong beak and the sharp claw. This process is a denial of all moral principles. Suffering is the lot of all sentient creatures; it constitutes an essential constituent part of the cosmic process. The methods of struggle for existence characteristic of the ape and the tiger, are its distinguishing features. "In the case of mankind, (in the primitive stage), self-assertion, the

in his *Collected Essays* and also in the *Essays, Ethical and Political*, Macmillan's popular edition, 1903.

[26] The word "agnostic" was introduced for the first time by a small group of doubting writers, who gathered about the publisher of the magazine *Nineteenth Century*, James Knowles. They preferred the name of "agnostics," i. e., those who deny "gnosis," to the name of "atheists."

unscrupulous seizing upon all that can be grasped, the tenacious holding of all that can be kept, which constitute the essence of the struggle for existence, have answered." (p. 51.)

And so on in the same vein. In short, the lesson which nature teaches is the lesson of "unqualified evil."

Thus, evil and immorality—this is what we can learn from Nature. It is not that the good and the evil approximately balance each other in Nature: no,—the evil predominates and triumphs. We cannot learn from Nature even that the sociality and the self-restraint of the individual are the mighty implements of success in the cosmic process of evolution. In his lecture Huxley categorically denied such an interpretation of life; he persistently endeavoured to prove that "cosmic nature is no school of virtue, but the head-quarters of the enemy of ethical nature." (*Ibid.*, p. 75.) "The practice of that which is ethically best—what we call goodness or virtue—involves a course of conduct which, in all respects, is opposed to that which leads to success in the cosmic struggle for existence. . . . It repudiates the gladiatorial theory of existence." (pp. 81–82.)

And amidst this cosmic life, which had been lasting for innumerable thousands of years and which had been continually teaching lessons of struggle and immorality, there suddenly arises without any natural cause, and we know not whence, the "ethical process," i. e., the moral life which was implanted in man in the later period of his development, we know not by whom or by what, but at any rate, not by Nature. "Cosmic evolution," Huxley insists, "is incompetent to furnish any better reason why what we call good is preferable to what we call evil than we had before." (p. 80.) Nevertheless, for some unknown reason, there begins in human society "social progress" which does not constitute a part of the "cosmic process" (i. e., of universal life), but "means a checking of the cosmic process at every step and the substitution for it of another, which may be called the ethical process; the end of which is not the survival of those who

284

may happen to be the fittest, in respect of the whole of the conditions which obtain, but of those who are ethically the best." (p. 81.) Why, whence, this sudden revolution in the ways of nature which is concerned with organic progress, i. e., the gradual perfecting of structure? Huxley does not say a word about this, but he continued to remind us persistently that the ethical process is not at all the continuation of the cosmic; it appeared as a counterbalance to the cosmic process and finds in it "a tenacious and powerful enemy."

Thus Huxley asserted that the lesson taught by Nature is in reality a lesson of evil (p. 85), but as soon as men combined into organized societies there appeared, we know not whence, an "ethical process," which is absolutely opposed to everything that nature teaches us. Later, the law, customs, and civilization continued to develop this process.

But where are the roots, where is the origin of the ethical process? It could not originate from observation of Nature, because, according to Huxley's assertion, Nature teaches us the opposite; it could not be inherited from pre-human times, because among the swarms of animals, before the appearance of man, there was no ethical process even in an embryonic form. Its origin, consequently, lies *outside of Nature.* Hence, the moral law of restraining personal impulses and passions originated like the Mosaic Law—not from already existing customs, not from habits that had already become ingrained in human nature, but it could appear only as a divine revelation, that illuminated the mind of the law-giver. It has a superhuman, nay, more than that, a supernatural origin.

This conclusion so obviously follows from reading Huxley, that immediately after Huxley delivered his lecture at Oxford, George Mivart, a noted and able evolutionist, and at the same time an ardent Catholic, printed in the magazine, "Nineteenth Century," an article in which he congratulates his friend upon his return to the teachings of the Christian Church. After citing the passages given above, Mivart wrote: "Just so! It would be difficult to declare more emphatically that ethics could never have formed part and parcel of the general process of evolution." [27]   Man could not voluntarily and consciously invent the ethical idea. "It was *in* him, but not of him." (p. 207.)   It comes from the "Divine Creator."

And really, it is one of the two; either the moral conceptions of man are merely the further development of the moral habits of mutual aid, which are so generally inherent in social animals that they may be called a *law* of Nature,—and in that event our moral conceptions, in so far as they are the product of reason, are nothing but the conclusion arrived at from man's observation of nature, and in so far as they are the product of habit and instinct, they constitute a further development of instincts and habits inherent in social animals.   Or our moral conceptions are revelations from above, and all further investigations of morality become merely interpretation of the divine will.   Such was the inevitable conclusion from this lecture.

And then, when Huxley published his lecture, "Evolution and Ethics," in the form of a pamphlet provided with long and elaborate notes, he included one note [28] in which he completely surrenders his position and destroys the very essence of his lecture, for he acknowledges in this note that the ethical process constitutes "part and parcel of the general process of evolution," i. e., of the "Cosmic Process," in which there are already contained the germs of the ethical process.

Thus it turns out that everything that was said in the lecture about the two opposite and antagonistic processes, the natural and the ethical, was incorrect.   The sociality of animals already contains the germs of moral life, and they merely continue to be developed and perfected in human societies.

By what path Huxley came to such an abrupt change in his views, we do not know.   It may only be supposed that it was done

[27] St. George Mivart, *Evolution in Professor Huxley,* "Nineteenth Century," August 1893, p. 198.
[28] Note 19 in the pamphlet; note 20 in the *Collected Essays* and in the *Essays, Ethical and Political.*

under the influence of his personal friend, Professor Romanes of Oxford, who acted as chairman during Huxley's lecture on "Evolution and Ethics." At that very time Romanes was working on an extremely interesting research on the subject of morality in animals.

As an extremely truthful and humanitarian man, Romanes probably protested against Huxley's conclusions and pointed out their utter lack of correct foundations. Possibly it was under the influence of this protest that Huxley introduced the addition which refuted the very essence of what he had advocated in his lecture. It is very regrettable that death prevented Romanes from completing his work on morality among animals; he had gathered extensive material for this task.[29]

(The manuscript of the eleventh chapter ends with these words)

---

[29] When I decided to deliver a lecture in London on Mutual Aid among Animals, Knowles, the publisher of the "Nineteenth Century," who had become greatly interested in my ideas and had discussed them with his friend and neighbour, Spencer, advised me to invite Romanes as chairman. Romanes accepted my suggestion and very kindly consented to act as chairman. At the end of the lecture, in his closing address, he pointed out the significance of my work and summarized it in the following words: "Kropotkin has unquestionably proved that although external wars are waged throughout the whole of nature by all species, internal wars are very limited, and in most species there is the predominance of mutual aid and co-operation in various forms. The struggle for existence, says Kropotkin, is to be understood in the metaphorical sense. . . ." I was seated behind Romanes and I whispered to him: "It was not I, but Darwin who said so, in the very beginning of the third chapter, 'On Struggle for Existence.'" Romanes immediately repeated this remark to the audience and added that this is just the right way to interpret Darwin's term,—not in a literal but in a figurative sense. If only Romanes could have succeeded in working for another year or two we should undoubtedly have had a remarkable work on animal morality. Some of his observations on his own dog are astounding, and have already gained wide renown. But the great mass of facts that he gathered would be still more important. Unfortunately, no one among the English Darwinists has as yet utilized and published this material. Their "Darwinism" was no more profound than that of Huxley. [Note by Lebedev, the Russian Editor.]

CHAPTER XII

(Continued)

THE nineteenth century approached the problem of morality from a new viewpoint—that of its *gradual development* in mankind, beginning with the primitive period. Regarding all nature as the result of the activity of physical forces and of evolution, the new philosophy had to interpret morality from the same point of view.

The ground for such an interpretation of morality had been already prepared at the end of the eighteenth century. The study of the life of the primitive savages, Laplace's hypothesis as to the origin of our solar system, and especially the theory of evolution in the plant and the animal world,—which was already indicated by Buffon and Lamarck, and then, in the twenties of the last century promulgated by Geoffroy-Saint-Hilaire,—the historical works in the same direction written by the Saint-Simonians, especially Augustin Thierry, and finally the positivist philosophy of Auguste Comte—all these taken together prepared the way for the assimilation of the theory of evolution in the entire plant and animal worlds, and, consequently, as affecting the human race as well. In 1859 appeared Charles Darwin's famous work in which the theory of evolution found a complete and systematic elaboration.

Before Darwin, in 1850, the theory of evolution, though by no means completely developed, was put forth by Herbert Spencer in his "Social Statics." But the thoughts that he expressed in this book were so sharply at variance with the conceptions then current in England, that Spencer's new ideas were disregarded. Spencer was accorded appreciation as a thinker, only when he began to publish under the collective name of "Synthetic Philosophy" a

288

series of remarkable philosophical researches in which he expounded
the development of our solar system, the development of life on the
earth, and finally the development of mankind, its thought and its
societies.

Ethics, as Spencer very justly held, was to constitute one of the
divisions of the general philosophy of nature. He first analyzed the
basic principles of the cosmos and the origin of our solar system,
which came into existence as the result of the activity of mechanical
forces; then the principles of biology, i. e., of the science of life in
the form it assumed on the earth; then the principles of psychology,
i. e., the science of the psychic life of animals and of man; next,
the principles of sociology, i. e., the science of sociality; and finally,
the principles of ethics, i. e., the science of those mutual relations of
living beings which have the nature of *obligation* and which therefore, were for a long time confused with religon.[1]

Only toward the end of his life, in the Spring of 1890, when the
greater part of his "Ethics" was already written, Spencer published
two magazine articles in which for the first time he spoke of
sociality and morality in animals,[2] whereas up to that time he had
concentrated his attention on the "struggle for existence" and
interpreted it in its application to animals as well as to men, as the
struggle of each against all for the means of subsistence.

Then, although these ideas were already expressed by him in his
"Social Statics," Spencer published in the 'nineties a little book,
"The Individual versus the State," in which he expounded his views
against the inevitable State centralization and oppression. On this
point he closely approached the first theorist of anarchism, William
Godwin, whose book, "Enquiry Concerning Political Justice," was
so much more remarkable in that it appeared at the moment of the

---

[1] In accordance with such an interpretation of philosophy, prior to be-
ginning his *Principles of Ethics*, Spencer published under the general title of
Synthetic Philosophy the following series of works: *First Principles, The
Principles of Biology, The Principles of Psychology, The Principles of
Sociology*.

[2] [See note 4, page 35.]—Trans. Note.

triumph in France of revolutionary Jacobinism, i. e., of the un-limited power of the revolutionary government. Godwin was in complete agreement with the Jacobin ideals of political and economic equality,[3] but he took a negative attitude toward their endeavour to create the all-absorbing State, which would destroy the rights of the individual. Spencer stood, similarly, against the despotism of the State, and he expressed his views on this subject in 1842.[4]

Both in his "Social Statics" and "The Principles of Ethics," Spencer expounded the fundamental idea that Man, in common with the lower creatures, is capable of indefinite change by adaptation to conditions. Therefore, through a series of gradual changes, man is undergoing transformation from a nature appropriate to his aboriginal wild life, to a nature appropriate to a settled, civilized life. This process is effected by the repression of certain primitive traits of the human organism, such, for example, as the warlike traits of character that are no longer needed in view of the changed conditions and owing to the development of more peaceful relations.

Gradually, under the influence of the external conditions of life and of the development of the internal, individual faculties, and with the increasing complexity of social life, mankind evolves more cultural forms of life and more peaceful habits and usages, which lead to a closer co-operation. The greatest factor in this progress Spencer saw in the feeling of *sympathy* (or *commiseration*).

More or less harmonious coöperation implies, of course, a certain limitation on individual freedom, which results from sympathetic regard for the freedom of others. Gradually there evolves in society an equitable individual conduct, and an equitable social order, in which each individual acts in conformity with the law of equal freedom for all the members of society. In proportion as men become accustomed to social life they develop mutual sympathy,

---

[3] See the first edition of the *Enquiry concerning Political Justice.* In the second edition (in octavo) the communistic passages were omitted, probably on account of the court prosecutions instituted against Godwin's friends. [London, 1796; first ed., Lond., 1793.]—Trans. Note.

[4] See, *The Proper Sphere of Government*, London, 1842.

which later constitutes what is called "the moral sense." Parallel with the development of this moral sense there arise in man intellectual perceptions of right human relations, which become clearer as the form of social life becomes better. Thus is attained the reconciliation of individual natures with social requirements. Spencer hopes that social life will progress in such a manner as eventually to achieve the greatest development of *personality* (*"individuation,"* i. e., the development of individuality, and not of "individualism"), together with the greatest development of *sociality*. Spencer is convinced that evolution and progress will lead to a social equilibrium so balanced that each, in fulfilling the wants of his own life, will spontaneously and voluntarily aid in fulfilling the wants of all other lives.[5]

The aim of ethics, as Spencer understood it, is the establishment of rules of moral conduct on a *scientific basis*. The placing of moral science on such a foundation is particularly necessary now, when the authority of religion is dwindling and moral teachings are being deprived of this support. At the same time, moral teaching must be freed from prejudices and from monastic asceticism, which have been very detrimental to the proper understanding of morality. On the other hand, ethics should not be weakened by the hesitation to reject completely a narrow egoism. Morality, resting on a scientific basis, satisfies this requirement, for scientifically derived ethical principles coincide in all ways with the ethical principles otherwise derived,—a fact which, unfortunately, the religious people categorically refuse to recognize, and are even offended when this coincidence is pointed out to them.

Having thus indicated the aim of ethics, Spencer approached the moral problem, taking as his starting point the simplest observa-

[5] In this exposition I follow very closely what Spencer himself wrote in the preface to the 1893 edition, in connection with the combined weight of his *Social Statics* and his *Principles of Ethics*. It will be seen that his *"evolutionist ethics,"* which he expounded in the *Social Statics*, shaped itself in his mind before the appearance of Darwin's *Origin of Species*. But the influence of Auguste Comte's ideas upon Spencer is unquestionable.

tions. In order to understand human conduct and mode of life,—they must be regarded, in a sense, as an organic whole, beginning with the animals. As we pass from the simplest forms of life to the higher and more complicated, we find that their conduct and their mode of existence become better and better adapted to the environment. These adaptations, moreover, always aim either at the strengthening of *individual vitality,* or the strengthening of the vitality of the species, the latter becoming more and more closely connected with the preservation of the individual in proportion as we approach the higher forms in the animal world. And indeed, the parents' care of their offspring is already a case of close connection between individual self-preservation and the preservation of the species; and this care increases and assumes the character of personal attachment as we approach the higher forms of animal life.

Unfortunately, it must be remarked that, carried away by the theory of struggle for existence, Spencer did not at this time devote sufficient attention to the fact that in every class of animals some species show a development of mutual aid, and in proportion as this factor acquires greater importance in the life of the species, the individual span of life is lengthened and at the same time experience is accumulated, which aids the species in its struggle with its enemies.

But mere adaptation to external conditions is insufficient, continued Spencer: the course of evolution is paralleled by the general improvement in the forms of life. The struggle for existence among the individuals diminishes among men, in proportion as the militant and predatory stage is replaced by what may be called *industrial co-operation.* And in the course of this process the rudiments of moral judgments appear.

What do we call good or bad? We call good that which fulfills its purpose; and we call bad that which does not answer its purpose, does not fit it. Thus, the good house is one which properly shelters us from cold and storm. We apply the same criterion to our actions: "You did well to change your wet clothes," or "You were wrong in trusting that person," whereby we mean that our actions were or were not suited to their end. But this is just what constitutes the gradual development of our conduct.

There are also different kinds of aims. They may be purely personal, as in the two cases mentioned, or they may be broadly social. They may involve the fate not only of an individual, but also of the species. (§ 8.)

All aims, moreover, are concerned not only with the preservation of life, but also with the intensification of *vitality,* so that the problem becomes broader and broader and *the good of society more and more tends to include the good of the individual.* Consequently, we call conduct good when it contributes to the fullness and variety of our life and of the life of others—that which makes life full of pleasurable experiences, i. e., richer in content, more beautiful, more intense.[6] This is the way in which Spencer explains the origin and the gradual development of the moral conceptions in man; he does not seek them in abstract metaphysical conceptions or in the dictates of religion, or finally, in the comparative evaluation of personal pleasures and advantages, as is proposed by the utilitarian thinkers. Like Comte, Spencer considers the moral conceptions just as much a necessary product of social development, as is the progress of reason, art, knowledge, musical taste, or the aesthetic sense. One might add to this that the further development of the herd instinct, which evolves into the feeling of a "reciprocal bond," of the solidarity or the mutual dependence of all upon every one, and of each upon all, is as much an inevitable result of social life, as the development of reason, the power of observation, sensibility to impressions, and other human faculties.

Thus it is unquestionable that the moral conceptions of man have been accumulating in the human race from the remotest time. Their rudiments manifested themselves among animals by virtue

---

[6] In short, says Spencer, "that perfect adjustment of acts to ends in maintaining individual life and rearing new individuals, which is effected by each without hindering others from effecting like perfect adjustments, is, in its very definition, shown to constitute a kind of conduct that can be approached only as war decreases and dies out." (§ 6.)

of their social life. But why did the course of evolution follow this direction and not the opposite? Why not the direction of struggle of each against all? To this question the evolutionist ethics should, in our opinion, reply:—because such a development led to the preservation of the species, to its survival, whereas the inability to develop these faculties of sociality, in the case of animals as well as of human tribes, fatally led to the inability to survive in the general struggle against nature for existence, and consequently, led to extinction. Or, as Spencer answers together with all the eudemonists:—because man found pleasure in these acts that lead to the good of society; and he pointed out to those who take the religious stand, that the very words of the Gospel, "Blessed are the merciful"; "Blessed are the peace-makers"; "Blessed is he that considereth the poor,"—already imply the state of blessedness, i. e., the pleasure from performing such acts. (§ 14.) This answer does not, of course, preclude an objection on the part of intuitional ethics, which can and does say that "it was the will of the gods or of the Creator that man should feel particularly gratified when his acts lead to the good of others, or when men obey the commands of the deity."

No matter what criterion is assumed for the judging of actions— be it high perfection of character or rectitude of motive,—we will see, continues Spencer, "that definition of the perfection, the virtue, the rectitude, inevitably brings us down to happiness experienced in some form, at some time, by some person, as the fundamental idea." . . . "So that no school can avoid taking for the ultimate moral aim a desirable state of feeling called by whatever name— gratification, enjoyment, happiness." (§ 15.) The evolutionist ethics, however, cannot fully agree with this explanation, for it cannot admit that the moral element constitutes nothing but the *accidental* accumulation of habits that were helpful to the species in its struggle for existence. Why is it, asks the evolutionist philosopher, that not the egoistic but the altruistic habits give man greatest gratification? Do not the sociality which we observe everywhere in nature, and the mutual aid which is developed through social life,—do not they constitute a means so general in the struggle for existence that egoistic self-assertion and violence prove weak and impotent before them? Therefore, do not the feelings of sociality and of mutual aid, from which gradually and inevitably our moral conceptions had to develop,—do not they constitute just as *fundamental a property* of human or even of animal nature, as the need of nourishment?

I shall discuss these two questions in detail in the theoretical part of this book, for I consider them fundamental in ethics. I will only note for the present that Spencer left these basic questions unanswered. It was only later that he took them up for consideration, so that the controversy between the naturalist, evolutionist ethics, and the intuitional, (i. e., inspired from above), he left unsettled. But he fully proved *the necessity of placing the principles of morality on a scientific basis,* as well as the lack of such a basis in the ethical systems previously advanced. (§§ 18–23.)

Spencer pointed out that in studying the various systems of moral science, one is astounded at the absence in them of the conception of causality in the realm of the moral. The ancient thinkers held that moral consciousness is implanted in man by God or by the gods, but they forgot that if the acts which we call bad, because they are contrary to the will of the Deity, had not *per se* entailed harmful consequences, we should never have discovered that disobedience to the divine will has a harmful effect upon society, and that the fulfillment of the divine will leads to good.

But equally wrong are the thinkers who, like Plato, Aristotle, and Hobbes, see the source of good and evil in the laws established through compulsion by the ruling power, or through the social covenant. If this were really the case, we would have to acknowledge that there is no intrinsic distinction between the consequences of actions, both good and evil, because the classification of all actions into good and evil is made by the ruling power, or by men themselves, when concluding the covenant. (§ 19.)

Similarly, says Spencer, when philosophers explain the moral element in man through a revelation from above, they tacitly admit thereby that human acts and their results are not connected by inevitable and natural casual relations which we can *know* and which can take the place of divine revelation. (§ 20.)

Even the Utilitarians, continues Spencer, are not completely free from this error, for they only partially recognize the origin of moral conceptions in natural causes. He then proceeds to make clear his thought by the following example:—every science begins by accumulating observations. The ancient Greeks and the Egyptians were able to predict the position of various planets on a certain day long before the discovery of the law of universal gravitation. This knowledge was obtained through observation, without any idea as to the causes. And only after the discovery of the law of gravitation, after we learned the causes and the laws of planetary motion, only then did our determinations of their movements cease to be empirical, and become scientific, rational. The same applies to the utilitarian ethics. The utilitarians, of course, recognize the existence of some causal connection, by virtue of which we consider certain acts good and some others bad; but they fail to explain wherein this connection lies. It is not, however, sufficient to say that certain acts are useful to society and that others are harmful; this is a mere statement of fact, whereas we want to know the general cause of morality—the general criterion whereby we may distinguish between the good and the bad. We seek a rational generalization in order to derive the general rules of conduct from a clearly defined general cause. Such is the aim of the science of morality—Ethics. (§ 21.)

Of course, the ground was prepared for Ethics through the development of the other sciences. We have now come to consider moral phenomena *as phenomena of evolution, which are in accord with the physical, biological, and social laws.* (§§ 22–23.)

In general, Spencer definitely took the viewpoint of the utilitarian morality, and he asserted that since the good in life is that which increases happiness, and the bad that which decreases it, it follows that morality in mankind is unquestionably that which increases the element of happiness in life. No matter how religious or political prejudices may tend to obscure this idea, says Spencer, all the various systems of morality have been built always upon this fundamental principle. (§ 11.)

The chapters devoted by Spencer to the consideration of conduct from the physical and from the biological point of view, are very instructive, for they clearly show, by means of examples taken from life, what attitude a science based on the theory of evolution should take with respect to the interpretations of morality.[7]

In these two chapters, Spencer gives the explanation of the *natural origin* of those fundamental facts that enter into every moral teaching. We know, for example, that a certain logical sequence of actions, a *coherence*, constitutes one of the distinguishing features of human morality, together with a *definiteness* (we can never predict the actions of men of weak, vacillating will); then comes balance in actions, *equilibrium* (we do not expect from a morally developed man a fitful, unbalanced conduct, irreconcilable with his past life), coupled with the *adaptability* to the varied environment. Finally, there is also a need of *variety* and *fullness* of life. This is what we expect from a developed individual. The existence of these faculties serves us as the criterion for the moral evaluation of men. These qualities attain greater development in animals, as we pass from the most primitive organisms to more complex ones, and finally to man.

Thus, distinctly moral qualities evolve in the course of the gradual development of animals. Similarly, in mankind, as we pass from the primitive, savage state to the more complex forms of social life, we observe the gradual evolving of a *higher type of man*. But the

[7] There is a long-felt need for a brief popular exposition of Spencer's ethics, with a good introduction which would point out its defects.

higher type of man can develop only in a society of highly developed men. A full, richly varied individual life can manifest itself only *in a society that lives a full and varied life.*

Such are the conclusions reached by Spencer considering the qualities which we call moral, from the viewpoint of the *greatest fullness of life,* i. e., from the biological point of view. And the facts lead him to conclude that there undoubtedly exists a natural inner connection between that which affords us pleasure and that which brings increased vitality, and consequently, between the intensity of emotional experiences and the duration of life. And this conclusion is, of course, a direct contradiction to the current conceptions of the supernatural origin of morality.

Spencer further points out that there are certain types of pleasures that were evolved during the time when the predatory system prevailed in human societies; but gradually, with the transition from the militant system to the peaceful, industrial system, the evaluation of the pleasant and the unpleasant undergoes a change. We no longer find the same pleasure in fighting and in military cunning and murder, as does a savage.

In general, it was easy for Spencer to show to what an extent pleasure and joy in life increase vitality, creativeness, and productivity, adding, therefore, to the happiness of life; whereas sorrow and suffering decrease vitality. Needless to say, excess of pleasure may temporarily or even permanently lower vitality, working capacity, and creativeness.

The failure to recognize this latter truth,—a failure for which theology (and also the warlike spirit of primitive societies) is to blame,—not only gives a wrong direction to all reasoning about morality, but is detrimental to life itself. Life does not inquire as to the motives that lead a man to live a physically debilitating life; it punishes the over-devoted scientist as much as the habitual drunkard.

It is clear, then, that Spencer distinctly ranged himself on the side of the "eudemonists" or "hedonists," i. e., of those who see in

298

the development of morality a striving after the greatest happiness, the greatest fullness of life. But it is still not clear why man finds his greatest pleasure in the kind of life which we call moral. The question arises: is there not in the very nature of man something that gives the preference to pleasure derived from the "moral" attitude toward others? Spencer leaves this question unanswered.

The very essence of Spencer's ethical teaching is, however, contained in his chapter on psychology, on the psychic experience which, in the course of the slow development of mankind, led to the elaboration of certain conceptions which are called "moral."

As always, Spencer begins with the simplest case. An aquatic creature senses the approach of something. This excitation produces in the creature a simple sensation, and this sensation calls forth a movement. The creature either hides, or rushes at the object, depending on whether it takes it for an enemy or sees in it a prey.

We have here the simplest form of that which fills our whole life. Something external produces in us a certain sensation, and we respond with action, an act. For example, we read in the newspaper an advertisement of an apartment to let. The advertisement describes the conveniences of the apartment and we form a certain mental picture of it, which produces a certain sensation, followed by action: we either make further inquiries about the apartment, or give up the idea of taking it.

But the case may be much more complicated. And indeed, "our mind consists of feelings and the relations among feelings. By composition of the relations and ideas of relations, intelligence arises. By composition of the feelings and ideas of feelings, emotion arises." (§ 41.) While a lower animal, or an undeveloped savage, rashly attacks the supposed prey,—a more developed man or a more experienced animal weighs the consequences of the act. *We find the same course in all moral acts.* A thief does not weigh all the possibilities and the consequences of his act, but a conscientious man considers them not only in application to himself

299

but also to the other man, and not infrequently even to all others, to society. And finally, in the case of intellectually developed man, the acts which we call judicial are frequently determined by very complex considerations of remote aims, and in such cases they become more and more ideal.

Of course, exaggeration is possible in all things. Reasoning may be carried to extreme conclusions. This happens to those who, in rejecting the present joys for the sake of the future, reach the point of asceticism and lose the very ability to live an active life. But we are not concerned with exaggerations. The important point in our discussion is that it gives us an idea of the origin of moral judgments and of their development simultaneously with the development of social life. It shows us how more complex, and consequently broader judgments attain preponderance over the simpler and the primitive ones.

In the life of human societies a very long period of time must, of necessity, elapse before the majority of the members learn to subordinate their first spontaneous impulses to the considerations of more or less remote consequences. The habit of subordinating one's unconscious tendencies to social considerations on the bases of personal experience, develops first in separate individuals, and then the great multitude of such individual inductions combines into tribal morality, supported by tradition and transmitted from generation to generation.

At first primitive men develop fear of the anger of their fellow-savages; then fear of the leader (usually the military leader), who is to be obeyed if war against the neighbouring tribe is to be waged; and finally, fear of ghosts, i. e., the spirits of the dead, who are believed to be constantly influencing the affairs of the living. These three kinds of fear restrain the striving of the savage for the immediate satisfaction of his desires, and they finally evolve into those phenomena of social life which we now call public opinion, political power, and church authority. However, a distinction should be made between these restraining factors, and the moral sentiments and habits proper which developed from them,—for moral sentiment and conscience have in view *not the external consequences of the act upon others, but the internal—upon the man himself.*

In other words, as Spencer wrote to Mill, the fundamental moral intuition of the human race is the result of the accumulated experience of the utility of *certain kinds of mutual relations.* It is only gradually that this intuition came to be independent of experience. Thus, at the time when Spencer was writing this part of his "Principles of Ethics," (in 1879), he saw no inner cause of the moral element in man. He made the first step in this direction only in 1890, when he wrote for the magazine, "Nineteenth Century," two articles on Mutual Aid, citing some data on the moral feelings in certain animals.[8]

Further, in considering the development of the moral conceptions from the sociological point of view, i. e., from the viewpoint of the development of social institutions, Spencer first of all pointed out that, since men live in societies, they inevitably become convinced that it is in the interests of each member of society to support the life of society, even if at times such action is contrary to one's personal impulses and desires. But, unfortunately, he still based his reasoning on that false idea, which had become established from the time of Hobbes, that primitive men lived not in societies, but singly or in small groups. With respect to the later evolution of mankind, he adhered to the simplified view established by Comte,—the gradual transition of modern societies from the warlike, militant state, to the peaceful, industrial community.

Due to this circumstance, he wrote, we find among modern mankind two codes of morality: *"Hate and destroy your enemy,"* and *"Love and aid your fellow-man." "Be obedient to the militant State,"* and, *"Be an independent citizen and strive for limitation of the power of the State."*

Even among modern civilized peoples subjection of women and children is permitted, although protests are heard and demands

[8] [See note 4, page 35.]—Trans. Note.

made for equality of rights of both sexes before the law. All this taken together leads to antinomy, to halfway morality, which consists of a series of compromises and bargains with one's conscience.

Contrariwise, the morality of the peaceful social system, if we are to express its essence, is extremely simple; it may even be said to consist of truisms. Obviously, that which constitutes evil in society includes all acts of aggression of one member of society against the other, for if we are to tolerate such acts, the stability of the social bond is weakened. It is also obvious that the maintenance of society requires the mutual coöperation of men. And, what is more, if coöperation is not practiced for the defence of the group, it will not be forthcoming for the gratification of the most pressing needs: food, dwelling, hunting, etc. All consideration of the usefulness of society will be lost. (§ 51.)

No matter how few the needs of society, and no matter how primitive the means of their satisfaction, coöperation is necessary: it manifests itself among the primitive peoples in hunting, in the cultivation of land in common, etc. And then, with the higher development of social life, there appears a form of co-operation in which the tasks of the different members of society are not alike, though they all pursue a common aim. And finally, another form of co-operation develops under which both the nature of the work and its aims are different, but under which this work contributes, nevertheless, to the general welfare. Here we already meet with the subdivision of labour, and the question arises:—"How are the products of labour to be divided?" There can be but one answer to this question: under voluntary agreement, so that the compensation for work will make possible the replenishing of the energy expended, just as occurs in nature. To this we must add:—"and in order to make it possible to expend energy upon work which may not be as yet recognized as necessary, and which gives pleasure to individual members of society, but which may in time prove useful to society as a whole."

This, however, is not enough, continues Spencer. An industrial society is conceivable in which men lead a peaceful life and fulfil all their contracts, but which lacks co-operation for the common good, and in which no one is concerned about the public interests. In such a society the limit of the evolution of conduct is not attained, for it may be shown that the form of development *which supplements justice with beneficence,* is a form adapted to an imperfect social system. (§ 54.)

"Thus the sociological view of Ethics supplements the physical, biological, and psychological views." (§ 55.) Having thus established the fundamental principles of ethics from the standpoint of evolution, Spencer wrote an additional chapter in which he answers the attacks upon utilitarianism, and, among other things, discusses the part played by justice in the elaboration of the moral conceptions.[9]

In arguing against the acceptance of justice as the basis of the moral, the utilitarian Bentham wrote: "But justice, what is it that we are to understand by justice?—and why not happiness, but justice? What happiness is, every man knows. . . . But what justice is,—this is what on every occasion is the subject matter of dispute. Be the meaning of the word justice what it will, what regard is it entitled to, otherwise than as a means of happiness?" ("Constitutional Code," ch. xvi, Section 6).

Spencer answered this question by pointing out that all human societies—nomadic, permanently settled, and industrial,—strive after

---

[9] In objecting to hedonism, i. e., to a teaching which explains the development of the moral conceptions by rational striving after happiness, personal or social, Sidgwick pointed out the impossibility of measuring the pleasant and the unpleasant effect of a given act according to the scheme devised by Mill. In answering Sidgwick, Spencer came to the conclusion that the utilitarianism which considers in each particular case what conduct will lead to the greatest sum of pleasurable sensations, i. e., the individually empirical utilitarianism, serves only as an introduction to rational utilitarianism. That which served as the means for attaining welfare, gradually becomes the aim of mankind. Certain ways of reacting to the problems of life become habitual, and man no longer has to ask himself in each particular case: "What will give me greater pleasure, to rush to the aid of a man who is in danger, or to refrain from so doing? To answer rudeness with rudeness, or not?" A certain way of acting becomes habitual. (§§ 57–58.)

happiness, although each uses different means to attain that aim. But there are certain necessary conditions that are *common to them all*—harmonious co-operation, absence of direct aggression, and absence of indirect aggression in the form of breach of contract. And these three conditions together reduce themselves to one: *maintenance of fair, equitable relations.* (§ 61.) This assertion on the part of Spencer is very significant, for it stresses the fact that widely different moral systems, religious as well as non-religious, including the evolution theory, agree in recognizing equity as the basic principle of morality. They all agree that the aim of sociality is the *well-being of each and of all,* and that *equity* constitutes the necessary means for attaining this well-being. And, I will add, —no matter how often the principle of equity was violated in the history of mankind, no matter how assiduously legislators up to the present day have made every effort to circumvent it, and moral philosophers to pass it over in silence—nevertheless, the recognition of equity lies at the basis of all moral conceptions and even of all moral teachings.

Thus, in replying to the utilitarian, Bentham, Spencer reached the essence of our interpretation of justice, i. e., the *recognition of equity.* This was the conclusion already come to by Aristotle, when he wrote: *"the just will therefore be the lawful and the equal; and the unjust the unlawful and the unequal."* The Romans similarly identified justice with equity, "which is a derivative of *aequus,* the word *aequus* itself having for one of its meanings, just or impartial.[10] (§ 60.) This meaning of the word Justice has been completely preserved in modern legislation, which forbids direct aggression, as well as indirect, in the form of breach of contract, both of which would constitute inequality. All these considerations,

---

[10] Spencer refers here also to the seventeenth Psalm of David, first and second verses:
"Hear the *right,* O Lord. . . . Let thine eyes behold the things that are *equal."* [The Russian text, as quoted by Kropotkin from the Synod version, differs from the English given here.]—Trans. Note.

concludes Spencer, "show the *identification of justice with equalness.*" (§ 60.)

Particularly instructive are the chapters devoted by Spencer to the discussion of egoism and altruism. In these chapters the very foundations of his ethics are expounded.[11]

To begin with, different races of men at different times were not in agreement in their interpretations of pleasure and pain. That which was held to be a pleasure ceased to be considered as such; and inversely, that which was considered a burdensome procedure becomes a pleasure under new conditions of life. Thus, for example, we now find pleasure in sowing, but not in reaping. But the conditions of work are being changed and we begin to find pleasure in things which were formerly considered wearisome. It may be said in general that any work necessitated by the conditions of life can, and in time will, be accompanied by pleasure.

What, then, is altruism, i. e., if not defined as love for others, then, at least, concern about their needs; and what is egoism, i. e., self-love?

"A creature must *live* before it can act." Therefore the maintenance of its life is the primary concern of every living being. "Egoism comes before altruism," wrote Spencer. "The acts required for continued self-preservation, including the enjoyment of benefits achieved by such acts, are the first requisites to universal welfare. This permanent supremacy of egoism over altruism, is further made manifest by contemplating life in course of evolution." (§ 68.) Thus the idea that every individual shall gain or lose in accordance with the properties of his own nature, whether inherited or acquired, becomes more and more sound. This is equivalent to recognizing that "egoistic claims must take precedence of altruistic claims." (§§ 68–69.) This conclusion, however, is incorrect, even

[11] These are the titles of the chapters: The Relativity of Pains and Pleasures. Egoism versus Altruism. Altruism versus Egoism. Trial and Compromise. Conciliation.

if for the sole reason that the modern development of society tends toward enabling each one of us to enjoy not only personal benefits, but to a much greater extent, social benefits.

Our clothes, our dwellings and their modern conveniences, are the products of the world's industry. Our cities, with their streets, their schools, art galleries, and theatres are the products of the world's development during many centuries. We all enjoy the advantages of the railroads:—note how they are appreciated by a peasant who, for the first time, sits down in a rail-coach after a long journey afoot in the rain. But it was not he who created them.

But all this is the product of collective, and not of individual creation, so that the law of life directly contradicts Spencer's conclusion. This law states that with the development of civilization man becomes more and more accustomed to take advantage of the benefits acquired not by him, but by humanity as a whole. And he experienced this at the earliest period of the tribal system. Study a village of the most primitive islanders of the Pacific, with its large *balai* (common house), with its rows of trees, its boats, its rules of hunting, rules of proper relations with the neighbours, etc. Even the surviving remnants of men of the Glacial Period, the Esquimaux, have a civilization of their own and their own store of knowledge *elaborated by all, and not by an individual.* So that even Spencer had to formulate the fundamental rule of life to admit the following restriction": *the pursuit of individual happiness within the limits prescribed by social conditions."* (§ 70, p. 190.) And indeed, in the period of the tribal mode of life,—and there never was a period of living in solitude,—the savage was taught from early childhood that *isolated life and isolated enjoyment of it are impossible.* It is on this basis, and not on the basis of egoism, that his life shapes itself, just as in a colony of rooks or in an ant-hill.

Speaking generally, the part of Spencer's book devoted to the defence of egotism (§§ 71–73) is very weak. A defence of egotism was undoubtedly needed, all the more since, as Spencer showed at the beginning of his treatise, the religious moralists made many unreasonable demands upon the individual. But Spencer's arguments reduced themselves to a vindication of the Nietzschean "blond beast," rather than to a justification of a "sound mind in a sound body." This is why he arrives at the following conclusion: "That egoism precedes altruism in order of imperativeness, is thus clearly shown," (§ 74)—a statement so indefinite as either to convey no information or leading to false conclusions.

It is true that in the next chapter, "Altruism vs. Egoism," Spencer, following the court-of-law system of accusation and defence, endeavoured to emphasize the great importance of altruism in the life of nature. Among birds, in their efforts to protect their young from danger at the risk of their own lives, we at once have evidence of true altruism, even if still semi-conscious. But the risk would be the same whether the feeling is conscious or unconscious. Thus Spencer was compelled to acknowledge that *"self-sacrifice is no less primordial than self-preservation."* (§ 75.)

In the later stages of evolution of animals and men, there is more and more complete transition from the unconscious parental altruism to the conscious kind, and there appear new forms of the identification of personal interests with the interests of a comrade, and then of society.

Even the altruistic activities contain the element of egoistic pleasure, as is exemplified in art, which tends to unite all in a common enjoyment. "From the dawn of life, then, egoism has been dependent upon altruism as altruism has been dependent upon egoism." (§ 81.)

This remark of Spencer's is perfectly true. But if we are to accept the word altruism, introduced by Comte, as the opposite of egoism, what, then, is ethics? What was it that morality, evolving in animal and human societies, was striving for, if not for the opposition to the promptings of narrow egoism, and for bringing up humanity in the spirit of the development of altruism? The very expressions "egoism" and "altruism" are incorrect, because there can be no pure altruism without an admixture of personal pleasure

—and, consequently, without egoism. It would therefore be more nearly correct to say that ethics aims at *the development of social habits and the weakening of the narrowly personal habits.* These last make the individual lose sight of society through his regard for his own person, and therefore they even fail to attain their object, i. e., the welfare of the individual, whereas the development of habits of work in common, and of mutual aid in general, leads to a series of beneficial consequences in the family as well as in society.

Having considered in the first part of his book ("The Data of Ethics") the origin of the moral element in man from the physical, biological, psychological, and sociological viewpoint, Spencer then proceeded to analyze the essence of morality. In man and in society, he wrote, there is a continual struggle between egoism and altruism, and the aim of morality is the reconciliation of these two opposing tendencies. Men come to this reconciliation, or even to the triumph of social tendencies over the egoistic tendencies, through the gradual modification of the very bases of their societies.

With reference to the origin of this reconciliation Spencer, unfortunately, continued to adhere to the view expressed by Hobbes. He thought that once upon a time men lived like certain wild animals, such as tigers, (very few animals, it must be said, lead this type of life now), always ready to attack and to kill one another. Then, one fine day, men decided to unite into a society, and since then their sociality has been developing.

Originally the social organization was military, or militant. Everything was subjected to the demands of war and struggle. Military prowess was regarded as the highest virtue, the ability to take away from one's neighbours their wines, their cattle, or any other property, was extolled as the highest merit, and, as a consequence, morality shaped itself in accordance with this ideal. Only gradually did the new social system begin to develop, the industrial system in which we are now living, although the distinguishing features of the militant system have by no means completely disappeared. But at present the characteristic features of the industrial system are already being evolved, and with them a new morality in which such features of peaceful sociality as sympathy obtain the ascendancy; at the same time there appeared many new virtues, unknown to the earlier mode of life.

The reader can ascertain from many works of contemporary and earlier writers, mentioned in my book, "Mutual Aid," to what an extent Spencer's conception of primitive peoples is wrong or even fantastic. But this is not the question. It is particularly important for us to know the later course of development of the moral conceptions in man.

At first, the establishment of rules of conduct was the domain of religion. It extolled war and the military virtues: courage, obedience to superiors, ruthlessness, etc. But side by side with religious ethics the *utilitarian* ethics began to develop. Traces of it are to be noticed in Ancient Egypt. Later, in Socrates and Aristotle, morality is separated from religion and the element of social *utility*, i. e., of utilitarianism, is introduced into the evaluation of human conduct. This element struggles against the religious element throughout the Middle Ages, and then, as we have seen, from the time of the Renaissance, the utilitarian bias again comes to the foreground, and gains special strength in the second half of the eighteenth century. In the nineteenth century, from the time of Bentham and Mill, says Spencer, "we have utility established as the sole standard of conduct," (§ 116),—which is, by the way, quite incorrect, for Spencer himself deviates somewhat in his ethics from so narrow an interpretation of morality. The habit of following definite rules of conduct, as well as religion and the evaluation of the utility of various customs, gave rise to feelings and conceptions adapted to certain moral rules, and in this manner was developed the preference for the mode of conduct which leads to social welfare; then came non-sympathy or even disapproval of the conduct that leads to the opposite results. In confirmation of this opinion, Spencer cites (§117) examples from the books of Ancient India and from Confucius, which show how morality evolved, irrespective of

309

the promise of reward from above. This development, according to Spencer, was due to the survival of those who were better adapted than others to the peaceful social system.

However, Spencer saw nothing but utility in the entire progress of the moral sentiments. He noted no guiding principle originating in reason or in feeling. In a certain system men found it useful to wage wars and to plunder, and they accordingly developed rules of conduct that elevated violence and plunder to the level of moral principles. The development of the industrial-commercial system brought with it a change in feelings and conceptions, as also in the rules of conduct,—and a new religion and a new ethics followed. Together with these there came also that which Spencer calls the aid to ethics ("pro-ethics," i. e., *in lieu* of ethics), a series of laws and of rules of conduct, at times preposterous, like the duel, and at times of a very indefinite origin.

It is interesting to note that Spencer, with a conscientiousness characteristic of him, pointed out certain facts which could not be explained from his point of view exclusively by the utilitarian course of morality.

As is well known, throughout the whole of the nineteen centuries that elapsed after the first appearance of the Christian teaching, military predatoriness never ceased to be extolled as the highest virtue. To our own time Alexander the Great, Karl, Peter I., Frederick II., Napoleon, are regarded as heroes. And yet, in the Indian "Mahabharata," especially in the second part, a very different course of conduct was advocated:

"Treat others as thou would'st thyself be treated.
Do nothing to thy neighbour, which hereafter
Thou would'st not have thy neighbour do to thee.
A man obtains a rule of action by looking on his neighbour as himself."

The Chinese thinker, Lao-Tsze, also taught that "peace is the highest aim." Persian thinkers and the Hebrew book of Leviticus taught these things long before the appearance of Buddhism and Christianity. But the greatest contradiction to Spencer's theory is found in that which he himself conscientiously noted in connection with the peaceful mode of life of such "savage" tribes as, for example, the primitive inhabitants of Sumatra, or the Tharus of the Himalayas, the league of the Iroquois, described by Morgan, etc. (§ 128.) [12] These facts, as well as the numerous instances that I pointed out in my "Mutual Aid" in connection with the savages and mankind during the so-called "barbarian," i. e., during the "tribal" period, and the multitude of facts that are contained in the existing works on anthropology,—all these are fully established. They show that while, during the founding of new states or in states already existing, the ethics of plunder, violence, and slavery was in high esteem among the ruling classes, there existed among the popular masses from the time of the most primitive savages, *another ethics: the ethics of equity*, and, consequently, of *mutual benevolence*. This ethics was already advocated and exemplified in the most primitive animal epos, as was pointed out in the second chapter of this book.

In the second part of his "Principles of Ethics," in the division, "The Inductions of Ethics," Spencer came to the conclusion that moral phenomena are extremely complex and that it is difficult to make any generalization concerning them. And, indeed, his conclusions are vague, and there is but one thing he definitely attempts to prove,—namely, that the transition from the militant system to the peaceful, industrial life leads to the development of a series of peaceful social virtues, as had been already pointed out by Comte. From this follows, wrote Spencer, "that the [innate] moral-sense doctrine in its original form is not true, but it *adumbrates* a truth, and a much higher truth,—namely, that the sentiments and ideas current in each society become adjusted to the kinds of activity predominating in it." (§ 191.)

The reader has probably noticed the unexpectedness of this almost platitudinous conclusion. It would be more nearly correct to summarize the data given by Spencer, and a mass of similar data ob-

---

[12] [L. H. Morgan, *League of the . . . Iroquois*, Rochester, 1851.]—Trans. Note.

tained by the study of primitive peoples, in the following form: *The basis of all morality lies in the feeling of sociality, inherent in the entire animal world, and in the conceptions of equity, which constitutes one of the fundamental primary judgments of human reason.* Unfortunately, the rapacious instincts that still survive in men from the time of the primitive stages of their development interfere with the recognition of the feeling of sociality and the consciousness of equity as the fundamental principle of the moral judgments. These instincts were not only preserved but even became strongly developed at various periods of history, in proportion as new methods of acquiring wealth were being created; in proportion as agriculture developed instead of hunting, followed by commerce, industry, banking, railroads, navigation, and finally military inventions, as the inevitable consequence of industrial inventions,—in short, all that which enabled certain societies, that forged ahead of others, to enrich themselves at the expense of their backward neighbours. We have witnessed the latest act of this process in the fearful war of 1914.

The second volume of Spencer's ethics is devoted to the two fundamental conceptions of morality—to Justice, and to that which goes beyond mere justice and which he called "Beneficence—negative and positive," i. e., what we would call magnanimity, though this term, like the other, is not quite satisfactory. Even in animal societies— wrote Spencer in the chapters which he inserted in his "Ethics" in 1890—we can distinguish good and bad acts, and we call good, i. e., altruistic, those acts that benefit not so much the individual as the given society and which aid the preservation of other individuals, or of the species in general. From these evolves that which may be called "sub-human justice," which gradually attains an always higher degree of development. Egoistic impulses become restrained in society, the stronger begin to defend the weak, individual peculiarities attain greater importance, and, in general, types essential for social life are produced. Thus, various forms of sociality are developed among the animals. There are, of course, some exceptions, but these gradually die out.

Furthermore, in the two chapters on Justice, Spencer shows that this feeling at first grew out of personal, egoistic motives (fear of the vengeance of the wronged or of his comrades, or of the dead tribesmen) and that, together with the intellectual development of men, there arose gradually the feeling of mutual sympathy. Then the rational conception of justice began to be evolved, although its development was, of course, impeded by wars,—at first among tribes, then among nations. With the Ancient Greeks, as may be seen in the writings of their thinkers, the conception of justice was very definite. The same applies to the Middle Ages, when murder or maiming was atoned for by compensation to the wronged, in unequal amounts depending on the class to which they belonged. And only at the end of the eighteenth and the beginning of the nineteenth century do we read in Bentham and Mill:—"everybody to count for one, nobody for more than one." This conception of equity is now adhered to by the socialists. Spencer, however, does not approve this new principle of *equality*, which, I will add, has been recognized only since the time of the first French Revolution;—he sees in it a possible extinction of the species. (§ 268.) Therefore, while not rejecting this principle, he seeks a compromise, as he had repeatedly done in various divisions of his synthetic philosophy.

In theory he completely recognizes the equality of rights, but, reasoning along the same lines as when he wrote about the association and the transcendental theories of intellect, he seeks in life a reconciliation between the desirable equity and the inequitable demands of men. From generation to generation, wrote Spencer, there took place the adaptation of our feelings to the requirements of our life, and as a result, a reconciliation of the intuitional and the utilitarian theories of morality was effected.

In general, Spencer's interpretation of justice is as follows: "Every man is free to do that which he wills, provided he infringes not the equal freedom of any other man. Liberty of each is limited only by the like liberties of all." (§ 272.)

"If we bear in mind," wrote Spencer, "that though not the immediate end, the greatest sum of happiness is the remote end, we see clearly that the sphere within which each may pursue happiness has a limit, on the other side of which lie the similarly limited spheres of actions of his neighbours." (§ 273.) This correction, says Spencer, is gradually introduced in the course of the mutual relations among human tribes and within each tribe; and in proportion as it becomes habitual in life there develops the desired conception of justice.

Some primitive tribes, in a very low stage of development, have, nevertheless, a far clearer perception of justice than the more developed peoples, who still preserve the habits of the earlier militant system in their life as well as in their thinking. It is unquestionable that,—if the Evolution-hypothesis is to be recognized, —this naturally formed conception of justice, acting upon the human mind for an enormously long period of time, produced directly or indirectly a definite organization of our nervous system and originated thereby a definite mode of thinking, so that the conclusions of our reason derived from the experiences of countless numbers of men are just as valid as the conclusions of an individual derived from his personal experiences. Even if they are not correct in the literal sense of the word, they may, nevertheless, serve to establish the truth.[13]

---

[13] If this paragraph (§ 278) were not so long it would be well worth citing in full. The next two paragraphs are also important for the understanding of Spencer's ethics in connection with the question of justice. He wrote on the same subject in the ninth chapter, "Criticisms and Explanations," while answering Sidgwick's objections to Hedonism, i. e., to the theory of morality based on the pursuit of happiness. He agreed with Sidgwick that the measurements of pleasures and pains made by the utilitarians need confirmation or checking by some other means, and he called attention to the following:—as man develops the means for gratifying his desires, the latter become increasingly complex. Very often man pursues not even the aim itself (certain pleasures, for example, or wealth), but the means leading to it. Thus a reasonable, rational utilitarianism is being gradually developed

MORAL TEACHINGS—XIX CENTURY

With this Spencer terminates the discussion of the bases of ethics and passes to their application in the life of societies, from the viewpoint of absolute as well as of relative ethics, of that which evolves in actual life (chapters IX to XXII). After this he devotes seven chapters to the discussion of the State, its essence and its functions. Like his predecessor, Godwin, he subjects to severe criticism the modern theories of the State, and the subordination of all of social life to it.

Spencer was perfectly right in introducing into ethics the discussion of the form into which social life had shaped itself; before his time this subject was given very little consideration. Men's conceptions of morality are completely dependent upon the form that their social life assumed at a given time in a given locality. Whether it be based on the complete subjection to the central power—ecclesiastical or secular—on absolutism or on representative government, on centralization or on the covenants of the free cities and village communes; whether economic life be based on the rule of capital or on the principle of the co-operative commonwealth—all this is reflected in the moral conceptions of men and in the moral teachings of the given epoch.

In order to be convinced of the truth of this statement it is sufficient to scrutinize the ethical conceptions of our time. With the formation of large states and with the rapid development of manufacturing, industry, and banking, and through them of the new ways of acquiring wealth, there also developed the struggle for domination and the enrichment of some through the toil of others. For the serv-

from the spontaneous striving for pleasure. And this rational utilitarianism urges us toward a life which is in accordance with certain fundamental principles of morality. It is incorrect to assert, as Bentham did, that justice, as the aim of life, is incomprehensible to us, whereas happiness is quite comprehensible. The primitive peoples have no word expressing the conception of happiness, whereas they have a quite definite conception of justice, which was defined by Aristotle as follows: "The unjust man is also one who takes more than his share." To this I will add that the rule here stated is in reality very strictly observed by savages in the most primitive stage known to us. In general, Spencer was right in asserting that justice is more comprehensible than happiness as the rule of conduct.

ing of these ends, bloody wars have been continually waged for the last one hundred and thirty years. Hence the questions of State power, of the strengthening of diminishing of this power, of centralization and decentralization, of the right of the people to their land, of the power of capital, etc.,—all these problems became burning questions. And in their solution in one or the other direction depends inevitably the solution of the moral problems. The ethics of every society reflects the established forms of its social life. Spencer, therefore, was right in introducing into ethics his inquiry into the State.

First of all he established the premise that the forms of the State, i. e., the modes of political life, are changeable, like everything else in nature. And indeed, we know from history how the forms of human societies have varied:—the tribal system, the federations of communities, centralized states. Then, following Auguste Comte, Spencer pointed out that history displays two types of social organization: the warlike or militant form of the state, which, according to Spencer, predominated in primitive societies; and a peaceful, industrial form, the transition to which is now being gradually effected by the civilized part of humanity.

Having recognized the equal freedom of every member of society, men had also to acknowledge political equality of rights, i. e., the right of men to select their own government. But it happened, remarks Spencer, that even this is not sufficient, for such a system does not obliterate the antagonistic interests of different classes. Spencer comes to the conclusion that modern humanity, despite the advantages of what is known as political equality of rights, will fail to secure real equity in the near future. (§ 352.)

I shall not discuss here Spencer's ideas as to the rights of citizens in the State; he conceived them as they were understood by the average middle-class person in the 'forties of the last century; therefore, he was strongly opposed to the recognition of the political rights of women. We must consider, however, Spencer's general idea of the State. The State was created by war, he asserts.

"Where there neither is, nor has been, any war there is no government." (§ 356.) All governments and all ruling power originated in war. Of course, an important rôle in the formation of the State power was played not only by the need of a chief in case of war, but also by the need of a judge for adjudication of interclan disputes. Spencer recognized this need, and yet he saw the principal cause for the rise and development of the State in the necessity of having a leader in time of war.[14] It takes a long war to convert the government's ruling power into a military dictatorship.

It is true that Spencer's ideas are reactionary in many respects, even from the viewpoint of the authoritarians of our time. But in one respect he went even further than many radical authoritarians, including the communistic group of state-apologists, when he protested against the unlimited right of the State to dispose of the person and liberty of the citizens. In his "Principles of Ethics" Spencer devoted to this subject a few pages marked by profound ideas about the rôle and the importance of the State; here Spencer is a continuator of Godwin, the first advocate of the anti-State teaching, now known under the name of anarchism.

"While the nations of Europe," wrote Spencer, "are partitioning among themselves parts of the Earth inhabited by inferior peoples, with cynical indifference to the claims of these peoples, it is foolish

[14] In general, Spencer, like many others, applied the word "State" indiscriminately to various forms of sociality, whereas it should be reserved for those societies with the hierarchic system and centralization, which evolved in Ancient Greece from the time of the empire of Philip II., and Alexander the Great,—in Rome, toward the end of the Republic and the period of the Empire,—and in Europe from the fifteenth and sixteenth centuries.

On the other hand, the federations of tribes and the free mediæval cities, with their leagues, which originated in the eleventh and twelfth centuries and survived up to the formation of the States proper with their centralized power, should rather be called "free cities," "leagues of cities," "federations of tribes," etc. And indeed, to apply the term "State" to Gaul of the time of the Merovingians, or to the Mongolian federations of the time of Jenghis-Khan, or to the mediæval free cities and their free leagues, leads to an utterly false idea of the life of those times. (See my *Mutual Aid*, chapters v, vi, and vii.)

to expect that in each of these nations the government can have so tender a regard for the claims of individuals as to be deterred by them from this or that apparently politic measure. So long as the power to make conquests abroad is supposed to give rights to the lands taken, there must of course persist at home the doctrine that an Act of Parliament can do anything—that the aggregate will may rightly impose itself on individual wills without any limit." (§ 364.)

However, such an attitude toward human personality is nothing but a survival of former times. The present aim of civilized societies is to enable everyone "to fulfil the requirements of his own nature without interfering with the fulfilment of such requirements by others." (§ 365.) And in analyzing this situation Spencer came to the conclusion that the function of the State should be limited *exclusively to maintaining justice.* Any activity beyond that will constitute a transgression of justice.

But, concludes Spencer, it is not to be expected for a long time to come that party politicians, who promise the people all kinds of benefits in the name of their party, will pay attention to those who demand the limitation of government interference in the life of individuals. Nevertheless, Spencer devotes three chapters to the discussion of "The Limits of State-Duties," and in the conclusion to these chapters he attempted to show how preposterous are the efforts of legislators to eradicate the variations in human nature by means of laws. With this end in view the criminal absurdities, like those perpetrated in former times for the purpose of converting all men to one faith, are being repeated to the present day, and the Christian peoples, with their countless churches and clergy, are just as vengeful and warlike as the savages. Meanwhile, life itself, irrespective of governments, leads toward the development of the better type of man.

Unfortunately, Spencer failed to point out in his Ethics what it is in modern society that chiefly supports the greed for enrichment at the expense of backward tribes and peoples. He passed over lightly the fundamental facts that modern civilized societies afford a broad opportunity, without quitting the homeland, to reap the benefits of the toil of propertyless men, compelled to sell their labour and themselves in order to maintain their children and household. On account of this possibility, which constitutes the very essence of modern society, human labour is so poorly organized and so uneconomically utilized that its productiveness, both in agriculture and in industry, remains to this day much smaller than it can and should be.

Labour, and even the life of the workers and peasants, are valued so low in our days that the workers had to conduct a long and weary struggle merely to obtain from their rulers factory inspection and the protection of the workers against injuries by machinery and against the poisoning of adults and children by noxious gases.

While coming forth as a fairly brave opponent of the political power of the State, Spencer, though he had the sufficient authority of a number of predecessors in the field of economics, remained, nevertheless, timid in this field, and like his friends of the liberal camp, he merely protested against the monopoly of land. Through fear of revolution he did not dare come out openly and bravely against the industrial exploitation of labour.

Spencer devotes the last two parts of his "Principles of Ethics" to "The Ethics of Social Life," subdividing it into two parts: "Negative Beneficence" and "Positive Beneficence."

At the very beginning of his work (§ 54), Spencer noted that justice alone will not suffice for the life of society, that justice must be supplemented by acts—for the good of others or of the whole of society—*for which man does not expect reward.*

To this category of acts he gave the name of "beneficence," "generosity," and he pointed out the interesting fact that, in the course of the changes that are now taking place in social life, many cease to recognize "the line of demarcation between things which are to be claimed as rights and things which are to be accepted as benefactions." (§ 389.)

Spencer was particularly afraid of this "confusion" and he willingly wrote against the modern demands of the toiling masses. These demands, in his opinion, lead "to degeneracy," and, which is even more harmful, "to communism and anarchism." Equality in compensation for labour, he wrote, leads to communism, and then comes "the doctrine of Ravachol" advocating that "each man should seize what he likes and 'suppress,' as Ravachol said, everyone who stands in his way. There comes anarchism and a return to the unrestrained struggle for life, as among brutes." (§ 391.)

It is necessary to strive to mitigate the severity of the law of extermination of the least adapted, which, according to Spencer, exists in nature, but this "mitigation" should be left to *private charity*, and not to the State.

At this point Spencer ceases to be a thinker and reverts to the point of view of the most ordinary person. He completely forgets the inability of the great mass of men to procure the necessities of life,—an inability developed in our societies through the usurpation of power and through class legislation; although in another passage he himself very sagely speaks against the usurpation of land in England by its present owners. But he is worried by the thought that in modern Europe too much is demanded in the way of legislation for the benefit of the toiling masses. And in attempting to separate that which is rightfully due to the masses from that which may be given them only out of beneficence, he forgets that the causes of pauperism and of low productivity among the masses lie precisely in the rapacious system, established through conquests and legislation, so that we must at present destroy the evils accumulated by the State and its laws.

Spencer's teaching has undoubtedly suffered also from the mistaken interpretation of the "struggle for existence." He saw in it only the *extermination* of the non-adapted, whereas its principal feature should be seen in the survival of those who adapt themselves to the changing conditions of life. As I have already pointed out elsewhere,[15] the difference between these two interpretations is enor-

15. See *Mutual Aid among animals and men, as a factor of Evolution.*

mous. In one case the observer sees the struggle between the individuals of the same group—or, more accurately,—he does not see, but mentally pictures to himself such a struggle. In the other case he *sees* the struggle with the hostile forces of nature or with other species of animals, and this struggle is *conducted by animal groups in common, through mutual aid.* And anyone who will attentively observe the actual life of animals (as was done, for example, by Brehm, whom Darwin rightly called a great naturalist) will see what a vast part is played by *sociality in the struggle for existence.* He will be compelled to acknowledge that among the countless species of animals, those species or those groups survive that are more sensitive to the demands of the changeable conditions of life, those that are *physiologically more sensitive* and more prone to variation, and those that show the *greater development of the herd instinct and of sociality,* which first of all leads, as was justly pointed out by Darwin,[16] to the better *development of the mental faculties.*

Spencer, unfortunately, did not note this circumstance, and although in the two articles which he printed in the magazine, "Nineteenth Century," in 1890, he at last partially corrected this error by demonstrating sociality among animals, and its importance,[17] (these two articles are included in the second volume of his "Principles of Ethics"), nevertheless, the entire structure of his ethical theory, which was elaborated at an earlier time, suffered from the faulty premise.

[16] In his *Descent of Man.* where he materially revised his former views on the struggle for existence, expressed in *The Origin of Species.*

[17] [Both articles have a common title, *On Justice,* and are divided into five sections, as follows: March number: 1) Animal Ethics; 2) Sub-Human Justice; April number: 3) Human Justice; 4) The Sentiment of Justice, 5) The Idea of Justice.]—Trans. Note.

CHAPTER XIII

DEVELOPMENT OF MORAL TEACHINGS—XIX CENTURY
(Concluded)

Among the numerous attempts made by philosophers and thinkers of the second half of the nineteenth century to build ethics on a purely scientific basis, we must examine most carefully the work of the gifted French thinker, J.-M. Guyau (1854–1888), who, unfortunately, died very young. Guyau aimed to free morality from all mystical, supernatural, divine revelations, from all external coercion or duty, and on the other hand, he desired to eliminate from the realm of morality the considerations of personal, material interests or the striving for happiness, upon which the utilitarians based morality.

Guyau's moral teaching was so carefully conceived, and expounded in so perfect a form, that it is a simple matter to convey its essence in a few words. In his very early youth Guyau wrote a substantial work on the moral doctrines of Epicurus.[1] Five years after the publication of this book, Guyau published his second highly valuable book, "La Morale anglaise contemporaine."[2]

In this work Guyau expounded and subjected to critical examination the moral teaching of Bentham, the Mills (father and son), Darwin, Spencer, and Bain. And finally, in 1884, he published his remarkable work, "Esquisse d'une morale sans obligation ni sanc-

---

[1] *La Morale d'Épicure et ses rapports avec les doctrines contemporaines* (*The Moral Teaching of Epicurus and its relation to the modern theories of morality*). This work appeared in 1874 and was awarded the prize of the French Academy of Moral and Political Sciences.

[2] The first edition appeared in 1879.

[3] *A Sketch of Morality independent of Obligation or Sanction.* Translated from the French by Gertrude Kapteyn. Watts & Company, London, 1898. [All the references will be to this edition.]

tion," [3] which astonished scholars by its novel and just conclusions and by its artistic beauty of exposition. This book went through eight editions in France and was translated into all the languages of Europe.

Guyau places at the basis of his ethics the conception of life in the broadest sense of the word. Life manifests itself in growth, in multiplication, in spreading. Ethics, according to Guyau, should be a teaching about the means through which Nature's special aim is attained,—the growth and the development of life. The moral element in man needs, therefore, no coercion, no compulsory obligation, no sanction from above; it develops in us by virtue of the very need of man to live a full, intensive, productive life. Man is not content with ordinary, commonplace existence; he seeks the opportunity to extend its limits, to accelerate its tempo, to fill it with varied impressions and emotional experiences. And as long as he feels in himself the ability to attain this end he will not wait for any coercion or command from without. "Duty," says Guyau, is "the consciousness of a certain inward *power*, by nature superior to all other powers. To feel inwardly the greatest that one is *capable* of doing is really the first consciousness of what it is one's duty to do." [4]

We feel, especially at a certain age, that we have more powers than we need for our personal life, and we willingly give these powers to the service of others. From this consciousness of the superabundance of vital force, which strives to manifest itself in action, results that which we usually call self-sacrifice. We feel that we possess more energy than is necessary for our daily life, and we give this energy to others. We embark upon a distant voyage, we undertake an educational enterprise, or we give our courage,

As was shown by Alfred Fouillée in his book, *Nietzsche et l'immoralisme*, Nietzsche drew freely on Guyau's essay, and he always had a copy on his table. On Guyau's philosophy see the work by Fouillée, *Morale des idées-forces*, and other writings by the author. [Especially, *La Morale, l'Art et la Religion d'après Guyau.*]—Trans. Note.

[4] *A Sketch of Morality independent of Obligation or Sanction*, Book I, chapter iii, page 91. [Further references will be indicated briefly, as follows: (I, iii, 91).]

our initiative, our persistence and endurance to some common undertaking.

The same applies to our sympathizing with the sorrows of others. We are conscious, as Guyau puts it, that there are more thoughts in our mind, and that there is in our heart more sympathy, or even more love, more joy and more tears, than is required for our self-preservation; and so we give them to others without concerning ourselves as to the consequences. Our nature demands this—just as a plant has to blossom, even though blossoming be followed by death.

Man possesses a "moral fecundity." "The individual life should diffuse itself for others, and, if necessary, should yield itself up. . . . This expansion is the very condition of true life." (Conclusion, p. 209.) "Life has two aspects," says Guyau: "According to the one, it is nutrition and assimilation; according to the other, production and fecundity. The more it takes in, the more it needs to give out; that is its law."

"Expenditure is one of the conditions of life. It is expiration following inspiration." Life surging over the brim is true life. "There is a certain generosity which is inseparable from existence, and without which we die, we shrivel up internally. We must put forth blossoms; morality, disinterestedness, is the flower of human life." (I, ii, 86–87.)

Guyau also points out the attractiveness of struggle and risk. And indeed, it suffices to recollect thousands of cases where man faces struggle and runs hazards, at times even serious ones, in all periods of life, even in grey-haired age, for the very fascination of the struggle and the risk. The youth Mzyri is not the only one to say, in recalling a few hours of life in freedom and struggle:

> "Yes, gaffer, I have lived; and had my life
> Not counted those three wondrous days,—
> 'Twere sadder in a thousand ways
> Than all your feeble eld betrays." [5]

[5] [Lermontov's poem, *Mzyri*.]—Trans. Note.

MORAL TEACHINGS—XIX CENTURY

All the great discoveries and explorations of the globe and of nature in general, all the daring attempts to penetrate into the mysteries of life and of the universe, or to utilize in a new form the forces of nature, whether through distant sea-voyages in the sixteenth century, or now through aerial navigation—all the attempts to rebuild society on the new bases, made at the risk of life, all the new departures in the realm of art,—they all originated in this very thirst for struggle and risk which at times took possession of separate individuals, and at times of social groups, or even of entire nations. This has been the motive power of human progress.

And finally, adds Guyau, there is also a *metaphysical risk*, when a *new* hypothesis is advanced in the realm of scientific or social investigation or thought, as well as in the realm of personal or social action.

This is what supports the moral structure and the moral progress of society; the heroic act, "not only in battle or in struggle," but also in the flights of daring thought, and in the reconstruction of personal as well as of social life.

As regards the sanction of the moral conceptions and tendencies that spring up in us,—in other words, that which imparts to them an *obligatory character*,—it is well known that men had all along sought such confirmation and sanction in religion, in commands received from without and supported by the fear of punishment or by the promise of reward in the life to come. Guyau, of course, saw no need of this, and he devoted, accordingly, a number of chapters in his book to explaining the origin of the conception of obligation in the moral rules. These chapters are so excellent in themselves and so artistic in expression that they should be read in the original. Here are their fundamental thoughts:

First of all, Guyau pointed out that there is within us an inner approval of moral acts and a condemnation of our anti-social acts. It has been developing from the remotest past by virtue of social life. Moral approval and disapproval were naturally prompted in man by instinctive justice. And finally, the feeling of love and fraternity inherent in man, also acted in the same direction.[6]

In general, there are two kinds of tendencies in man: those of one kind are still unconscious tendencies, instincts, and habits, which give rise to thoughts that are not quite clear, and on the other hand, there are fully conscious thoughts and conscious propensities of will. Morality stands on the border line between the two; it has always to make a choice between them. Unfortunately, the thinkers who wrote on morality failed to notice how largely the conscious in us depends upon the unconscious. (I, i, 79.)

However, the study of customs in human societies shows to what an extent man's actions are influenced by the unconscious. And in studying this influence we notice that the instinct of self-preservation is by no means sufficient to account for all the strivings of man,— as is postulated by the utilitarians. Side by side with the instinct of self-preservation there exists in us another instinct:—the striving toward a more intensive, and varied life, toward widening its limits beyond the realm of self-preservation. Life is not limited to nutrition, it demands mental fecundity and spiritual activity rich in impressions, feelings, and manifestations of will.

Of course, such manifestations of will,—as some of Guyau's critics justly remarked,—may act, and frequently do act, against the interests of society. But the fact is that the anti-social tendencies (to which Mandeville and Nietzsche ascribed such great importance) are far from being sufficient to account for all human strivings that go beyond the limits of mere self-preservation, because side by side with the anti-social tendencies there exists also a striving for *sociality*, for life harmonizing with the life of society as a whole, and the latter

[6] To what an extent these remarks of Guyau, which he unfortunately did not develop further, are correct, has been already shown in the second chapter of this book, where it is pointed out that these tendencies of man have been the natural outcome of the social life of many animal species, and of early man, and also of the sociality that developed under such conditions, without which no animal species could survive in the struggle for existence against the stern forces of nature.

tendencies are no less strong than the former.   Man strives for good neighbourly relations and for justice.

It is to be regretted that Guyau did not develop more thoroughly these last two thoughts in his fundamental work; later he dwelt on these ideas somewhat more in detail in his essay, "Education et hérédité." [7]

Guyau understood that morality could not be built on egoism alone, as was the opinion of Epicurus, and later of the English utilitarians.   He saw that inner harmony alone, and *"unity of being"* (*l'unité de l'être*) will not suffice: he saw that morality includes also the instinct of sociality.[8]   Only, he did not assign to this instinct its due importance, unlike Bacon, and Darwin, who even asserted that in man and in many animals this instinct is *stronger* and acts more permanently than the instinct of self-preservation.   Guyau also failed to appreciate the decisive rôle played in cases of moral indecision by the ever-expanding conception of justice, i. e., of equity among human beings.[9]

Guyau explains the consciousness of the *obligatory* nature of morality, which we unquestionably experience within ourselves, in the following manner:

"It is sufficient to consider the normal directions of psychic life; there will always be found a kind of inner pressure exercised by the activity itself in these directions."   Thus "moral obligation, which has its root in the very function of life happens to come in principle before thinking consciousness, and springs from the obscure and unconscious depths of our being."   (I, iii, 97.)

[7] These additions were inserted in the seventh edition. J.-M. Guyau, *Education and Heredity*, translated by W. S. Greenstreet, London, 1891.

[8] "Morality," wrote Guyau, "is nothing else than unity of being. Immorality, on the contrary, is the dividing into two—an opposition of different faculties, which limit each other."   (Book I, ch. iii, p. 93).

[9] In a word, we think of the species, we think of the conditions under which life is possible to the species, we conceive the existence of a certain normal type of man adapted to these conditions, we even conceive of the life of the whole species as adapted to the world, and, in fact, the conditions under which that adaptation is maintained. (*Education and Heredity*, Chapter II, Division III, p. 77.)

ETHICS: ORIGIN AND DEVELOPMENT

The sense of duty, he continues, is not invincible; it can be suppressed. But, as Darwin showed, it remains within us, it continues to live, and it reminds us of its existence whenever we have acted contrary to the sense of duty; we feel inner dissatisfaction and there arises in us a consciousness of moral aims. Guyau cites here a few excellent examples of this power, and he quotes the words of Spencer, who foresaw the time when the altruistic instinct would develop in man to such an extent that we will obey it without any visible struggle, (I may remark that many are already living in this manner), and the day will come when men will dispute among themselves for the opportunity to perform an act of self-sacrifice. "Self-sacrifice," wrote Guyau, "takes its place among the general laws of life. . . . Intrepidity or self-sacrifice is not a mere negation of self and of personal life; it is this life itself raised to sublimity." (II, i, 125.)

In the vast majority of cases, self-sacrifice takes the form not of complete sacrifice, not the form of sacrificing life, but merely the form of danger, or of the renunciation of certain advantages. In struggle and in danger man hopes for victory. And the anticipation of this victory gives him the sensation of joy and fullness in life. Even many animals are fond of play connected with danger: thus, for example, certain species of monkeys like to play with crocodiles. And in men the desire to combat against odds is very common:—man has at times a need to feel himself great, to be conscious of the might and the freedom of his will. He acquires this consciousness through struggle—struggle against himself and his passions, or against external obstacles. We are dealing here with physiological needs, and quite commonly the feelings that prompt us to deeds of peril grow in intensity in proportion as the danger grows.

But the moral sense urges men not only toward the risk; it guides their actions even when they are threatened by *inevitable death*. And on this point history teaches mankind—at least those who are ready to benefit by its lessons, that "self-sacrifice is one of the most precious and most powerful forces in history. To make humanity,

—this great indolent body,—progress one step, there has always been needed a shock which has crushed individuals." (II, i, 127.)

Here Guyau wrote many delightful pages in order to show how natural self-sacrifice is, even in cases where man faces inescapable death, and entertains, moreover, no hope of reward in the after life. It is necessary, however, to add to these pages that the same situation prevails among all the social animals. Self-sacrifice for the good of the family or of the group is a common fact in the animal world; and man, as a social creature, does not, of course, constitute an exception.

Then Guyau pointed out another property of human nature, which at times takes, in morality, the place of the sense of prescribed duty. This is the *desire of intellectual risk,* i. e., the faculty of building a daring *hypothesis,*—as was demonstrated by Plato,—and of deriving one's morality from this hypothesis. All the prominent social reformers were guided by one or the other conception of the possible better life of mankind, and although unable to prove mathematically the desirability and the possibility of rebuilding society in some particular direction, the reformer, who is in this respect closely akin to the artist, devoted all his life, all his abilities, all his energy to working for this reconstruction. In such cases, wrote Guyau, "hypothesis produces practically the same effect as faith—even *gives rise to a subsequent faith,* which, however, is not affirmative and dogmatic like the other". . . . Kant began a revolution in moral philosophy when he desired to make the will "autonomous," instead of making it bow before a law exterior to itself; but he stopped half way. He believed that the individual liberty of the moral agent could be reconciled with the universality of the law. . . . The true "autonomy" must produce individual originality, and not universal uniformity. . . . The greater the number of different doctrines which offer themselves to the choice of humanity, the greater will be the value of the future and final agreement (II, ii, 139–140), As to the "unattainability" of ideas, Guyau answered this question in poetically inspired lines:—"The further the ideal is removed from reality, the more desirable it seems. And as the desire itself is the supreme force, the remotest ideal has command over the maximum of force." (II, ii, 145.)

But bold thinking that does not stop halfway, leads to equally energetic action. "Religions all say, 'I hope because I believe, and because I believe in an external revelation.' We must say: 'I believe because I hope, and I hope because I feel in myself a wholly internal energy, which will have to be taken into account in the problem.' . . . It is action alone which gives us confidence in ourselves, in others, and in the world. Abstract meditation, solitary thought, in the end weaken the vital forces." (II, ii, 148.)

This is, according to Guyau, what was to take the place of sanction, which the defenders of Christian morality sought in religion and in the promise of the happier life after death. First of all, we find within ourselves the approval of the moral act, because our moral feeling, the feeling of fraternity, has been developing in man from the remotest times through social life and through observation of nature. Then man finds similar approval in the semi-conscious inclinations, habits, and instincts, which, though still not clear, are deeply ingrained in the nature of man as a social being. The whole human race has been brought up under these influences for thousands and thousands of years, and if there are at times periods in the life of mankind when all these best qualities seem to be forgotten, after a certain time humanity begins again to strive for them. And when we seek the origin of these feelings, we find that they are implanted in man even deeper than his consciousness.

Then, in order to explain the power of the moral element in man, Guyau analyzed to what an extent the ability for self-sacrifice is developed in him, and showed how largely a desire for *risk* and *struggle* is inherent in human beings, not only in the minds of leaders, but also in the concerns of everyday life. These passages constitute some of the best pages in his essay.

Generally speaking, it is safe to say that in his treatise on the bases of morality without obligation and without the sanction of religion, Guyau expressed the modern interpretation of morality and of its problems in the form it was taking in the minds of educated men towards the beginning of the twentieth century.

It is clear from what has been said that Guyau did not intend to unfold all the bases of morality, but merely aimed to prove that morality, for its realization and development, has no need of the conception of *obligation*, or, in general, of any *confirmation from without*.

The very fact that man seeks to bring intensity into his life, i. e., to make it varied,—if only he feels within himself the power to live such a life,—this very fact becomes in the interpretation of Guyau a mighty appeal *to live just such a life*. On the other hand man is urged along the same path by the desire and the joy of risk and of concrete *struggle*, and also by the *joy of risk in thinking*, (metaphysical risk, as Guyau called it). In other words, man is urged in the same direction by the pleasure which he feels as he advances toward the *hypothetical* in his thoughts, his life, his action, i. e., toward that which is only conceived by us as possible.

This is what replaces in naturalistic morality the sense of *obligation* accepted by the religious morality. As regards sanction in naturalistic morality, i. e., as regards its confirmation by something higher, something more general, we have the natural feeling of approval of moral actions, and an intuitional semi-consciousness, *the moral approval*, which originates in the conception of justice, still unconscious, but inherent in all of us. And finally, there is the further approval on the part of our inherent feelings of *love* and *fraternity*.

This is the form which conceptions of morality took for Guyau. If they had their origin in Epicurus, they became considerably deepened, and instead of the Epicurean "wise calculation" we already have here a naturalistic morality, that has been developing in man by virtue of his social life. The existence of such a morality was understood by Bacon, Grotius, Spinoza, Goethe, Comte, Darwin, and partly by Spencer, but it is still persistently denied by those who prefer to talk about man as of a being who, though created "in God's image," is in reality an obedient slave of the Devil, and who can be induced to restrain his innate immorality only by threats of whip and prison in this life, and by threats of hell in the life to come.

CHAPTER XIV

CONCLUSION

WE shall now attempt to summarize our brief historical survey of the various moral teachings.

We have seen that from the time of Ancient Greece up to the present day, there were two principal schools in Ethics. Some moralists maintained that ethical conceptions are inspired in man from above, and they accordingly connected ethics with religion. Other thinkers saw the source of morality in man himself and they endeavoured to free ethics from the sanction of religion and to create a realistic morality. Some of these thinkers maintained that the chief motive power of all human actions is found in that which some call *pleasure,* others *felicity* or *happiness,* in short, that which gives man the greatest amount of enjoyment and gladness. All action is toward this end. Man may seek the gratification of his basest or his loftiest inclinations, but he always seeks that which gives him happiness, satisfaction, or at least a hope of happiness and satisfaction in the future.

Of course, no matter how we act, whether we seek first of all pleasure and personal gratification, or whether we intentionally renounce immediate delights in the name of something better, *we always act in that direction in which at the given moment we find the greatest satisfaction.* A hedonist thinker is therefore justified in saying that all of morality reduces itself to the seeking by each man of that which gives him most pleasure, even if we should, like Bentham, choose as our aim the greatest happiness of the greatest number. It does not follow from this, however, that after having acted in a certain way, I shall not be seized with regret—perhaps for a lifetime,—that I have acted in this and not in some other manner.

This, if I am not mistaken, leads us to the conclusion that those writers who assert that "each one seeks that which gives him greatest satisfaction" have not attained a solution, so that the fundamental question of determining the bases of morality, which constitutes the principal problem of all research in this field, remains open.

Neither is this question answered by those who, like the modern utilitarians Bentham, Mill, and many others, say: "In abstaining from replying to an injury with injury, you have simply avoided an unnecessary unpleasantness, a self-reproach for lack of self-control and for rudeness, which you would not approve with respect to yourself. You followed the path which gave you the greatest satisfaction, and now you, perhaps, even think: 'How rational, how *good* was my conduct.'" To which some "realist" might add: "Please do not talk to me of your altruism and your love for your neighbour. You have acted like a clever egoist,—that is all." And yet the problem of morality has not been carried a step farther, even with all these arguments. We have learned nothing about the origin of morality and have not discovered whether a benevolent attitude toward our fellow-men is desirable, and if desirable, to what an extent it is so. The thinker is as before faced with the question: "Is it possible that morality is but an accidental phenomenon in the life of men, and to a certain extent also in the life of the social animals? Is it possible that it has no deeper foundation than my casual benevolent mood followed by the conclusion of my reason that such benevolence is profitable to me, because it saves me from further unpleasantness? Moreover, since men hold that not every injury is to be met with benevolence, and that there are injuries which no one should tolerate, no matter upon whom they are inflicted, is it really possible that there is no criterion by means of which we can make distinctions among various kinds of injuries, and that it all depends on calculation of personal interest, or even simply on a momentary disposition, an accident?"

There is no doubt that "the greatest happiness of society," advocated as the basis of morality from the earliest period of the life of

334

the human race, and particularly put forward in recent time by the rationalist thinkers, is actually the primary basis of all ethics. But this conception, taken by itself, is too abstract, too remote, and would not be able to create moral habits and a moral mode of thought. That is why, from the most remote antiquity, thinkers have always sought a more stable basis of morality.

Among primitive peoples the secret alliances of the sorcerers, shamans, soothsayers (i. e., the alliances of the scientists of that time) resorted to *intimidation*, especially of women and children, by various weird rites, and this led to the gradual development of religions.[1] And religions confirmed the usages and the customs which were recognized as useful for the life of the whole tribe, for they served to restrain the egoistic instincts and impulses of individuals. Later, in Ancient Greece, various philosophical schools, and still later in Asia, Europe, and America, more spiritual religions worked toward the same end. But beginning with the seventeenth century, when in Europe the authority of religious principles began to decline, a need arose for the discovery of different grounds for the moral conceptions. Then, following Epicurus, some began to advance the principle of personal gain, pleasure, and happiness under the name of hedonism or eudemonism,—while others, following chiefly Plato and the Stoics, continued more or less to seek support in religion, or turned to *commiseration, sympathy,* which unquestionably exists in all the social animals, and which is so much more developed in man, as a counterbalance to egoistic tendencies.

To these two movements Paulsen added in our time, "Energism," the essential feature of which he considers "self-preservation and the realization of the highest goal of the will: the freedom of the

[1] Among many tribes of North American Indians, during the performance of their rites, should a mask fall from the face of one of the men so that the women can notice it, he is immediately slain, and the others say that he was killed by a spirit. The rite has the direct purpose of intimidating women and children. [Kropotkin uses the present tense,—but it is probable that this pleasant custom has fallen into disuse.]—Trans. Note.

rational ego, and the perfect development and exercise of all human powers." [2]

But "energism" too, fails to answer the question why "the conduct of some men and their manner of thought arouse pleasurable or unpleasurable feelings in the spectator." Or why the pleasurable feelings can gain preponderance over the other variety, and then become habitual and thus regulate our future acts. If this is not a mere accident, then why? What are the causes by virtue of which moral tendencies obtain the ascendancy over the immoral? Are they in utility, in calculation, in the weighing of various pleasures and in the selection of the most intense and most permanent of them, as Bentham taught? Or are there in the very structure of man and of all social animals, causes impelling us pre-eminently toward that which we call morality,—even though, under the influence of greed, vanity, and thirst for power we are at the same time capable of such infamy as the oppression of one class by the other, or of such acts as were often perpetrated during the late war: poisonous gases, submarines, Zeppelins attacking sleeping cities, complete destruction of abandoned territories by the conquerors, and so on?

And indeed, does not life and the whole history of the human race teach us that if men were guided solely by considerations of personal gain, then no social life would be possible? The entire history of mankind shows that man is an unmitigated sophist, and that his mind can find, with astounding ease, every manner of justification for that which he is urged to by his desires and passions.

Even for such a crime as the war of conquest in the twentieth century, which should have horrified all the world,—even for this crime the German Emperor and millions of his subjects, not excepting the radicals and the socialists, found a justification in its usefulness to the German people; and some other still more adroit sophists even saw in it a gain for all humanity.

[2] Friedrich Paulsen, *A System of Ethics*, trans. by Frank Thilly, New York, 1899. [These lines are not a single quotation, but a combination of phrases from different parts of Paulsen's book. See particularly, pp. 223–224, 251, 270–271.]—Trans. Note.

CONCLUSION

Paulsen includes among the representatives of "energism" in its various forms such thinkers as Hobbes, Spinoza, Shaftesbury, Leibnitz, Wolff, and the truth, says he, is apparently on the side of energism. "In recent times," continues Paulsen, "the evolutionist philosophy comes to the following point of view: a certain ideal type and its expression in activity, is the actual goal of all life and of all striving." [pp. 272-4.]

The arguments by which Paulsen confirms his idea are valuable in that they throw light on certain sides of moral life from the viewpoint of will, to the development of which the writers on ethics did not give sufficient attention. These arguments, however, fail to show wherein the *expression in activity of the ideal type* differs in moral questions from the seeking in life of the "greatest sum of pleasurable sensations." [p. 272.]

The former is inevitably reduced to the second, and can easily reach the point of the "I-want-what-I-want" principle, if not for the existence in man of a sort of restraining reflex that acts in moments of passion,—something like aversion to deception, aversion to domination, the sense of equality, etc.

To assert and to prove, as Paulsen does, that deceit and injustice lead man to ruin is unquestionably proper and necessary. This, however, is not enough. Ethics is not satisfied with the mere knowledge of this fact; it must also explain *why the deceitful and unjust life leads to ruin.* Is it because such was the will of the Creator of nature, to which Christianity refers, or because lying always means *self-debasement,* the recognition of oneself as inferior, weaker than the one to whom the lie is told,—and consequently, by losing self-respect, making oneself still weaker? And to act unjustly means to train your brain to *think unjustly,* i. e., to mutilate that which is most valuable in us—the faculty of correct thinking.

These are the questions that must be answered by the ethics that comes to replace the religious ethics. Therefore, it is not possible to solve the problem of conscience and its nature, as Paulsen did, by simply saying that conscience is in its origin nothing but a "consciousness of custom," prescribed by up-bringing, by the judgment of society as to what is proper and improper, commendable or punishable; and finally, by the religious authority. [p. 363.] It is explanations of this sort that gave rise to the superficial negation of morality by Mandeville, Stirner, and others. The fact is, that while the mode of life is determined by the history of the development of a given society, conscience, on the other hand, as I shall endeavour to prove, has a much deeper origin,—namely in the consciousness of equity, which physiologically develops in man as in all social animals. . . .

(The manuscript ends with these words)
[N. Lebedev's Note].

APPENDIX (to page 173).

HERE is how Shaftesbury describes himself in his work "The Moralists,"—"being in respect of *virtue* what you lately called a *realist;* he [i. e., the author] endeavours to show, 'that it is really something *in itself,* and in the nature of things: not arbitrary or *factitious,* not constituted from without, or dependent on *custom, fancy* or *will;* not even on the Supreme Will itself, which can no way govern it; but being *necessarily good* is governed by it, and ever uniform with it.' " (Part II, Section III, pp. 52–53.)

In another passage, Shaftesbury wrote: "Nor does the fear of Hell, or a thousand terrors of the Deity imply conscience; unless where there is an apprehension of what is *wrong,* odious, morally deformed, and ill-deserving. And where this is the case, there *conscience* must have effect, and punishment of necessity be apprehended; even though it be not expressly threatened." ("An Inquiry Concerning Virtue," Book II, Part II, Section I, p. 305.)

Here is another passage from his "Characteristics":—"You have heard it, my friend, as a common saying, that interest governs the world. But, I believe, whoever looks narrowly into the affairs of it will find that passion, humour, caprice, zeal, faction, and a thousand other springs, which are counter to self-interest, have as considerable a part in the movements of this machine." ("Characteristics," Part III, Section III, p. 77.) It is hard to believe, continues Shaftesbury, that no allowance whatsoever should be made for "the better and more enlarged affections; that nothing should be understood to be done in kindness or generosity, nothing in pure good-nature or friendship, or through any social or natural affection of any kind; when perhaps the mainsprings of this machine will be found to be either these very natural affections themselves, or a compound kind derived from them, and retaining more than one half of their nature." (*Ibid.*, pp. 77–78.) And he ridiculed Hobbes and other defenders of the egoistical interpretation of life. "For in this we should all agree, that happiness was to be pursued, and in fact was always sought after; but whether found in *following Nature*, and giving way to common affection, or in suppressing it, and turning every passion towards *private* advantage, a narrow *self-end*, or the preservation of mere *life*, this would be the matter in debate between us." (pp. 80–81.) "A man is by nothing so much *himself* as by his *temper* and the character of his passions and affections. If he loses what is manly and worthy in these, he is as much lost to himself as when he loses his memory and understanding." (p. 81.)

I will add also the following remark:—Shaftesbury naturally did not recognize free will. "For let Will be ever so free," he wrote, "Humour and Fancy, we see, govern it." (Treatise III, "Advice to an Author," Part I, Section II, p. 122.)

INDEX

INDEX

INDEX

Diderot, 186, 190, 191, 192, 213
Diodorus Siculus, 201 n.
Diogenes Laertius, 107, 183
Discours de la Méthode (Descartes), 178 n., 181
Discourse concerning . . . Obligations of Natural Religion (Clarke), 168
Discourse on Universal History (Turgot), 196
Dostoievsky, 128 n.
Draper, John W., 130 n.
Droit . . . du citoyen, Le (Mably), 193, 193 n.
Duncan, Davis, 68 n.

Eckermann, 21, 21 n., 209
Économie sociale (Pecqueur), 267 n.
Éducation et Hérédité (Guyau), 327, 327 n.
Empirik und Skepsis in Humes Philosophie (Pfleiderer), 202 n.
Encyclopædia of the Philos. sciences (Hegel), 186, 191, 227 n.
Encyclopædists, French, 7, 9, 109, 144, 168, 172, 180, 186, 187, 190, 191, 192, 213, 223, 224, 234, 246, 249, 261, 265, 268, 269
Engels, 267
Entretiens de Phocion (Mably), 193
Epictetus, 103, 109, 110 n., 111, 113, 209
Epicureans, 13, 102, 104, 105, 107-109, 113, 183, 184, 211
Epicurus, 82, 88, 96, 103-109, 111, 114, 115, 115 n., 139, 144, 145, 154, 176, 183, 184, 184 n., 185, 211, 223, 237, 238, 275, 322, 327, 331, 335
Epistle on Tolerance (Locke), 162 n.
Eskimo Tribes, The (Rink), 123 n.
Espinas, Alfred Victor, 38 n., 49 n., 65 n.
Esquimaux, The, 68, 77, 123 n., 306
Esquisse d'une morale sans obligation ni sanction (Guyau), see *Morality without Sanction or Obligation*
Essais (Montaigne), 139 n., 179
Essais de Théodicée (Leibnitz), 177 n.
Essais philosophiques (Descartes), 181
Essai sur l'origine des connaissances humaines (Condillac), 189 n.
Essay concerning Human Understanding (Locke), 162, 162 n., 163 n.

Essays, Ethical and Philosophical (Huxley), 283 n., 286 n.
Essays . . . on several subjects (Hume), 198, 199 n.
Ethica (Aristotle), 98, 98 n., 99, 99 n., 101, 101 n., 102, 102 n.
Ethics (Spinoza), 157 n., 160 n., 161, 162
Ethics (Wundt), 28 n., 224 n.
Ethik David Humes, Die (Gizycki), 202 n.
Eucken, 112, 112 n., 229, 231
Eudemonism, 103, 335
Eudemonists, 96, 99
Evolution and Ethics (Huxley), 13 n., 49, 282, 286, 287
Evolution in Professor Huxley (Mivart), 286 n.
Evolutionism, 231
Exercitationes (Gassendi), 184 n.
Exodus, 125 n.
Exploration of the Great Salt Lake (Stansbury), 34 n.

Fable of the Bees (Mandeville), 34, 238
Faraday, 256
Farrer, James A., 192 n.
Feuerbach, 8, 231, 255-259
Fichte, 225, 226, 229, 248, 256
Forel, Auguste, 65 n., 66 n.
Fouillée, Alfred, 9, 9 n., 11 n., 21, 21 n. 65 n., 323 n.
Fourier, 248, 250, 265, 266, 267
Fourierism, 81
Frederick II., 310
French Revolution, The (Kropotkin), 193 n.

Galileo, 137, 138, 180 n.
Gassendi, Pierre, 109, 149, 184, 184 n., 185, 275
Gautama, 117, 118
Gehrich, G., 29 n.
Geoffroy-St. Hilaire, 288
Geschichte der Ethik (Jodl), see *History of Ethics*
Geschichte der Materialismus (Lange), see *History of Materialism*
Geschichte der neueren Philosophie (Höffding), 32 n.
Geschichte der Religion in Altertum (Tiele), 29 n.

343

INDEX

344

INDEX

345

INDEX

INDEX

347

INDEX

348